IN
AMERICA

FROM WICKED AMUSEMENT TO NATIONAL OBSESSION

David K. Wiggins, PhD
George Mason University

Editor

Human Kinetics

Library of Congress Cataloging-in-Publication Data

Sport in America : from wicked amusement to national obsession / David
  K. Wiggins, editor.
    p.   cm.
  Includes bibliographical references and index.
  ISBN 0-87322-520-1
  1. Sports--United States--History. 2. Sports--Social aspects-
-United States--History. I. Wiggins, David Kenneth, 1951-
GV583.S6823 1995
796'.0973--dc20   94-16363
                                  CIP

ISBN: 0-87322-520-1

Developmental Editor: Larret Galasyn-Wright; **Assistant Editors:** John Wentworth, Julie Lancaster, and Dawn Roselund; **Proofreader:** Susan Dove; **Typeset-
ter & Page Layout:** Julie Overholt; **Text Designer:** Judy Henderson; **Indexer:**
Barbara Cohen; **Cover Designer:** Jack Davis; **Printer:** United Graphics

Printed in the United States of America   10 9 8 7 6 5 4

Human Kinetics
Web site: www.HumanKinetics.com

United States: Human Kinetics
P.O. Box 5076
Champaign, IL 61825-5076
800-747-4457
e-mail: humank@hkusa.com

Canada: Human Kinetics
475 Devonshire Road, Unit 100
Windsor, ON N8Y 2L5
800-465-7301 (in Canada only)
e-mail: orders@hkcanada.com

Europe: Human Kinetics
107 Bradford Road
Stanningley
Leeds LS28 6AT, United Kingdom
+44 (0)113 255 5665
e-mail: hk@hkeurope.com

Australia: Human Kinetics
57A Price Avenue
Lower Mitcham, South Australia 5062
08 8277 1555
e-mail: liaw@hkaustralia.com

New Zealand: Human Kinetics
Division of Sports Distributors NZ Ltd.
P.O. Box 300 226 Albany
North Shore City, Auckland
0064 9 448 1207
e-mail: blairc@hknewz.com

To Reet Howell,
friend, mentor, and lasting inspiration

Contents

Preface

During the last 2 decades there has been a proliferation of quality research examining the history of sport in America. Although varying in style and approach, this research contributed significantly to the literature concerned with the development of sport as both informal play and as organized competition. As a result, we now have a better understanding of such diverse topics as the relationship between urbanization and sport; the influence of ethnic and racial groups on sport; the role of women in sport; the interdependence among sport, physical education, and other health professions; and the role of consumer culture in sport development. *Sport in America: From Wicked Amusement to National Obsession* brings to one volume scholarly explorations of these and many aspects of American sport history.

Although it is certainly capable of serving as a stand-alone text, I originally conceived the book to supplement existing surveys such as Benjamin Rader's *American Sports: From the Age of Folk Games to the Age of Spectators* (Prentice Hall, 1983); Better Spears and Richard A. Swanson's *History of Sport and Physical Activity in the United States* (William C. Brown, 1988); William J. Baker's *Sports in the Western World* (University of Illinois Press, 1988); and Elliott J. Gorn and Warren Goldstein's *A Brief History of American Sports* (Hill and Wang, 1993). Such use of this anthology will fill the gaps left by these volumes and provide students a wider perspective by introducing them to scholars employing different strategies and approaches to historical research.

The chapters in this collection have been compiled from academic journals, monographs, and edited books and arranged chronologically rather than topically to help give readers a historical sense of the changing patterns of sport. The book is divided into fives parts, opening with sport's influence on early America and ending with its impact on society today. Intervening sections include: Health, Exercise, and Sport in a Rapidly Changing Society, 1820-1870; Sport in the Era of Industrialization and Reform, 1870-1915; and Sport, Consumer Culture, and Two World Wars, 1915-1945. The chapters within these parts are far-reaching and contain both narrowly focused research and broadly conceived studies.

Although it's impossible to include research touching every topic and involving every approach, I tried to include only high quality work representing the central thrust of scholarship in the field and dealing with sport in its broadest possible sense. Included, for instance, are chapters on fighting in the Southern back country; the promotion of sport and active games in antebellum America; the relationship between sport and consumer culture in the 1920s; the growth of televised sport; the cultural symbolism of prizefighting; and the history of anabolic steroids in sport.

Finally, I should point out that to accommodate the space required to reprint these 19 essays, all notes that accompanied the original articles have been deleted.

While this choice was certainly not the most desirable, it was nonetheless necessary and preferable to eliminating actual articles. Because these notes were often quite extensive and contain important reference material, you are encouraged to further explore the original articles.

Acknowledgments

Many people have helped me with this project. I appreciate all the hints and cogent suggestions provided by my colleagues in sport history. I am also grateful to Susan Pufnock of George Mason University for typing much of the manuscript (and for boosting my ego with flattering poems). Last, I would like to thank Brenda, Jordan, and Spencer for their continued support and for making me realize what's important in life.

PART 1
❖
THE PATTERN OF SPORT IN EARLY AMERICA

Sport in early America was marked by regional variations. The divergent cultural traditions and religious beliefs brought by settlers to the New World converged with differing forms of labor, gender relations, and a host of other factors indigenous to this country to produce patterns of sport that varied in both form and style from one geographical location in America to another. The pattern of sport in New England was certainly different from other areas of the country because of Puritan magistrates who brought with them from the old country a belief in the sanctity of hard, honest work and opposition to "unwholesome amusements" that did not lead to the glorification of God. The admonitions of Puritan leaders contributed to a social environment in New England where sport participation was often viewed with suspicion, if not overt hostility.

Much of the latest research, however, guards us against viewing the Puritans' many edicts as a wholesale condemnation of sport. Scholars have pointed out that not all sports were condemned by the Puritans, noting that their admonitions were based on a number of intervening variables and open to various interpretations. Some academicians have even claimed that the Puritans contributed to the development of modern sport. These various claims are the focus of chapter 1, Allen Guttmann's essay, "Puritans at Play? Accusations and Replies." Utilizing an impressive mix of primary and secondary sources, Guttmann agrees that the Puritans were not opposed to all forms of sport, but he parts company with those scholars who assert that the Puritans were responsible for furthering the development of sport. He supports his position in part by arguing that many of the recreations acceptable to the Puritans could not be classified as sport at all but forms of "calisthenics." In addition, the Puritans' justification for sport participation was always based on instrumental rather than intrinsic reasons. The Puritans were simply incapable, according to Guttmann, of rationalizing sport merely for the sake of the activity or the joy it brought the participant.

Guttmann does not differentiate between men and women in his analysis of sport and Puritan culture. It is clear, however, that women were involved in a number of recreational and sporting activities in early American society. The extent and type of involvement of women in early American sport is the focus of chapter 2, Nancy Struna's essay, "Gender and Sporting Practice in Early America, 1750-1810." In one of the latest in her line of essays on early American sporting practices, Struna examines both the consumption and production of sport forms in the context of gender relations during the late eighteenth and early nineteenth centuries. She concludes, after a careful analysis of estate inventories, tavern licenses, and literary sources, that while men had the material resources and organizational control over sport, women in post-1750 America helped shape the role of leisure practices and had access to more commercialized sport and recreational activities than is commonly assumed by historians.

CHAPTER 1

❖

Puritans at Play?
Accusations and Replies

Allen Guttmann

''The Puritan,'' quipped Thomas Babington Macaulay, ''hated bear-baiting, not because it gave pain to the bear, but because it gave pleasure to the spectators.'' Several generations of British historians have shared Macaulay's witticism with their students. For decades American professors asked their classes to read Vernon Louis Parrington's influential study, *Main Currents of American Thought* (1927), which characterized the Puritans as a gloomy lot whose attitude toward play was best represented by kill-joy Cotton Mather on a rampage against the sin of mixed dancing. How can one forget Parrington's chapter on ''The Mather Dynasty,'' which concludes: ''The New England of the dreams of Increase and Cotton Mather was sick to death from morbid introspection and ascetic inhibitions; no lancet or purge known to the Puritan pharmacopeia could save it. Though father and son walked the streets of Boston at noonday, they were only twilight figures, communing with ghosts, building with shadows.'' Parrington's readers have sometimes had the impression that the Puritans came to America mostly to provide the gloom subsequently illuminated by Benjamin Franklin, Thomas Jefferson, and other representatives of the Enlightenment.

Parrington has long since ceased to be viewed as an authority. Perry Miller, Edmund Morgan, and a whole congregation of younger historians have shown that the conventional wisdom about Puritanism was mostly nonsense, but Miller's monumental analysis of the Puritan mind, Morgan's discussion of the Puritan family, and numerous reconstructions of seventeenth-century social structure and religious institutions have done little to dispel the notion that the Puritans were serious to the point of solemnity. That classic story of grim retribution, *The Scarlet Letter,* has also helped to darken the image. Small wonder that the term ''puritan'' remains a popular synonym for ''spoilsport.''

Most sports historians have agreed that the English and American Puritans, a dour lot for whom frolic was akin to sacrilege, hindered the development of modern sports. In *Sport and Society: Elizabeth to Anne* (1969), Dennis Brailsford was as direct as, although considerably less witty than, Macaulay: "The Puritans saw their mission to erase all sport and play from men's lives." *A World History of Physical Education* (1971), the widely used text by D. B. Van Dalen and Bruce L. Bennett, summarizes the reasons for the Puritans' opposition to sports. In the first place, the Puritans' religious sanction of labor and their "detestation of idleness" removed play from the sphere of socially approved behavior. "The ideal of serving God through steady application to work came to imply that any innocent amusement was a waste of time and talents." Then there was "the Puritans' desire to eliminate any activity tainted with Catholicism."

Finally, most radically, the "determination to improve morals through spiritual vigilance and external discipline" rigidified into "a fanatic proscription of nearly every natural desire of man." The social historian Foster Rhea Dulles was more moderate, writing in *America Learns to Play* (1940) that the "intolerance of Puritanism was superimposed upon economic necessity to confine life in New England within the narrowest possible grooves. Massachusetts and Connecticut banned dice, cards, quoits, bowls, ninepins, 'or any other unlawful game in house yard, garden or backside,' singling out for special attention 'the Game called Shuffle Board, in howses of Common Interteinment, whereby much precious time is spent unfruitfully.' " Dulles admitted that the builders of Bay Colony and the founders of Connecticut had their playful impulses and that the Puritans "failed to eradicate the early Americans' natural urge for play," but their influence on American culture was ostensibly such that subsequent generations had to *learn* what animals and children know instinctively, i.e., how to play.

Since historians have a penchant for the Hegelian game of assertion and counterassertion, the humanistic indictment of the Puritans as theocratic spoil-sports has, inevitably, brought forth a host, or at least a small band, of defenders, most of them Germans. Some scholars brighten the reputation of the Puritan rank and file and tarnish the image of the Puritan leadership. Hans Peter Wagner, for instance, has argued persuasively that "Puritan theology proved ineffective in relation to sport." His evidence, drawn largely from ministerial appeals to the "unregenerate," can, however, be taken as implied support for the case against the clergy, whose "interpretation of recreation found no echo among the body of laymen." While it may have been true that "by the end of the seventeenth century New England had a rich recreational life," Wagner admits that much of this life was a thorn in the eye of the righteous. Christian Graf von Krockow has seized upon Max Weber's interpretation of the Protestant ethic in order to suggest a parallel between the "secular asceticism" (*innerweltliche Askese*) of Puritanism and the self-imposed denials of an athletic regimen. Two other German scholars have sought more directly to refute the accusation that Puritanism retarded the development of modern sports. Gerhard Schneider has written, "In no way have Puritan measures hindered men in the healthy, reasonable physical exercise. . . . The contributions of Puritanism to the shaping of modern physical exercises, including SPORTS, can no longer be overlooked." Erich Geldbach agrees that alleged "opposition between sport and the Puritans does not correspond to the historical facts."

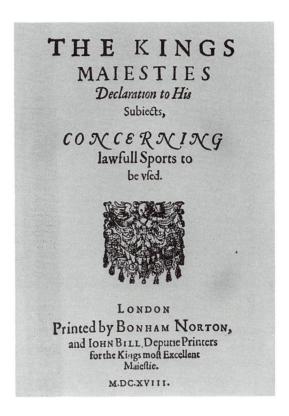

Title page of King James I's "Book of Sports," a document that challenged Puritan teachings by encouraging participation in lawful recreation and honest amusements. Courtesy of the Library of Congress.

Before joining the Hegelian game and suggesting a resolution to the clash of contradictory opinion, it is imperative to look at the historical record. This is no easy task, partly because the Puritan divines sought to float the arc of their theology on an ocean of words. Since the awesome contrast between goodness and wickedness, leading to salvation and damnation, obsessed the theologians far more than the precise distinction between sports and other forms of recreation (such as dancing, playing cards, or holding hands beneath the orchard boughs), Puritan attitudes are not always clear. In fact, the Puritans seem to have written so little about sports per se that twentieth-century historians usually discuss some larger category like amusements and diversions. But the Puritans did mention sports often enough for the attentive student to determine their views.

Puritan Attitudes and Actions

As early as 1583, Philip Stubbes had thundered against the game of folk-football. In *Anatomy of Abuses* he portrayed it as liable to produce "fighting, brawling,

contention, quarrel-picking, murther, homicide, and great effusion of blood.''
This condemnation tells us little about specifically Puritan attitudes because
sixteenth-century folk-football was indeed akin to mayhem; even the exemplary
humanist Thomas Elyot denounced the sport as ''nothing but beastly fury and
extreme violence.'' A more narrowly Puritan complaint appeared seven years
later, in the lament that ''Sabbath days and holy days . . . are spent full heathen-
ishly, in taverning, trippling [sic], gaming, playing and beholding of bear-baitings
and stage-plays.'' Concerned about the violent passions unleashed among the
spectators at animal sports, most Puritans condemned weekday as well as Sunday
cockfighting and bearbaiting. Contrary to Macaulay's quip, the Puritans were
not indifferent to the pain suffered by the animals. ''What christen [sic] heart,''
wrote Philip Stubbes, ''can take pleasure to see one poor beast to rent, teare,
and kill another, and all for his foolish pleasure?'' Such Christian charity did
not characterize all Puritan opposition to animal sports. The Reverend Edward
Burghall made gleeful journal entries whenever the spectators at such beastly
amusements were injured or killed. Such mishaps proved that God will not
be mocked.

By 1617, isolated protests against such Sabbath desecrations had become
consolidated into a powerful movement effectively restricting them. When James
I returned to England that year, after a visit to his native Scotland, he was
petitioned by the common people of Lancashire, who complained that Puritan
bans had blocked them from their traditional Sunday amusements. The king
granted the petitioners temporary relief and, a year later, issued the famous
Declaration of Sports, also known as the *Book of Sports,* in which he took issue
generally with those who argued ''that no honest mirth or recreation is lawful
or tolerable in Our Religion.'' If the common people of England were not to
enjoy their recreation on the one day of the week when they were not hard at
work, when were they to relax? James, like rulers before and after him, was also
mindful of the necessity for military preparedness. The ''common and meaner
sort of people'' had need of ''such exercises as may make their bodies more
able for warre, when Wee, or Our Successors, shall have occasion to use them.''
James ordered, therefore, ''That, after the end of Divine Service, Our good people
be not disturbed, letted, or discouraged from any lawfull recreation, Such as
dancing, either of men or women, Archery for men, leaping, vaulting, or any
other such harmlesse Recreation, nor from having of May Games, Whitson Ales,
and Morris-dances, and the setting up of Maypoles, and other sports therewith
used.'' Many Puritan clergymen refused to read the *Declaration* from their pulpits.
Recalcitrance cost some their positions, but the Puritan resistance was so powerful
that James prudently retired from the fray.

When Charles I reissued his father's declaration in 1633, the Puritan response
was even more determined. When the balance of power shifted from Cavalier
to Roundhead, Parliament damned the *Declaration* and ordered it burned. A year
later, in 1644, Parliament ordained ''That no person or persons shall hereafter
upon the Lords-Day, use, exercise, keep, maintain, or be present at any wrastlings,
shooting, Bowling, Ringing of Bells for Pleasure or Pastime, Masque, Wake,

otherwise called Feasts, Church-Ale, Dancing, Games, Sport or Pastime whatso-ever. . . .'' Cavalier-sponsored folk festivals, including Robert Dover's famous Cotswold games (which took place on Thursday and Friday of Easter Week), were banned for the duration of the Commonwealth, only to be revived in 1660, when Charles II gave his *nihil obstat* to ''Merrie England.''

The Puritans of the New World were at least as strict as those of the Old. The Court of Assistants of Massachusetts Bay reacted with typical severity in 1630, when it ordered that John Baker ''be whipped for shooteing att fowle on the Sabbath day.'' In 1647, the General Court of the colony outlawed shuffleboard; prohibition of bowling followed in 1650. Vermonters who ran, rode, jumped, or danced on Sunday were subject to ten lashes and a forty-shilling fine.

One of the best-known passages in William Bradford's *Of Plimouth Plantation* contains the governor's response to the Christmas revelry of 1621. A number of newcomers to the colony announced that it was against their consciences to work on December 25. Referring to himself in the third person, Bradford commented,

> So the Governor told them that if they made it matter of conscience, he would spare them till they were better informed; so he led away the rest and left them. But when they came home at noon from their work, he found them in the street at play, openly; some pitching the bar, and some at stool-ball and such like sports. So he went to them and took away their implements and told them that was against his conscience, that they should play and others work. If they made the keeping of it a matter of devotion, let them keep their houses; but there should be no gaming or reveling in the streets.

No trace here of the Catholic notion that revelry can be associated with worship, much less of the American Indian sacralization of play.

In another episode, one of the most famous in early American history, Bradford had to deal with the obstreperous Thomas Morton. Morton, who seems to have had some of the same hedonistic impulses as Robert Dover, defied the Puritans and challenged Bradford's control of the colony. Asserting that the Indians were ''more full of humanity than the Christians,'' Morton set up a maypole at ''Mare Mount'' and invited the Indians to join him in a frolic. This was too much for Bradford:

> And Morton became Lord of Misrule, and maintained (as it were) a School of Atheism. . . . They . . . set up a maypole, drinking and dancing about it many days altogether, inviting the Indian women for their consorts, dancing and frisking together like so many fairies, or furies, rather; and worse practices. As if they had anew revived and celebrated the feasts of the Roman goddess Flora, or the beastly practices of the mad Bacchanalians. Morton likewise . . . composed sundry rhymes and verses, some tending to lasciviousness, and others to the detraction and scandal of some persons, which he affixed to this idle or idol maypole.

While Bradford's language was a curious mix of outrage and wordplay, his actions were unambiguous. He dispatched Captain Miles Standish, whom Morton irreverently referred to as "Captain Shrimp" (Standish was not a tall man). After a scuffle, the maypole was cut down. Morton endured a brief imprisonment, which did nothing to dampen his love of revelry, and was then sent on his merry way.

Nearly a century later, when Puritan rigor had already been weakened by proponents of a less medieval worldview, Judge Samuel Sewall commented in his diary that he had ventured out on a Monday evening to interrupt the unregenerate at play on what is now known as Mount Vernon: "Dissipated the players at Nine-Pins at Mount-Whoredom. . . . Reproved Thomas Messenger for entertaining them."

From these episodes of English and American history one may conclude that the Puritans were indeed hostile to any kind of traditional amusement on the Sabbath and to certain kinds of "heathenish" recreation, such as dancing about the maypole, regardless of the day of the week. How, then, can historians maintain that the Puritans contributed to the rise of modern sports? The argument takes us from the political realm to the theological domain. It is common knowledge that the Puritans of seventeenth-century New England considered themselves Englishmen and English women guided in their thought and behavior by English scholars. It is at least arguable that the wilderness in which they lived influenced their actions less than did their intellectual tradition of Puritan theology. The English authorities whom they consulted for a godly view of worldly sports agreed that all work and no play made Everyman a poor Christian. In the words of John Downame, who published *A Guide to Godliness* in 1622, shortly before he joined the Puritan exodus to New England, "Let us know, that honest recreation is a thing not onely lawfull, but also profitable and necessary." Downame added that the bow cannot be always spanned, a metaphor that had already occurred to a more influential authority, William Perkins, who wrote in *The Whole Treatise of the Cases of Conscience* (1614) that "rest from labour with the refreshing of the bodie and mind, is necessary, because man . . . is like a bow, which being always bent and used, is soone broken in pieces." Perkins listed archery, running, wrestling, and fencing among amusements "verie commendable, and not to be disliked." Downame added hunting, hawking, fishing, and fowling. Richard Baxter, who was highly esteemed by the American Puritans, included a section on sports and recreations in his *Christian Directory*. In this influential work Baxter defined lawful recreation as "the use of some Natural thing or Action, not forbidden us, for the exhilerating of the natural Spirits by the Fantasie, and due exercise of the natural parts, thereby to fit the body and mind for ordinary duty to God. It is some delightful exercise."

Edward Elton, interpreting *Gods Holy Mind Touching Matters Morall,* announced confidently in 1625, "There are such movings of the body as bee honest and delightfull exercise of the minde, and serve to the refreshing of the body and minde, as Shooting, Tennis-playing, Stoolball-playing, Wrestling, Running, and such like." Even William Prynne, whose ferocious *Historiomastix* (1633) excoriated playgoers, had some favorable words for more innocent amusements: "Besides, though men are debard from Stage-playes, Dicing, or mixed lascivious Dancing, or any unlawfull sports, they have store of honest . . . recreations still remaining, with which to refresh themselves; as walking, riding, fishing, fowling, hawking, hunting, ringing, leaping, vaulting, wrestling, running, shooting." Apart from the omission of animal sports, the inventory might have been found in the sermons of an Anglican divine.

The American Puritans had somewhat less to say on the relation of play to worship. Increase Mather wrote in 1688, "For a Christian to use Recreation is very lawful, and in some cases a great Duty." His son Cotton admitted, even as he scolded those who "unnecessarily frequent the Tavern," that the Elect required a modicum of innocent recreation: "We would not be misunderstood, as if we meant to insinuate, that a due Pursuit of Religion is inconsistent with all manner of Diversion: No, we suppose there are Diversions undoubtedly innocent, yea profitable and of use, to fit us for Service, by enlivening and fortifying our frail Nature, Invigorating the Animal Spirits, and brightening the Mind, when tired with a close Application to Business." Cotton Mather's own preference for sedentary diversion was probably intensified when he deviated from his customary regimen and went fishing on Spy Pond. He fell in.

Among the innocent sports, folk-football, which Boston had banned in 1657, was tolerated if the players restrained themselves from breaking one another's bones and were careful not to disturb the peace of more meditative colonists. Shooting matches were looked upon with special favor. The danger of attack by hostile Indians, with or without the Indians' French allies, was present for most of the century. The magistrates and ministers of the colony agreed that a trained militia was essential, and one way to liven up the hours of drill was to institute shooting competitions.

The Puritan affirmation of honest amusements was not, however, unqualified. Indeed, Richard Baxter followed his endorsement of recreation with no less than eighteen restrictions, "the want of any one of them will *make* and *prove* to be *unlawful*." This and every similar list contained the proviso that the Sabbath be devoted to prayer, meditation, and good works rather than to worldly diversions and heedless gambols. When some of the New England "saints" endeavored to justify Sunday sports by reference to Holy Scripture, Cotton Mather was appalled: "Never did anything sound more sorrowfully or more odious since the day the World was first bless'd with such a day." A year later, in 1704, Jeremiah Dummer added his condemnation: it was "strange to see how zealously some Learned men contend for the indulgence of *Sports and Pastimes* on the Lords day in direct contrariety to the Prophet Isaiah." In addition to the adamant defense of the Sabbath, there was always the stipulation that sports and other recreations must be of the right sort. No pastime was to be condoned if it became the occasion for gambling, drunkenness, idleness, cupidity, cruelty, wastefulness, extravagance, or lascivious behavior. The divines were also careful to warn, in Perkins's words, that recreation "must be moderate and sparing." Most insistently, the saints reminded each other that they were placed upon this earth in order to serve and glorify God. In Baxter's view of lawful sport or recreation, "The *end* which you really intend in using it, must be to fit you for your *service to God*; that is, either for your Callings, or for his *worship,* or for some work of obedience in which you may *please* and *Glorify* him." Thomas Gouge, author of *The Young Man's Guide Through the Wilderness of This World to the Heavenly Canaan* (1672), used more colloquial language to express this same sense of the purpose of sports and recreation. They "should be as Sauces to your Meat, to sharpen your appetite unto the duties of your Calling and not to glut yourselves with them, so as to make your selves the more unfit, both for the duties of your callings, and of Gods service." We can be sure that clerical New England nodded its approval of such sentiments.

Can these authentically Puritan opinions be construed as an affirmation of sports? Wagner is surely correct in asserting that there was always a discrepancy between what the clergy dictated and what the farmers, bakers, smiths, and wheelwrights of New England did. It is difficult to believe that ordinary New Englanders always heeded ministerial admonitions, sought invariably to "performe service unto God" in their sports, and never lost themselves in the excitement of the contest. It is improbable that the majority of Puritans, English or American, gave much thought to Election, or even to Innate Depravity, as they ran, jumped, wrestled, shot, and whacked away at the stoolball. But that is not really the issue. Did the Puritan elite encourage the development of modern sports, as Schneider and Geldbach maintain? Or did they not? The debate is over their attitudes and intentions, not over the putative behavior of their indentured servants.

There is no reason to accept the popular notion that Puritan ministers were sullenly opposed to any kind of play. The Puritans were not "puritanical" in the twentieth-century Menckenesque sense of the word, and Brailsford certainly did them an injustice when he wrote that they saw it as "their mission to erase all sport and play from men's lives." Their asceticism has been exaggerated. They were certainly stern and capable of self-denial, but they allowed for "reasonable and lawful" pleasures and were disinclined to inflict upon themselves the mortifications of Saint Anthony in the desert or Saint Simeon upon his pillar. The divines were in agreement on the lawfulness, necessity, and propriety of a wide range of physical diversions. To acknowledge this, however, is not to agree that the Puritans contributed to the rise of modern sports. In the first place, most allowable recreations were not sports at all but versions of what was, in the nineteenth century, called "calisthenics." Other acceptable pastimes (running, wrestling, and ball games) were indeed sports under almost any definition, but the Puritan affirmation of such activities lacked the enthusiasm of a Robert Dover (not to speak of the reckless abandon of a Thomas Morton). The acceptance of sports was *sotto voce* in comparison to the thundered denunciations of sinners in the hands of an angry God. When the clergy did list sports among the other "lawful recreations," their justification was traditionally Christian. Within the Puritans' hierarchical worldview, sports were instrumental—means to an end (rest, recreation, diversion, defense), rather than ends in themselves. The theological justification for rest, recreation, and diversion was that *mens sancta* required *corpus sanum*. That sports might also be done for the intrinsic pleasure of a "peak experience" or the quest for "excellence of the body" was a thought too hedonistic to be contemplated by the Puritan mind. Downame was typical when he demanded that his fellow men "performe service unto God" in their "lawful sports and recreations" as well as in their vocations. We can be sure he contemplated nothing remotely like the modern feast-of-fools theology that predicates God as the spirit of play.

There is, therefore, good reason to reject Schneider's and Geldbach's unconventional argument that Puritanism actually *furthered* the development of sports. While negative universals are always susceptible to disproof by further research, I am not aware of a single document in which a Puritan minister or magistrate demonstrates any enthusiasm for sports per se. Puritan attitudes toward sports were—not surprisingly—premodern. It may have been that their root-and-branch hostility to traditional pastimes, like maypoles and Morris dances, inadvertently cleared the way for the growth of modern forms of recreation just as their "Protestant ethic" of hard work and sober thrift contributed—in Max Weber's analysis—to the eventual emergence of modern capitalism, which was certainly one of the last things the Puritans consciously intended. Whether modern capitalism might have developed more quickly *without* the Puritan efforts to establish a Bible-based commonwealth is for others to debate. That the English and American Puritans retarded the emergence of modern sports, which "took off" only when Puritan magistrates were replaced by more worldly rulers, seems undeniable. To argue the contrary, as the revisionists have done, is a distortion of the historical facts.

CHAPTER 2

Gender and Sporting Practice in Early America, 1750–1810

Nancy L. Struna

In the latter half of the eighteenth and the early years of the nineteenth centuries, the recreational scene in what was becoming the United States was markedly different from what had been the case 100 years earlier. Well-organized thorough-bred races on formal tracks had supplanted impromptu quartermile sprints in many places along the Atlantic seaboard, and race weeks drew thousands of people to small towns and bustling cities. In the more recently settled backcountry, especially in the South, colonists constructed a variety of human and animal contests, notably baits, cockfights, and gouging matches, which tested the mettle of the contestants and appealed to the gambling interests of many. Elsewhere, foot and boat races, card games, spinning and ax-throwing matches, sledding and skating events, and even cricket games emerged, both within and outside of the context of community celebrations. The largest cities, like New York and Philadelphia, even offered commercial "pleasure gardens"; and virtually every crossroads had at least one tavern, which had been and remained the recreational center for many early Americans. By 1810, a city like Baltimore, the country's third largest, had more than 300 licensed tavernkeepers, or approximately one for every 150 inhabitants.

That late eighteenth- and early nineteenth-century Americans had begun to produce and consume more sporting practices than had their predecessors a century earlier seems certain, even from this brief description. Among the many things that are not clear about this expansionism, however, are its gender dimensions. The impressionistic evidence that undergirds the conclusion that there was an expansion in sporting practice between 1750 and 1810 suggests that it was largely a male phenomenon. Yet, most of these sources—especially, newspapers, diaries, and letters—were provided by men, so that is not particularly surprising. It does, however, require further testing.

The meanings of this expansion in sporting practice for gender relations and, in fact, the interplay between men and women over time constitute a second set

Reprinted from *Journal of Sport History*, 18:1, Spring, 1991. © The North American Society for Sport History. Reprinted by permission from The North American Society for Sport History.

of questions. Given that two of the major events of the era—the revolt against Britain and the transition to capitalism—did alter gender relations, particularly insofar as republican ideology, the disruption of family economies, and the changing relationship between work and leisure defined different roles and expectations for men and women, it seems possible to suggest that sporting practices may have incorporated those different roles and expectations. They may even have clarified male-female relations in particular ways.

The story that emerges in the following pages focuses on two aspects of the apparent post-1750 expansion in sport and other recreational forms: consumption and production. Such a division permits one to examine more fully the dimensions of gender and gender relations. That interplay, it appears, was complex, for even though men constituted the majority of producers and consumers, they neither defined nor conducted sporting practices independently of women. Instead, men and women negotiated both the content and the meanings of recreations. The consequences were gendered practices that eventually enabled men and women to sharpen, and even redefine, their social roles and to clarify their differences.

The Expansion of Sport

Several historians have suggested that major changes in personal and popular consumption occurred on both sides of the Atlantic during the eighteenth century. Early in the century the British middle ranks began to purchase what in the previous century would have constituted luxury goods for them, including china, stylistic household goods, wallpaper, books, fabrics, and even pets. By at least 1750 this ''consumer revolution'' had begun in the Anglo-American colonies, first with the landowning and mercantile gentry and then among middling and lower rank colonials. As Lois Carr, Lorena Walsh, and Gloria Main have concluded, the goods were numerous, non-essential items, and sufficiently widespread to suggest that the colonists had come to define an entirely different standard of living.

The effect of this popular consumption movement on late colonial popular culture more generally has not received any systematic attention from historians. It seems reasonable to suggest, however, that the presence of a variety of consumer goods probably underlay the broadening array of popular culture practices evident from the middle of the eighteenth century onward. Forms of and forums for music, theater, literary works, and art all expanded dramatically; and libraries, philosophic societies, fire and insurance companies, and academies and colleges formed. Modes of political action, forms of travel, eating and drinking facilities, and social organizations also proliferated and specialized.

It also seems reasonable to suggest that the apparent expansion of sporting practices was one aspect of this expanding popular culture and popular consumption movement. J.H. Plumb in particular has put forward just such an argument for sporting and other recreational practices on the British isles. There, horse racing became institutionalized within the social and political life of high society, cricket and boxing regularized and acquired specific ethics, and equipment and

Lucy (Randolph) Burwell, daughter of William and Anne (Harrison) Randolph of Virginia, was one of those upper-class women who possessed both the time and resources necessary to participate in sport and a variety of commercial entertainments in Early America. Courtesy of the Virginia Historical Society.

facilities became relatively common features in the lives of elite and low-born alike and the towns in which they lived.

Whether Anglo-American sporting practices altered in the face of changing consumption patterns and standards of living remains a question. Using the same sources that other historians have used to document changing types and ownership patterns of consumer goods, however, we should be able to explore this possibility by focusing on sporting goods, which indicate ownership and access and perhaps even behavior. These sources are estate inventories, which listed the real and personal property holdings of individuals at the time of their deaths. Estate inventories are not bias-free, particularly insofar as poorer and rural colonists tended to be underrepresented; nor did they probably register all of the goods used in sport, since not all such items were either recognizable or sport-specific.

They do, however, serve as one indicator of potential consumer behavior and, hence, suffice as one gauge of sporting consumption.

Table 2.1 summarizes the sporting goods content of the inventories registered in six counties in Maryland between 1770 and 1810. Before 1770 few sport-specific goods of any kind appeared in individual inventories, even though the same inventories did register the kinds of nonessential items that early American historians have described. The timing of their appearance thus suggests that sporting goods were probably even more nonessential than were other forms of personal property, in part perhaps because people could use make-shift items and because they participated in sport away from the confines of their homes.

By 1770, as recognizable items for sporting practice began to appear, they quickly became relatively numerous and varied. Some of these items, like the varieties of gaming tables, embellished parlors and libraries in large Georgian and smaller town houses alike. Sleighs and sulkeys replaced the once ubiquitous and multi-use sleds or sledges and wagons for winter and summer races and recreational outings, respectively, just as fowling pieces and hunting saddles supplanted muskets and ordinary riding saddles. Moreover, more people had access to these items, as the increase from six percent of estates with goods to more than a quarter of all estates by 1810 suggests.

Table 2.1   Sporting Goods in Maryland Estate Inventories, 1770-1810

Equipment	1770	1790	1810
Backgammon tables	1	6	5
Billiard tables	1	0	3
Card tables	0	9	45
Dice/box	0	0	1
Fishing hooks/lines	7	4	9
Fowling pieces	3	6	15
Hunting saddles	2	2	2
Packs of cards	0	5	2
Pleasure boat	0	0	1
Shuffleboard/checkers	0	0	4
Sleighs	1	5	7
Sulkeys	0	0	4
Totals	15	37	98
Estate N	239	206	361
Percent of estates with goods	6	18	27

Sources: Probate Records of Baltimore, Anne Arundel, Worcester, Frederick, Queen Anne, and St. Mary's counties, Hall of Records, Annapolis, Maryland.

Marylanders were not the only collectors of sporting goods between 1770 and 1810, as inventories from Suffolk County, Massachusetts described in Table 2.2 indicate.

As had been the case in Maryland, the Suffolk County inventories revealed a substantial increase in the total numbers of items and the percentage of estates with sporting equipment. There are differences between the two samples, of course; and those differences are suggestive, especially about the urban/rural dimensions of ownership. By 1810 Suffolk County had essentially become Greater Boston, and consequently most of the Suffolk inventories were Boston inventories. An examination of differences between rural and urban ownership patterns awaits a systematic analysis.

The estate inventories in both Maryland and Massachusetts help to confirm that the expansion in sporting practice indicated in newspapers and diaries was probably something other than the figment of contemporary imaginations. Neither increase, either of goods or of estates with goods, signals a consumer revolution of the dimensions evident in other consumer behavior studies, but the simple fact of the matter is that more people did have more sporting goods. Importantly as well, the owners of sporting goods were not all members of the colonial and early national upper ranks. Indeed, by 1810 more than sixty percent of the goods registered in Suffolk and Baltimore county estates belonged to middling rank decedents, a pattern that suggests that sporting goods were no longer luxuries.

Table 2.2   Sporting Goods in Suffolk County Estate Inventories, 1769-1810

Equipment	1769	1790	1810
Backgammon tables	2	3	7
Card tables	1	7	33*
Fishing goods	0	4	5
Fowling pieces	0	0	3
Packs of cards	0	0	9
Sleighs	1	4	6
Pigeon nets	1	2	0
"Hoyle's Games"	1	1	0
Totals	6	21	63
Estate N	108	145	93
Percent of estates with goods	6	14	68

Sources: Suffolk County Probate Records, Suffolk County Courthouse, Boston; 1770 inventories missing, so the ones for 1769 were used.
*The actual number of card tables was 68. Inventories also registered skates and sulkeys in 1790 and a pair of barbells in 1810.

The proliferation of sporting goods probably enabled late eighteenth- and early nineteenth-century Americans to incorporate sporting practices within their style of daily living. In doing so, such goods may have fueled the expansion of sporting practice that contemporary diarists and newspapers described. The availability of goods does not, however, account for all or even most of that expansion, especially since many sporting practices required little or no equipment. Moreover, colonists and early nationals often engaged in sport away from the home, or the farm, or the plantation—in public places where personal holdings, or the lack thereof, would not necessarily be evident or significant. Taverns, in particular, served as significant venues for sport. Consequently, an examination of tavern licensing patterns may provide another gauge of the post-1750 sporting expansion.

Taverns had always been a center of colonial social life in early America. Settlers and visitors to the colonies alike went to them for food, drink, lodging, conversation, and conviviality. Most towns and crossroads had at least one tavern; and over the course of the seventeenth and early eighteenth centuries, the numbers of taverns increased in proportion to the popular demand and an area's economic base. Tavernkeepers, in turn, often acquired particular responsibilities, such as for arbitrating disputes, and respect. They also often curried the favor of local magistrates, who controlled licenses, and customers. Accommodating the latter group was, for many tavernkeepers, the more critical task, for their livelihood depended on the patronage of people who came to refresh and relax themselves with food, drink, talk, and recreation. Consequently, many tavernkeepers found ways either to skirt the laws concerning sporting practices, especially gambling, or to harness the popular interest in recreations by organizing and promoting particular practices. Many tavernkeepers furnished tables and cards and permitted gambling, which they could limit by the amount of credit they extended. A few tavernkeepers built cockpits and alleys, and some arranged horse races and baits. One man, Benjamin Berry, even built a business of legendary proportions in west central Virginia by retaining locals to serve as fistfighters in bouts against all comers.

There is virtually no evidence to suggest that connection between taverns and sporting practice diminished over time in early America. In fact, particularly after the middle of the eighteenth century as the population grew and the economy diversified, the sporting business of tavernkeepers also expanded. In cities like New York, Philadelphia, and Charleston where taverns catered to specific groups of people, to laborers or mechanics or trading and shipping magnates, the owners arranged activities ranging from baits to billiards that their clients preferred. Elsewhere small, barely subsisting rural taverns held shooting contests; and middling rank tavernkeepers in villages and hamlets even began to import or buy from local craftspeople tables, cards, and dice.

Historians may never know the full extent of sporting practice in early American taverns or even how much of the late eighteenth and early nineteenth century sporting expansion occurred in the taverns. We can begin, however, to understand the possible dimensions of what was really the producer side of this expansion by examining licensing patterns. Such patterns do not speak directly to actual sporting practice, but they may be adequate indicators of opportunity, insofar as they focus on the people who might have permitted and even promoted sport in any given colony. In the case of Maryland these patterns are made possible by the existence of county court records, which record the names of people who obtained their licenses on an annual basis. Using the records of Baltimore County, which are more complete than are some other counties, one is able to identify who obtained licenses, when they got them, where they resided, and for how many years they kept the license. The records do not, of course, speak either to the actual use of the license or to individuals who kept unlicensed taverns.

By counting the numbers of licenses granted for the first time to any individual, we can chart the numbers of individuals who first received their license in a given decade. The Baltimore County data, both actual numbers of tavernkeepers licensed in each decade and scaled numbers to account for years in which the records are missing, appear in Figure 2.1.

Whether one examines the actual numbers of licenses given for the first time in any decade or the numbers that are scaled to account for missing years, he or she will see a similar and quite dramatic rise between 1750 and 1810. The actual numbers of licenses increased from sixty-eight in the 1750s to 1008 between 1801 and 1810, which represents a fifteen-fold increase. The scaled numbers, which rose from 108 in the earliest decade to 1440 in the final one, reflect a slightly smaller rise. Either of these sets of figures, however, suggests that the

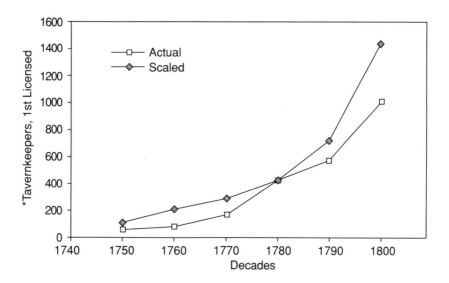

Figure 2.1 Numbers of Baltimore County tavernkeepers, first licensed.
Note. Numerous years of the court minutes no longer exist (1750-54, 1765-67, 1769-71, 1773-74, 1776, 1798-99, 1805-07); consequently, the scaled data are estimates (proportional within decades) helpful only in suggesting the probable number of all people who received licenses.
Source: Baltimore County Court Minutes, Hall of Records, Annapolis, Maryland.

number of tavernkeepers receiving licenses to do business for the first time increased significantly.

Precisely why the numbers of tavernkeepers who acquired licenses for the first time rose so dramatically, especially from 1780 onward, remains unknown. Immigration from abroad and in-migration from other parts of Maryland and other colonies probably swelled the numbers of prospective taverners. Both movements clearly changed the demographics of Baltimore County itself, which experienced approximately a tenfold rise in population. The energy and growth of Baltimore City itself may also have attracted prospective tavernkeepers. Little more than a village in 1760, it became the nation's second major entrepôt for goods and people, after New York City, by 1810. Other factors, including the relatively low cost of setting up a tavern, the instability of the trade, the prime location of Baltimore County on the north-south travel axis, and the relatively stable economy of the region, also probably encouraged the rising tide of tavernkeepers.

This pattern of increasing numbers of licensed tavernkeepers may have emerged in other colonies and states along the Atlantic seaboard, as well. Evidence from a neighboring county, Anne Arundel, suggests precisely that, albeit on a smaller scale. Anecdotal evidence from travelers and diarists also indicates that in other regions licensed taverns proliferated rapidly, as did specialized coffee and boarding houses and in unlicensed taverns, between 1750 and 1810.

The Dimensions of Gender

Contemporary accounts suggest that the post-1750 expansion in sporting practice was largely a white male phenomenon. Diaries and newspapers, especially, report that men arranged the matches and constituted a majority of both participants and spectators. These sources, as well as the numerous letters and public records, also encourage one to conclude that men organized clubs and formalized rules for sports, controlled the legislatures and courts that continued to try to regulate sporting behavior, and determined times and contexts for events. Even the events that engaged both sexes—such as horse races, card games, balls, and recreational "outings" that involved things like sleighing and fishing—appear as the products of male initiative.

Is this impression fact or artifact? This question arises for the simple reason that most of the evidence underlying this inference derives from public and private literary sources produced by men. Women, and men of lower rank and of color who lacked writing skills or the means of acquiring such skills, neither constructed nor appeared in such records in proportion to their numbers. Consequently, these sources probably misrepresent the dimensions of gender—the sex ratio was nearly equal—in many parts of late colonial and early national America.

Estate inventories and tavern licenses do, however, enable us to explore the possible gender dimensions of this movement. Though not without a male bias, both sets of records do include evidence about women. The county courts, of course, had a vested interest in gathering the information contained in these records from as many people as possible. Estate inventories were the basis for inheritance taxes levied by counties, and license applicants always paid an annual fee that went into the coffers of the county and, in some cases, the colony or state.

Because they list individuals by name, estate inventories permit us to see who owned sporting goods. Table 2.3 compares the percentages of selected goods registered in male and female estate inventories in Baltimore and Suffolk counties.

In both counties men owned all the registered sporting equipment in 1770 and a large majority of it in 1810. Although this pattern of ownership does not speak to the matter of use, it does indicate access and perhaps control of the means of participation, for in early America the owners of property held the rights to use and conveyance. In the case of sporting equipment, those owners and controllers were predominantly men.

Still, the 1790 and 1810 inventories do indicate that some women did own sporting goods. Even though the numbers are small—twelve percent of the Suffolk County estates and four percent of the Baltimore County estates with goods belonged to women in 1810—they encourage one to ask how women came to own this equipment? Did they purchase or receive it as a gift and, hence, exercise control over the equipment? Or did they acquire it through inheritance from their husbands? If the latter case were true, the presence of equipment in women's inventories might indicate men's experience rather than their own. Historians have no way of knowing for certain how women gained possession of these goods, but one can suggest whether they acquired them by inheritance or purchase (or gift) by distinguishing the owners who were either married or widowed from those who were unmarried. Table 2.4 presents this comparison for Suffolk County.

In 1790 when women's inventories first registered sporting goods, the women who owned sporting goods were either married women or widowed. Not until after the turn of the century did single women's estates in Suffolk County contain recognizable sporting goods. This pattern, coupled with the nature of the actual

Table 2.3   Percentage of Total Selected Sporting Goods in Baltimore and Suffolk County Inventories, by Gender

Decade	1769/70	1790	1810
% equipment in male estates			
Baltimore	100	89	96
Suffolk	100	94	88
% equipment in female estates			
Baltimore	0	11	4
Suffolk	0	6	12

Sources: Probate Records of Baltimore County, Hall of Records, Annapolis, Maryland; Suffolk County Probate Records, Suffolk County Courthouse, Boston, Massachusetts.

Table 2.4   Percentage of Married/Unmarried Women's Estates With Sporting Goods, Suffolk County

Decade	1790	1810
Married/widows	100	80
Single women	0	20

Source: Suffolk County Probate Records, Suffolk County Courthouse, Boston, Massachusetts.

items, reinforces the prospect that women inherited the sporting goods registered in their estates rather than having purchased them and that men controlled this aspect of the consumption of sport.

If records of the actual producers of sporting goods existed, we could more adequately determine whether most goods were made for and purchased by men. Unfortunately, few such records have survived the ravages of time; and the ones that have, especially ships' manifests and merchants accounts, merely confirm what goods were for sale rather than who purchased them. Given the goods on the market, the types and percentages of that equipment in men's estates, and the kinds of events commonly described in literary sources, however, we may conclude that men were the major consumers of particular sports, especially sports like billiards, cards, races, fishing, and hunting.

To understand more fully the gender dimensions of this post-1750 sporting expansion, we do, however, need to know something about men's and women's roles as suppliers in the market. In a society undergoing a transition to capitalism, such as late eighteenth- and early nineteenth-century America was, consumers and suppliers played critical and symbiotic roles in the construction of new standards of living and new social practices. A portrait of who made goods and organized and promoted services for whom in this emergent capitalist system, however, is just beginning to emerge. At this point, the picture highlights men making and promoting goods and services for men and women often operating independently of men to provide goods and services necessary to life but neither effectively capitalized nor efficiently incorporated within capitalist structures. A similar pattern may have shaped the post-1750 sporting expansion, as well. As owners, and presumably purchasers, men clearly outnumbered women, but whether they dominated the market as producers remains to be seen.

At this point, the only records of a supply-side group that are complete enough to permit a systematic gender analysis are those of tavernkeepers. Figure 2.2 presents the total numbers of men and women who received licenses for the first time to operate taverns in Baltimore County, Maryland.

The numbers of both men and women licensed for the first time as tavernkeepers rose steadily across the period, an increase that reflected the general population growth of the county. Men and women did not, however, acquire their first

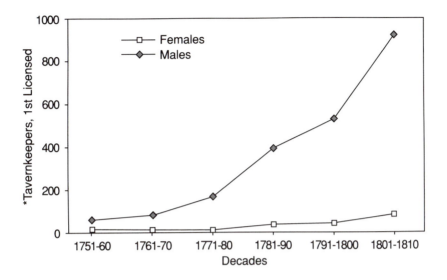

Figure 2.2 Numbers of first-time tavern licenses in Baltimore County, by gender.
Source: Baltimore County Court Minutes, Hall of Records, Annapolis, Maryland.

licenses at the same rate. The numbers of women increased from eight to ten by
the 1770s, to forty-five in the 1790s, and to eighty-two in the first decade of the
nineteenth century. The number of male licensees, on the other hand, more than
tripled by the 1770s (164) and then tripled again by the 1790s (532). Finally,
after the turn of the century, Baltimore County had slightly more than eleven
male first-time tavern licensees for each female who obtained one.

This licensing pattern requires careful, even conservative interpretation at this
point. On the one hand, of course, the fact that someone obtained a license does
not insure that he or she ever operated a tavern. Second, this pattern derives only
from the experiences in one county, and the patterns in other places may have
varied. Still, one conclusion that the Baltimore County licensing history suggests,
that many more men than women were likely to obtain licenses, seems valid.
Contemporary literary accounts from the period support it, as does the licensing
pattern in neighboring Anne Arundel County. There, males licensed as tavernkeepers increased from sixty-seven percent of the total in the 1750s to eighty-
one percent in the 1790s. An analysis of Baltimore County tavernkeepers who
obtained licenses for two or more years reveals a similar pattern. Men took out
eighty-seven percent of the licenses in the 1750s and ninety-five percent in the
first decade of the nineteenth century. Over the sixty-year period, as well, of the
1098 people who obtained licenses for at least two years, 1044 were men.

It seems reasonable to suggest, then, that the tavern trade was increasingly
run by men and, as the descriptions of activities in the taverns reveal, probably
for men. This probability, coupled with the equipment ownership patterns in
which men also dominated, encourages one to conclude that men, at the very

least, had the material base and the public presence that enabled them to define and direct much of the sporting expansion after 1750. One might also be tempted to conclude that women were minority players on this stage, particularly insofar as tavernkeeping and ownership of sporting goods are gauges of their roles as suppliers and consumers, and that the post-1750 sporting expansion really was largely a male phenomenon.

Gender Relations

Prior histories of sport in early America—and, in fact, most histories of sport at other times in American life—have encouraged us to make precisely this conclusion: sporting practice has primarily been a male phenomenon. Men have constituted the majority of participants, and they have written most of the rules and created most of the organizations. Sporting practice, in turn, has been incorporated within the rituals of manhood and the institutions of men. Carried to the extreme, this nearly formulaic linking of sport and men has even produced a distinctive social type, or trope, that modernizationists define as "modern sport."

As secure as this conclusion is in the writings of historians, however, it may baldly, and badly, misstate the reality of history. It surely does so in the case of early America, where women were agents in the making of sporting practices in ways and to an extent beyond what either their numbers or historians' prior reading of the literary evidence have suggested. For certain, colonial and early national women participated in recreational forms, although not always in full view of contemporary chroniclers. But they also played a role in the construction of what have traditionally been described as men's sporting practices, particularly insofar as their labor often underlay men's leisure and insofar as their behaviors and expectations shaped those of men. Moreover, as the eighteenth century lengthened, women assumed an increasingly visible public presence in formalized and often commercialized recreations for both sexes. Promoters targeted women as prospective participants and consumers, and organizers encouraged women to attend events.

The full extent of women's involvement in the post-1750 sporting expansion may never be known, but it seems clear that, just as did men, women participated in more numerous forms of sport. This was particularly true for middle and upper rank women, among whom the changing nature of work, improved modes of travel, and the tightening of kin and neighborhood bonds produced time and opportunity for recreations. Their own diaries and letters reveal that they played cards and gambled, and they fished, skated, ran foot races, and went sledding. Just prior to the Revolution, when domestic production became all-important, and until mechanization removed it from the domestic scene, women of all ranks transformed the necessary work of spinning into competitive contests. They divided themselves into groups, either by neighborhood or skill, and set out to produce as many skeins of yarn as possible. Invariably, as well, someone would produce a prize for the winning side.

Women's participation in sport extended well beyond the confines of the home and domestic production, particularly to the era's most commonly discussed practices, horseback riding and racing. Wherever horses were common, and whether or not sidesaddles were available, girls and women took to riding as if it were an ordinary expectation. In a place like post-war Charleston, of course, it was, or so it seemed to the Venezuelan-born traveler, Francisco de Miranda, who concluded that riding was the women's "favorite diversion." But women did more than ride; they also raced, occasionally "with the best male riders for a wager" or among themselves. In 1791, as the Frenchman Ferdinand Bayard observed some women challenge one another to a race near Bath, Virginia, he concluded that all of the contestants were "skillful and fearless riders."

The most telling comment about late colonial and early national women equestrians, however, may be one made on the eve of the Revolution. Having observed the members of the Virginia family of Robert Carter, as well as their friends and relatives, for over a year in his role as tutor, Philip Fithian concluded that the females of the family "are passionately fond of Riding." Contemporaries must have recognized a similar emotion and interest among the wives and daughters of other Virginia and Maryland planters and merchants, and they responded accordingly. Between the 1760s and the 1780s—as thoroughbred racing formalized, as race weeks replaced race days, and as the crowds of spectators rose from several hundred to several thousand people—the jockey clubs and individual entrepreneurs changed the face of racing in the Chesapeake in substantive ways. They initiated "Ladies purses," or specific events often on the third and final day of racing. They also designated seats for women and improved and expanded facilities at the course for them, even to the point of constructing "a commodious House" where women could escape inclement weather, rest, or find other entertainments.

What all of this suggests, of course, is that horse racing in the Chesapeake, and eventually in other sections of the eastern mid-Atlantic and the deep South, was not primarily or even predominantly a male practice. Men were the most visible, public contestants, but they were not the only ones. Nor did they alone construct the racing scene; women were evident along the rail, and women's interests shaped the structure of events. The net effect was a strikingly different sporting practice than was the case in some other places. In New England, for example, where trotting and pacing races were more common than thoroughbred events, there is no evidence that women displayed much interest in the matches, nor is there any evidence that race organizers catered to women. The same is true about the various forms of racing that emerged in the southern piedmont regions and in western Pennsylvania and New York. The disinterest of women in racing in these areas, and perhaps even the disinterest in women's interests, may help to explain why horse racing, in any of its other forms, never appeared to be as popular or as important in the cultures and social lives of the people of those areas as did thoroughbred races in the Chesapeake.

Recreational practices in some of these other regions did, however, incorporate women from the 1750s onward. In Salem, Massachusetts, for example, women and men went sailing and then returned to shore for supper and an evening at backgammon or cards. Wintry evenings in the mid-Atlantic states, as well as in New England, permitted sleigh rides and races, while southerners organized balls and card parties. Rural families throughout the country regularly celebrated the end of a harvest with frolics, which included dancing and games. In northern New Jersey and the Hudson River region of New York, the "pinkster" holiday, a Dutch- and African-influenced time of dancing and drinking, among other things, became an annual event for the young and old of both sexes.

In many of these events and celebrations, women's experiences extended beyond their traditional, or at least pre-1750, roles as provisioners in what were family and neighborhood gatherings. They cast the lines and drew seines, they dealt cards and rode to the hunt, and, of course, they sang and danced. They were, in effect, active participants, and perhaps even partners, in practices that may have proliferated and regularized at least in part because of women's presence, in greater numbers, and their interests in establishing new gender relations. For certain, the structure of these events suggests that women, and men, chose to construct practices that minimized the physical differences between them and maximized shared experiences.

In the process of constructing these shared experiences, late colonial and early national Americans also altered the place and significance of recreational practices in general and of sports in particular. Horse races, for example, ceased to be tied to elections and court days and emerged as central rituals in the culture of the Chesapeake. Fishing parties and sleigh rides and races in many regions emerged from the shadows of ordinary food gathering and necessary travel-linked tasks and became independent, and joyful, social practices. Balls, also, expanded beyond their earlier settings in officious celebrations of royal anniversaries, birthdays, and military and political victories. In fact, for middle and upper rank early Americans after 1750, particularly those who either lived or visited for lengthy periods in urban areas, balls organized in the context of subscription assemblies became the central social events, even the hallmark of emergent bourgeoisie society.

This last point requires some expansion. Not all women exerted the same degree of influence in the early American sporting culture, nor did all women experience similar changes in their relationships with men. Slave women, for certain, clearly remained subordinate to the whims and whips of their masters, both black and white; and, except for holiday celebrations and weekend or evening breaks, they rarely had the opportunity to construct their own recreational forms. White servants, also, had little effect on the expanding sporting culture, except insofar as they, like slave women, provided the work which underlay the leisure of their mistresses and masters and insofar as they took advantage of, and were taken advantage of in, the expanding sphere of bawdy houses and laborers' commercial entertainments. Finally, women who lived on the fringes of late colonial and early national society, in the most recently settled frontier regions, did not find their experiences substantially different from those of their ancestors a century or more earlier. Often isolated on farmsteads and with children and farms to tend, they knew little of the outside world or its recreations. Weddings and Christmas aside, theirs was a world dominated by men and expressed in gouging and drinking and shooting.

Farm women in the longer settled and more heavily populated regions of early America, as well as the wives and daughters of village artisans and seafarers, played a more visible role in the construction of late eighteenth- and early nineteenth-century recreations than did any of these women who were on the margins of society. Their work, which was often independent of men's but interdependent with the family and village economy and society, often left them with the means and the opportunity to participate and even to arrange frolics and quiltings and picnics or barbecues. Young women, especially, sought out or joined neighboring youths, of both sexes, in various recreations. Their mothers, in turn, became the managers and moral monitors of their pleasure-seeking offspring. They knew what historians of the family and women's experience have only recently begun to recognize: that recreation occasionally resulted in procreation.

Neither their recreations nor their roles in shaping recreations altered as rapidly or as substantively for farm and village women, however, as both did for urban women, especially those in the middle and upper ranks. These women, of course, were the co-creators of balls and assemblies, and they had access to the card and billiard tables and the fowling pieces and sleighs that merchants sold and their husbands acquired. They also possessed the resources and the time to enjoy the increasing variety of commercial entertainments, from tumbling and equestrian exhibitions to pleasure gardens to bathing apparatus, that urban entrepreneurs devised.

Particularly after the Revolution, as capitalist enterprise permeated many facets of urban life, the wives and daughters of the new nation's shopkeepers, bankers, civil servants, merchants, and factory owners found themselves in a new situation. In New York, Philadelphia, Baltimore, and Charleston, the organizers of commercial recreational facilities actively pursued the participation of women, as well as that of men. The owners of buildings with rooms large enough for assemblies advertised in the papers and stressed the decorous behavior and good food that awaited dancers. Charles Quinan, who operated Queen Ann's in Philadelphia, installed "flying coaches" for women and, for their escorts, "horse(s)" that whirled about—all apparently in an effort to draw customers. Not surprisingly, as well, in New York City where the competition for bourgeoisie customers was great, one operator of a pleasure garden went a step beyond his competitors. Having just completed a "grand Amphitheatre" for the July 4th celebration at his Vauxhall Garden, Joseph Delacroix ended his description of the proposed entertainments with this warning: "No gentleman will be admitted without (being) accompanied by a lady."

Delacroix's statement suggests two expectations that men in his profession held about consumers of commercial recreations at the turn of the century. First, male patrons were not entirely trustworthy; their moral judgments were suspect, and they could be rowdy. Second, only women could effectively curb the passions of the men and prevent them from overdrinking, bothering other customers, or getting into arguments or fights. Put another way, he expected his urban female customers to assume precisely the kind of role that farm and village women had assumed, the role of moral arbiter, of social manager. He was not alone. Other men, including the members of jockey clubs, organizers of assemblies, theater managers, and exhibition and museum promoters actively appealed to prospective female consumers, especially in the decades immediately after the Revolution. They did so, in part of course, because they accepted the role for women that republican ideology expressed, the role as republican mothers, as caretakers of the new nation's virtue.

Republicanism and capitalism thus heightened, rather than diminished, the significance and directions of male-female negotiations in the construction of post-Revolutionary recreations. Men owned the vast majority of sporting goods and dominated as tavernkeepers, merchants, and leisure organizers, but women were clearly essential to the use of those goods and the consumption of recreations. For certain, women provided much of the labor that freed men for leisure, and they existed as a substantive body of clients to whom commercial promoters appealed. Moreover, with women responsible for the nation's virtue, they ultimately affected the definition of two different but interrelated codes of behavior evident in early national sporting life.

The first of these codes was that of the ''sportsman.'' In contemporary terms, a sportsman engaged only in particular sports, especially the outdoor events of hunting, fishing, quoits, and horse racing and a few indoor games like billiards and whist. He was also one who set limits on the kill—as ''one brace of woodcocks and two of partridges''—kept the inevitable wager small, and displayed generosity, courtesy, and bravery. The sportsman, in short, was a masculine type embued with masculine values; and he appealed to those leading men, like John Stuart Skinner and John Randolph, who had both a political and an economic stake in distinguishing themselves from propertyless wage-laborers and servants in the young nation.

Men like Skinner and Randolph also had a stake in distinguishing themselves— and their sports—from women. Rank differences with all their implications for economic and political order and power, rather than gender differences, provided the rationale; but gender provided the means, via the second code constructed by early national middle and upper rank Americans: the cult of domesticity. Rooted in the image of the republican mother, which first expressed virtue as a feminine characteristic and what the important female virtues were, the cult of domesticity prescribed female dependency highlighted by domestic exercises and very few active, outdoor recreations. As championed by Skinner's contemporary, Catharine Beecher, the cult of domesticity envisioned forms and forums for recreations among women that were antithetical to Skinner's own tabulation of the rural ones embraced by a sportsman.

This story thus ends with an ironic twist to what was a lengthy and complex series of negotiations between men and women about the content of early national recreations and their respective roles in them. The code of the sportsman and the cult of domesticity emerged as opposing categories of experiences in a world of "separate spheres" among upper and middle class Anglo-Americans. Historically, however, they are not separable, for men and women like Skinner and Beecher negotiated the experiences collapsed in these social types. They did so, of course, in a social, economic, and political context that was far different from the one Mittleberger had encountered in the 1750s or even Bayard knew in the 1790s. Capitalism had penetrated more deeply into American life, and the sexual division of labor and leisure had broadened. In such an era, the participant of active rural sports, the sportsman, which Skinner championed and the domestically inclined and morally upright women whom Beecher upheld declared the all-important differences between men and women. Each also made a statement about gender relations.

Suggested Readings

Blanchard, Kendall. *The Mississippi Choctaws at Play.* Urbana, IL: University of Illinois Press, 1981.

Brailsford, Dennis. *Sport and Society: Elizabeth to Anne.* London: Routledge & Kegan Paul, 1969.

Brobeck, Stephen. "Revolutionary Change in Colonial Philadelphia: The Brief Life of the Proprietary Gentry." *William and Mary Quarterly,* 33(1976): 410-434.

Carson, Jane. *Colonial Virginians at Play.* Charlottesville, VA: University of Virginia Press, 1965.

Cheska, Alyce. "Native American Games as Strategies of Societal Maintenance." In *Forms of Play of Native North Americans,* edited by Edward Norbeck and Claire R. Farrer. St. Paul, MN: West Publishing, 1979, 227-247.

Culin, Stewart. *Games of the North American Indians.* Washington, DC: U.S. Government Printing Office, 1907.

Isaac, Rhys. *The Transformation of Virginia, 1740-1790.* Chapel Hill: University of North Carolina Press, 1982.

Jable, J. Thomas. "The English Puritans: Suppressors of Sport and Amusement?" *Canadian Journal of History of Sport and Physical Education,* 7(1976): 33-40.

Jable, J. Thomas. "Pennsylvania's Blue Laws: A Quaker Experiment in the Suppression of Sport and Amusements, 1682-1740." *Journal of Sport History,* 1(1974): 107-121.

Kennard, June A. "Maryland Colonials at Play: Their Sports and Games." *Research Quarterly,* 41(1970): 389-395.

Ledbetter, Bonnie S. "Sports and Games of the American Revolution." *Journal of Sport History,* 6(1979): 29-40.

Oxendine, Joseph. *American Indian Sports Heritage.* Champaign: Human Kinetics, 1988.

Salter, Michael A. "Play in Ritual: An Ethnohistorical Overview of Native North America." *Stadion,* 3(1977): 230-243.

Struna, Nancy L. "The Formalizing of Sport and the Formation of an Elite: The Chesapeake Gentry, 1650-1720." *Journal of Sport History,* 13(1986): 212-234.

Struna, Nancy L. "Puritans and Sport: The Irrevitable Tide of Change." *Journal of Sport History,* 4(1977): 1-21.

Struna, Nancy L. "Sport and Society in Early America." *The International Journal of the History of Sport,* 5(1988): 292-311.

Wagner, Peter. "Literary Evidence of Sport in Colonial New England." *Stadion,* 2(1976): 233-249.

Wagner, Peter. "Puritan Attitudes Toward Physical Recreation in Seventeenth Century New England." *Journal of Sport History,* 6(1979): 29-40.

Wagner, Peter. *Puritan Attitudes Toward Recreation in Early Seventeenth-Century New England.* Frankfurt: Peter Lang, 1982.

PART 2

HEALTH, EXERCISE, AND SPORT IN A RAPIDLY CHANGING SOCIETY, 1820–1870

The rapid changes in American society during the mid-nineteenth century greatly influenced sport. Burgeoning industrialization, influx of immigrants, sectional conflict between the North and South, religious revivalism, common school movement, women's rights crusades, and a host of other reform movements combined to effect both a change in the nature of sport and a shift in attitude toward health and exercise. Common to other periods in American history, the changing view of health, exercise, and sport during this time took various forms depending on such factors as gender, social class, economic status, geographical location, and urban and rural differences. While men in the outreaches of the southern backcountry defended their honor through gouging matches, and slaves on remote plantations established their own culture through participation in different recreational activities, others were expressing newfound concern for the health of women, and sportsmen in New York City were making organizational changes in harness racing that would ultimately lead to modernization of the sport.

Of all the sports Americans participated in during this period, perhaps none was more violent than the gouging matches among men in the southern backcountry. This style of fighting, reported with remarkable regularity by travelers to the region, had no rules except for a ban on weapons and promoted "maximum disfigurement" and the severing of body parts. Why this form of fighting became so popular is Elliott Gorn's focus in his essay, " 'Gouge and Bite, Pull Hair and

Scratch': The Social Significance of Fighting in the Southern Backcountry,'' which is chapter 3. Gorn explains that ''rough-and-tumble'' fighting flourished in the southern backcountry because of primitive legal institutions, feeble market economy, nature of daily work, lack of moral uplift of the domestic family, and ''intensely communal'' as well as highly competitive styles of life. Rough-and-tumble fighting was a symbolic act that allowed men in the southern backcountry to prove their self-worth, retain their social standing in the community, and defend their reputations against others in the all-male subculture.

Rough-and-tumble fighting was not evident in the slave community of the Old South. As pointed out in chapter 4, my essay, ''Sport and Popular Pastimes: Shadow of the Slavequarter,'' the recreational and sporting activities of slaves living on both farms and large plantations were marked by little violence, a more cooperative than competitive orientation, and emphasis on group involvement. Participation in recreational and sporting activities was the medium through which slaves maintained kinship ties, perpetuated existing friendships, expressed individual fears and anxieties, and commented on the peculiarities of their masters and their families. Dancing in their own particular style, roaming fields and woods in search of game, swimming in nearby lakes and streams, and testing their physical strength in numerous games allowed slaves to transcend their institutionally defined role and create a unique culture within the restricted confines of the plantation community.

While men in the southern backcountry were inflicting bodily damage on one another and slaves coped with the cruelties of the plantation system through recreational activities, efforts were being made by intellectuals to improve the health of American citizens. Recognizing the poor physical condition of Americans caused by their inactive lifestyles and the squalid conditions of burgeoning cities, intellectuals and other advocates of reform ignited a movement directed at improving the health of individuals through proper diet, fresh air, abstention from alcohol and tobacco, and promotion of exercise, active games, recreation, physical education, and athletics.

The health movement, evidenced by educational programs, books, and scholarly journals on exercise and physical development, was directed toward women as well as men. Increased attention was being paid to the health of women in America, and this was reflected in the concern for their physical development. In chapter 5, Roberta Park traces this early interest in the physical development of women in her essay, '' 'Embodied Selves': The Rise and Development of Concern for Physical Education, Active Games and Recreation for American Women, 1776-1865.'' Through analysis of the writings of such people as William B. Fowle, Dio Lewis, Frances Wright, Emma Willard, Catharine Beecher, Sarah Josepha Hale, Margaret Fuller, Andrew Combe, and William A. Alcott, Park correctly places the concern for women's health in the context of the expanding medical profession, educational reform, and the women's rights movement. ''With varying degree of intensity,'' notes Park, these individuals called attention to the health of women through the promotion of active games, calisthenics, exercise, dress reform, instruction in physiology and anatomy, and advocacy of more healthful schools and homes.

Concern for the health of women, and other Americans for that matter, was inextricably bound up with problems arising from the burgeoning cities in America. British travelers and other social commentators were correct in placing much of the blame for the poor health of Americans on the growth of cities and its associated ills. The city also provided, however, the fertile soil needed for the blossoming of commercialized sport. As several scholars have pointed out, cities provided the elements required for the rise of highly organized sport in America.

The most important sport to emerge from the city and its environs was harness racing. Commonly associated with the country fair, harness racing actually emerged from the urban setting, particularly New York City, to become America's most popular commercialized sport. The development of harness racing in America's largest city is the focus of chapter 6, Mel Adelman's essay, "The First Modern Sport in America: Harness Racing in New York City, 1825-1870." Adelman argues that between 1825-1870 harness racing was transformed into an organized sport characterized by formal organizations, standardized rules, national competitions, role differentiation, public information, and statistics and records.

CHAPTER 3

"Gouge and Bite, Pull Hair and Scratch": The Social Significance of Fighting in the Southern Backcountry

Elliott J. Gorn

"I would advise you when You do fight Not to act like Tygers and Bears as these Virginians do—Biting one anothers Lips and Noses off, and *gowging* one another—that is, thrusting out one anothers Eyes, and kicking one another on the Cods, to the Great damage of many a Poor Woman." Thus, Charles Woodmason, an itinerant Anglican minister born of English gentry stock, described the brutal form of combat he found in the Virginia backcountry shortly before the American Revolution. Although historians are more likely to study people thinking, governing, worshiping, or working, how men fight—who participates, who observes, which rules are followed, what is at stake, what tactics are allowed—reveals much about past cultures and societies.

The evolution of southern backwoods brawling from the late eighteenth century through the antebellum era can be reconstructed from oral traditions and travelers' accounts. As in most cultural history, broad patterns and uneven trends rather than specific dates mark the way. The sources are often problematic and must be used with care; some speculation is required. But the lives of common people cannot be ignored merely because they leave few records. "To feel for a feller's eyestrings and make him tell the news" was not just mayhem but an act freighted with significance for both social and cultural history.

As early as 1735, boxing was "much in fashion" in parts of Chesapeake Bay, and forty years later a visitor from the North declared that, along with dancing, fiddling, small swords, and card playing, it was an essential skill for all young Virginia gentlemen. The term "boxing," however, did not necessarily refer to

This essay was originally printed in the *American Historical Review*, 90, February, 1985, and is reprinted here by permission of the author.

the comparatively tame style of bare-knuckle fighting familiar to eighteenth-century Englishmen. In 1746, four deaths prompted the governor of North Carolina to ask for legislation against "the barbarous and inhuman manner of boxing which so much prevails among the lower sort of people." The colonial assembly responded by making it a felony "to cut out the Tongue or pull out the eyes of the King's Liege People." Five years later the assembly added slitting, biting, and cutting off noses to the list of offenses. Virginia passed similar legislation in 1748 and revised these statutes in 1772 explicitly to discourage men from "gouging, plucking, or putting out an eye, biting or kicking or stomping upon" quiet peaceable citizens. By 1786 South Carolina had made premeditated mayhem a capital offense, defining the crime as severing another's bodily parts.

Laws notwithstanding, the carnage continued. Philip Vickers Fithian, a New Jerseyite serving as tutor for an aristocratic Virginia family, confided to his journal on September 3, 1774:

> By appointment is to be fought this Day near Mr. *Lanes* two fist Battles between four young Fellows. The Cause of the battles I have not yet known; I suppose either that they are lovers, and one has in Jest or reality some way supplanted the other; or has in a merry hour called him a *Lubber* or a *thick-Skull,* or a *Buckskin,* or a *Scotsman,* or perhaps one has mislaid the other's hat, or knocked a peach out of his Hand, or offered him a dram without wiping the mouth of the Bottle; all these, and ten thousand more quite as trifling and ridiculous are thought and accepted as just Causes of immediate Quarrels, in which every diabolical Strategem for Mastery is allowed and practiced.

The "trifling and ridiculous" reasons for these fights had an unreal quality for the matter-of-fact Yankee. Not assaults on persons or property but slights, insults, and thoughtless gestures set young southerners against each other. To call a man a "buckskin," for example, was to accuse him of the poverty associated with leather clothing, while the epithet "Scotsman" tied him to the low-caste Scots-Irish who settled the southern highlands. Fithian could not understand how such trivial offenses caused the bloody battles. But his incomprehension turned to rage when he realized that spectators attended these "odious and filthy amusements" and that the fighters allayed their spontaneous passions in order to fix convenient dates and places, which allowed time for rumors to spread and crowds to gather. The Yankee concluded that only devils, prostitutes, or monkeys could sire creatures so unfit for human society.

Descriptions of these "fist battles," as Fithian called them, indicate that they generally began like English prize fights. Two men, surrounded by onlookers, parried blows until one was knocked or thrown down. But there the similarity ceased. Whereas "Broughton's Rules" of the English ring specified that a round ended when either antagonist fell, southern bruisers only began fighting at this point. Enclosed not inside a formal ring—the "magic circle" defining a special place with its own norms of conduct—but within whatever space the spectators

The violent nature of fighting in the southern backcountry is vividly depicted in this woodcut from *The Crockett Almanac, 1840.*
Courtesy of the Lilly Library, Indiana University.

left vacant, fighters battled each other until one called enough or was unable to continue. Combatants boasted, howled, and cursed. As words gave way to action, they tripped and threw, gouged and butted, scratched and choked each other. "But what is worse than all," Isaac Weld observed, "these wretches in their combat endeavor to their utmost to tear out each other's testicles."

Around the beginning of the nineteenth century, men sought original labels for their brutal style of fighting. "Rough-and-tumble" or simply "gouging" gradually replaced "boxing" as the name for these contests. Before two bruisers attacked each other, spectators might demand whether they proposed to fight fair—according to Broughton's Rules—or rough-and-tumble. Honor dictated that all techniques be permitted. Except for a ban on weapons, most men chose to fight "no holts barred," doing what they wished to each other without interference, until one gave up or was incapacitated.

The emphasis on maximum disfigurement, on severing bodily parts, made this fighting style unique. Amid the general mayhem, however, gouging out an opponent's eye became the sine qua non of rough-and-tumble fighting, much like the knockout punch in modern boxing. The best gougers, of course, were adept at other fighting skills. Some allegedly filed their teeth to bite off an enemy's appendages more efficiently. Still, liberating an eyeball quickly became a fighter's surest route to victory and his most prestigious accomplishment. To this end, celebrated heroes fired their fingernails hard, honed them sharp, and oiled them slick. " 'You have come off badly this time, I doubt?' " declared an alarmed passerby on seeing the piteous condition of a renowned fighter. " 'Have I,' says he triumphantly, shewing from his pocket at the same time an eye, which he had extracted during the combat, and preserved for a trophy."

As the new style of fighting evolved, its geographical distribution changed. Leadership quickly passed from the southern seaboard to upcountry counties and the western frontier. Although examples could be found throughout the South, rough-and-tumbling was best suited to the backwoods, where hunting, herding, and semisubsistence agriculture predominated over market-oriented, staple crop production. Thus, the settlers of western Carolina, Kentucky, and Tennessee, as well as upland Mississippi, Alabama, and Georgia, became especially known for their pugnacity.

The social base of rough-and-tumbling also shifted with the passage of time. Although brawling was always considered a vice of the "lower sort," eighteenth-century Tidewater gentlemen sometimes found themselves in brutal fights. These combats grew out of challenges to men's honor—to their status in patriarchal, kin-based, small-scale communities—and were woven into the very fabric of daily life. Rhys Isaac has observed that the Virginia gentry set the tone for a fiercely competitive style of living. Although they valued hierarchy, individual status was never permanently fixed, so men frantically sought to assert their prowess—by grand boasts over tavern gaming tables laden with money, by whipping and tripping each other's horses in violent quarter-races, by wagering one-half year's earnings on the flash of a fighting cock's gaff. Great planters and small shared an ethos that extolled courage bordering on foolhardiness and cherished magnificent, if irrational, displays of largess.

Piety, hard work, and steady habits had their adherents, but in this society aggressive self-assertion and manly pride were the real marks of status. Even the gentry's vaunted hospitality demonstrated a family's community standing, so conviviality itself became a vehicle for rivalry and emulation. Rich and poor might revel together during "public times," but gentry patronage of sports and festivities kept the focus of power clear. Above all, brutal recreations toughened men for a violent social life in which the exploitation of labor, the specter of poverty, and a fierce struggle for status were daily realities.

During the final decades of the eighteenth century, however, individuals like Fithian's young gentlemen became less inclined to engage in rough-and-tumbling. Many in the planter class now wanted to distinguish themselves from social inferiors more by genteel manners, gracious living, and paternal prestige than by patriarchal prowess. They sought alternatives to brawling and found them by imitating the

English aristocracy. A few gentlemen took boxing lessons from professors of pugilism or attended sparring exhibitions given by touring exponents of the manly art. More important, dueling gradually replaced hand-to-hand combat. The code of honor offered a genteel, though deadly, way to settle personal disputes while demonstrating one's elevated status. Ceremony distinguished antiseptic duels from lower-class brawls. Cool restraint and customary decorum proved a man's ability to shed blood while remaining emotionally detached, to act as mercilessly as the poor whites but to do so with chilling gentility.

Slowly, then, rough-and-tumble fighting found specific locus in both human and geographical landscapes. We can watch men grapple with the transition. When an attempt at a formal duel aborted, Savannah politician Robert Watkins and United States Senator James Jackson resorted to gouging. Jackson bit Watson's finger to save his eye. Similarly, when "a low fellow who pretends to gentility" insulted a distinguished doctor, the gentleman responded with a proper challenge. "He had scarcely uttered these words, before the other flew at him, and in an instant turned his eye out of the socket, and while it hung upon his cheek, the fellow was barbarous enough to endeavor to pluck it entirely out." By the new century, such ambiguity had lessened, as rough-and-tumble fighting was relegated to individuals in backwoods settlements. For the next several decades, eye-gouging matches were focal events in the culture of lower-class males who still relished the wild ways of old.

"I saw more than one man who wanted an eye, and ascertained that I was now in the region of 'gouging,' " reported young Timothy Flint, a Harvard educated, Presbyterian minister bound for Louisiana missionary work in 1816. His spirits buckled as his party turned down the Mississippi from the Ohio Valley. Enterprising farmers gave way to slothful and vulgar folk whom Flint considered barely civilized. Only vicious fighting and disgusting accounts of battles past disturbed their inertia. Residents assured him that the "blackguards" excluded gentlemen from gouging matches. Flint was therefore perplexed when told that a barbarous-looking man was the "best" in one settlement, until he learned that best in this context meant not the most moral, prosperous, or pious but the local champion who had whipped all the rest, the man most dexterous at extracting eyes.

Because rough-and-tumble fighting declined in settled areas, some of the most valuable accounts were written by visitors who penetrated the backcountry. Travel literature was quite popular during America's infancy, and many profit-minded authors undoubtedly wrote with their audience's expectations in mind. Images of heroic frontiersmen, of crude but unencumbered natural men, enthralled both writers and readers. Some who toured the new republic in the decades following the Revolution had strong prejudices against America's democratic pretensions. English travelers in particular doubted that the upstart nation—in which the lower class shouted its equality and the upper class was unable or unwilling to exercise proper authority—could survive. Ironically, backcountry fighting became a symbol for both those who inflated and those who punctured America's expansive national ego.

Frontier braggarts enjoyed fulfilling visitors' expectations of backwoods depravity, pumping listeners full of gruesome legends. Their narratives projected a satisfying, if grotesque, image of the American rustic as a fearless, barbaric, larger-than-life democrat. But they also gave Englishmen the satisfaction of seeing their former countrymen run wild in the wilderness. Gouging matches offered a perfect metaphor for the Hobbesian war of all against all, of men tearing each other apart once institutional restraints evaporated, of a heart of darkness beating in the New World. As they made their way from the northern port towns to the southern countryside, or down the Ohio to southwestern waterways, observers concluded that geographical and moral descent went hand in hand. Brutal fights dramatically confirmed their belief that evil lurked in the deep shadows of America's sunny democratic landscape.

And yet, it would be a mistake to dismiss all travelers' accounts of backwoods fighting as fictions born of prejudice. Many sojourners who were sober and careful observers of America left detailed reports of rough-and-tumbles. Aware of the tradition of frontier boasting, they distinguished apocryphal stories from personal observation, wild tales from eye-witness accounts. Although gouging matches became a sort of literary convention, many travelers compiled credible descriptions of backwoods violence.

"The indolence and dissipation of the middling and lower classes of Virginia are such as to give pain to every reflecting mind," one anonymous visitor declared. "Horse-racing, cock-fighting, and boxing-matches are standing amusements, for which they neglect all business; and in the latter of which they conduct themselves with a barbarity worthy of their savage neighbors." Thomas Anburey agreed. He believed that the Revolution's leveling of class distinctions left the "lower people" dangerously independent. Although Anburey found poor whites usually hospitable and generous, he was disturbed by their sudden outbursts of impudence, their aversion to labor and love of drink, their vengefulness and savagery. They shared with their betters a taste for gaming, horse racing, and cockfighting, but "boxing matches, in which they display such barbarity, as fully marks their innate ferocious disposition," were all their own. Anburey concluded that an English prize fight was humanity itself compared to Virginia combat.

Another visitor, Charles William Janson, decried the loss of social subordination, which caused the rabble to reinterpret liberty and equality as licentiousness. Paternal authority—the font of social and political order—had broken down in America, as parents gratified their children's whims, including youthful tastes for alcohol and tobacco. A national mistrust of authority had brought civilization to its nadir among the poor whites of the South. "The lower classes are the most abject that, perhaps, ever peopled a Christian land. They live in the woods and desarts and many of them cultivate no more land than will raise them corn and cabbages, which, with fish, and occasionally a piece of pickled pork or bacon, are their constant food. . . . Their habitations are more wretched than can be conceived; the huts of the poor of Ireland, or even the meanest Indian wig-wam, displaying more ingenuity and greater industry." Despite their degradation— perhaps because of it—Janson found the poor whites extremely jealous of their republican rights and liberties. They considered themselves the equals of their best-educated neighbors and intruded on whomever they chose. The gouging match this fastidious Englishman witnessed in Georgia was the epitome of lower-class depravity:

> We found the combatants . . . fast clinched by the hair, and their thumbs endeavoring to force a passage into each other's eyes; while several of the bystanders were betting upon the first eye to be turned out of its socket. For some time the combatants avoided the *thumb stroke* with dexterity. At length they fell to the ground, and in an instant the uppermost sprung up with his antagonist's eye in his hand!!! The savage crowd applauded, while, sick with horror, we galloped away from the infernal scene. The name of the sufferrer was John Butler, a Carolinian, who, it seems, had been dared to the combat by a Georgian; and the first eye was for the honor of the state to which they respectively belonged.

Janson concluded that even Indian "savages" and London's rabble would be outraged by the beastly Americans.

While Janson toured the lower South, his countryman Thomas Ashe explored the territory around Wheeling, Virginia. A passage, dated April 1806, from his *Travels in America* gives us a detailed picture of gouging's social context. Ashe expounded on Wheeling's potential to become a center of trade for the Ohio and upper Mississippi valleys, noting that geography made the town a natural rival of Pittsburgh. Yet Wheeling lagged in "worthy commercial pursuits, and industrious and moral dealings." Ashe attributed this backwardness to the town's frontier ways, which attracted men who specialized in drinking, plundering Indian property, racing horses, and watching cockfights. A Wheeling Quaker assured Ashe that mores were changing, that the underworld element was about to be driven out. Soon, the godly would gain control of the local government, enforce strict observance of the Sabbath, and outlaw vice. Ashe was sympathetic but doubtful. In Wheeling, only heightened violence and debauchery distinguished Sunday from the rest of the week. The citizens' willingness to close up shop and neglect business on the slightest pretext made it a questionable residence for any respectable group of men, let alone a society of Quakers.

To convey the rough texture of Wheeling life, Ashe described a gouging match. Two men drinking at a public house argued over the merits of their respective horses. Wagers made, they galloped off to the race course. "Two thirds of the population followed:—blacksmiths, shipwrights, all left work: the town appeared a desert. The stores were shut. I asked a proprietor, why the warehouses did not remain open? He told me all good was done for the day: that the people would remain on the ground till night, and many stay till the following morning." Determined to witness an event deemed so important that the entire town went on holiday, Ashe headed for the track. He missed the initial heat but arrived in time to watch the crowd raise the stakes to induce a rematch. Six horses competed, and spectators bet a small fortune, but the results were inconclusive. Umpires' opinions were given and rejected. Heated words, then fists flew. Soon, the melee narrowed to two individuals, a Virginian and a Kentuckian. Because fights were

common in such situations, everyone knew the proper procedures, and the combatants quickly decided to "tear and rend" one another—to rough-and-tumble—
rather than "fight fair." Ashe elaborated: "You startle at the words tear and
rend, and again do not understand me. You have heard these terms, I allow,
applied to beasts of prey and to carnivorous animals; and your humanity cannot
conceive them applicable to man: It nevertheless is so, and the fact will not
permit me the use of any less expressive term."

The battle began—size and power on the Kentuckian's side, science and craft
on the Virginian's. They exchanged cautious throws and blows, when suddenly
the Virginian lunged at his opponent with a panther's ferocity. The crowd roared
its approval as the fight reached its violent denouement:

> The shock received by the Kentuckyan, and the want of breath, brought
> him instantly to the ground. The Virginian never lost his hold; like those
> bats of the South who never quit the subject on which they fasten till they
> taste blood, he kept his knees in his enemy's body; fixing his claws in his
> hair, and his thumbs on his eyes, gave them an instantaneous start from
> their sockets. The sufferer roared aloud, but uttered no complaint. The
> citizens again shouted with joy. Doubts were no longer entertained and
> bets of three to one were offered on the Virginian.

But the fight continued. The Kentuckian grabbed his smaller opponent and held
him in a tight bear hug, forcing the Virginian to relinquish his facial grip. Over
and over the two rolled, until, getting the Virginian under him, the big man
"snapt off his nose so close to his face that no manner of projection remained."
The Virginian quickly recovered, seized the Kentuckian's lower lip in his teeth,
and ripped it down over his enemy's chin. This was enough: "The Kentuckyan
at length *gave out,* on which the people carried off the victor, and he preferring
a triumph to a doctor, who came to cicatrize his face, suffered himself to be
chaired round the ground as the champion of the times, and the first *rougher-
and-tumbler.* The poor wretch, whose eyes were started from their spheres, and
whose lip refused its office, returned to the town, to hide his impotence, and get
his countenance repaired." The citizens refreshed themselves with whiskey and
biscuits, then resumed their races.

Ashe's Quaker friend reported that such spontaneous races occurred two or
three times a week and that the annual fall and spring meets lasted fourteen
uninterrupted days, "aided by the licentious and profligate of all the neighboring
states." As for rough-and-tumbles, the Quaker saw no hope of suppressing them.
Few nights passed without such fights; few mornings failed to reveal a new
citizen with mutilated features. It was a regional taste, unrestrained by law or
authority, an inevitable part of life on the left bank of the Ohio.

Foreign travelers might exaggerate and backwoods storytellers embellish, but
the most neglected fact about eye-gouging matches is their actuality. Circuit
Court Judge Aedamus Burke barely contained his astonishment while presiding
in South Carolina's upcountry: "Before God, gentlemen of the jury, I never saw

such a thing before in the world. There is a plaintiff with an eye out! A juror with an eye out! And two witnesses with an eye out!'' If the "ringtailed roarers" did not actually breakfast on stewed Yankee, washed down with spike nails and epsom salts, court records from Sumner County, Arkansas, did describe assault victims with the words "nose was bit." The gamest "gamecock of the wilderness" never really moved steamboat engines by grinning at them, but Reuben Cheek did receive a three-year sentence to the Tennessee penitentiary for gouging out William Maxey's eye. Most backcountrymen went to the grave with their faces intact, just as most of the southern gentry never fought a duel. But as an extreme version of the common tendency toward brawling, street fighting, and seeking personal vengeance, rough-and-tumbling gives us insight into the deep values and assumptions—the *mentalité*—of backwoods life.

Observers often accused rough-and-tumblers of fighting like animals. But eye gouging was not instinctive behavior, the human equivalent of two rams vying for dominance. Animals fight to attain specific objectives, such as food, sexual priority, or territory. Precisely where to draw the line between human aggression as a genetically programmed response or as a product of social and cultural learning remains a hotly debated issue. Nevertheless, it would be difficult to make a case for eye gouging as a genetic imperative, coded behavior to maximize individual or species survival. Although rough-and-tumble fighting appears primitive and anarchic to modern eyes, there can be little doubt that its origins, rituals, techniques, and goals were emphatically conditioned by environment; gouging was learned behavior. Humanistic social science more than sociobiology holds the keys to understanding this phenomenon.

What can we conclude about the culture and society that nourished rough-and-tumble fighting? The best place to begin is with the material base of life and the nature of daily work. Gamblers, hunters, herders, roustabouts, rivermen, and yeomen farmers were the sorts of persons usually associated with gouging. Such hallmarks of modernity as large-scale production, complex division of labor, and regular work rhythms were alien to their lives. Recent studies have stressed the premodern character of the southern uplands through most of the antebellum period. Even while cotton production boomed and trade expanded, a relatively small number of planters owned the best lands and most slaves, so huge parts of the South remained outside the flow of international markets or staple crop agriculture. Thus, backcountry whites commonly found themselves locked into a semisubsistent pattern of living. Growing crops for home consumption, supplementing food supplies with abundant game, allowing small herds to fatten in the woods, spending scarce money for essential staples, and bartering goods for the services of part-time or itinerant trades people, the upland folk lived in an intensely local, kin-based society. Rural hamlets, impassable roads, and provincial isolation—not growing towns, internal improvements, or international commerce—characterized the backcountry.

Even men whose livelihoods depended on expanding markets often continued their rough, premodern ways. Characteristic of life on a Mississippi barge, for example, were long periods of idleness shattered by intense anxiety, as deadly snags, shoals, and storms approached. Running aground on a sandbar meant backbreaking labor to maneuver a thirty-ton vessel out of trouble. Boredom weighed as heavily as danger, so tale telling, singing, drinking, and gambling filled the empty hours. Once goods were taken on in New Orleans, the men began the thousand-mile return journey against the current. Before steam power replaced muscle, bad food and whiskey fueled the gangs who day after day, exposed to wind and water, poled the river bottoms or strained at the cordelling ropes until their vessel reached the tributaries of the Missouri or the Ohio. Hunters, trappers, herdsmen, subsistence farmers, and other backwoodsmen faced different but equally taxing hardships, and those who endured prided themselves on their strength and daring, their stamina, cunning, and ferocity.

Such men played as lustily as they worked, counterpointing bouts of intense labor with strenuous leisure. What travelers mistook for laziness was a refusal to work and save with compulsive regularity. "I have seen nothing in human form so profligate as they are," James Flint wrote of the boatmen he met around 1820. "Accomplished in depravity, their habits and education seem to comprehend every vice. They make few pretensions to moral character; and their swearing is excessive and perfectly disgusting. Although earning good wages, they are in the most abject poverty; many of them being without anything like clean or comfortable clothing." A generation later, Mark Twain vividly remembered those who manned the great timber and coal rafts gliding past his boyhood home in Hannibal, Missouri: "Rude, uneducated, brave, suffering terrific hardships with sailorlike stoicism; heavy drinkers, coarse frolickers in moral sties like the Natchez-under-the-hill of that day, heavy fighters, reckless fellows, every one, elephantinely jolly, foul witted, profane; prodigal of their money, bankrupt at the end of the trip, fond of barbaric finery, prodigious braggarts; yet, in the main, honest, trustworthy, faithful to promises and duty, and often picaresquely magnanimous." Details might change, but penury, loose morality, and lack of steady habits endured.

Boatmen, hunters, and herdsmen were often separated from wives and children for long periods. More important, backcountry couples lacked the emotionally intense experience of the bourgeois family. They spent much of their time apart and found companionship with members of their own sex. The frontier town or crossroads tavern brought males together in surrogate brotherhoods, where rough men paid little deference to the civilizing role of women and the moral uplift of the domestic family. On the margins of a booming, modernizing society, they shared an intensely communal yet fiercely competitive way of life. Thus, where work was least rationalized and specialized, domesticity weakest, legal institutions primitive, and the market economy feeble, rough-and-tumble fighting found fertile soil.

Just as the economy of the southern backcountry remained locally oriented, the rough-and-tumblers were local heroes, renowned in their communities. There was no professionalization here. Men fought for informal village and county titles; the red feather in the champion's cap was pay enough because it marked him as first among his peers. Paralleling the primitive division of labor in backwoods society, boundaries between entertainment and daily life, between spectators and participants, were not sharply drawn. "Bully of the Hill" Ab Gaines from the Big Hatchie Country, Neil Brown of Totty's Bend, Vernon's William Holt, and Smithfield's Jim Willis—all of them were renowned Tennessee fighters, local heroes in their day. Legendary champions were real individuals, tested gang leaders who attained their status by being the meanest, toughest, and most ruthless fighters, who faced disfigurement and never backed down. Challenges were ever present; yesterday's spectator was today's champion, today's champion tomorrow's invalid.

Given the lives these men led, a worldview that embraced fearlessness made sense. Hunters, trappers, Indian fighters, and herdsmen who knew the smell of warm blood on their hands refused to sentimentalize an environment filled with threatening forces. It was not that backwoodsmen lived in constant danger but that violence was unpredictable. Recreations like cockfighting deadened men to cruelty, and the gratuitous savagery of gouging matches reinforced the daily truth that life was brutal, guided only by the logic of superior nerve, power, and cunning. With families emotionally or physically distant and civil institutions weak, a man's role in the all-male society was defined less by his ability as a breadwinner than by his ferocity. The touchstone of masculinity was unflinching toughness, not chivalry, duty, or piety. Violent sports, heavy drinking, and impulsive pleasure seeking were appropriate for men whose lives were hard, whose futures were unpredictable, and whose opportunities were limited. Gouging champions were group leaders because they embodied the basic values of their peers. The successful rough-and-tumbler proved his manhood by asserting his dominance and rendering his opponent "impotent," as Thomas Ashe put it. And the loser, though literally or symbolically castrated, demonstrated his mettle and maintained his honor.

Here we begin to understand the travelers' refrain about plain folk degradation. Setting out from northern ports, whose inhabitants were increasingly possessed by visions of godly perfection and material progress, they found southern upcountry people slothful and backward. Ashe's Quaker friend in Wheeling, Virginia, made the point. For Quakers and northern evangelicals, labor was a means of moral self-testing, and earthly success was a sign of God's grace, so hard work and steady habits became acts of piety. But not only Yankees endorsed sober restraint. A growing number of southern evangelicals also embraced a life of decorous self-control, rejecting the hedonistic and self-assertive values of old. During the late eighteenth century, as Rhys Isaac has observed, many plain folk disavowed the hegemonic gentry culture of conspicuous display and found individual worth, group pride, and transcendent meaning in religious revivals. By the antebellum era, new evangelical waves washed over class lines as rich and poor alike forswore such sins as drinking, gambling, cursing, fornication, horse racing, and dancing. But conversion was far from universal, and, for many in backcountry settlements like Wheeling, the evangelical idiom remained a foreign tongue. Men worked hard to feed themselves and their kin, to acquire goods and status, but they lacked the calling to prove their godliness through rigid morality. Salvation and self-denial were culturally less compelling values, and the barriers against leisure and self-gratification were lower here than among the converted.

Moreover, primitive markets and the semisubsistence basis of upcountry life limited men's dependence on goods produced by others and allowed them to maintain the irregular work rhythms of a precapitalist economy. The material base of backwoods life was ill suited to social transformation, and the cultural traditions of the past offered alternatives to rigid new ideals. Closing up shop in mid-week for a fight or horse race had always been perfectly acceptable, because men labored so that they might indulge the joys of the flesh. Neither a compulsive need to save time and money nor an obsession with progress haunted people's imaginations. The backcountry folk who lacked a bourgeois or Protestant sense of duty were little disturbed by exhibitions of human passions and were resigned to violence as part of daily life. Thus, the relative dearth of capitalistic values (such as delayed gratification and accumulation), the absence of a strict work ethic, and a cultural tradition that winked at lapses in moral rigor limited society's demands for sober self-control.

Not just unconverted poor whites but also large numbers of the slave-holding gentry still lent their prestige to a regional style that favored conspicuous displays of leisure. As C. Vann Woodward has pointed out, early observers, such as Robert Beverley and William Byrd, as well as modern-day commentators, have described a distinctly "southern ethic" in American history. Whether judged positively as leisure or negatively as laziness, the southern sensibility valued free time and rejected work as the consuming goal of life. Slavery reinforced this tendency, for how could labor be an unmitigated virtue if so much of it was performed by despised black bondsmen? When southerners did esteem commerce and enterprise, it was less because piling up wealth contained religious or moral value than because productivity facilitated the leisure ethos. Southerners could therefore work hard without placing labor at the center of their ethical universe. In important ways, then, the upland folk culture reflected a larger regional style.

Thus, the values, ideas, and institutions that rapidly transformed the North into a modern capitalist society came late to the South. Indeed, conspicuous display, heavy drinking, moral casualness, and love of games and sports had deep roots in much of Western culture. As Woodward has cautioned, we must take care not to interpret the southern ethic as unique or aberrant. The compulsions to subordinate leisure to productivity, to divide work and play into separate compartmentalized realms, and to improve each bright and shining hour were the novel ideas. The southern ethic anticipated human evil, tolerated ethical lapses, and accepted the finitude of man in contrast to the new style that demanded unprecedented moral rectitude and internalized self-restraint.

The American South also shared with large parts of the Old World a taste for violence and personal vengeance. Long after the settling of the southern colonies, powerful patriarchal clans in Celtic and Mediterranean lands still avenged affronts to family honor with deadly feuds. Norbert Elias has pointed out that postmedieval Europeans routinely spilled blood to settle their private quarrels. Across classes, the story was the same:

> Two associates fall out over business; they quarrel, the conflict grows violent; one day they meet in a public place and one of them strikes the

other dead. An innkeeper accuses another of stealing his clients; they become mortal enemies. Someone says a few malicious words about another; a family war develops. . . . Not only among the nobility were there family vengeance, private feuds, vendettas. . . . The little people too—the hatters, the tailors, the shepards—were all quick to draw their knives.

Emotions were freely expressed: jollity and laughter suddenly gave way to belligerence; guilt and penitence coexisted with hate; cruelty always lurked nearby. The modern middle-class individual, with his subdued, rational, calculating ways, finds it hard to understand the joy sixteenth-century Frenchmen took in ceremonially burning alive one or two dozen cats every Midsummer Day or the pleasure eighteenth-century Englishmen found in watching trained dogs slaughter each other.

Despite enormous cultural differences, inhabitants of the southern uplands exhibited characteristics of their forebears in the Old World. The Scots-Irish brought their reputation for ferocity to the backcountry, but English migrants, too, had a thirst for violence. Central authority was weak, and men reserved the right to settle differences for themselves. Vengeance was part of daily life. Drunken hilarity, good fellowship, and high spirits, especially at crossroads taverns, suddenly turned to violence. Traveler after traveler remarked on how forthright and friendly but quick to anger the backcountry people were. Like their European ancestors, they had not yet internalized the modern world's demand for tight emotional self-control.

Above all, the ancient concept of honor helps explain this shared proclivity for violence. According to the sociologist Peter Berger, modern men have difficulty taking seriously the idea of honor. American jurisprudence, for example, offers legal recourse for slander and libel because they involve material damages. But insult—publicly smearing a man's good name and besmirching his honor—implies no palpable injury and so does not exist in the eyes of the law. Honor is an intensely social concept, resting on reputation, community standing, and the esteem of kin and compatriots. To possess honor requires acknowledgment from others; it cannot exist in solitary conscience. Modern man, Berger has argued, is more responsive to dignity—the belief that personal worth inheres equally in each individual, regardless of his status in society. Dignity frees the evangelical to confront God alone, the capitalist to make contracts without customary encumbrances, and the reformer to uplift the lowly. Naked and alone man has dignity; extolled by peers and covered with ribbons, he has honor.

Anthropologists have also discovered the centrality of honor in several cultures. According to J.G. Peristiany, honor and shame often preoccupy individuals in small-scale settings, where face-to-face relationships predominate over anonymous or bureaucratic ones. Social standing in such communities is never completely secure, because it must be validated by public opinion whose fickleness compels men constantly to assert and prove their worth. Julian Pitt-Rivers has added that, if society rejects a man's evaluation of himself and treats his claim to honor with ridicule or contempt, his very identity suffers because it is based on the judgment of peers. Shaming refers to that process by which an insult or any public humiliation impugns an individual's honor and thereby threatens his sense of self. By risking injury in a violent encounter, an affronted man—whether victorious or not—restores his sense of status and thus validates anew his claim to honor. Only valorous action, not words, can redeem his place in the ranks of his peer group.

Bertram Wyatt-Brown has argued that this Old World ideal is the key to understanding southern history. Across boundaries of time, geography, and social class, the South was knit together by a primal concept of male valor, part of the ancient heritage of Indo-European folk cultures. Honor demanded clan loyalty, hospitality, protection of women, and defense of patriarchal prerogatives. Honorable men guarded their reputations, bristled at insults, and, where necessary, sought personal vindication through bloodshed. The culture of honor thrived in hierarchical rural communities like the American South and grew out of a fatalistic worldview, which assumed that pain and suffering were man's fate. It accounts for the pervasive violence that marked relationships between southerners and explains their insistence on vengeance and their rejection of legal redress in settling quarrels. Honor tied personal identity to public fulfillment of social roles. Neither bourgeois self-control nor internalized conscience determined status; judgment by one's fellows was the wellspring of community standing.

In this light, the seemingly trivial causes for brawls enumerated as early as Fithian's time—name calling, subtle ridicule, breaches of decorum, displays of poor manners—make sense. If a man's good name was his most important possession, then any slight cut him deeply. "Having words" precipitated fights because words brought shame and undermined a man's sense of self. Symbolic acts, such as buying a round of drinks, conferred honor on all, while refusing to share a bottle implied some inequality in social status. Honor inhered not only in individuals but also in kin and peers; when members of two cliques had words, their tested leaders or several men from each side fought to uphold group prestige. Inheritors of primal honor, the southern plain folk were quick to take offense, and any perceived affront forced a man either to devalue himself or to strike back violently and avenge the wrong.

The concept of male honor takes us a long way toward understanding the meaning of eye-gouging matches. But backwoods people did not simply acquire some primordial notion without modifying it. Definitions of honorable behavior have always varied enormously across cultures. The southern upcountry fostered a particular style of honor, which grew out of the contradiction between equality and hierarchy. Honorific societies tend to be sharply stratified. Honor is apportioned according to rank, and men fight to maintain personal standing within their social categories. Because black chattel slavery was the basis for the southern hierarchy, slave owners had the most wealth and honor, while other whites scrambled for a bit of each, and bondsmen were permanently impoverished and dishonored. Here was a source of tension for the plain folk. Men of honor shared freedom and equality; those denied honor were implicitly less than equal— perilously close to a slave-like condition. But in the eyes of the gentry, poor whites as well as blacks were outside the circle of honor, so both groups were subordinate. Thus, a herdsman's insult failed to shame a planter since the two men were not on the same social level. Without a threat to the gentleman's honor, there was no need for a duel; horsewhipping the insolent fellow sufficed.

Southern plain folk, then, were caught in a social contradiction. Society taught all white men to consider themselves equals, encouraged them to compete for power and status, yet threatened them from below with the specter of servitude and from above with insistence on obedience to rank and authority. Cut off from upper-class tests of honor, backcountry people adopted their own. A rough-and-tumble was more than a poor man's duel, a botched version of genteel combat. Plain folk chose not to ape the dispassionate, antiseptic, gentry style but to invert it. While the gentleman's code of honor insisted on cool restraint, eye gougers gloried in unvarnished brutality. In contrast to duelists' aloof silence, backwoods fighters screamed defiance to the world. As their own unique rites of honor, rough-and-tumble matches allowed backcountry men to shout their equality at each other. And eye-gouging fights also dispelled any stigma of servility. Ritual boasts, soaring oaths, outrageous ferocity, unflinching bloodiness—all proved a man's freedom. Where the slave acted obsequiously, the backwoodsman resisted the slightest affront; where human chattels accepted blows and never raised a hand, plain folk celebrated violence; where blacks could not jeopardize their value as property, poor whites proved their autonomy by risking bodily parts. Symbolically reaffirming their claims to honor, gouging matches helped resolve painful uncertainties arising out of the ambiguous place of plain folk in the southern social structure.

Backwoods fighting reminds us of man's capacity for cruelty and is an excellent corrective to romanticizing premodern life. But a close look also keeps us from drawing facile conclusions about innate human aggressiveness. Eye gouging represented neither the "real" human animal emerging on the frontier, nor nature acting through man in a Darwinian struggle for survival, nor anarchic disorder and communal breakdown. Rather, rough-and-tumble fighting was ritualized behavior—a product of specific cultural assumptions. Men drink, together, tongues loosen, a simmering old rivalry begins to boil; insult is given, offense taken, ritual boasts commence; the fight begins, mettle is tested, blood redeems honor, and equilibrium is restored. Eye gouging was the poor and middling whites' own version of a historical southern tendency to consider personal violence socially useful—indeed, ethically essential.

Rough-and-tumble fighting emerged from the confluence of economic conditions, social relationships, and culture in the southern backcountry. Primitive markets and the semisubsistence basis of life threw men back on close ties to kin and community. Violence and poverty were part of daily existence, so endurance, even callousness, became functional values. Loyal to their localities, their occupations, and each other, men came together and found release from life's hardships in strong drink, tall talk, rude practical jokes, and cruel sports. They craved one another's recognition but rejected genteel, pious, or bourgeois values, awarding esteem on the basis of their own traditional standards. The glue that held men together was an intensely competitive status system in which the most prodigious drinker or strongest arm wrestler, the best tale teller, fiddle player, or log roller, the most daring gambler, original liar, skilled hunter, outrageous swearer, or accurate marksman was accorded respect by the others. Reputation was everything, and scars were badges of honor. Rough-and-tumble fighting demonstrated unflinching willingness to inflict pain while risking mutilation—all to defend one's standing among peers—and became a central expression of the all-male subculture.

Eye gouging continued long after the antebellum period. As the market economy absorbed new parts of the backcountry, however, the way of life that supported rough-and-tumbling waned. Certainly by mid-century the number of incidents declined, precisely when expanding international demand brought ever more upcountry acres into staple production. Towns, schools, churches, revivals, and families gradually overtook the backwoods. In a slow and uneven process, keelboats gave way to steamers, then railroads; squatters, to cash crop farmers; hunters and trappers, to preachers. The plain folk code of honor was far from dead, but emergent social institutions engendered a moral ethos that warred against the old ways. For many individuals, the justifications for personal violence grew stricter, and mayhem became unacceptable.

Ironically, progress also had a darker side. New technologies and modes of production could enhance men's fighting abilities. "Birmingham and Pittsburgh are obliged to complete . . . the equipment of the 'chivalric Kentuckian,' " Charles Agustus Murray observed in the 1840s, as bowie knives ended more and more rough-and-tumbles. Equally important, in 1835 the first modern revolver appeared, and manufacturers marketed cheap, accurate editions in the coming decade. Dueling weapons had been costly, and Kentucky rifles or horse pistols took a full minute to load and prime. The revolver, however, which fitted neatly into a man's pocket, settled more and more personal disputes. Raw and brutal as rough-and-tumbling was, it could not survive the use of arms. Yet precisely because eye gouging was so violent—because combatants cherished maimings, blindings, even castrations—it unleashed death wishes that invited new technologies of destruction.

With improved weaponry, dueling entered its golden age during the antebellum era. Armed combat remained both an expression of gentry sensibility and a mark of social rank. But in a society where status was always shifting and unclear, dueling did not stay confined to the upper class. The habitual carrying of weapons, once considered a sign of unmanly fear, now lost some of its stigma. As the backcountry changed, tests of honor continued, but gunplay rather than fighting tooth-and-nail appealed to new men with social aspirations. Thus, progress and technology slowly circumscribed rough-and-tumble fighting, only to substitute a deadlier option. Violence grew neater and more lethal as men checked their savagery to murder each other.

CHAPTER 4

Sport and Popular Pastimes: Shadow of the Slavequarter

David K. Wiggins

The institution of slavery in antebellum America was an oppressive and dehumanizing system characterized by intense labor and terrible cruelties. But slavery was not all toil and to fully come to grips with the real nature of the bondsmen's day to day existence, the quest for an understanding of all aspects of the plantation system is imperative. The intent of this study, then, is to broaden the understanding of slave culture through the medium of sport and popular pastimes and to determine the meaning of these two activities for a people who were so often restricted and circumscribed in their daily lives.

What is immediately apparent from this analysis is that however dehumanizing the plantation became for slaves, their struggle for survival never became so severe that it destroyed their creative instincts or prevented them from establishing their own unique culture. In spite of their degraded condition slaves were still able to find sources of enjoyment and ways of manifesting it. They took a cultural kind of pride in being able to rejoice and have fun through various sports and pastimes no matter the treatment given them by their masters. Participation in various recreational activities allowed slaves a degree of individual autonomy and self-respect while at the same time nurturing their belief in group solidarity and sense of themselves as a district body with common concerns, philosophies, and lifestyles. "The sternest and most covetous master cannot frighten or whip the fun out of us," remembered the slave Josiah Henson. "In those days I had many a merry time and would have had had I lived with nothing but moccasins and rattlesnakes in Okafenoke Swamp." "Even with all the hardships that the slaves had to suffer," recalled Henry Wright, who labored on a large Georgia plantation, "they still had time to have fun and to enjoy themselves. . . ."

Planters frequently allowed their slaves to have Saturday night parties. On many plantations these parties occurred on a weekly basis, although the planters material offerings would be minimal in these particular situations. Many masters would furnish a fiddler, a barrel of liquor and meat for a barbecue, "and left the

From the *Canadian Journal of History of Sport and Physical Education,* Vol. 11, May, 1980. © 1980 Canadian Journal of History of Sport and Physical Education. Reprinted by permission.

slaves alone to enjoy themselves." These parties were given in the specific hope of keeping the slaves home during the week. "Saturday nights were always the time for dancing and frolicking," remembered Robert Henry of Georgia. "The master sometimes let them use a barn loft for a big square dance." Celestia Avery, who also labored on a Georgia plantation, said that her master "allowed his slaves to have a frolic every Saturday night and folks would get broke down from so much dancing. . . ." "The most fun was on Saturday night when massa 'lowed us to dance," remembered Toby Jones of South Carolina. "There was lots of banjo pickin' and tin pan beatin' and dancin' and everybody would talk about when they lived in Africa and done what they wanted."

Sometimes the whites of the plantation would attend the Saturday night parties and either enjoy themselves vicariously or actually take part in the festivities. A number of slaveholders would actually arrange and direct these frolics. Slaves obviously could not prevent their masters from participating in the parties but they usually resented their presence. "Us danced most e'ry Sattiday night an' us made de rafters shake wid us foots," remembered Preston Klein of Alabama. "Lots o' times ole missus would come to de dances an' look on; an' when er brash nigger boy cut a cute bunch ev steps, de men folks would give 'em a dime or so." "We had parties Saturday nights," recalled Wes Brady of Texas, "and massa come out and showed us new steps. . . ." Sara Colquitt of Alabama remembered that they "could have all de fun us wanted on Sa'dday nights, and us sho' had it cutting monkeyshines and dancing; sometimes our mistess' would come down early to watch us dance."

If the slaves were not permitted to have Saturday night parties they would either gather at a secluded spot a sufficient distance from the "big house" or, with or without a pass, travel to a neighborhood plantation that was having one. "Massa am good but he don't 'low de parties," reminisced Albert Hill of Georgia. "But we kin go to massa Dillions place next to us and dey has lots of parties and de dances." "A way off from de big house, down in de partur' der wuz about de bigges' gully what I ever seed," recalled Martha Abrams of South Carolina. "Dat wuz de place whar us collected mos' every Sa'day night for our lil'night of fun from de white folks hearin.' . . ." Ellen Campbell of Georgia remembers that on Saturday nights they would have a big frolic ". . . and de niggers from Hammonds place, Phinizy place, Eve place, Clayton place, all git togedder for a big dance."

It was the unauthorized parties held during the week that slaves enjoyed the most. Lack of consent meant lack of surveillance and meddling, save the patrollers who might catch wind of a party and break up the evening's festivities. Many planters placed a nine o'clock curfew on their slaves. But the overseers seldom checked the cabins more than once, so the slaves merely played "possum" and slipped out later in the evening. "It was a rule for the overseer to come at nine o'clock and lock the cabin doors," recalled the slave William Webb. "He would call each person by their name and they had to answer, to let him know they were in their cabins. We had old fashioned dirt chimneys; we would crawl out upon the roof, git down, and be away till nearly day break." "Through the week

The joy that slaves found in various dance forms is illustrated in this drawing from the *Century Magazine*, November 1887.
Courtesy of the Library of Congress.

we'd fall into our quarters," remembered Eli Coleman of Texas. "De patterollers come walk all over us, and we'd be plumb still, but after they done gone some niggers gits up and out." Tom Hollard, who also lived on a Texas plantation, said they would "go and fall right in at the door of the quarters at night, so massa and the patterollers thinks we's real tired and let us alone and not watch us. That very night we'd be plannin' to slip off somewheres to see a negro gal or our wife, or to have a big time. . . ."

Slaves placed a high value on continuing their parties all night long. A celebration that couldn't be sustained all night was a disgrace to themselves and their plantation community. "Negroes would go off all night," recalled Jefferson Franklin, who labored on a large Georgia plantation. "It would be work time when they got back, and they went to the field and tried to keep on going but the good Lord soon cut them down." "Many a time I danced till broad daylight," remembered Sarah Waggoner of Missouri, "and den when I worked I was so sleepy I'd nod and nod. . . ." Sarah Byrd of Georgia said they would "frolic all night long sometimes and when the sun rose in the morning we would be lying around or sitting on the floor.''

Many slaves, of course, could afford to party all night considering they had mastered the art of ''goldbricking'' during the day. Most planters realized that once slaves decided how much work they were going to perform they renounced to work any harder. The prominent Virginia planter William B. Randolph received a letter from his overseer in 1833 complaining of the slaves not putting in a full days work. ''I will try to give you a full account of my proceedings,'' wrote the overseer. ''As soon as you left the plantation I had much trouble and vexations with the negroes, they with some exceptions—were unruly and wandering about at night and in the day they were sleepy. Of course it was almost impossible to make them do anything like a days work, refusing to do any more than they pleased.'' Frederick Law Olmsted described how many of the slaves on the Virginia plantation he visited would ''go through the motions'' during the day:

> He [slaveholder] afterwords said that his negroes never worked so hard as to tire themselves—always were lively and ready to go off on a frolic at night. He did not think they ever did half a fair days work. They could not be made to work hard: they never would lay out their strength freely, and it was impossible to make them do it. This is just what I have thought when I have seen slaves at work—they seem to go through the motions of labor without putting strength into them. They keep their powers in reserve for their own use at night, perhaps.

Tellingly, nothing bothered the planters more than the week-night excursions of their slaves. They obviously preferred to have them rest up for the next day's labor, rather than running all over the countryside partying. Every effort was made, then, to cut down on the slave's nocturnal activities. The Mississippi slaveholder William Ethlebert Erwin told his overseer that ''at nine o'clock every night the horne must be blown—which is to be a signal for each to retire to his or her home and there to remain until the morning—but should he or she be called for and found out of their places they shall be dealt with accordingly.'' Fletcher Srygley, who spent several years travelling in the South, remembered that ''every negro was kept in his place and no one was allowed to go beyond the bounds of his masters plantation without a written pass. Some negroes had a habit of secretly visiting the negroes of other plantations by night. To break this up the overseers of every section organized themselves and patrolled the country.'' Bennet H. Barrow attempted to make his Louisiana plantation so comfortable that his slaves would not find it necessary to visit other plantations during the week. ''The quarter was the center of his slave world . . . and if he was made comfortable at home, if the essentials of happiness were provided for him there would be little inclination for him to leave. . . .''

An important concern of planters was the demoralizing effect that neighboring slaves might have on their own. They continually railed against the certain loss of morale and destruction of discipline that would result among their well-regulated slaves if they were allowed to socialize with "strange negroes." Nap McQueen of Texas said that the neighboring slaveholders did not want their bondsmen to associate with them because they were treated too well. "Some of dem on dose plantations say dey ain't want Massa McQueens niggers 'round de place, 'cause deys free, dey fed too good and all and dey afraid it made dere slaves unsatisfy. . . ." Green Willbanks of Georgia remembered that "there were certain plantations where we were not permitted to go and certain folks were never allowed on our place. Old boss was particular about how folks behaved on his place; all his slaves had to come up to a certain notch. . . ."

Most planters found their attempts at preventing interplantation visiting a losing proposition. Despite the many rules that were set up, slaves of all ages would slip off to visit their friends and join in a barbecue or dance at a neighboring plantation. For most slaves it was not always enough to just sit around a blazing fire with their family or retire to their cabins after a day's work. "As soon as his burdens are laid down," remembered the British traveller Timothy Flint, "or his toils for a moment suspended, he sings, he seizes his fiddle, he dances. When their days are passed in continued and severe toil their nights—for like cats and owls they are like nocturnal animals—are passed in wandering about from plantation to plantation in visiting, feasting, and conversation." "You know it is against the law for them to go without a pass from their master or overseer," stated Sarah Williams, the wife of a North Carolina planter, "nevertheless they do go. Some of our hands will work all day and then walk eight or ten miles to dance all night." "In spite of all the work and strictness," reminisced a slave from Tennessee, "a majority of the niggers would slip from place to place after night and find a little pleasure. . . ."

Members of the slavequarters often related humorous tales concerning their illicit parties and social gatherings. Appropriately enough the figure in most of the stories was the master. Nancy Jackson, who toiled on a Tennessee plantation, related a story about one of their dances:

> I remember one big time we done had in slavery. Massa was gone, and then we found out he wasn't gone. He left the house intending to go on a visit, and missy and her children were gone and us niggers gave a big ball the night they were all gone. The leader of that ball had on massa's boots, and he sang a song he made up: 'Ole massa's gone to Philiman York and wont be back till July 4th to come; the fact of it I don't know he'll be back at all; Come on you Niggers and join this ball.'
>
> The night they gave that ball, massa had blacked his face and slipped back in the house, while they were singing and dancing and he sat by the fireplace all the time. Directly he spat and the nigger who had on his boots recognized him and tried to climb the chimney.

Neal Upson of Georgia told a comical tale of a fellow house slave who had a rather unfortunate experience:

One time a houseboy from another plantation wanted to come to one of our dances so his marster told him to shine his boots for Sunday and fix his hoss for de night and den he could git off for de frolic. Abraham shined his marsters boots till he could see hisself in em and dey looked so grand he was tempted to try em on. Dey was a little tight but he thought he could wear em and he wanted to show hisself off in em at de dance. Dey warn't so easy to walk in and he was 'fraid he might git em scratched up walking through de fields, so he snuck his marsters hoss out and rode to de dance. When Abraham rid up der in dem shiny boots he got all de gals 'tention, none of 'em wanted to dance wid de other niggers. Dat Abraham was sho struttin' til somebody run in and told him his hoss had done broke it's neck. He had tied it to a limb and sho 'nough, some way, dat hoss had done got tangled up and hung it's own self. Abraham begged de other nigger boys to help him take de daid hoss home, but he had done tuk deir gals and he didn't git no help. He had to walk 12 long miles home in dem tight shoes. . . .''

The above examples help to illustrate not only the slave's ability to laugh at themselves, but the pleasure they derived from momentarily assuming a superior but fanciful position to their masters. By temporarily reversing their social roles, slaves were able to briefly relieve any aggressions and hostilities they held toward their owners. The slaves' daily suppression and inability to express their innermost feelings could be withstood more gracefully if they occasionally had opportunities to conduct their own ''fashionable balls'' and wear their own ''shiney boots.'' The slaves knack for capriciously transcending their masters' authority helped momentarily to liberate them from that pressure and assisted them in coping with the realities of the plantation community. A tremendous feeling of relief resulted from rebelling and ''putting one over'' on the ''Lord of the Manor.''

The central feature of slave gatherings were a variety of different dances. The slaves repeatedly spoke of their love for dancing in the narratives. ''Used to rather dance than eat,'' remembered Pick Gladdeny of South Carolina, ''started out at sundown and git back to the Whitneys at daybreak, den from dar run all de way to Squire Hardy's for a dance.'' An ex-slave from Tennessee said that all he ''cared about was fiddling and dancing. It was come day, go day, God send Sunday, with me.'' ''When we were under bondage they said we could have prayer meetings out,'' remembered another slave from Tennessee, ''but I was right young and little then and all I cared was to dance. . . .''

The slaves apparently found the European Reels, minuets, and schottishes too sedate and formalized for them, even though there are occasional references to these dances in the narratives. The dances in the slavequarters closely resembled African dances in terms of method and style. They were frequently performed from a flexed, fluid, bodily position as opposed to the stiffly erect position of European dancers; often imitated and portrayed such animals as the buzzard, eagle, crow, and rabbit in realistic detail; placed great emphasis upon satire, improvisation, and freedom of individual expression; concentrated on movement outward from the pelvic region which whites found so despicable; and most importantly were performed to a propulsive, swinging rhythm which animated the whole body. "One would think they had steam engines inside of them," remarked the traveler Lewis Paine, "to jerk them about with so much power; for they go through with more motions in a minute, than you could shake two sticks at in a month. . . . It is useless to talk about fellows, minstrels or any other band of merely artificial 'Ethiopians' for they will bear no comparison with the plantation negroes." "Their dancing is truly remarkable," remarked the traveler William Howard Russell. "It consists of a double shuffle in a thumping ecstacy, with loose elbows, pendulus paws, angulated knees, heads thrown back and backs arched inwards. . . ."

Slaves performed a number of "animal" dances. These dances took many forms, but the one mentioned most often was the "Buzzard Lope," which was performed on the isolated Sea Island region off the coast of Georgia. Two historians have suggested that it may have been similar to a West African buzzard dance. This explanation is certainly credible. The slaves living on Sea Island cotton plantations had contact with few whites except the overseer and his family, and very little contact with slaves from the mainland. Shut off from contact with the outside world because of lack of transportation, they were unfamiliar with many of the cultural traits of the whites and therefore were more likely to maintain the cultural peculiarities of their forebears. Many of the ex-slaves from the Sea Island region recalled performing the buzzard lope, but none of them described how it was executed. Song-collector Lydia Parrish did see the dance performed in 1915 by a family living on Sapelo Island:

On Sapelo Island, I found in the Johnson family a combination of the old dance form with rather more modern steps. . . . Of the twins, Naomi did the patting while Isaac did the dancing; an older brother rhythmically called out the cues in a sharp staccato, and another one lay on the floor of the wide veranda representing a dead cow. Anyone who has seen turkey buzzards disposing of carr' on' will recognize the aptness of the following directions. . . .

March around!
Jump across!
Get the eye!
So glad!
Get the guts!
Go to eatin'!
All right—cow mos' gone!
Dog comin'!
Look aroun' for mo' meat!
All right—belly full!
Goin to tell the res'!

Mrs. Parrish observed that the performance she witnessed was apparently a combination of the slave version and the original African interpretation of the dance. Of religious origin, the slaves added a few steps of their own to the "Buzzard Lope" and ultimately created an entirely secular, rural, and rhythmically hand clapping type of dance.

There are numerous examples in the narratives of slaves performing dances in which water was carried on the head. A bucket or glass of water balanced on the head was frequently used as a means to determine the winner in contests or challenge dances in the slave quarters. These dances are also highly suggestive or analogous to the African custom of carrying things on the head. "Sometimes the slaves would have a jig contest," remembered Lewis Jones of Texas. "That's when they put the glass of water on the head and saw who could jig hardest without spilling the water." "A prize was given to the person who could buck dance the steadiest with a tumbler of water balanced on the head," recalled Emmaline Heard of Georgia. "A cake or quilt was often given as the prize."

One of the most popular dances in the slavequarters was "juba." It was another dance of African origin and has often been mentioned in conjunction with the West Indies as a sacred dance. In its original African form the "juba" was primarily a competitive dance of skill. Two men stepped forward in a circle of dancers and proceeded to exhibit their skill at the juba step—a sort of eccentric shuffle. Meanwhile the men in the surrounding circle performed the same step before and after each performance of the two men in the center; in the interim clapping rhythmically and encouraging the competitors with song and verse. In the South it evolved into a dance called "Patting Juba" which was characterized by a special routine of slapping the hands, knees, thighs, and body in a rhythmic pattern accompanied by a variety of songs. The emergence of "patting" seems to have been inevitable since most planters, for fear of revolts, forbid their slaves from having drums. Solomon Northup, who toiled for a number of years on a Louisiana plantation, remembered "Patting Juba":

> A slave dance does not cease with the sound of the fiddle, but in that case they set up a music peculiar to themselves. This is called patting, accompanied with one of those unmeaning songs, composed rather for its adaption to a certain tune or measure, than for the purpose of expressing any distinct idea. The patting is performed by striking the hands on the knees, then striking the hands together, then striking the right shoulder with one hand, the left with the other—all the while keeping time with the feet and singing:
>
> > Juba dis and juba dat'
> > Juba kill a yaller cat.
> > Juba up and juba down;
> > Juba runnin' all aroun.'

Dr. William B. Smith gave a vivid description of the "Juba" dance he had witnessed on a Northern Virginia plantation:

I had never seen Juber clapped to the banjor before, and you may suppose I looked upon such a novel scene, with some degree of surprise. Indeed I contemplated the dancing group, with sensations of wonder and astonishment. The clappers rested the right foot on the heel, and its clap on the floor was in perfect unison with the notes of the banjor, and palms of the hands on the corresponding extremities. While the dancers were all jigging it away in the merriest possible gaiety of heart having the most ludicrous twists; wry erks, and flexible contortions of the body and limbs, that human imagination can divine. . . . The rude ballad set to Juber, corresponds admirably with the music and actors in this wild fantastic dance. While the clappers were laboring in the performance of their office, they responded at the same to the notes of the banjor.

> Juber up and juber down,
> Juber all around de town,
> Juber dis, and juber dat,
> And juber roun' the simmon vat.
> Hoe corn! Hill tobacco!
> Get over double trouble, juber boys juber.

The dance in the slavequarters was often simply a test of physical prowess and a method of winning praise from one's peer group. Slaves took great pride in their ability to perform arduous "movements" and vicariously enjoyed the exploits of their fellow dancers. In fact, members of the slavequarters tended to look down upon the whites for the lack of style in their dancing. Slaves normally thought of themselves as being superior and more energetic dancers than the whites and always welcomed the opportunity to display their pre-eminence. Lewis Paine, who spent several years traveling through Georgia relates a story which illustrates the slave's attitude:

> After the log rolling was over someone calls for a fiddle, but if one is not to be found, some one pats "juber." This is done by placing one foot a little in advance of the other raising the ball of the foot from the ground, and striking it in regular time, while in connection the hands are struck slightly together and then upon the thighs. . . . All indulge in the dance. The slaves as they become excited, use the most extravagent gestures—the music increases in speed—and the whites soon find it impossible to sustain their parts and they retire. This is just what the slaves wish, and they send a general shout which is returned by the whites acknowledging the victory. Then they all sing out now 'show de white man what we can do!'

Slaves not only utilized the dance to prove their superiority but also made use of this sport form to satirize the cultural mannerisms of the whites. The Episcopalian minister Jonathan Whipple described a group of slaves in Virginia "who spent Christmas day marching up and down the streets in great style. Already have they paraded with a corps of staff officers with red sashes, mock epauletters, and goose quill feathers; they are followed by others some dancing, some walking, and some singing, if any negro refuses to join them they seize him and have a mock trial and sentence him to a flogging which is well laid on.'' Shephard Edmonds recalled how the slaves in Tennessee would perform the cakewalk: ''It was generally on Sundays, when there was little work, that the slaves both young and old would dress up in hand-me-down finery to do a high-kicking, prancing walk-around. They did a take-off on the high manners of the white folks in the 'big house,' but their masters, who gathered around to watch the fun, missed the point.'' The *South Carolina Gazette* of 1772 related an account of a slave dance on the outskirts of Charleston: ''The entertainment was opened by the men copying the manners of their masters and the women, those of their mistresses, and relating some highly curious anecdotes, to the inexpressible diversion of that company. Then they danced, betted, gamed, swore, quarelled, fought and did everything that the most modern accomplished gentlemen are not ashamed of. . . . Whenever or wherever such nocturnal rendezvous are made, may it not be concluded, that their deliberations are never intended for the advantage of the white people?''

Several religious denominations of the South, particularly the Methodists, implored their slave congregations to give up the sinful practice of dancing. Many slaves spoke of the inharmonious relationship between their love for dancing and concurrent devotion to practical piety. ''I was a sinner and loved to dance,'' remembered Alice Alexander of Oklahoma. ''I remember I was on the floor one night dancing and I had four daughters on the floor with me and my son was playing de music—that got me! I just stopped and said, 'I wouldn't cut another step and I haven't. . . .' '' ''After I joined the church, I didn't have no desire to dance no more,'' recalled an ex-slave from Tennessee. ''You know what my religion done for me; it cleared my soul for all eternity. . . .'' Another ex-slave from Tennessee remembered that in spite of her praying she went to dances. ''One night, I went to a dance, but I didn't feel right and strange to say, every time I got on the floor to dance a round, the fiddle string would break; all of a sudden while I was in my place ready to dance I heard a voice on the inside that said, 'Do you remember the promise you made to me?' ''

Despite the selected instances of religious opposition, for the majority of slaves dancing was too popular to be discontinued. For one thing, many planters encouraged their slaves to dance and certainly did not want them to give it up unless it was voluntary. The slaveholder James H. Hammond, for instance, wrote in his plantation journal of 1857 that ''church members are privileged to dance on all holiday occasions and the class leader or deacon who may report them shall be reprimanded or punished at the discretion of the master.'' The more pious slaves also satisfied their troubled conscience by substituting the ''ring shout'' for their wicked secular dances. They convinced themselves that they did not dance the shout, ''for as everyone knows, you cross your feet when you dance; and since they did not tolerate crossing of feet, they clearly were not dancing.'' ''Dancing was considered a very wicked amusement for a church member," remembered the slave Fanny Bergen, "although there was no harm for a member to dance if he did not cross his feet." Wash Wilson, who toiled on a Texas plantation, recalled that "us 'longed to de church, all right, but dancin' ain't sinful 'ffen de foots ain't crossed. Us danced at de order meetings but us sho didn't have us foots crossed."

The "Ring Shout" was derived from the African Circle dance and is one of the best-known examples of an African survival in the United States. Several contemporary observers gave brief accounts of how the "Ring Shout" was performed in the praise-houses of the slavequarters. Laura M. Towne, who spent three years on the Sea Islands of Georgia, gave this description:

> We went to the shout, a savage, heathenish dance out in Rina's house. Three men stood and sang, clapping, and gesticulating. The others shuffled along on their heels, following one another in a circle and occasionally bending the knees in a kind of curtsey. They began slowly, a few going around and more gradually joining in, the song getting faster and faster, till at last only the most marked part of the refrain is sung and the shuffling, stamping, and clapping get furious. The floor shook so that it seemed dangerous. . . . As they danced they, of course, got out of breath, and the singing was kept up principally by the three apart, but it was astonishing how long they continued and how soon after a rest they were ready to begin again. . . .

The white Unitarian minister Henry George Spaulding saw the "Ring Shout" performed when he visited Port Royal, South Carolina during the Civil War:

> Three or four, standing still, clapping their hands and beating time with their feet, commence singing in unison one of the peculiar shout melodies, while the others walk around in a ring, in single file, joining also in the song. Soon those in the ring leave off their singing, the others keeping it up the while with increased vigor, and strike into the shout step, observing most accurate time with the music. . . . They will often dance to the same song for twenty or thirty minutes. . . .

In the final analysis, the slave's "Ring Shouts," and secular dances as well, appeared to assist them in coping with their fears and anxieties. Through their various dance forms the slaves were able to express, at least symbolically, their most deeply held feelings which normally could not be verbalized in the restricted environment of the plantation community. The psychological release that the dance afforded helped to lighten the slaves burden of hardship. The British traveler Alex Mackey, who journeyed through the southern states in 1846, said that the slaves "should be encouraged to dance rather than interfered with. In the evening after the work of the day is over, they will thus enjoy themselves in groups—some dancing with an earnestness which would lead one to the belief that they considered it the main business of life. But all this playfulness of disposition is sometimes only a mask used to relieve a burning thirst for free-dom. . . .'' Another British traveler said that ''it was usual for a people to express their natural inclinations in their favorite amusements, among which the national dance occupies the foremost rank. . . . The original negro dance is stamped with the marks of brutal sensuality restlessness, an vexations.'' ''We liked better the dances of our own particular race,'' remembered the slave Robert Anderson, ''in which we tried to express in motion the particular feelings within our own selves. . . . The slaves became proficient in such dances, and could play a tune with their feet, dancing largely to an inward music, a music that was felt but not heard.''

When the slaves were not spending their free time ''cuttin' de steps'' on the dance floor, they were usually engaged in a hunting or fishing excursion. The men, and less frequently the women, loved to roam the fields and streams of their home plantation in search of their favorite animal or fish. Hunting and fishing was an ideal way for slaves to supplement their usual monotonous diet. The majority of slaves, particularly those living on smaller plantations, were not normally provided with the kinds of food by their masters that would sustain them through their weekly labors. By growing vegetable gardens, picking wild fruits, raising livestock and poultry, stealing various victuals from their masters, and through hunting and fishing the slaves were often able to procure an adequate amount of rations. Silas Jackson, deemed the religious leader of the slaves on his Maryland plantation, remembered that ''all of the slaves hunted or those who wanted, hunted rabbits, opossums or fished. These were our choice food, as we did not get anything special from the overseer.'' George Eason, who labored on a small Georgia plantation, recalled that ''the amount of food given each slave was inadequate as a general rule. . . . The slaves increased their food by hunting and fishing. . . .'' ''The weekly allowance of meal scarcely sufficed to satisfy us,'' remembered Solomon Northup. ''It was customary with us, as it is with all in that region, where the allowance is exhausted before Saturday night, or is in such a state as to render it nauseous and disgusting, to hunt in the swamps for coon and opossum. . . . There are planters whose slaves, for months at a time, have no other meat than such as is obtained in this manner.''

Very severe laws were passed in the southern states restricting the slaves right to hunt, primarily because whites did not want them to possess guns. White dominance could be maintained more easily if the slaves were denied arms. Despite these constraints, planters were liberal in allowing their bondsmen the privilege of roaming the fields of the plantation in search of game; especially if they were expected to share a portion of the day's kill with their master. It was not uncommon for slaveholders to permit their older and more trusted slaves to use their guns for hunting excursions, as well as their prized dogs. In reality, the southern slaveholders were more influential than the law in determining the extent to which the activities of the slaves were curtailed. ''Marster 'lowed my daddy ter hunt wid a gun,'' remembered Zeb Crowder of North Carolina, ''and he killed a lot 'o rabbits, squirrels, an' game.'' The southern novelist William Gilmore Simms, who owned plantations around the Charleston area of South

Carolina, wrote in his journal that there were five slaves on his woodland plantations who kept "guns in their possession" and were "uncanny in bagging wild turkeys, ducks, and deer."

Even without permission from their masters, slaves were too dependent on the meat they procured from hunting to give up the sport very easily. Slave fathers also must have gained a degree of status by adding delicacies to the family table, as well as finding it very gratifying personally. Slaves continually mentioned the unauthorized nightly hunting excursions they would engage in when they were sure their master was securely snuggled in his bed or out of hearing distance from the "baying hounds." James Bolton of Georgia remembered that "slaves weren't supposed to go hunting at night and everybody know you can't catch no possums except at night. Just the same we had plenty possums and nobody asked how we caught them." "Our marster he wouldn't 'low us to go hunting," recalled Benny Proctor of Texas, "but some time we slips off at night and ketch possums anyway." Dennis Simms, who lived on a small Maryland plantation, remembered that "Even without permission from our master or overseer, we would go hunting and catch a coon or possum and a pot pie would be a real treat. . . ."

Rarely having the privilege to use guns, slaves were compelled to become experts at trapping rabbits, squirrels, turkeys, and other small animals. There are also occasional references in the narratives of slaves snaring deer and bears. "Us got squirrels and rabbits the best ways us could," stated Tom Hawkins of Georgia, "catch them in traps, hit them with rocks, and trailed them with dogs." Carter Jackson said that "deer were thick them days" on the Alabama plantation where he lived. "They would set up sharp stebs inside the pea field and them young bucks jumped over the fence and stabbed themselves. That the only way to cotch them cause they so wild. . . ." Joe Higgerson, who labored on a small Missouri plantation, recalled that he used to build "turkey pens and dig a trench, put feed in dere and cover it over wid brush and de turkeys would come to feed, and we would trap 'em. . . . Then I've trapped quail too, in rail pens, built ten feet square. . . ."

The slaves favorite type of hunting were the nocturnal racoon and opossum chases. Of the two animals, the opossum were more numerous and easier to catch without dogs. The slaves also considered it more palatable than the "tough" and "stringy" racoon. Dogs were normally used to hunt both animals, though very little training was needed to teach them how to "tree" properly. Elmina Foster, who owned a small plantation in North Carolina, said the "opossum was a favorite with the slaves as a food which they greatly relished. At night the woods often rang out with the baying of hounds and the songs of slaves, whose voices were melodious, with always something of a melancholy strain,when they were out hunting." Isam Morgan reminisced about his Alabama plantation where the slaves would "go out at night wid a big sac an' a pack of houn's an' twarn't long befo' we done treed a 'poosum; after we done treed him, de dongs would stan' aroun' de tree an' bark. Iffen de tree was big, one of de niggers hadda climb up it an' git old mr. possum hisself."

Members of the slavequarters frequently mentioned different ethereal experiences they had while out opossum hunting. Many slaves were convinced that a spirit world played an integral role in the terrestrial world. In fact, some slaves appeared to believe in a world where physical and spiritual forces grappled for supremacy. There were more than a few slaves who actually felt the ghosts and mysterious spirits held the upper hand. "Uncle Ben was a great possum hunter, but he died fore I get big enough to go huntin' wid him," remembered John Glover of South Carolina. "He went possum huntin' every night till something went up de tree one night en possum talk to him. . . ." Andrew Means, who labored on a small South Carolina plantation, said that he never seed a ghost, but one night when me and another fellow was going possum hunting, I saw something, but I don't know what it was. De dogs treed a possum and laid down at de foot of the tree and something flew down out of the top of de trees and fought de dogs. It looked bigger than a bear maybe it was a ghost. . . ." Will Dill, who also toiled on a South Carolina plantation, said he never saw a ghost "unless it was one night when we boys was out with our dogs possum hunting. The dogs treed a possum, so I went up to shake it out, but when I looked down to see what I shook out it got bigger and bigger; I scrambled down the tree right away. . . ."

Besides their hunting trips, slaves thoroughly enjoyed the opportunity to fish in nearby streams or lakes. They caught a variety of different fish, the most popular being the catfish. The slave Timothy Smith remembered that "as soon as they came in from the fields he would be out playing, hunting, or fishing. I seen delightful times in those days." "As we lived on the rivers we ate any kind of fish we caught," recalled Susanna James, who toiled on a small Maryland plantation, "and everybody would go fishing after work." Ida Prine of Alabama " 'members when they would be plowin' down by de ribber, when it come dinner time an' whilst de mules eatin' us go down to de ribber an fish. Den eb'ry Sat'day ebenin's us'd fish; us kotch trout, gyar, jack, an' carp. . . ."

Slaves utilized a variety of different methods to catch fish, including set hooks, trot lines, nets, seines, and baskets. The basket or "trap" were especially useful, since slaves wasted little time tending them. Trot lines and set hooks could be left untended as well, but most slaves preferred to work them a few hours during the evening to inhibit pillage by alligators. All these methods were ideal for the slaves, since their maintenance did not interfere with their daily tasks. Gus Feaster and the other slaves on his South Carolina plantation used to make "mud baskets for cat fish; tie grapevines on dem and put dem in de river. We catch some wid hooks." The author Paul Ravesies, who spent the majority of his childhood in Alabama, remembered that the slaves would trap catfish "from the Warrior River in baskets plaited with white-oak strips, wide at the bottom and narrow at the top; a yielding funnel composed of the same material admitted the fish easily, but closed against their exit. . . . These baskets tied to overhanging limbs by grapevines were let down upon the bottom of the river and allowed to remain for several days before taken up. . . ." Robert Mallard, the son of a wealthy South Carolina planter, stated that the slaves would "churn" for fish by knocking the ends out of flour barrels then "thus provided would range themselves across a canel, and moving in concert would each bring his barrel at intervals down to the bottom. The moment a fish was covered, its presence was betrayed by its beating against the stoves in its effort to escape; when the fisherman instantly covered his barrel with his breasts, and with his hands speedily captured it. . . ."

Slaves found fishing to be not only a source of simple amusement but a means of obtaining extra spending money. The slaves on Charles Balls' plantation had the privilege of selling whatever they caught. Some of them "sold as many fish . . . as enabled them to buy coffee, sugar, and other luxuries for their wives." William Hayden acquired money by fishing on his small plantation in Kentucky. "I applied myself," said Hayden, "during my leisure moments to fishing, at which I was generally successful. These fish I coveyed to market, and obtained a considerable sum of spending money." In fact, the slave was so successful in fishing that white commercial fishermen often complained they were monopolizing the fishing holes and putting them out of business. In 1831, for instance, fifty-six petitioners of New Bern, North Carolina requested the legislature to pass a law that would prevent slaves from fishing unless in the company of a white person. "The petitioners declared themselves to be much injured both in their advocations, and in the management of their farms and negroes, by the large gangs of slaves, who come up from the town of New Bern and the neighborhood thereof, in boats . . . to sell, buy traffick, and fish."

Despite the legal attempts to circumvent slave fishing, the majority of planters were not bothered by their bondsmen receiving money for their "angling" exploits. In fact, as long as it was done during their own time, the planters encouraged and occasionally even payed their own slaves for the fish they caught. The British traveler A Dey Puy Van Buren said "the negroes never failed to send in some of the finest of the fish to their masters, for which they often received money. . . ." Another British traveler Sir Charles Lyell wrote that when the "slaves were disposed to exert themselves, they got through the days task in five hours, and then amused themselves in fishing . . . the master often paying for the catch." Frederick Law Olmsted told the story of an overseer who refused to pay a slave for the fish he had caught on the grounds he had garnered his catch during a work day. "The manager sent to him some of the fish for his own use," stated Olmsted, "and justified himself to me for not paying for it on the ground that the slave had undoubtedly taken time which really belonged to his owner to set his baskets. . . . They must do it at night when they were excused from labor for their owner. . . ."

Advancing age or labor requirements rarely diminished the slaves competitive spirit or love for the physical activities they had engaged in as children. There were obvious restrictions placed on their leisure time, but slaves continued to play almost every day of their lives and thoroughly enjoyed the opportunity to participate in various diversions.

The narratives are fraught with examples of slaves gambling. The more peccant slave men placed bets on everything from dice and card games to local horse races and cock fights. Of course there was frequently the problem of having enough to bet with and the fear that the slaves of the more devout planters would be reprimanded for their gaming. Charlie Crump of North Carolina reminisced that "crap shooting wuz de style den, but a heap of times dey can't find nothin' ter bet." Midge Burnett, who also lived on a North Carolina plantation, recalled that on moonlight nights "yo' could hear a head of voices an' when yo' peep ober de dike dar am a gang of niggers a shootin' craps an' bettin' eber' thing day has stold from de plantation . . ." The southern traveler George William Featherstonaugh related the story of a white man named Bob Chatwood who made a practice of pursuading "negroes that he was acquainted with to steal whatever they could from their masters, convert it into money, and then play with him at all fours. . . . There was a black amateur, greatly adept at the game, quite equal to Bob at it; and upon every occasion, when they were playing together, the negro would win every game."

Most southern states in the early antebellum period had no specific laws concerning the gambling of slaves. But by 1830, a number of strict laws had been passed which forbad slaves from gambling. The legislatures of North Carolina passed a law in 1830, for example, that "prohibited slaves from playing at any game of cards, dice, nine-pins, or any game of hazard or chance, for any money, liquor, or any kind of property, whether the same be staked or not upon pain of receiving thirty-nine lashes." A subsequent act in 1838 required that white people joining a slave in a game of chance for property be fined or imprisoned for six months. A South Carolina law of 1850 made it unlawful for a white person to play any game of chance with slaves whether for money, liquor, or property. No matter the legal restrictions, gambling remained popular among the slaves. The temperament of their masters, as well as the economic, social, and political condition of their community, was more important in determining the extent to which slaves were allowed to gamble.

Slaves welcomed the opportunity to engage in very informal and spontaneous boat and horse races. If slave boat crews happened to pass on the way to a coastal market they would invariably challenge one another to a test of speed. Similarly, slaves were anxious to prove the swiftness of their respective horses by running races on the avenues that led to the quarters. "My father owned large twelve-oared boats, in which we made frequent trips to the towns of Beaufort and Savannah," recalled Mary Howard Schoolcraft, whose father owned a large plantation in South Carolina. "The most delightful music I ever listened to was the wild songs of those athletic boatmen on the water; and should their chance to pass us a river yacht our men would ply their oars with renewed energy and challenge their neighbors to a race." Frederick Law Olmsted witnessed a horse race while he was traveling through the states of the southern seaboard. "While returning to the plantation I met six negroes," stated Olmsted. One of them a woman—riding on horseback. Soon afterwards I saw them stop, and two rode back some distance, and then raced their horses, the others cheering as they passed them." James Battle Avirett, the son of a wealthy Virginia slaveholder, told the story of a horse race he witnessed on his father's plantation: "Uncle Phillip and Cicero are to try the speed of their respective horses. . . . Presently you hear in trumpet tones the word 'go' and off they speed along the whole length of the avenue through the open gateway of the enclosure as rapidly as the horses can put their feet to the ground both running under whip and spur.''

Slaves loved to refresh themselves by swimming in nearby rivers and lakes. Irrespective of the circumstances, members of the slavequarter revived and invigorated themselves by going on swimming excursions. The southern climate was ideal for this activity. ''Didn't work in hot sun in June, July, or August,'' declared Aaron Ford of South Carolina, ''cause in slavery time dey allow us to take out at 10 or 11 o'clock an go swimmin.' '' Midge Burnett of North Carolina recalled that ''Dar was a ribber nearby de plantation, an' we niggers swam dar ever' Sadday. . . .'' Bill Crump, who also toiled on a North Carolina plantation, said they ''wucked in de fiel's from sunup ter sundown mos' o' de time, but we had a couple of hours at dinner time ter swim or lay on de banks. . . . Ober about sundown marster let us go swim ag'in iffen we wanted ter do it.''

There are frequent references in the narratives of adult slaves wrestling and fighting each other. These contests, however, were usually arranged by and performed solely for the enjoyment of whites. Confrontations certainly occurred in the slavequarters between people who were trying to settle personal arguments and differences, but these fights were not frequent and cannot be classified as sport. Slaves refrained from such fights because they recognized the need to care for one another and remain together as a familiar group regardless of the circumstances. Physical abuse of one slave by another was considered a threat to the general well-being of other members of the slavequarter community.

Those younger adults who had enough energy left after a hard day's work were probably more inclined to expend it in foot races, various jumping contests, and a host of other sports and athletic pursuits. Slaves delighted in challenging their peers to contests and participating in games that tested their physical prowess and sports skills. The ability to perform well in sporting competitions insured slaves the respect of their peers and a degree of status as well as leadership in the slavequarter community. Josiah Henson felt there was no one who could compete with him at work and sport. ''I could run faster and jump higher than anybody about me,'' reminisced Henson. Erving Lowery of South Carolina said the slaves would travel to neighboring plantations on Sunday and spend ''the day in jumping contests and foot races.'' William Wells Brown remembered that many slaves would attend the numerous religious revivals but the majority would spend their free time at the dances, cockfights, jumping contests, foot races, and other amusements that presented themselves.

In sum, slaves played and participated in a variety of diversions with a remarkable degree of intensity. The chance to frolic with neighboring slaves, opportunities to dance in their own particular style, freedom to roam the fields and woods in search of game, and the privilege of testing their physical strength was a source of great fun and enjoyment for members of the slavequarter. Through certain physical activities slaves were better able to realize particular social needs that could not be accomplished in any other fashion. Their various parties and social gatherings helped to insure their identity as individuals and as a community.

It was the medium through which they experienced necessary social intercourse, met new people, and perpetuated existing friendships. It gave them the opportunity to share personal experiences, express individual fears and anxieties, discuss local gossip, reminisce about their departed kinsmen, keep alive important love affairs, and dream about what life would be like in freedom.

It was not always dancing per se that was important to members of the slavequarter, but an instrument that was used to express their innermost fears and anxieties, demonstrate their physical prowess, ridicule whites, and communicate their thoughts and feelings to fellow slaves. In other words, dancing appeared to have a cathartic effect in that it provided a release of tension precipitated by their degraded condition. Not having many opportunities to vent their displeasure, slaves often used the dance to vicariously comment on themselves and their masters. Furthermore, slave dancing illustrates their view of themselves as a unique body of people with their own values and lifestyles. They never did identify with the slaveholders interests but only recognized their masters ultimate authority.

The opportunity to hunt and fish meant a great deal to slaves because it was a chance to help supplement their families' monotonous diet. Slave men realized a much needed feeling of self-worth and satisfaction by adding delicacies to the family table. Often precluded by their masters from contributing to their families material welfare, slave men relished the chance to hunt and angle for food. Slave men must have also enjoyed the comraderie and parity of their fellow "sportsmen." There was nothing quite like sitting around a blazing fire relating the tales of the phantom-like racoon or the sixteen foot catfish that "got away." Slave men, furthermore, found these two activities satisfying because it allowed them the opportunity to teach their older children the intracacies involved in hunting and fishing. There were not many activities in the plantation community where slave fathers and sons could share in the excitement of common pursuits.

Like most people, members of the slavequarter never lost their love for competitive activities. They took pleasure in challenging their fellows to various contests that would test their physical abilities. Slaves were unique, however, in that they generally preferred less combative pursuits instead of the more violent activities like boxing and wrestling. Slaves would normally engage in these activities only when their master wished to have some fun and forced different bondsmen to battle each other. Despite the personal animosities and jealousies individual slaves held toward each other, they normally refrained from unduly harming another member of the quarters. They realized the importance of sticking together as a familial group and were compelled by circumstances to tolerate the idiosyncrasies of individual members of the slavequarter community. At the center of the slaves' social philosophy was a necessary belief in cooperation and community spirit. There was simply no room in the slaves' world for cruel rivalry, physical violence, and ruthless domination.

CHAPTER 5

"Embodied Selves": The Rise and Development of Concern for Physical Education, Active Games and Recreation for American Women, 1776–1865

Roberta J. Park

The 1970s were not the first time that concerted efforts were made in the United States to draw attention to the lack of equality afforded women in social, educational, political, and economic life. Neither was it the first time that efforts were made to improve the general condition of women. Nor was it the first time that there were endeavors to draw attention to the physical needs and abilities of women or attempts to improve their health and "physical education." Stirrings for expanded educational opportunities, for better health care, for the recognition of women as worthy corporal beings and for "women's rights" had already reached noticeable proportions in the United States in the decades preceding the Seneca Falls Convention of 1848, often called, the single most important event of the nineteenth century women's rights movement. Such efforts grew in number and intensity until the dislocations of the Civil War temporarily impeded their progress.

Surely, these early endeavors did not advocate the type of *athletic sport* which has occupied so much of the Title IX discussion of the 1970s. The type of organized sport with which we in the twentieth century are so familiar did not develop (for men, much less for women) until at least the mid-1800s. Many of these early proposals, however, did encourage a variety of simple games and active pastimes (as well as calisthenics) for girls and women, and it seems reasonable to argue that, at the least, they helped to establish a climate favorable to the development of both curricular physical education and extracurricular

From the *Journal of Sport History,* 5:2 (Summer, 1978). © 1978 The North American Society for Sport History. Reprinted by permission.

sports for females in the late nineteenth and the twentieth centuries. The acknowledgement that girls and women might appropriately ''take more active exercise'' was important in fostering the social and cultural circumstances which opened to them the more strenuous and spectacular forms of activity which characterize the formalized and structured sports available to women in the twentieth century.

The Eighteenth Century Beginnings

During the eighteenth and nineteenth centuries American women possessed relatively few political, legal, even social, rights. Like their counterparts abroad, they were bound by law to their husbands. The same reasoning which could be—and was—used to invoke and sanction ''. . . the principle of inequality in the distribution of wealth amongst men . . . to be acquiesced in as a permanent condition of society,'' could also be used to support the contention that women were not equal to men. This did not mean, of course, that women were unaware of the disparity between their rights and those accorded men, nor that they were disinterested in trying to remedy the situation. In the minds of many women (and some men) the proposition that all men were created equal, which the Declaration of Independence had supposedly promised, became translated into the contention that, *if all men were created equal, why not women?* While it might have been industrialization which made it possible for women to finally gain emancipation in the twentieth century, an important and early influence was the stream of ideas which flowed from the eighteenth century ''Enlightenment'' and was articulated in works like Thomas Paine's *Rights of Man* and the writings of liberals like William Godwin and the famous—or infamous—Mary Wollstonecraft.

The America which by its Declaration of Independence had proclaimed that all men were created equal did not, in 1776, extend this same concept to members of the female sex. On May 7, 1776 Abigail Adams wrote to her husband John, observing that while the founding fathers were: ''. . . proclaiming peace and good-will to men . . .,'' they insisted upon ''. . . retaining absolute power over wives.'' Two years later Mrs. Adams again wrote to her husband lamenting the ''. . . trifling, narrow, contracted education . . .'' which women in America received and the way the subject of female education was either neglected or ridiculed. In August 1775 the *Pennsylvania Magazine* published an article entitled ''An Occasional Letter on the Female Sex'' in which the author encouraged greater acknowledgement of the rights of women, even though their duties in life might differ from those of men. The *Massachusetts Magazine* implied, in 1789, that attitudes were becoming more favorable toward the subject of female education. In 1790 this same journal began a series entitled ''On the Equality of the Sexes'' in which Judith Sargent Murray, writing under the name ''Constantia'', deplored the depressed conditions to which women had been subordinated, and proclaimed that if women were to be ''. . . allowed an equality of acquirement, let serious studies equally employ our minds, and we shall bid our

EXERCISES FOR THE CHEST AND LUNGS.

EXERCISE 1.

LET all the pupils take a given station, and at such distances that they can throw out their arms without touching each other. Then let the teacher give words of command as here indicated.

Word of Command—" Military Position !"

The directions here given are the same as those used by drill-sergeants in training military men, and therefore it is called the *Military Position.*

Fig. 1.

Let the heels be half an inch apart, and the feet turned out so as to form *an angle of sixty degrees.*

Let the knees be straight.

Let the shoulders be thrown back, the arms hang close to the body, the hands open to the front, the elbows turned in and close to the sides.

Let the chest be advanced, and the lower part of the body drawn back.

Let the head be erect, and the weight of the body be thrown onto the front part of the feet, as in *Fig.* 1.

This position brings the ear, shoulder, hip, knee, and ankle into a line, as is illustrated in this figure.

This drawing from Catharine Beecher's *Physiology and Calisthenics* (New York: Harper and Brothers, 1870), illustrates the "military position" advocated by Beecher and many other proponents of exercise and calisthenics.
Courtesy of the Library of Congress.

souls arise equal in strength." It was, Mrs. Murray contended, the limited education, employment and recreation permitted to women which had ". . . enervate[d] the body and debilitate[d] the mind . . ." Another early spokesman favoring a somewhat improved female education was Dr. Benjamin Rush, physician and Professor of Chemistry at the University of Pennsylvania. As a member of the all-male Board of Visitors of the Ladies' Academy of Philadelphia, Dr. Rush addressed a gathering of students and their families in 1787, declaring that in this newly created republic, ". . . ladies should be qualified to a certain degree by a peculiar and suitable education, to concur in instructing their sons in the principles of liberty and government." Concerned about the health of young ladies, he stipulated that dancing might be pursued as a form of healthful activity.

The first sustained argument in favor of the "rights of women" to be published in America is usually held to have been written by Charles Brockden Brown, often called the first professional man of letters in the United States. Brown's *Alcuin: A Dialogue* was published in 1798. (The first two portions of this small book also appeared in serial form in 1798 under the title "The Rights of Women.") Brown considered the customary separation of the sexes to be most injurious, observing that boys and girls ". . . associate in childhood without restraint, but the period quickly arrives when they are obligated to take different paths . . .," and this does not benefit either. From their earliest years, Brown maintained, men and women require the same type of care and instruction and it is illogical to believe that one sex will find physical vigor, suppleness and health more valuable than will the other sex. Since the limbs and organs of both sexes are basically the same, he held, there must, obviously, be one best diet, regimen and type and amount of exercise to develop the human body regardless of the sex of the individual.

The Early 1800s

In a pioneer, frontier country, such as America was at the beginning of the nineteenth century, it is certain that large numbers of women found themselves in circumstances where strenuous physical demands were made upon them daily. Many frontier women, and probably a high percentage of town women, were physically worn out by the demands of family responsibilities and domestic occupations. Especially in the Northeast many worked long hours in mills and at similar employments. (A distinction was made, of course, between "women" and "ladies"). How much time most American females actually had for a cultivation of their minds or bodies, even if custom had deemed such activity appropriate, is highly questionable. The most serious impediment to their progress, however, was the prevailing attitude which relegated them to a dependent and subordinated life. The expected, one might almost say the ordained, role for women in the nineteenth century was marriage and motherhood. Moreover, during the "Victorian period" the image of the helpless female became increasingly pronounced. The extent to which this ethic prevailed was noted by many foreign observers. Harriet Martineau, who visited America in the 1820s and 1830s, offered a prime example when she observed that in America, ". . . wifely and motherly occupations may be called the sole business of women. . . ."

A cautiously-phrased request for the amelioration of such limitations was provided in 1818 by Hannah Crocker Mather in her *Observations on the Real Rights of Women*. While the author acknowledged that the duties in life of each sex might properly differ, she contended that God "has endowed the female mind with equal powers and faculties . . ." to those given to men. After they have completed their domestic duties, women have a right to improve their literary and scientific abilities. Mrs. Crocker was also aware of the need for greater attention to women's bodily welfare. "The constitution and habit of the body," she wrote, "has a very great effect on the mind of either sex. . . ." The relationship between a sound body and a sound mind is no different for women than for men and those who are most vigorous and animated are usually also more cheerful and able.

By the third decade of the nineteenth century a general zeal for social reform of various kinds had become evident in America. Religious revivalism and temperance movements flourished, abolitionism was gaining momentum, reformers established a variety of utopian settlements, the common school movement was under way, and incipient "women's rights" crusades were forming. While the vast number of Americans still accepted the thesis that women were inferior to men—hence, that it was legitimate to limit their activities and opportunities—a growing number found such inequality to be objectionable, if not downright intolerable. There were outspoken "feminists" like Frances Wright, agitators for special causes like Emma Willard and Catharine Beecher, reformers like the Grimké sisters (who combined advocacy of women's rights with other social causes), and those like Margaret Coxe who were much more conventional in their views. Some were champions of suffrage and more or less total equality; others were scandalized by such requests, believing that woman's role in life differed from that of man. There was, however, one subject upon which most of the ladies—and a considerable number of men—were in rather general agreement; this was improved education for members of the female sex—(even though they might disagree considerably as to what form that education should take). For the very liberal, women had the right to full development of all their abilities; for the more conservative, it was clear that an education which was limited to morality and "the accomplishments" would be of little value in managing a household (and should a husband die, a widow must be able to insure that her young sons received a proper education). Some type of improved female education seemed indicated. Educational, popular, and even some medical journals took up the subject, devoting a surprising amount of attention to matters of health and "physical education."

When William Russell began publication of the *American Journal of Education* in 1826 female education, physical recreations, and physical education received extensive attention. The first issue carried a five-page article entitled "Physical Education." Russell promised to keep his readers informed of the importance of physical education and to introduce ". . . all the information that can be desired. . . ." To comply with this promise Russell utilized three approaches: a) original articles; b) articles reprinted from domestic and foreign journals; c) reviews of books on the subject of gymnastics, calisthenics and physical education. The first issue of the *American Journal of Education* also championed the cause of improved education for members of the female sex, discussing the Boston High School for Girls (established in 1821) and the desirability of a ". . . provision for a higher education of our daughters at the public expense. . . ." The June 1826 issue questioned why proper physical education should be denied to girls, noting that ". . . great sufferings frequently ensue, from the neglect of those early habits which increase strength and fortify the constitution." Having judged the vigorous gymnastic exercises imported from Europe to be inappropriate for women, the author of this article called for some other type of regular system of exercises for them. The November 1826 issue included an article reprinted from *The Boston Medical Intelligencer* entitled "Gymnastic Exercise for Females." It was written by William B. Fowle, founder of the Boston Female Monitorial School, who as early as 1824 had introduced there regular and systematic exercises for the girls. Fowle suggested that the term "hygienic exercises" might replace the term "gymnastics" because most people associated the latter with heavy exertions inappropriate for girls. The January 1827 issue of the *American Journal of Education,* quoting from *Parent's Friend,* declared: "Girls should have plenty of amusements: they should run races, play out of doors and in the garden . . . jump, run, halloo . . . exert the good spirits and vivacity so natural to their age. . . ." The May and June 1827 issues discussed "Suggestions to Parents: Physical Education" and "Education of Females," respectively.

Comprehensive book reviews of Voarino's and Hamilton's treatises on physical education for girls were published in the July 1827 issue, along with the declaration that, ". . . our principal object, at present . . . is to bring forward the subject of regular exercise for girls. . . ." During the five years that Russell served as editor (1826-1831) the *American Journal of Education* devoted substantial attention to the subject of "physical education for girls." This practice was continued by William Woodbridge, who assumed the editorship in 1831. Lydia Sigourney wrote in Woodbridge's *American Annals of Education* that mothers must devote proper attention to the physical welfare of their daughters and decried the use of tight and deforming corsets. The January 1833 issue encouraged teachers to join in the sports of the children. The July 1836 issue contained an article entitled "Physical Education of Females" extracted from a 1835 summer session address delivered by Dr. John Andrews, M.D. at the Steubenville, Ohio Female Seminary, wherein Dr. Andrews outlined the relationship between body and mind and stressed the ". . . necessity of judicious regulations in reference to labor, to diet, to dress, to exercise and repose. . . ."

Russell's *American Journal of Education* and Woodbridge's *American Annals of Education* were by no means the only educational publications to take up the matter of healthful exercise and active recreations for members of the female sex. The *Massachusetts Teacher* from 1849 to 1856, for example, remarked upon the subjects, often borrowing articles from works like *Household Words* and extracting from books like Catharine Beecher's *Letters to the People on Health and Happiness.* It praised the benefits of "out-of-door life" and "exercise in the open air" for women, discussed the interdependence of the intellectual and the physical, upheld the decision of the Massachusetts legislature that schools should teach physiology, admonished parents to ensure for their children ". . . the proper consideration of the laws of life and health," and suggested that teachers, as well as pupils, should ". . . devote a portion of each day to vigorous exercise. . . ." Other articles criticized the prevailing tendency to limit girls' physical activity to dancing and a few light calisthenics, suggesting, instead, games like shuttlecock and ". . . games in which their judgements shall teach them what they ought to do, and in which practice shall teach their hands to execute what their heads have planned.'' The December 1856 edition, quoting from the *Boston Medical and Surgical Journal*, declared: ''It is not merely a saunter that will benefit a young girl. . . . We had far rather see a girl romp than a sickly, over-imaginative, novel-reading, candy-eating creature. . . .'' The more vigorous outdoor activities which it was believed English girls engaged in were recommended, and parents were encouraged to set the proper example by joining in their children's sports. Horace Mann praised a gymnastic school for young ladies in the *Common School Journal,* which occasionally discussed physical education. Henry Barnard's *American Journal of Education,* which began publication in 1855, also included a number of similar articles in the decade before Civil War. In 1856, for example, Catharine Beecher's ''Health of Teachers and Pupils'' called for increased attention to physical training in a course ''designed to exercise every muscle of the body.'' No class of women, Ms. Beecher noted, suffered more from lack of exercise than did *female teachers.* Barnard published articles on playgrounds and gymnastic apparatus and on the benefits of physical education, of which Mason's ''Physical Exercise in School,'' with its concluding plea—''If we as teachers take this matter of physical exercise in school into serious consideration, determined to cultivate the physical well-being of our pupils as enthusiastically and systematically as we do the intellectual, we shall see even in our day, a better and happier, because healthier race . . .''—is a prime example. In 1862 and 1863 Barnard's *American Journal of Education* published Dio Lewis' ''New Gymnastics,'' which detailed a large number of specific exercises, provided examples of proper gymnasium costumes for women (and men), and declared that with proper exercise ''even the feeblest of girls'' could be transformed into ''. . . erect, ruddy, vigorous young women.''

Nor were educational journals alone in bringing the subjects of health and physical activity for members of the female sex to the attention of their readers. The *American Monthly Magazine* for 1829 included an article entitled ''Physical Education'' in which the author asserted that at perhaps no previous time in history had physicians more fully acknowledged the importance of physical exercise. Having contended that a ''. . . regular system of exercise, under the name of Physical Education, has lately been introduced and received by the public with unprecedented favor,'' the author declared that many of the exercises engaged in by men would be ''. . . equally applicable to the female. The difference, so striking in the appearance of the two in civilized life, is owing, in great measure, to the difference in their physical education; and may be ascribed to that cause rather than to any which nature has established.'' The *New York Free Enquirer* decried denying exercise to girls, and averred that when the physical and moral condition of women was improved the ''millenium'' would be realized. John Stuart Skinner, editor of the *American Farmer,* often included articles dealing with the importance of active exercise for females. Frequently drawing from contemporary journals, Skinner included assertions such as the one that most exercises appropriate for boys (with the exception of those termed ''athletic'') might be recommended for girls: ''Trundling a hoop, battledore, trapball, and every game which can exercise both the legs and the arms, and at the same time the muscles of the body, should be encouraged . . .''; for older girls, however, more propriety should be observed. Other articles in Skinner's journal suggested that those social restraints which interfered with young women receiving adequate exercise should be removed.

Efforts for Women by Women

While it must be acknowledged that during the 1800s there were numerous men who supported the concept of an improved condition for women, it was women themselves who supplied the major persistent voice of the movement toward greater freedom and opportunity. Of all the proclamations which were issued by women during the first decades of the nineteenth century concerning better education for their sex, a remarkable number called for greater attention to health and physical education. This was surely influenced by what Shryock had described as general advances in medicine and public health, and by popular health movements between 1800 and 1860. Expanding medical knowledge cannot alone, however, account for the magnitude of the women's concern. The recognition that women had bodies and that their bodies were the visible, tangible means by which they could be known as discrete persons must be seen, at the least, as equally important. Women, no less than men, were embodied spirit, and the desire for a recognition that they had intellectual, moral and *physical* abilities (and rights) recurs again and again in their writings and speeches.

Although British by birth, her adventures in the United States place Frances Wright among the notable American feminists of the early 1800s. She surely had an impact upon American society—both favorable and unfavorable. Her *Views of Society and Manners in America,* published in 1821, has been called one of the most celebrated travel memoirs of the early nineteenth century. Among her many undertakings she served as a co-editor of the *New Harmony Gazette* (later the *New York Free Enquirer*), and founded the ill-fated Nashoba communitarian settlement. In *Views of Society* Frances Wright wrote: ''I often lament that in the rearing of women so little attention should be commonly paid to the exercise of the bodily organs; to invigorate the body is to invigorate the mind, and Heaven knows that the weaker sex have much cause to be rendered strong in both. In this happiest country [women's] condition is sufficiently hard. . . . A vigorous intellect . . . is broken down by sufferings, bodily and mental.'' She believed that it was ''the union of bodily and mental vigor'' which gave to the American male his special energy of character, and that the benefits of ''wholesome exercise'' should also be accessible to women. While it was not necessary for women to emulate all men's activities, ''they might, with advantage, be taught in early youth to excel in the race, to hit a mark, to swim, and in short to use every exercise which could impart vigor to their frames and independence to their minds.'' In her *Course of Popular Lectures,* published in 1829, Ms. Wright declared that women should be regarded as human beings and that ''the fair and thorough development of all the facilities, physical, mental, and moral . . ." must be assured; girls have "equal claims" to the development of *all* their faculties.

Few American women in the early 1800s were as outspoken as was Frances Wright. Emma Willard, a staunch advocate of improved education for women, was never a supporter of women's political rights. In 1819 Mrs. Willard approached Governor De Witt Clinton of New York with an appeal for state-aided schools for girls. Her *Plan for Improving Female Education* suggested that dancing was a suitable instruction because it provided exercise—"needful to the health"—and recreation—necessary for the "cheerfulness and contentment of youth." She also suggested that their employment at domestic duties would "afford a healthy exercise" as well as help reduce the costs of the girls' education. While it was never Mrs. Willard's intention that women receive the same education as men, their responsibilities for raising children and "elevating the community" made it necessary to seek the "perfection of their moral, intellectual and physical nature." The considerable success of her Troy Female Seminary drew attention to Emma Willard's views concerning the proper education of girls. So, also, did the success of Mary Lyon, whose work is often mentioned along with that of Emma Willard. Mary Lyon had already had a variety of teaching experiences before her Mount Holyoke Seminary opened in 1837. In summers, commencing in 1824, she joined the staff of the Adams Female Seminary where her friend Zilpah Grant was preceptress. Apparently, calisthenics formed part of the curriculum at Adams for it was reported that Ms. Grant damaged her achilles tendon in 1827 while teaching calisthenics. The girls at Mount Holyoke received twenty minutes of calisthenics and performed one hour of domestic duties each day. Housework helped reduce the pupils' cost and, as a by-product, it provided the girls with physical exercise. In July 1838 Ms. Lyon wrote: "The daily work brings one hour of regular exercise . . . [and] seems to give them a relish for exercise . . . they walk more here of their own accord. . . ."

In 1831 a treatise entitled *Course of Calisthenics for Young Ladies,* purported to have been written by an American mother, was published at Hartford, Connecticut. The author, who is designated only by the letter "M", dedicates the work to ". . . Mothers and Instructresses, with the earnest wish, that the subject [of calisthenics] may receive the attention that it deserves. . . ." The small volume takes the form of a series of letters intended initially for the ". . . benefits of the author's own family." A variety of exercises (i.e., the triangle; the wand; weight exercises; postural exercises; exercises for "grace of motion"; exercises to increase muscular strength; the "oscillator"; exercises to relieve the effects of tight lacing) are included, accompanied by numerous illustrations. The author also observed that calisthenic exercises like "la Grace" promoted cheerfulness and contributed to overall health. Not only were these exercises deemed useful for the home; "M" hoped that ". . . the time . . . is not far distant, when Calisthenics will be introduced into every female school in the United States."

Among the earliest American women to formulate an extensive system of calisthenic exercises and endeavor to have these incorporated into the education

of girls was Catharine Esther Beecher. She was certainly one of the more prominent figures in the cause of improved education for American women in the
decades before the Civil War. Sklar contends that Catharine Beecher's Hartford
Seminary was considered by her contemporaries to be, ''. . . one of the most
significant advances made in early nineteenth century education for women. . . .''
Although a tireless agitator in favor of their better education, Ms. Beecher was
convinced that a woman's proper role in life consisted in being a wife and mother;
hence, women needed an education which differed in a number of particulars
from that given to men. She was opposed to overt participation by women in social
movements, and especially to the growing agitation for equal political rights.

Ms. Beecher was highly critical of the typical female seminary of her day,
insisting that it was *action,* not *ornament,* which should be the goal for a woman;
she favored more practical studies, calisthenics and better health care. In works
like *A Treatise on Domestic Economy* (1841) she provided practical instruction
on family health, infant care, children's education and home management. Her
best-known works dealing with the subject of ''physical education'' were *Letters
to the People on Health and Happiness* (1855), *Physiology and Calisthenics for
Schools and Families* (1856) and *Calisthenic Exercises for Schools, Families
and Health Establishments* (1856). The last-mentioned work opened with the
statement: ''The design of this book is to teach the methods by which children
may be trained *at school,* so as to become healthful, strong, graceful, and good-
looking.'' After devoting numerous chapters to a discussion of the organs of the
body, the ''laws'' of health, and abuses of the body and their remedies, Ms.
Beecher then described sixty-two exercises for the schoolroom, accompanying
all but three with illustrations of girls (and a few of boys) performing them. Ms.
Beecher was always especially concerned about postural and physiological abuses
which prevailing fashions were apt to inflict upon girls and women; she discussed
various causes of structural deformities (and the means of avoiding these), and
suggested exercises designed to alleviate such problems.

Ms. Beecher had considerable practical experience in her career as an educator.
In 1829 she published an essay entitled *Suggestions Respecting Improvements
in Education* in which the goals of her Hartford Female Seminary were described.
Here she outlined many of the themes which she later expanded upon: ''It is to
mothers and to teachers that the world is to look for the character of . . . each
ensuing generation.'' However, women have rarely been systematically prepared
for these important duties. ''Have you been taught anything of the structure, the
nature, and the laws of the body, . . .'' she asked. ''Were you taught to understand
the operations of diet, air, exercise and the modes of dress on the human frame?
Have the causes which are continually operating to prevent good health . . . ever
been made the subject of any instruction?'' These are the questions to which
Ms. Beecher set about providing answers. In this early essay she also set forth
her views on the proper operation of a boarding school for girls. The ''formation
of personal habits and manners,'' the formation of the disposition and conscience,
and the ''business of physical education'' all needed special attention, she insisted.

She also suggested that a school should have an assistant who could provide young ladies with instruction in calisthenics.

Catharine Beecher resigned her position at the Hartford Female Seminary in 1831 and opened the Western Female Institute in 1832. She also established several other rather short-lived schools. It was her enduring conviction that women needed economic independence, and an avowed aim of her Women's Educational Association was the establishment of teaching positions for women so that they might become financially independent. Her textbooks on physiology and calisthenics enjoyed a wide circulation and surely had a valuable role in introducing the American people to the need for physical education and health education at home and at school; her articles appeared in numerous popular and educational publications, some of which reached a very wide reading audience.

Interest in improved health, physical education and active recreations for members of the female sex was by no means limited to educators. Ladies who enjoyed success in the literary field were also supporters. One of the earlier to make a successful career of literature was Lydia Sigourney. Her effusive and flowery books and articles were widely read by women in the 1830s and 1840s. Louis Godey paid her five hundred dollars a year merely to use her name in association with his *Lady's Book.* In 1833 Mrs. Sigourney published *Letters to Young Ladies,* her most popular prose work, in which she stated: ''Since without health, both industry and enjoyment languish . . . it is desirable to multiply those modes of exercise, which are decidely feminine.'' She objected to allowing fashion to impair health and advocated a balance between what she called the modern penchant for neglecting the body and making it a slave to the mind and the Spartan example of excessive concern for the physical. She recommended walking, riding, sea-bathing and an assortment of vigorous domestic tasks for young girls, speaking favorably of Mary Lyon's Mount Holyoke Seminary and the work of Catharine Beecher, Sarah Josepha Hale and Mme de Genlis, the famous French educator of the late eighteenth century.

Mrs. Sigourney was a frequent contributor to Godey's *Lady's Book,* which was edited for nearly forty years by Sarah Josepha Hale. At the height of its popularity this magazine boasted a circulation of over 150,000 copies, being a style-and taste-setter for large numbers of American women. After a brief teaching experience Sarah Josepha Hale settled down to family life. In 1827 the Reverend John Blake, principal of Boston's Cornhill School for Young Ladies, encouraged her to accept the editorship of the *American Ladies' Magazine.* Its first issue carried her optimistic declaration: ''In this age of innovation, perhaps no experiment will have an influence more important on the character and happiness of our society, than the granting to females the advantages of a systematic and thorough education.'' She further asserted that insufficient attention was devoted to ''. . . the physical strength of women; or to that course of instruction and treatment which relates to the vigor and improvement of their bodily powers.'' Although she accepted the prevailing belief that there was a ''divinely ordered gulf'' between the sexes (criticizing feminists like Frances Wright and the movement for female suffrage), Mrs. Hale held several progressive views concerning women's sphere. She was a tireless champion of improved education, praising the work of innovators like Emma Willard and Mary Lyon. Under her editorship the *American Ladies' Magazine* printed numerous comments concerning educational innovations. The January 1829 issue, for example, described the benefits of play for young children; the November 1829 issue included an announcement of the Greenfield High School for Young Ladies in which it was stated: "Our system of Education embraces the three-fold object of Physical, Intellectual and Moral culture. . . . Physical health and its attendant cheerfulness promote a happy tone of moral feeling, and they are quite indispensable to successful intellectual effort. We are ambitious that our pupils should return to their homes [with] . . . an increased share of muscular vigor and youthful freshness." The use of the battledore, cornella, rope-skipping, swinging, walking and country rides were mentioned. The January 1830 edition stated, in a long excerpt from *The Journal of Health* entitled "Physical Education of Girls": "The bodily exercises of the two sexes ought, in fact, to be the same. As it is important to secure to both, all the corporal advancements which nature has formed them to enjoy . . . girls should not be confined to a sedentary life. . . ." They need freedom to enjoy the exercise of their muscles as much as do boys.

In 1836 Louis Godey pursuaded Mrs. Hale to join him as editor of his very popular *Lady's Book.* In spite of her own conforming inclinations (and Godey's policy of avoiding controversial topics), Mrs. Hale did not falter in her efforts to improve the lot of American women, (at least along the lines which *she* deemed proper). Boyer has judged: "On the great theme of education for women she never wavered. . . . In an era when a delicate pallor was considered fascinating and an early death romantic, she tirelessly urged upon her readers the virtues of exercise, fresh air, proper diet, and sensible dress. . . ." In July 1841 Mrs. Hale wrote an article of her own for Godey's *Lady's Book,* quoting extensively from a Glasgow physician and adding that in her estimation she found the views ". . . judicious, and well calculated to promote the physical improvement of Children":

> . . . females, from their earliest years, should be allowed those sports and amusements in the open air, so necessary to a proper development of their bodies, and which are now confined entirely to boys. . . . Until girls are 14 or 15 years old, they should be allowed to play in the open air at least *six hours* every day. . . . They should be allowed to run, throw the ball, and play at battledore. . . . All these exercises call the different muscles into action, strengthen the limbs, and impart a healthy tone to the different organs; the blood circulates freely, the nervous system is invigorated.

She vowed that physical exercise, active recreations and playful games would be discussed in subsequent issues and, indeed, Sarah Josepha Hale did for many years use her "Editor's" section (as well as a careful selection of articles) to discourse upon several of her favorite topics, not the least of which were improved health and proper physical education for members of the female sex.

Among the more notable American ladies of the first half of the nineteenth century was Margaret Fuller, whose *The Great Lawsuit: Man versus Men, Woman Versus Women* and *Woman In the Nineteenth Century* became "bibles" of the women's rights movements. During her short lifetime she was author, teacher, literary critic for the *New York Tribune,* foreign correspondent, intellectual conversationalist and a pioneer in feminist proclamations. She associated with the New England Transcendentalists and helped Emerson and Thoreau edit *The Dial.* As did others of this "Transcendental movement," she believed that a sound body was indispensible for the proper development of the mind and that *all* the human faculties (mental, spiritual, physical) must be freely and harmoniously developed. Disappointed that his first child had not been a boy, Margaret's father set for her the most demanding tasks; her diaries reflect her concerns about the ill-effects of a childhood devoted to excessive reading, late hours and inactivity. She often referred to what she believed was a growing emphasis in favor of physical education in the United States: "If we had only been as well brought up in these respects," she declared; "I can't help but mourn sometimes, that my bodily life should have been so destroyed by the ignorance of both my parents." In her *Life Without and Life Within* she commented favorably upon a lecture delivered by Dr. John Warren, M.D. on the subject "Physical Education and the Preservation of Health," wherein Dr. Warren maintained: ". . . gymnastic exercises, especially in the open air, are needed by everyone who is not otherwise led to exercise all parts of the body by various kinds of labor"; even if adults were not interested in their own health, she insisted, they ought to be concerned that their children had ample playful activity.

It is abundantly clear that the majority of American women did not share the very liberal views espoused by a Frances Wright or a Margaret Fuller. Writers like Margaret Coxe, whose *Claims of the Country on American Females* was published in 1842, adhered to a much more traditional concept of woman's proper sphere. Her *Young Lady's Companion* (1842), for example, was praised for the ". . . wise moderation [which] pervades the work; the aim is always at the promotion of the very best features of female and Christian character." Indeed, it was on the basis of the more traditional argument that the major reason for women to receive a proper physical education was because it was their Christian duty to raise physically healthy and morally sound children that she included a chapter entitled "Hints to American Females on the Physical Culture of Youth." "Judicious, systematic, physical culture is needed for our daughters no less than for our sons. . . .," she declared; "it is a requisite to promote the health, happiness, and moral excellence of both." Girls were ill-prepared for the arduous tasks of domestic life because all too often, ". . . exercise which would invigorate the frame, is discouraged as unlady-like and rude. . . ." If a woman failed to fulfill her "wifely duties" a husband was likely to look elsewhere for sexual satisfaction, thereby destroying the normal and proper fabric of society. All this might ensue because of the "inattention of mothers to the physical culture of females."

Although the majority of American men and women might adhere to the more traditional views expressed by Margaret Coxe, by the 1840s active stirrings for greater female emancipation were clearly evident. When Lucretia Mott and Elizabeth Cady Stanton were denied the right to be seated at the World Anti-Slavery Convention in London in 1840, so many contend, the Seneca Falls "Women's Rights" Convention of 1848 was born. When preparing for this now-famous convention Mrs. Stanton paraphrased the Declaration of Independence: "We hold these truths to be self evident; that all men and women are created equal. . . . The history of mankind is the history of repeated injuries and usurpations on the part of man toward woman. . . ." Mrs. Stanton repeated the same sentiments on July 19, 1848 in her maiden speech before the first "women's rights" convention in America at Seneca Falls, New York: ". . . the time [has] come for the question of women's wrongs to be laid before the public . . . woman alone can understand the height, the depth, the length and the breadth of her degredation." From the Seneca Falls Convention until the Civil War numerous women—and not a few men—dedicated to the cause of expanded "rights" for members of the female sex labored to achieve increased freedom for American women. A proper education was clearly seen to be one of the corner-stones. Lucretia Mott, for example, in her *Discourse on Women* (1849) declared: ". . . the demand for a more extended education will not cease, until girls and boys have equal instruction in all the departments of useful knowledge . . . let women receive encouragement for the proper cultivation of all her powers . . . strengthening her physical being by proper exercise and observance of the laws of health. . . ."

Since the public press and most journals did relatively little to further their cause (and sometimes tried to impede it), the women had to rely upon abolitionist newspapers and a variety of journals published for and by themselves. The first issue of *The Una,* published by Paulina Wright Davis, included an article entitled "Woman As Physically Considered," in which the author declared: "Our aim in these remarks is to come to the physical organization of the sexes, and to prove that woman is not man's inferior." Although men might be stronger, they were not necessarily superior beings; in fact, in some respects the physical ability of women is ". . . decidedly superior to the sex which rules and oppresses her." While reporting upon the deliberations of various women's rights conventions, *The Una* (like other similar publications), often observed that women, as well as men, had a right to the highest mental and *physical* development. When Amelia Bloomer began publication of *The Lily* in 1849 its masthead carried the statement "Devoted to the Interests of Women." The topics which it most frequently discussed were: temperance; women's rights; suffrage; health and physical education for women; dress reform; access to the professions—especially medicine. *The Lily* declared in its May 1, 1849 issue that there was too great an inclination to urge the enlightenment of women solely, ". . . as a sure means of improving man, rather than as in itself an intrinsic excellence. . . ." With increasing frequency the desire to see women regarded as human beings with *their own* worth and integrity was stressed. The June 1, 1849 issue condemned the lack of concern regarding the health and physical education of American women: "Shame on us, that we, who boast of having raised women in the nineteenth century to the position in life which she ought to hold, so educated her that not one of her powers, physical or mental, can even attain a full and healthy action . . . has not a girl a physical system to be developed and matured and invigorated?'' Pitching the quoit, throwing the ball, sliding down hills, roaming through hills, it was held, had all been denied to girls on the excuse that these were ''unfeminine'' when, instead, active exercise, games and sports should have been encouraged. Jane G. Swisshelm (publisher of her own newspaper, *The Saturday Visiter*) complained that women sewed too much instead of exercising in the fresh air, and suggested that the ''laxity of parental authority'' in America was due to ''. . . the absorbing pursuit of money that occupies the minds of men]and] from the want of physical education of women, and the place assigned them as intellectual inferiors. . . .'' A considerable number of the articles which appeared in *The Lily* were contributed by Elizabeth Cady Stanton, the dedicated and extremely active advocate of women's rights, who frequently wrote under the name of ''Sunflower.'' In April 1850 Mrs. Stanton discussed the topic ''man's claim to physical superiority.'' As had Mary Wollstonecraft before her, Mrs. Stanton declared: ''We cannot say what the woman might be physically, if the girl were allowed all the freedom of the boy, in romping, swimming, climbing, and playing hoop and ball. . . . Physically as well as intellectually, it is *use* that produces growth and development.'' A writer using the pseudonym ''Veritas'' discussed ''Improper Education of Women'' in the April 1855 issue, declaring that women had a right to be educated morally, mentally and physically; girls should not be excluded from ''. . . the open air and field sports, which would develop and invigorate both physical and mental powers,'' for such hoydenish activities help insure that women may become intelligent and self-reliant.

The clothing styles worn by women throughout the nineteenth century seriously inhibited their freedom of movement. Tight lacings interfered with circulation and could lead to structural deformities; long skirts swept the ground and were unhygienic; fashion might burden women with ten or more pounds of garments. In 1851 *The Lily* began an earnest discussion of the ''new costume.'' This outfit, which came to be known as ''bloomers'' for Mrs. Amelia Bloomer who advocated and tried to popularize it, consisted of full pantaloons and a shortened skirt. Writing in July 1851, Mrs. Stanton declared an intention to free women from the constraints of their traditional costume and permit free use of lungs, limbs, spine and ribs; such discussions continued throughout 1851 and 1852. By 1854, however, the ''new costume,'' and the debate which surrounded it in the public press, had generated so much adverse publicity that it was feared that criticisms of dress reform might interfere with other advances. Most of the ladies abandoned their new dress, but meetings of the National Dress Reform Association did continue. *The Lily,* reporting on such a meeting in August 1856, once again declared that the cause of the poor health of so many American girls and women could be attributed to ''fashionable long-skirted garments.''

Women's Rights Conventions proliferated in the years immediately following the Seneca Falls Convention of 1848. The Ohio Convention of 1851 issued a declaration that not only were women deprived of a liberal education, they were also ''. . . either deprived of healthy physical exercise and development . . . [or]

. . . overpowered by domestic drudgery. . . ." The proceedings of the 1885 National Women's Rights Convention, resolved that "the right to acquire knowledge should be limited only by the capacity of the individual," and that social attitudes which excluded women from the best colleges, universities and schools of law, divinity and medicine were unendurable. At an evening session of this same Convention Mrs. Frances Gage declared to those assembled that American women still had great need for better education, greater independence, more opportunities for employment, and improved physical strength.

One of the causes vigorously pursued by several of the ladies who favored augmented opportunities was the right to be trained for and granted access to the so-called "male professions." Of these, medicine received the most frequent discussion in the women's journals. (This exclusion of women from the learned professions—law, theology and medicine, had been criticized in the Declaration of Principles adopted at Seneca Falls in 1848). The first woman in the United States to be graduated from a proper medical school was Elizabeth Blackwell. Admitted to Geneva College against the unanimous opposition of the faculty, she graduated in 1849 at the head of her class but found it impossible to secure a position in the medical establishment. With the support of private capital she finally opened the New York Infirmary in 1857, staffed entirely by women. In 1851, Dr. Blackwell delivered a course of lectures in New York on bodily hygiene and physical education—two topics which were of particular interest to her throughout her medical career. These lectures were published in 1852 as *The Laws of Life, with Special Reference to the Physical Education of Girls*. In her introduction Dr. Blackwell declared that her object was ". . . to call your attention to the importance of this subject—physical education of the young—and to urge upon you the means by which our present degeneracy may be checked. . . ." It was her further conviction that women no less than men could not live as "disembodied spirit," and since the self was expressed through the physical, the body must be properly cared for.

With her extensive medical training, Dr. Blackwell was more scientifically informed than most women concerning the physiological and anatomical benefits of exercise; in fact, *The Laws of Life* reads very much like a basic physiology of exercise textbook written for the layman. Four "basic laws of health" are discussed by the author: the law of *exercise* (or movement) in life; the law of *order* in exercise; the *balance* of exercise; the law of *use* in exercise. Dr. Blackwell criticized the typical school curriculum for its failure to devote adequate attention to the child's physical development, stating: ". . . education of the mind shall always be subordinate to our education of the body, until the body has completed its growth." Children were subjected to poor ventilation, improperly constructed desks and lack of exercise; often they were not properly fed; towns neglected to provide any kind of playgrounds for them. Because of lack of understanding of the laws of health, the health of girls had been impaired before they reached maturity; therefore, they became feeble wives and mothers. To all this improper and neglected physical education of American females, Dr. Blackwell contrasted the type of physical education provided women in other nations (i.e., Sparta,

Athens, England). She insisted that the school system in America must be changed and, ". . . a system of scientific gymnastic training should be adopted—every kind of active sport encouraged. . . ."

Various Medical and Quasi-Medical Contributions

During the nineteenth century "the laws of health" did receive increasing attention from members of the medical profession, as well as in a spate of health fads which arose around the third decade of the century. Shryock has characterized the decades from 1820 to 1860 as ones of growth in all types of medical institutions, as well as in the establishment of a variety of medical journals and health periodicals. Students began to go abroad in large numbers to study at Paris—at that time probably the most advanced center for medicine and public health—and to London where various sanitary and health reforms were underway. Although in the United States training by apprenticeship was still more common than attendance at medical school, faculties were growing and chairs of physiology were being established. Both doctors and laymen authored books and pamphlets on the general subject of health, many of which devoted considerable attention to matters of hygiene and physical education. In all this, women received a measure of benefit. In fact, in many ways, both the health problems of women *and* the implied—if not always stated—propriety of regarding women as worthy corporal entities was given expanded attention.

The *Boston Medical Intelligencer* for May 1825 published an article entitled "Physical Education," written by Dr. James Field, M.D. of London, in which lack of exercise in relation to curvature of the spine among girls was discussed. Dr. Field asserted that ". . . a certain degree of *hoydenism* . . . skipping and scampering . . ." must be allowed, and that girls should play games like battledore, tennis and trap-ball. The prevailing notions of female fragility and helplessness, he contended, were entirely erroneous. In 1826 Dr. John G. Coffin, M.D. (who contributed articles on physical education to Russell's *American Journal of Education*) assumed publication of the *Boston Medical Intelligencer,* wherein William B. Fowle's article on the exercises provided girls at his Boston Female Seminary appeared. Fowle expressed his hope that ". . . the day [was] not far distant when gymnasiums for women will be as common as churches in Boston. . . ." Dr. Coffin added his own support, proclaiming that Fowle's was ". . . the first account we have seen of gymnastics having been successfully practiced in any school for girls in any part of the United States." Dr. Coffin admonished his reader, asking whether anything had been done ". . . in the last half century in the American Union, to render our women what they are capable of being made, healthy, efficient, and happy beings?"

The Boston Medical and Surgical Journal for December 1835 described the problems inflicted upon a little girl due to lack of exercise, urged parents to pay attention to the natural laws of growth and health, and drew attention to Dr. Andrew Combe's *Principles of Physiology Applied to the Preservation of Health and the Improvement of Physical and Mental Education.* In early 1836 this same journal published an article entitled "Physical and Moral Evils of the Present System of Female Education In the United States" in which the author criticized the present system for education for not devoting sufficient attention to the physical education of girls: "They are sent to school when they are three or four years old, confined there for hours together in one position, and when they are released for the day, instead of being allowed to play like boys, they must return home. . . ." Among the many faults of the typical female education, the author declared, one of the most unfortunate was the failure to provide young ladies with adequate active exercise in the open air.

The *Health Journal and Advocate of Physiological Reform* discussed topics like "the Graham System," ventilation of school houses, the relationship of tight-lacing to spinal deformities, and offered hints on exercise to young ladies. It reprinted "Physical Education of Girls" from the *Journal of Health* and "Physical Education" from the *New England Farmer.* This latter article stipulated that daughters would profit from "vigorous exercise, and that too in the open air. . . ." It also frequently excerpted from (or at least mentioned) works like Caldwell's *Thoughts on Physical Education,* Combe's *Principles of Physiology.* . . . and William Alcott's extensive writings on health and physical education. The *American Medical Intelligencer* also reviewed Caldwell's *Thoughts On Physical Education;* and the *New York Medical and Physical Journal* reviewed works like Dr. William P. Dewees' *A Treatise on the Diseases of Females.* The *Water Cure Journal* discussed "Healthy Children" from William Alcott's *Golden Rule,* reported that Horace Mann had decried ". . . the destructive practice of depriving children of fresh air and exercise. . . ," reprinted "Evils of Tight-Lacing" from the *Boston Journal of Health,* and excerpted "Health of Females" from Lydia Sigourney's *Letters to Mothers* (including her plea for earnest play and active sports for little girls). From *Jerrold's Magazine,* the *Water Cure Journal* borrowed "Physical Education" (noting the need for physical exercise on the part of both boys and girls); from the *New York Sun* it took "Out-of-Door Exercise for Females" (observing that foreigners often remarked upon a lack of health among American women). Sylvester Graham's *Journal of Health and Longevity* also mentioned Mrs. Sigourney's observations on the health of girls, discussed the ill-effects of tight lacing, and noted the importance of fresh air and exercise for girls. Graham's insistence that proper hygiene was dependent upon the observance of sound physiological rules (even though his views often tended to extremes), helped foster support for various dietary, dress and exercise reforms for women. Several Ladies Physiological Reform Societies were organized, and a few of the more outspoken, like Paulina Wright Davies (founder of *The Una*), even had the temerity to give lectures on physiology.

The need to devote greater attention to the observance of sound physiological and anatomical principles, especially on behalf of the female sex, was a subject treated by several medical doctors in the first six decades of the nineteenth century. Dr. E.W. Duffin's *The Influence of Modern Physical Education of Females in Producing and Confirming Deformity of the Spine* was well-received in the United States. (This was one of the works to which "M" referred in *Course of Calisthenics for Young Ladies*). Duffin was concerned about the high incidence of postural and structural difficulties among women, and believed calisthenic exercise could be invaluable in the prevention and correction of many of these problems. In a small treatise published in 1833 Dr. Charles Caldwell declared that since much of the perfection of the American race was dependent upon liberal exercise in the open air, ". . . a much larger amount of it than is taken by children at school, especially female children, is essential." Although he would have women avoid "masculine activities," they could benefit from things like horseback riding, walking, dancing, gardening and doing housework. As did many of his contemporaries, Caldwell inveighed against the tight and constraining clothing worn by women. This small volume was cited or quoted in numerous health journals in the 1830s and 1840s. Another work which was frequently mentioned was Dr. Andrew Combe's *The Principles of Physiology Applied to the Preservation of Health and the Improvement of Physical and Mental Education;* this was issued in the Harper Brothers Home Library series at fifty cents per copy, thus making it financially attractive. Dr. Combe was vitally concerned that the American people develop a better understanding of the laws of health. He thoroughly endorsed physical activity for growing children, believing that active sports were superior to things like walking, and that the sociability in games encouraged the children to continue to participate. Instead of being confined to formal walks, Combe maintained, girls would be both ". . . delighted and benefited by spending two or three hours a day in spirited exercise." He disapproved of the prevailing assumption that the physical educa-tion of the two sexes should differ so radically (although he held that the type and amount of exercise should be adjusted to the needs of the individual); he also referred with disapproval to the number of structural deformities which could all too often be found among pupils in female seminaries. Another medical commentator on the evils caused by a deficient physical education for girls was Dr. John Bell, whose *Health and Beauty: An Explanation of the Laws of Growth and Exercise* . . . was published in 1838. Health, beauty, education, even humanity, Bell declared, are all based upon proper development of the natural structures of the human body. Unfortunately, false notions of grace and feminine reserve had prevented girls from engaging in anything more than the most formal and limited exercise—which proved to be monotonous and heartless. Happily, Bell observed, methodological exercises (gymnastics for boys; calisthenics for girls), were receiving greater attention. He, too, discussed the hazards of stays and confining clothing and advocated a type of dress which would allow young girls ample opportunity to freely exercise their muscles. The absence of city playgrounds—especially for girls—he held, made necessary the establishment of programs of methodical exercise in schools. In 1846 Dr. John Warren's *Physical Education and the Preservation of Health* (based upon a lecture he had delivered to the American Institute in 1830) became available to America's reading public. Although its benefits might be understood in theory, Warren asserted, regular exercise was too much neglected in *practice*. Girls were discouraged at an early age from engaging in natural physical activities and taught to spend their leisure quietly at home, much to the detriment of their health and well being. This practice, combined with the type of clothing which they wore, resulted in the structural illnesses which were all too apparent among American women in the early 1800s. Girls should walk, dance, play battledore, play ball with both hands, exercise with the triangle and dumbbells, and use the parallel bars. "Every seminary of young persons," Warren declared, "should be provided with the instruments for these exercises."

The salubrious reciprocity among physical, mental and moral health was stressed by several physicians. A prime exemplar of this attitude was Dr. William A. Alcott, one of the most active health reformers of the first half of the nineteenth century. A prolific writer in the cause of both health and social reform, Alcott was also an editor of several journals, including Woodbridge's *American Annals of Education* (to which he also contributed articles on physical education) and the *Boston Health Journal and Advocate of Physiological Reform*. As a young man Alcott accepted a teaching position, thereupon beginning an association with an activity which would be of deep interest to him throughout his lifetime. In *Confessions of a School Master* (1839) he declared: "Indeed this [school keeping] was always nearest my heart. I had only resorted to another profession as a discipline to my mind, and that I might have, as the common saying is, 'two strings to my bow'. . . ." Alcott soon became convinced that both morality and health were being sacrificed to the intellect in America; in the stiffling atmosphere of the school house children's and teachers' health was impaired. This was deemed especially serious by Alcott, who always believed that health and Christian salvation were intimately related; healthy bodies meant healthy spirits. "The redemption of the intellectual and moral world and the physical conditions of mankind must proceed together," he insisted. In 1849 Alcott's *The Young Woman's Guide to Excellence* (which the author claims was written in 1839) was published. "Excellence" was the thing to strive for in life, he declared, because it brings happiness; it is to be sought in all spheres: moral; intellectual; physical. He was convinced that human happiness was far more dependent upon daily exercise of the whole muscular system than most people realized. He objected to tight clothing because of the physiological and structural harm it could cause; walking, gardening, housekeeping, dancing and riding were described as the best forms of exercise for females. In *Letters to a Sister,* however, Alcott noted that gardening and walking were not sufficient: "You need something more active, as jumping, running, and the like." The benefits of calisthenics for young ladies in cities he mentioned in his *Library of Health*. Chapter III of his *Young Woman's Book of Health,* entitled "Errors in the Physical Education of Young Women," condemned the attitudes which relegated American females to a condition of delicacy and nervousness and stipulated that "woman ought to possess at least twice as much muscular power as she now does." His *Laws of Health,* which provided an extensive discussion of the how, when and why of muscular exercise, likewise questioned whether women's inferior strength and endurance might not be due as much to their "mis-education" as to their natures. Alcott was also a staunch supporter of overall improvement in female education; he believed that women merited a much more comprehensive education than the type they usually received, and would have them study subjects like physiology; hygiene; anatomy; chemistry; natural history; philosophy; domestic and political economy; and higher mathematics.

While many theorized concerning the importance of systematic exercise, Dr. Dioclesian Lewis took various steps to facilitate actual participation. Lewis had studied at Harvard Medical School—from which he did not graduate—and had served as a physician's apprentice. (An honorary degree from a small homeopathic hospital conferred upon him the title "Dr."). In 1852 "Dio" Lewis joined the Sons of Temperance and soon achieved a reputation as a temperance and health lecturer. He developed his own system of calisthenic exercises (which he called the "new gymnastics"), based upon the use of hand apparatus and set to music, borrowing many of these movements from foreign and domestic sources. In August 1860 Lewis introduced his new system at a meeting of the American Institute of Education in Boston, (this was reported in the October *Massachusetts Teacher*), and a resolution was passed recommending the introduction of Dr. Lewis' gymnastics into the schools. To train the necessary teachers, he opened the Normal Institute for Physical Education on July 4, 1861, hiring medical men from Harvard to teach physiology and hygiene. (It is generally held that this was the first actual training school for gymnastics in the United States, and even though it closed in 1868 its graduates helped spread Dio Lewis' message concerning the need for an organized program of physical exercises to considerable numbers of American men and women). His "New Gymnastics" appeared in a two-part series in Barnard's *American Journal of Education* (and also in book form) in 1862. The gymnastic costume which he recommended for women bore a marked resemblance to the "new costume" which Amelia Bloomer had depicted in *The Lily* several years earlier. Concerned that "education as a whole must be made symmetrical," Lewis criticized the typical education for neglecting the body; even the feeblest of girls, he declared, would need little more than an hour a day of his "new gymnastics" to be ". . . transformed in two or three years from crooked, pale, nervous creatures, into ruddy, vigorous sound women."

The bombardment of Fort Sumter on April 12-13, 1861, launched the United States into four years of sectional strife which brought severe ruptures to the lives of many Americans. Efforts, of necessity, were directed toward problems occasioned by the dislocations of the Civil War. The women's movement was one of many to suffer from the upheaval. When the surrender was finally signed at Appomatox the advocates of "women's rights," many of whom had devoted themselves to other worthy causes during the hostilities, were shocked and dismayed to learn that the momentum which they believed they had seen developing in the decades preceeding the Civil War had slowed dramatically. They were even more distressed to learn at the American Equal Rights Association annual meeting in 1868 that the support which they had generated in the years prior to the war was now diverted, for political reasons, to the cause of *male* black suffrage. The women, in effect, were told they would have to wait. Elizabeth Cady Stanton, the indefatigable spokesman for women's rights, declared of the proposed 15th amendment to The Constitution of the United States: ". . . shall the freest Government on the earth be the first to establish an aristocracy based on sex alone?"

Although small and divided, the women's rights movement was not abandoned, nor was the issue of improved health and physical education. Elizabeth Cady Stanton was prophetic when she declared in 1882: "Woman is now in the transition period from the old to the new . . . all girls are not satisfied with the amusements society has to offer . . . statistics show that girls taking a college course are more healthy than those who lead listless lives in society." With the rise of institutions of higher learning in the decades following the Civil War women began to enter colleges and universities in substantial numbers, and by the 1880s and 1890s concern for the health and physical education of the college woman had resulted in the establishment of courses of calisthenics for them as well as in the beginning of women's college sports. In the broader society the rapid increase of interest in sports and the rise of the athletic club contributed to the renewed concern for health, physical education, recreation, play, games and active sports for American women. The early proponents of such causes (those who spoke out in their favor from 1776 to 1865) may have felt their efforts to have been vindicated.

Concluding Observations

It has been claimed that the amount of attention which is directed to a problem in any given period of history can be as telling as the actual incidence of the problem. If this is so, the problem of ill-health and lack of exercise among American women was a considerable one in the first half of the nineteenth century; at least, this seems to have been the opinion held by many men and women of the period. In *The Feminization of American Culture* Ann Douglas had made the observation that, "the cultural uses of sickness for the nineteenth century . . . lady are undeniable. To stress their ill-health was a way . . . to dramatize their anxiety that their culture found them useless; it supplied them, moreover, with a means of . . . obtaining psychological and emotional power even while apparently acknowledging the biological correlatives of their social and political unimportance." Most investigations of the health of women in the nineteenth century have focused upon questions of their delicateness and illness rather than upon the converse—the development of robust, vigorous health—the type of health which a proper regimen and physical education is supposed to help ensure.

Certainly, questions which, in one way or another, had to do with the delicateness, ill-health and "fashionable diseases" of American women were frequently raised in the first six decades of the nineteenth century. Throughout the entire century—indeed, well into the twentieth century—the biological functions of females, especially those associated with reproduction, were grossly misunderstood by medical doctors as well as by the general public. Traditional myths prevailed, and little scientific fact was known. In the 1880s and 1890s, the period of the rise of American higher education, many college authorities were fearful that the ''strains'' of academic work would be harmful to the psychological development of young women. It has been asserted, moreover, that many men (educators and doctors by no means excluded) consciously or unconsciously used the argument of the supposed inferiority of women to justify their own concepts of the lordly and superior male. The majority of American doctors would probably have agreed with the contentions of works like Dr. Edward Clarke's *Sex in Education* (1873) that women were inherently intellectually and physically inferior to men. This impression was one which also appears to have been held by substantial numbers of American women who, from childhood, had been constantly reminded of their frailties.

Not all Americans of the period from 1776 to 1865 were willing, however, to accept the argument that a woman's biology rendered her in any way inferior to men—different, yes; inferior, no! There were even more who took an intermediary position: women might be inferior to men both intellectually and physically, but not as inferior as tradition had forced them to be. Beginning at least as early as the last decade of the eighteenth century, an increasing number of American men and women argued that women were far more capable, stronger, healthier—and even wiser—than they were customarily pictured to be; or at least they could become so if their development were not arrested by social custom and false and limiting conceptions of their abilities.

To be sure, the concern for improved ''physical education'' for members of the female sex was part of the greater movement for social reform and augmented rights and opportunities for American women—a movement which had begun well before the Seneca Falls Convention of 1848 and has extended well into the seventh decade of the twentieth century. In addition to those who may have stressed ill-health as a way to ''. . . dramatize their anxiety that their culture found them useless . . .'' there were women—and men—who declared that women were not useless. Given the opportunity, they could become quite useful. Many also maintained that opportunities to lead a useful life was demanded by both common decency and by the provisions of the Declaration of Independence which, by declaring that ''all men were created equal,'' had implied women, too. Such opportunities included those which were concerned with hygiene, proper regimen and ''physical education.'' In the minds of many, since the *physical* constituted the tangible manifestation of the means by which individuals could be known as discrete, whole persons, it merited more attention. Greater freedom in the forms of their dress, exercise, recreation, and even sport could be interpreted as an indicator of women's overall increased freedom.

The evidence clearly indicates that a substantial amount of interest in the health and physical education of the female sex existed in the United States between 1776 and 1865. Men and women of a diversity of interests and persuasions spoke out, with varying degree of intensity, for greater attention to such things as:

calisthenics; playful games; exercise; less confining clothing; active recreations; instruction in physiology and anatomy; more healthful school and home environments; more physical activity in girls' seminaries. For some, such recommendations were modulated and cautious; for others, the demands were strident and persistent. In the views of several "feminists" the recognition of her physicality—the obvious corporeal, tangible evidence of woman's existence in the world—was of the utmost consequence. From the 1800s through 1850s, a time when most American women—like women abroad—were either overworked or were considered helpless and "delicate," when the anticipated role for a woman was wife and mother, the intensity of the requests for greater physical activity for girls and women reached remarkable proportions. The first concerted appeals came from individuals, beginning with Judith Sargent Murray's brief observations and Charles Brockden Brown's *Alcuin* (1798). By the 1820s various periodicals had begun to address the subject with some regularity. Educational journals like William Russell's *American Journal of Education* (the nation's first educational journal), the *Massachusetts Teacher* and Henry Barnard's *American Journal of Education* took an especially active role in fostering both improved female education and physical education for boys and girls. Journals as the *American Monthly Magazine* and the *American Farmer* did likewise. The *American Ladies' Magazine* and Godey's *Lady's Book* frequently advocated improved physical education and active games for American girls and women, even though the majority of the so-called "ladies' periodicals" still portrayed the Victorian image of the weak, helpless woman whose physical activity was confined to a leisurely walk or, perhaps, a ride in the country. Women authors like Lydia Sigourney and Margaret Fuller encouraged more playful physical activity. The rise of interest in medical questions in the 1820s in some ways facilitated the growth of the interest in and concern for the physical education of American women. The *Boston Medical Intelligencer,* the *Health Journal and Advocate of Physiological Reform* and the *American Medical Intelligencer* often carried articles on the subject. So did periodicals which might be better classified as "health fad" journals—those like the *Water Cure Journal* and Graham's *Journal of Health and Longevity.* After the first "women's rights" convention of 1848 a number of newspapers written by and for women began publication. *The Lily* and *The Una* discussed dress reform, health and physical education, and especially in the case of *The Lily* (and possibly largely due to the efforts of Elizabeth Cady Stanton), there were numerous assertions that to be considered as equals—worthy of the same status and treatment as that afforded men—the physical aspect of women's being must be respected. In fact, improved health and greater freedom in the choice of physical activities were among the major demands of many of the American "feminists" of the middle decades of the nineteenth century. Another of these demands was the right to be trained for and granted entrance to the so-called "male professions" (law, theology, medicine). In the case of Elizabeth Blackwell, the first woman in America to be graduated from a proper medical school, the health and physical education of girls and women was an issue of particular concern. Beginning in the 1830s and through the Civil War a growing number of medical doctors devoted some attention to the health and physical education of American women. In the case of men like William A. Alcott this attention was extensive. The majority of American doctors, however, persisted in the belief that women were delicate and inferior creatures—an attitude which may have had a retarding effect upon the development of more scientific knowledge concerning the physiology of women.

While most such proposals remained largely theoretical, women like Emma Willard, Mary Lyon and Catharine E. Beecher actually endeavored to provide opportunities for greater physical activity in their seminaries. So, apparently, did men like William B. Fowle and William A. Alcott and the directors of schools like the Greenfield High School for Young Ladies, where a variety of active games were said to take place.

Although the dislocations of the Civil War impeded the progress which those who advocated better physical education for girls and women thought they had begun to make; although the women were told at the 1868 meeting of the American Equal Rights Association that ''women's rights'' would have to wait until the cause of black *male* suffrage was settled—indeed, wait until the first decades of the twentieth century—a small, but determined, group persisted. It does not seem unreasonable to suggest that the efforts put forward between 1776 and 1865 provided an ideological milieu which was favorable to the development of curricular physical education and extracurricular sports programs for females in the last decades of the nineteenth and first seven decades of the twentieth century. The failures and successes of those who have sought to extend better health, improved physical education and expanded athletic sports opportunities to American girls and women from 1865 to 1978, is, however, a story which is beyond the scope of the present investigation.

CHAPTER 6

The First Modern Sport in America: Harness Racing in New York City, 1825–1870

Melvin L. Adelman

Historians have assigned the rise of sport in America to the last three decades of the nineteenth century. Although they found antecedents to this development in the antebellum period, especially during the 1850s, they presented the era as one of limited sporting activity. This perspective of the pre-Civil War years is unfortunately based on only a handful of studies and most of these examine the changing attitudes toward athletics. The sporting patterns in New York City between 1820 and 1870 revealed, however, a much more active sporting life than heretofore thought to have existed at that time. Far from mere prefigurings, the framework of modern sport was established during this half century.

The modernization of harness racing between 1825 and 1870 exemplifies the growth and transformation of sport during this period. An examination of the modernization of trotting can proceed by employing two ideal sporting types: one premodern and the other modern. These ideal sporting types need not be perfect representations of actual historical stages, but they may be distinguished by six polar characteristics (see Table 6.1). The modernization of sport entails the movement of the activity in the direction of the modern ideal type. This movement is generally, although not always, accompanied by a shift in the playing arena from an open to a close one, the increasing presence of spectators and the commercialization of the sport.

Prior to 1825, harness racing was a premodern sport. Trotting consisted primarily of informal road contests which took place mainly in the northeastern section of the country. The sport was unorganized, lacked standardized rules, attracted limited public attention and possessed no permanent records. By 1870, harness racing had become a modern sport. The creation of the National Trotting Association in that year indicates the development of harness racing into a highly organized sport, with fairly uniform rules and with contests taking place throughout

From the *Journal of Sport History*, 8:1 (Spring, 1981). © 1981 The North American Society for Sport History. Reprinted by permission.

Table 6.1   The Characteristics of Premodern and Modern Ideal Sporting Types

Premodern sport	Modern sport
1. *Organization*—is either nonexistent or at best informal and sporadic. Contests are arranged by individuals directly or indirectly (e.g., tavern-owners, bettors) involved.	1. *Organization*—formal organizations, institutionally differentiated at the local, regional and national level.
2. *Rules*—are simple, unwritten and based upon local customs and traditions. Variations exist from locale to locale.	2. *Rules*—are formal, standardized and written. Rules are rationally and pragmatically worked out and legitimized by organizational means.
3. *Competition*—locally meaningful contests only; no chance for national reputation.	3. *Competition*—national and international superimposed on local contests; chance to establish national and international reputation.
4. *Role differentiation*—low role differentiation among participants and loose distinction between playing and spectating roles.	4. *Role differentiation*—high role differentiation; emergence of specialists (professionals) and strict distinctions between playing and spectating roles.
5. *Public information*—is limited, local and oral.	5. *Public information*—is reported on a regular basis in local newspapers, as well as national sporting journals. The appearance of specialized magazines, guidebooks, etc.
6. *Statistics and records*—nonexistent.	6. *Statistics and records*—are kept, published on a regular basis and are considered important measure of achievement. Records are sanctioned by national associations.

the country. The modernization of trotting is further illustrated by the coverage harness racing received in the daily and sporting press, the emergence of statistics and records and the appearance in 1871 of the first stud book devoted exclusively to trotting. Finally, harness racing emerged as the first sport to be successfully commercialized. By the mid-nineteenth century, trotting replaced thoroughbred

A DISPUTED HEAT.
CLAIMING A FOUL

This drawing from the Currier and Ives collection shows a man "claiming a foul" following a trotting match.
Courtesy of the Library of Congress.

racing as this country's number one spectator sport. Not until after the Civil War did baseball challenge the supreme position of trotting; but by 1870, if not for awhile longer, harness racing remained the nation's leading spectator sport.

The contention that harness racing was the first modern sport in America does not mean that it was the initial sport to assume modern characteristics. Thoroughbred racing began to modernize during the eighteenth century when permanent jockey clubs were established. The modernization of this sport reached its pre-Civil War peak during the 1830s when the sport enjoyed a period of unprecedented growth and prosperity. By the mid-1840s, however, the process grounded to a halt when the sport collapsed throughout the North. With horse racing confined mainly to the South during the subsequent two decades, the modernization of the sport remained dormant until the revival of thoroughbred racing in the North in the years immediately following the Civil War. By 1870, nevertheless, the gestalt of horse racing was not as yet modern despite the significant steps in this direction during the antebellum period.

Conversely, the claims that harness racing had become a modern sport by 1870 does not mean to suggest that the modernization of trotting was complete by this date. Rather a key point of this article is that a certain stage is reached as a sport moves along the continuum from the premodern to the modern ideal form in which modern characteristics are sufficiently present to shape the structure and direction of the sport. At this juncture, the sport presents a modern configuration, one which shares more in common with its future than its premodern past. It is in this sense that harness racing had become America's first modern sport by 1870.

Harness racing conjures up a rural image, the sport of the county fair. Trotting was, however, an urban product. The sport first emerged on urban roads and developed its most salient modern characteristics in the city. New York played a more critical role in the development of harness racing than any other city. As early as 1832, the *Spirit of the Times* recognized that New York was the premier city in the breeding and training of trotting horses. Nearly a quarter of a century later, one frequent correspondent to this sporting journal maintained that trotting was indigenous to the Empire City and that there were "more fine horses here than can be found any where else in the world." The importance of New York to the growth of the sport did not derive solely from the concentration of the best stock in the metropolitan region. New York was the hub of harness racing throughout the period 1825 to 1870. In the nation's most populated city, there were more trotting tracks, more races, including a disproportionate number of the leading contests, and more prize money offered than in any other place in the country. Equally significant, the characteristics of modern harness racing initially appeared in New York. Here the sport was first organized and commercialized. As a result, New York set the pattern that was to be followed on a national scale.

I

Harness racing emerged as a popular pastime in New York and in other parts of the Northeast in the first quarter of the nineteenth century. Sport historians have maintained that the growth of trotting was directly related to the antiracing legislation passed by several northern states, including New York State, during this era. Denied the race course, lovers of fast horses took to the "natural track"—the highway. While the road was ill suited for the feet of the running horse, it was the natural home of the trotter. "It is no accident," a leading historian of the sport contended, "that the racing of trotters began in regions where horses could be 'raced' only in defiance of law."

New York State's antiracing law, passed in 1802, neither directly nor indirectly influenced the growth of trotting in the Empire City. As enforcement had been lax, horsemen did not have to take to the road as a substitute for the prohibited race course. Rather, trotting emerged at this time because improvements in the roads now made the sport possible. One historian noted that "it was only natural that the speed of the harness horse found its first testing ground upon the smooth hard roads whose networks radiated from the northeastern cities . . . especially those of the Boston-New York-Philadelphia regions."

Sportsmen began racing their "roadsters" (as street trotters came to be called) because it provided them with an amusement which was convenient, participatory and relatively inexpensive. Third Avenue quickly emerged as New York's major trotting area. Beginning outside the residential portion of the city at that time, the approximately five mile road was perfectly suited for these informal trials of speed. In close proximity to the homes of the horsemen, it was a convenient location for these contests which started upon the completion of the day's work and which usually lasted until dark. Moreover, numerous taverns dotted the highway where reinsmen could stop, arrange contests and discuss the latest sporting developments.

These impromptu contests appealed to the city's horsemen because they allowed personal participation. Unlike thoroughbred racing, where the owner and the rider of the horse had long been separated, trotting permitted the sportsman to demonstrate the prowess of his horse, as well as his own skill as a reinsman. Finally, the pastime did not require the capital outlay of thoroughbred racing. The trotter was not a "pure breed," but rather a horse drawn from the common stock that had the ability to trot. The plebian horses that engaged in these road races, moreover, were almost always used by their owners in their day-to-day activities.

Although early nineteenth century trotting consisted almost exclusively of these impromptu contests, permanent structures began to emerge. The first trotting tracks in the New York metropolitan region were mere extensions of the courses used for thoroughbred racing. The most significant of these tracks was located in Harlem and the first recorded performance by an American trotter took place there in 1806. Several years later, the first track constructed exclusively for trotting was built in Harlem next to the Red House Tavern. The course was the major resort for the Third Avenue road racing crowd and the track was probably constructed for their benefit. While racing took place on both courses, these tracks remained essentially training grounds for the city's roadsters.

More formalized matches, either on the city's roads or tracks, were a natural outgrowth of the impromptu races, or "brushes" as they were called, which took place on Gotham's streets. Since the press paid scant attention to these matches information exists on only a few of them. Probably the most important took place in 1818 when William Jones of Long Island, a prominent horseman, wagered Colonel Bond of Maryland a thousand dollars that he could produce a horse that would trot a mile in less than three minutes. The race caused great excitement among the city's sporting crowd. With odds against success, a horse named *Boston Pony* accomplished the feat in just less than the required time.

The formation of the New York Trotting Club (NYTC) in the Winter of 1824-1825 marks the first critical step in the modernization of harness racing. The first organized trotting club in America, there is no information on its members, although most were probably drawn from the men who raced their roadsters on Third Avenue and other roads in the New York metropolitan region. The creation of the NYTC was inspired by the success thoroughbred racing had enjoyed in New York after the State revoked its antiracing legislation in 1821. The NYTC drew its objectives and methods heavily from the experience of horse racing. Similar to the racing organization of its sister sport, the NYTC justified its association on utilitarian grounds (the sport's contribution to the improvement of the breed); instituted regular meetings twice yearly; and, constructed a race course (in Centerville, Long Island) to facilitate the growth of the sport.

Trotting in New York made significant advances as both a participatory and spectator sport in the two decades following the formation of the NYTC. In 1835, the *Spirit* noted that the "number of fast horses for which our city is so celebrated is steadily accumulating." With some exaggeration, one contemporary observer claimed that "there was scarcely a gentleman in New York who did not own one or two fast (trotting) horses." The rising cost of good roadsters further indicated the increasingly appeal of the sport. During the 1830s, the price of the best trotting horses doubled. In addition, trotting races on the city's tracks, especially the major ones, generated considerable excitement among New York's sporting crowd. In 1838, the *New York Herald* reported that the contest between *Dutchman* and *Ratner* created "as much interest in our city and neighborhood: as the intersectional horse race between *John Bascombe* and *Post Boy* held in New York two years earlier.

The emerging commercialization of trotting most accurately dramatizes the growth of the sport. By the mid-1830s, entrepreneurs began to tap the public interest in harness races that took place on New York's streets and tracks. The experience of the Beacon Course in nearby Hoboken, New Jersey illustrates the early introduction of the profit motive into trotting. This course was constructed in 1837 for thoroughbred racing. When the sport proved unprofitable the following year, the proprietors of the track started to promote harness racing for the sole purpose of reaping the financial rewards from the gate receipts. By the early 1840s, businessmen had replaced the original sponsors of trotting—the road runners and their associations—as the major promoters of the sport.

Although organized trotting made important progress in its first twenty years, it continued to take a back seat to horse racing. The coverage harness racing received in the press defined the secondary status of this turf sport. While trotting won the polite endorsement of New York newspapers, reports of races, even important ones, remained limited. Similarly, harness racing won the approval of sports editors John Stuart Skinner and Cadwallader Colden, but their monthly journals were devoted almost exclusively to thoroughbred racing and provided only the barest summaries and details of the developments on the trotting track. Only William T. Porter's *Spirit* paid any significant attention to trotting and even there the extent of the coverage did not correspond to the growth of the sport.

II

As thoroughbred racing collapsed throughout the North in the decade following the Depression of 1837, the sporting press took increasing note of the activities of the trotting horse. By the early 1840s, they suggested that the "ugly duckling" had become the legitimate rival of her more respected sister. In 1847, the *Herald* pointed out that "For several years past, trotting has been gradually taking the precedence of running in this part of the country; while one specie of amusement has been going into decay, the other has risen to heights never before attained."

Contemporaries claimed that the corresponding fates of the two turf sports were closely linked to the characteristics associated with the two different horses. In contrast to the aristocratic and foreign thoroughbred, the trotter was perceived as the democratic, utilitarian, and, by logical extension, the American horse. Implicit was the belief that harness racing surpassed horse racing as the leading turf sport because it more accurately captured the spirit of the American experience.

Henry W. Herbert (better known as Frank Forester) recognized the close connection between the nature of the horses and the popularity of the respective sports. Since cost restricted the ownership of thoroughbreds to wealthy men, horse racing could never be a popular sport. By contrast, the trotter was common to all and the "most truly characteristic and national type of horse" in America. In this country, the transplanted Englishman concluded, trotting "is the people's sport, the people's pastime, and consequently, is, and will be, supported by the people."

This perspective provides a good starting point in understanding the maturation of trotting if such terms as democratic, utilitarian and even American are broadly conceived. While contemporaries grossly exaggerated the extent to which the masses owned trotters, ownership of these plebian and relatively inexpensive horses was far more widespread than thoroughbreds. Precise data on the owners of trotting horses in New York is nonexistent, but available information does permit a profile to be logically deduced. The evidence indicates that only a small number of trotting men came from the "upper crust." Conversely, the cost and upkeep of trotting horses were still sufficiently high to generally exclude individuals who fell below the middle class. While broad parameters still exist, it appears that trotting owners came from the more prosperous segments of the middle class—men who lived a comfortable, but hardly opulent, lifestyle. Nevertheless, individuals of more moderate means could still own a roadster as a result of the limited price of the horse and their usage in daily activities. This was particularly the case for men working in New York's various food markets. Their involvement in harness racing gave credence to the common adage that "a butcher rides a trotter" often used to illustrate the democratic nature of the horse.

The fortunes of the two turf sports, the *Herald* repeatedly insisted, were connected to their utilitarian functions. The decline of horse racing stemmed from the fact that the thoroughbred had little practical benefit. The newspaper conceded that trotting "may not be attended with all the high zest and excitement" of running races, but it is "a more useful sport, as the qualities in the horse which it is calculated to develop are more intimately connected with the daily business of life." The growth of harness racing did reflect shifting patterns of travel. With the improvement of roads and wagons, the driving horse increasingly replaced the saddle horse as the basic means of convoy in the northeastern and Middle Atlantic states. As one scholar pointed out, there was "a direct correlation between the improved modes of transportation and their popular manifestations seen on the trotting track."

Since Americans believed that the true nature of the trotter—democratic and utilitarian—could only be developed in this country, they perceived the trotter as a native product although they were familiar with English antecedents. In 1853, the *Herald* wrote, "We are the first who have attached particular importance to the breeding of trotting horses, and in this respect . . . have shown the practical nature of our character." These assumptions may be passed off as American chauvinism, but the contention that both the horse and the sport were indigenous products does contain merit. Harness racing had been a popular pastime in England, but its emergence as a sport first occurred in the United States. Similarly, the establishment of a distinct breed of trotting race horse was an American creation, although this process was not completed until the late nineteenth century. More significantly, it was the perception of the trotter as the American horse, more than the reality, which was of critical importance to the growth of the sport. While harness racing never wrapped itself in the flag to the extent that baseball did, nationalistic overtones gave trotting a sanction absent in horse racing. Oliver Wendell Holmes, Sr. captured these sentiments. He noted that the running horse was a gambling toy, but the trotting horse was a useful animal. Furthermore, "horse racing is not a republican institution; horse-trotting is."

While the contemporary explanation provides a starting point, other critical factors must also be examined if a comprehensive analysis of the maturation of trotting is to be constructed. Trotting's supreme position in the turf world can be more productively analyzed in terms of three interacting forces: the increasing potential for commercialized amusements made possible by urban and economic expansion; the greater susceptibility of trotting to commercialization than any of its sporting counterparts; and, the more innovative nature of trotting.

The absence of surplus wealth and concentrated populations traditionally restricted the development of commercialized amusements. During the antebellum period, these two major barriers began to dissolve under the impact of urban and economic growth. The expanding economy throughout these years not only produced a significant rise in wealth, but, more importantly, broadened the availability of discretionary income among a wider segment of the population. The concentration of large numbers of people in one area facilitated the creation of a greater number of permanent institutions devoted to commercialized amusements. These newer forms of popular entertainment shared three essential properties: they were cheaper, depended on volume, and appealed to a wider segment of the populace. While commercialized amusements increased throughout the first four decades of the nineteenth century, their numbers multiplied rapidly in the two decades preceding the Civil War. As one scholar pointed out, commercialized amusements underwent "an expansion of new proportions" during the lengthy era of general prosperity between 1843 and 1860.

The plebian character of the trotter and its relatively inexpensive price made the sport more susceptible to commercialization. Since the trotter cost less than the thoroughbred, the prize money offered by track proprietors did not have to be as great for the owners of the trotters to cover their cost and make a profit. As late as 1860, purses in New York rarely exceeded $250 and contests could be run for as low as $10. The stakes were naturally higher in match or privately arranged races. By the 1850s, a few contests went for as much as five thousand dollars per side. In general, however, the amounts fell below that which existed for similar kinds of thoroughbred races. Clearly one does not find anything comparable to the stakes placed on the major intersectional thoroughbred contest, such as between *Eclipse* and *Henry* or *Boston* and *Fashion,* or for that matter the money that could be won in horse racing's larger sweepstake races.

The nature of the trotter facilitated the commercialization of the sport by making more races possible. Whereas a good thoroughbred might race six or seven times a year, the more durable trotter started at least twice as many races annually. Furthermore, a trotter's career lasted longer, many racing into their teens. More importantly, the trotter came from the common horse stock. Consequently, there were simply more of them to race. The impact of the greater numbers can be seen in terms of the respective racing sessions in New York. There were at most three weeks of thoroughbred racing in the city annually; but hardly a week would pass, except in the Winter months, without a trotting match taking place somewhere in the New York metropolitan region.

Finally, harness racing was not bogged down in the "aristocratic" trappings which characterized horse racing. In 1843, the *Spirit* recognized that trotting men were more innovative and aggressive than their horse racing counterparts. As a result of their greater "enterprise, industry and go *aheadiveness,*" the sporting journal predicted, harness racing "will soon be a formidable rival to thoroughbred racing in the North." Nearly a quarter of a century later, *Turf, Field and Farm,* essentially a thoroughbred journal, gave the same basic reasons and used exactly the same words in explaining the greater popularity of harness racing.

Trotting was more innovative than horse racing in two critical ways. The first was a product of the different social backgrounds of those involved in the respective sports. Engaged in thoroughbred racing were wealthy men and/or people from established families. Most of the owners of trotting horses and the proprietors of trotting tracks, however, appear to have been middle class in origin. The different social origins affected the entire tone of the two turf sports. While thoroughbred racing was run for and by the upper class, harness racing enticed a broader segment of the populace. The commercially minded proprietors of trotting tracks catered more readily to all ticket holders than those involved in their sister sport. One does not find connected with trotting complaints of exclusiveness, aristocracy and snobbishness levelled by the press against the leaders of thoroughbred racing. As a leading sporting journal noted, "Racing will never succeed in New York until it and its attended arrangements are put on a more democratic basis—something approaching the order of the first class trotting races. Then, like the trots, it will get the support of the people."

In addition, trotting was more innovative because the comparatively new sport was not inhibited by tradition. By the 1840s, horse racing in America had a long heritage on how a thoroughbred race should be conducted. The absence of institutional confinements made it easier for trotting to adjust to commercialization. Similar to their horse racing counterparts, trotting men initially valued a horse which combined speed and endurance. Early trotting contests were raced in heats from one to five miles. By the early 1840s, trotting men broke with this pattern. Most major contests were now one mile heats with the winner required to win three heats. Since the new system placed less strain on the trotter, the horse could race more frequently and thereby more races were possible. Furthermore, harness racing contests took place in a wider variety of styles, giving the sport greater diversity and interest.

Harness racing surged to the forefront of not only the turf world, but modern sport in general, because more than any other sport of the day it captured the flow of the American experience. In common with other forms of popular entertainment, the emergence of trotting as a spectator sport was a product of the two dynamic forces—urbanization and economic expansion—transforming and modernizing American life. The impact of these agents of change would have been far less had not trotting possessed properties which predisposed it towards commercialization. Here the nature of the horse played a critical role. Of equal significance was the fact that those who governed trotting, at least from the standpoint of sport, internalized the values of modern society. As such, they put a greater premium on innovation rather than tradition, and cash rather than class.

III

Harness racing progressed rapidly as a popular spectator sport both in New York and throughout the country in the two decades preceding the Civil War. While the changes in the social and economic conditions, discussed in the previous section, created the setting for the growth of the sport, performers attracted the crowds. During the early years of organized trotting, numerous horses left their mark on the history of the sport, but it was *Lady Suffolk* who set the standard of excellence and was the sport's first hero. The fifteen year career of *Lady Suffolk* (1838-1853), moreover, illustrates the condition and development of trotting during this period.

Foaled in 1833, *Lady Suffolk* was bred by Leonard Lawrence of Suffolk County, Long Island, from whence she drew her name. The *Lady* was a descendant of imported *Messenger,* the founding father of the American trotter, but no preparation was made for a trotting career. As a weanling she was sold for $60, then resold as a two year old for $90. At age four she was pulling a butcher or oyster cart when David Bryan purchased her for $112.50 for use in his livery stable. The prowess of the horse went undiscovered until none other than William T. Porter by chance rented her for a tour of the Long Island tracks. The editor of the *Spirit* was impressed with the *Lady*'s speed and good gait. He told Bryan that she had too much potential as a racer to be wasted in his stable. In the Spring of 1838, Bryan entered the *Lady* in her first race. The "Old Grey Mare," as she was later affectionately called, completed the mile contest in three minutes flat, winning the fabulous sum of eleven dollars.

Bryan owned *Lady Suffolk* until his death in 1851. Of Irish or Celtic origin, little is known of his background, save for his previous occupation. It is clear, however, that Bryan was the embodiment of the professional ethic which came to dominate the sport. As one historian wrote, "For Bryan, his *Lady Suffolk*, the most loved as well as the most admired horse of her time, was not, first and foremost, a sporting animal—she was a mint of money, a nugget of rich metal to be melted by him in the heat of competition and struck off into dollars." Bryan raced his grey mare mainly in the New York metropolitan area because this is where he lived and, even more importantly, because the city's courses provided the best financial opportunities. Similar to other professional trotting men of his day, however, Bryan campaigned with *Lady Suffolk* on the growing number of tracks throughout the country, going as far west as St. Louis and as far south as New Orleans.

Bryan had the reputation of being a poor reinsman and he placed excessive demands on *Lady Suffolk*. Nevertheless, he was an unqualified success by the new professional standards. He entered the *Lady* in 162 races and won between $35,000 and $60,000. The ability of *Lady Suffolk* to achieve victory, despite the clumsy and inept driving of her owner, derived from her saintly patience, an unbreakable spirit and a remarkable endurance. At age nineteen, her last full year on the turf, the Old Grey Mare demonstrated her tremendous stamina by coming to the start twelve times.

Harness racing had emerged as the nation's leading spectator sport by the time *Lady Suffolk* was retired in the early 1850s. During this decade, the sport emerged as an integral part of the county fair and the public's desire to see harness races resulted in the creation of an ever increasing number of trotting tracks throughout the country. By 1858, one sporting journal estimated that over seventy trotting courses existed in America.

Expanding coverage of harness racing corresponded with its growth. In New York, the daily newspapers naturally focused on contests within the metropolitan region, but the city-based sporting journals reported on races throughout the country. While trotting men had always been preoccupied with "time" as a measure of their horses' abilities and performances, statistics and records took on new importance when horsemen began touring the increasing number of tracks in search of fame and fortune. That these measurements served the interest of track promoters and fans of the sport was to a large extent responsible for their expanding value. Since a trotter might visit a city only once a year, proprietors of the courses could use the statistical reputation of a horse to encourage people to come see the race even though they may have never seen him perform. Similarly, statistics nourished fan interest by providing them with a method of evaluating a horse in the absence of personal observation or witnessing the horse race on only a handful of occasions.

Trotting men were not only familiar with unsurpassed performances, but were already cognizant of the concept of the record. In 1860, for example, *Flora Temple,* who succeeded *Lady Suffolk* as the "princess of the turf," sought to break *Dutchman*'s record (7:32.5) for three miles. Since "the watch never breaks and never tires," *Wilkes' Spirit of the Times* reported, the effort of *Flora Temple* (eventually unsuccessful) to surpass the time of the then dead horse evoked considerable speculation and discussion.

New York continued to dominate the development of harness racing even though the sport expanded nationally. At least seven trotting tracks existed in the metropolitan region, with three—Union, Fashion and Centerville Courses— hosting first class contests. More significantly, with the ever increasing importance of gate receipts, trotting in the Empire City drew the largest number of spectators. Between six and eight thousand spectators were usually present at each of the four to six leading matches held annually. However, when *Flora Temple* raced, attendance could jump into double figures. Within a period of seventeen days in 1859, her contests with *Ethan Allen* and then *Princess* drew crowds of 12,000 and 20,000, respectively.

The growth of harness racing as a sports spectacle did not occur without problems. As the commercial and professional ethic came to dominate the sport, suspicions of irregularities on the trotting track markedly increased. The question of the integrity of harness racing produced the first extensive discussion and concern about the honesty of professional-commercial sport. Cries of foul play on New York tracks were already heard as early as the 1830s. The *Spirit* claimed that the public are beginning to express concern about the improprieties on the trotting track and insisted that men of character must immediately rule off the track those who disgrace the sport or else the "trotting course and everything pertaining them must 'go to pot.' "

While complaints of irregularities persisted, the city's sporting press began to repeat these charges vociferously only in the 1850s. Fundamentally these statements did not vary from the theme, solution and dire predictions offered by the *Spirit* over a decade earlier. In 1857, the *New York Times* asserted that many owners of fast trotters would not allow their horses to compete in races since the courses had "fallen under the control of men who made use of them to subserve their own private interest."

During the next two decades, the New York press emphatically argued that the fixing of races was a common practice. So often were the charges made that by their sheer numbers this argument becomes a compelling one. Yet was it accurate? It would be naive to assume that no races were rigged, but the claims of widespread manipulation of contests seems grossly exaggerated. Evidence of these "clandestine arrangements" are significantly lacking. It is not surprising, therefore, that the arguments develop a predictable rhythm and break down into vague generalities. In contrast to the contention of rampant wrongdoings, I was impressed at the number of times the favorite, and especially the outstanding horses, won. Clearly, many of the assertions, which at times border on the incredulous, can be cast aside as sensationalist journalism. From time to time, moreover, statements in the press not only challenged the prevailing view, but often contradicted previous beliefs.

The rise of the "manipulation theory" derived from three interrelated factors: the nonexistence of investigative commissions; the nature of professional sport and the attitude toward professional athletes; and the primitive concept of ''upset.'' In absence of effective investigating commissions as we know them today, charges of irregularities were rarely examined. The lack of this critical institutional structure for the governance of sport facilitated the growth of rumor and innuendo and made personal judgment the sole criteria in deciding the honesty of a race. The case brought against James Eoff illustrates the obvious drawbacks of such a method in determining the integrity of a contest. In 1859, *Princess,* a California mare, was the first horse to make the trip from the West Coast to New York. With little time to recoup from the long journey, she was matched against *Flora Temple.* Hiram Woodruff, the leading antebellum reinsman and a spectator at the contest, wrote that ninety-five percent of the huge crowd felt that *Princess* lost because Eoff, her jockey, pulled the mare. So vociferous was the cry of ''fix'' that the Union Jockey Club, a thoroughbred organization which owned the course where the race took place, held a rare investigation. There Eoff claimed that the California mare tired because she had not recovered from her trip and could not be pushed any harder. Woodruff felt the explanation was a plausible and truthful one. He further pointed out that not one of the many people who felt the race had been thrown came forward to substantiate their charge.

The nature of professional athletics made creditable the assertion that races were fixed. Since the major purpose of the contest for the professional athlete is to make money, what guarantees exist that he would not manipulate the event to maximize his profit? A certain class bias against the professional athlete accentuated the suspicions inherent within the professional system. While no monolithic view of either the professional athlete or professional athletics existed, the prevailing attitude was that the public was assured honest contests only when the ''better class'' governed the sport.

The strong temptations confronting the professional athlete went far in explaining why the press so vehemently opposed what was known as ''hippodroming''—the making of contests for the sole purpose of splitting the gate receipts (in contrast to racing for stakes and purses). With no money depending on the outcome, and therefore with no incentive to win, these ''concocted affairs'' were perfect races to rig. As the *New York Clipper* pointed out, ''Many matches advertised for heavy stakes are merely for 'gate money' and so arranged that the winners are known to the 'initiated' before the event ever took place.''

The suspicions of wrongdoing were justifiably heightened by the less than candid policy of track promoters in billing what was essentially an ''exhibition'' as a match race for large stakes. This less than honest practice does not prove, however, that the contests were fixed. In 1860, the *Spirit* conceded that hippodroming had become a method of scheduling races, but it doubted ''if there is one-tenth part of the rascality on a trotting track that many people suppose.''

The development of hippodroming was a legitimate response to the financial considerations of both the owners of the horses and the proprietors of the courses rather than being the product of evil intent. Woodruff claimed that *Flora Temple* caused the new system. In a class by herself, the mare ''could not get a match on even terms, and was excluded from all purses.'' It is unlikely that *Flora*

Temple or any other horse initiated hippodroming. Instead it emerged from the inadequacy of the prevalent winner-take-all system. The new arrangements made it possible for a horse to be defeated and the owner still be able to cover part of his cost and possibly emerge with a profit. Consequently, it gradually facilitated an expansion in both the number of trotters and races. Equally important for the proprietors, it guaranteed the presence of the super horses that drew the huge crowds. "No matter how these 'little arrangements' are concocted," the *Clipper* was forced to conclude, "it is but fair to say that they generally made interesting races, and in that way the spectators are pleased."

The most striking fact about the literature of the day was the primitive understanding of the concept of "upset." Nineteenth century writers were conscious that luck played a factor in the outcome of athletic contests and that the more talented performer did not always win. On most occasions when the favorite lost, however, the press and the public offered some excuse for his defeat. As I perceive it, the concept of upset does not automatically entail that luck played a part in the underdog winning, although it may and often does. Rather it is premised on the realization that on certain occasions a competitor can achieve a level of performance which is not his usual standard and quite possibly may never be reached again.

Today it is axiomatic that on any given day any professional athlete or team could defeat any other professional athlete or team. Over the years, the vicissitudes of sport have sufficiently demonstrated the validity of this idea. The legitimacy of even the most unbelievable developments go unquestioned. Jargon ridden as this perspective has become in our mass communication sporting world, the internalization of this view by the fan and the press alike is mandatory if the integrity of professional sport is to be accepted. Precisely because such an attitude was absent in the early days of professional sport any unexpected occurrence frequently became translated into "fix."

Serious doubts must be raised of the prevalent view that widespread manipulation of races followed on the heels of the growth of professional-commercial harness racing. While dishonest contests occurred in New York, they were the exception rather than the rule. Nevertheless, professionalization did significantly alter the character of these contests. The emphasis of amateur turfmen on style and sportsmanship yielded to the sole objective of success as jockies adopted tricks and tactics which if not outright violations of the rules permitted the drivers to get all he could within them. Such practices were often chastised and contributed to the belief that there was a lack of propriety on the trotting track; but they foreshadowed the pattern which emerged in all professional sports. As one historian pointed out, these techniques were consistent with the dominant American values "in that it was results that counted, not how hard you tried or how sportingly you behaved."

IV

While commercialization became harness racing's leading characteristic by the 1850s, informal trials of speed persisted on New York's streets. With the growth of the city, however, severe restrictions began to be placed on the roadster. By the early 1860s, New York's road runners had moved from Third Avenue to Harlem Lane in the upper part of Manhattan. This location shortly began to succumb to the forces of progress. Dismayed by the prospect of the loss of New York's last good driving area, the editor of *Wilkes' Spirit* believed that it "was incumbent upon the city's authorities to supply the vacancy created by the occupation of Harlem Lane." As the headquarters of the fast trotter, anything less, he suggested, "would be a national loss, as well as a municipal sham and disgrace."

The call for government intervention might be considered a "far sighted" approach, but trotting men took steps more typical of the period. They established private organizations which bought or rented their own tracks. Unlike earlier trotting or jockey clubs, these organizations did not sponsor public or private races, although club members could and probably did arrange contests amongst themselves and their guests. Rather, they were formed to perpetuate an informal pastime no longer possible in the more formalized urban setting. The first of these clubs was the Elm Park Pleasure Grounds Association established in the late 1850s. The majority of the 400 members were prosperous businessmen, although there were a handful of men of considerable wealth, most notably Cornelius Vanderbilt and Robert Bonner.

Of New York's road drivers, none had a more dramatic impact on the development of harness racing than Robert Bonner. Born in Londonderry, Ireland in 1824, Bonner amassed his fortune by the time he was thirty as the owner of the *New York Ledger,* a weekly family journal. In 1856, his physician advised him to find an outdoor recreation for health reasons. Bonner then bought a horse and began driving it on New York's speedways. There he had a few brushes with Vanderbilt. What emerged was a friendly rivalry between these two for the ownership of the best trotters. The Bonner-Vanderbilt duel, a leading turf historian insisted, "marked the beginning of a change that provided the sport not only with strong financial backing but an efficient leadership." While the confrontation between the steamship and newspaper magnates did not initiate a new era, it symbolized and gave impetus to an already existing process.

In the battle between the two giants, Bonner emerged as the king of the road. He spent lavishly in purchasing some of the best trotters of his era. Between 1859 and 1870, Bonner bought thirteen horses at a total cost of $162,000. His prize purchase was *Dexter* clearly the number one trotter of his day. By the time he retired in 1890, the newspaper magnate had spent nearly half a million dollars for his horses, including $40,000 each for his stars *Maud S. and Pocahontas.*

Bonner's reputation as a horseman did not derive solely from his ownership of possibly the largest and best stable. A more significant reason, as the *New York Tribune* pointed out, was that he "did more to lift the trotting horse from disrepute to respectability than any other man." According to the universally accepted perspective, prior to Bonner's involvement, acceptable society viewed the owners of trotting horses as fast men "who spent their afternoons trotting from tavern to tavern . . . (and) had too much money in their pockets." Bonner was the critical figure in altering this negative impression. A man of unimpeachable character, the strict Scotch-Presbyterian did not smoke, drink or swear. Moreover, he so violently opposed gambling that he refused to enter his horses in public places. Consequently, Bonner could bring a dignity to the sport that other wealthy *nouveaux,* such as the salty Vanderbilt, never could. Through Bonner's influence, the ownership of trotting horses won an acceptable position in society, with the result that "Men of affairs, men of money, men of social position began to buy trotters, drive them on the road and even enter them for races on the public tracks."

That the possession of trotting horses gradually achieved greater respectability in New York society when men of wealth became involved in the sport is undeniable as it was almost inevitable. This development did not emerge from a shift in the attitude of the city's "upper crust," but rather from a shift in its composition. As older elites gave way to the onslaught of new wealth, they lost their position as the arbiters of culture. The ascending group, from whom trotting men were overwhelmingly drawn, dictated from its new position the acceptability of its own activity. The increasing involvement of New York's affluent in trotting, therefore, can be understood against the background of what a leading scholar of New York elites described as the plutocratic nature of the city's high society. Since New York society was easily accessible to the newly risen who were uncertain of the traditions and prerogatives of their new class and status, it produced an elite structure which encouraged the pursuit of publicity and created a fashionable style of conspicuous luxury. Although these traits did not emerge as the dominant characteristics of New York society until the 1870s, they were strongly present among the city's elite even prior to the Civil War.

Nouveaux riches New Yorkers became involved in trotting, as they would in other sports, as a means of status confirmation. Interesting differences existed, however, between trotting and other sporting activities. In the prevailing pattern, new wealth asserted its position by patronizing those sports which had an upper class heritage and/or could be afforded only by men of wealth. In the early years of trotting, the sport shared none of these characteristics. To function as other upper class sports, therefore, exclusiveness had to be created. Two interrelated processes accomplished this transformation: the purchasing of the best trotters at lavish prices and the rationalization of the breeding industry.

The willingness of wealthy men to pay premium prices resulted in their monopoly of the best trotters by the 1870s. The soaring cost of trotters was in part a product of the growth of the sport and the increasing number of bidders for what is a relatively fixed market; there can be only a few champions per period. However, the law of supply and demand, important though it may be, does not explain the surge in prices. For example, Bonner bought *Dexter* in 1867 for the incredible sum of $33,000 even though his seller, George Trussle of Chicago, had paid only $14,000 for the horse two years earlier. Another subtle but significant reason therefore existed for the rising cost. The fabulous sums trotting horses attracted was a critical part of the status game. To have obtained the best horses at anything less than these fantastic sums would have not satisfied the needs of these *parvenus* to demonstrate their wealth and status.

The rationalizations of the breeding industry further encouraged the concentration of good trotting horses in the hands of the wealthy. In the mid-nineteenth century, this business required little capital, organization or promotion. Some attention was paid to pedigree; however, lineage was usually guesswork, if not outright falsification. The small scale on which the business was run was not conducive to finely selective breeding, but its random nature had the valuable result of diffusing the blood of the best stock widely throughout the country. This haphazard method, one historian noted, "contributed to the sport a delightful element of uncertainty, discovery and surprise, the satisfaction of making something out of nothing." This business enabled David Bryan and William M. Rysdyk, a former farm hand, to make their fame and fortune from their horses *Lady Suffolk* and *Hambletonian,* respectively, at a cost of less than $250 for the two horses.

Within two or three decades, small breeders yielded to the larger stables owned by wealthy men for pleasure, profit or both. These well capitalized stock farms gathered the best trotters. Similar to other American industries in the latter part of the nineteenth century, the concentration of talent and wealth permitted the breeding of trotting horses to become a more rationalized process. For the small breeder, the swift trotter was essentially a sideline, although an important one, to the general stud services his horses provided. Above all, the major objective was the procreation of the race and the overall improvement of the breed. In the large stables, speed was the sole objective. Using innovative techniques, the big farms "became laboratories of speed." As one turf historian concluded, "A system of breeding that had diffused the qualities of the best sires so widely through the common horse stock was replaced by a system more narrowly concentrated but for that reason more likely to produce exceptional results."

During the 1870s, four more critical steps were taken to rationalize the breeding industry: (1) the creation of the first turf register devoted exclusively to the trotting horse (1871); (2) the appearance of the first sporting journal, *Wallace's Monthly Magazine,* concerned primarily with trotting affairs (1875); (3) the formation of the National Association of Trotting Horse Breeders (1876); and, (4) the establishment of a standard breed of trotting horse (1879). By the end of this decade, the rationalization of the breeding industry solidified the ownership of the leading trotters in the hands of wealthy men. Unable to compete with the big farms, the horses of the smaller breeders found themselves confined to tracks at county fairs. The day that a horse could be removed from a butcher's cart and become a world's champion was relegated to dime novels and serials in popular magazines.

Neither the shift in the social composition of the owners of trotting horses nor changes in the breeding industry undermined the popularity of harness racing. Since the initial growth of the sport was strongly linked to the inexpensive cost of the trotter and its broadly based ownership, why did trotting continue to enjoy widespread popular appeal in the aftermath of these profound alterations? The persistent perception of the trotter as the democratic and utilitarian horse, despite the changes, played a contributory role. As late as 1884, one newspaper insisted that the "millionaire horsemen with their mammoth establishments and invested thousands, represent but a small fraction of the money employed in this special industry." While the contention that the average farmer was the backbone of the sport was inaccurate, the tremendous growth of harness racing at the county fair, with its rural connotations, did give the sport a democratic aura.

The symbiotic relationship which already developed between the growth of harness racing, the changes in the breeding industry and the commercialization of the sport was an even more important factor. This linkage made it virtually impossible for the wealthy owners of trotters to create a sport run solely for their own class. While considerations of status contributed to elite involvement in this sport, financial concerns, for the overwhelming majority of these turfmen, were always present. To offset the surging cost of trotting horses required a corresponding expansion of the economic side of the sport. Consequently, trotting men continued to welcome the public and their money from gate receipts and gambling as a means of defraying their expenses and making a profit. The ongoing willingness of harness racing to cater to a broad segment of the population resulted in the perpetuation of trotting as the "people's pastime."

V

Harness racing underwent tremendous growth as a commercial-spectator sport in New York in the 1860s. The outbreak of the Civil War brought a brief pause to the general prosperity of the sport, but things were back into full swing by the Fall of 1862. During the following year, trotting in New York appeared to be one continuous stream of match races. Symbolized by a series of six races, each for $5,000, between *General Butler* and *George Patchen,* these match races attracted large audiences to the various courses. By 1864, the *Clipper* noted that the previous season was "Successful beyond precedent, alike in the quantity and quality of the sport which it produced."

More significant for the overall development of trotting than these glamorous races was the increasing size of the purses given by the proprietors and clubs of the various tracks. The prize money tendered at the Fashion Course, for example, more than tripled, increasing from $3,750 to $11,500, in the years between 1862 and 1870. By the start of the 1870s, the aggregate sum of the purses offered by New York's three leading tracks during their weekly sessions exceeded $25,000. In addition, the proprietors scheduled other purse contests from time to time. Races which went for no more than $250 during the 1850s, and were run for about $1,000 by the early 1860s, could go for as much as $5,000 by the end of the decade.

An increase in the number of horses coming to the start corresponded with the rise in prize money. Whereas four horses rarely entered a race in the 1850s, this had become the norm by the early 1860s and it was not uncommon to find as many as seven horses in a contest. When there were 78 entries for the ten races held at the Fashion Course in 1864, one sporting journal called it by far the greatest number ever known for a regular meeting. To facilitate the growing number of horses, the proprietors of the courses adopted the policy of sweepstake racing, long used in horse racing, with nominations to these contests sometimes coming as much as a year in advance.

The rapid expansion of harness racing not only in New York but throughout the nation during this decade, and especially after the Civil War, gave rise to several problems. According to the press, the most serious one remained the specter of the "fix." Calling upon the proprietors of the courses to cleanse and reform trotting of its evil elements, they continued to prognosticate dire consequences if their advice went unheeded. Nevertheless, no significant action was taken until the Naragansett (RI) Trotting Association called a convention of track operators in late 1869. Meeting in New York the following February, delegates from forty-six tracks in fifteen states established the National Trotting Association for the Promotion of the Interest of the Trotting Turf, later simplified to the National Trotting Association (NTA).

The dual objectives of the NTA were the creation of uniform government and the prevention and punishment of fraud. To facilitate the former goal, the NTA adopted rules which would be used at all tracks in the association. To expedite the later aim, the NTA attempted to buttress the power of local authorities by creating a board of appeals which would rule on all kinds of infractions. To give muscle to this court, it made the suspension on one track applicable to all courses within the federation.

Turf historians have accepted the desire to reform the evils of the turf as the major factor behind the creation of the NTA. Although they recognized the need for changes in the institutional structure of harness racing, they perceived this development as a means to the larger end. Since the contemporary press and these historians grossly exaggerated the degree to which races were fixed, the lofty ideals assigned by these writers must be questioned. At the time of the creation of the NTA, in fact, several individuals asked how the proprietors of the courses, who had at least tacitly accepted the fraudulent behavior even though they may not have been responsible for it, were going to lead a reform movement. Interestingly, the right of track operators to represent the "trotting fraternity" at this convention was based on their vested economic interest in the sport.

The formation of the NTA can be more appropriately examined as a response to what were the major problems of the turf: the inefficiency of uncoordinated local organizations and local rules to meet the needs of the proprietors of the courses and the owners of the horses. As early as 1858, *Porter's Spirit of the Times,* noting the growth of the sport, called for the creation of a national organization to govern harness racing. Only with the tremendous expansion of trotting in the years following the Civil War, however, did the extant institutional structures of harness racing become incapable of meeting the requirements of the sport. Far from being a means to an end, the new institutions were ends in themselves. The creation of the NTA, to borrow a popular historical phrase, was part of harness racing's "search for order."

Trotting had long been governed solely by local rules. This system did not prove excessively unwieldly when harness racing depended mainly on match races or consisted of contests with small fields comprised largely of neighborhood horses. With the growth of the sport, the older rules became inoperative. In 1862, the Fashion Course rewrote their rules to adjust to the more numerous starters. Such a simple matter as the positioning of the horses on the track prior to each heat, heretofore left to the individual driver, now had to be codified. Moreover, races began to be handicapped to maintain competitive balance between the increasing number of trotters present on the course. In the early 1860s, New York tracks began handicapping by weight, but not until the next decade was the more efficient system of time-classification introduced. The increase in the number of tracks throughout the country was far more significant in producing homogenity in the rules. To facilitate the easy movement of horses from course to course, standardization of the rules and regulations became necessary.

The NTA drew heavily on the experience of the New York tracks. Since the leading sporting journals were located in Manhattan, New York's rules were the ones published and therefore practiced on a goodly number of courses throughout the country even prior to the convention. Moreover, Isaiah Rynders, the only New Yorker on the nine man committee designated to draft the NTA's regulations, was the chairman of this group. John L. Cassady, a delegate at the convention and a leading commentator on the trotting scene, maintained that Rynders was the busiest and most influential member at the convention.

Rynders' presence and influence in the creation of the NTA raises further questions of those who viewed this association as a reform movement led by men in "white hats." A former Mississippi river boat gambler, the founder of the notorious Empire Club, a major New York gang, an active and influential member of Tammany Hall and a leading "shoulder hitter," he was the man, the *Times* claimed, who was most responsible for the "organized system of terrorism and ruffianism in city politics." Clearly, Rynders was the prototype (gambler, ruffian) of the individual who the press frequently complained wielded undo and a negative influence on the sport. If this was the man who was leading the reform, it may be asked from whom were they reforming the turf?

Besides the necessity of uniform rules, the expansion of harness racing made it imperative that the various tracks be coordinated. For New York's major courses it was not so much a question of the need to synchronize their respective schedules as it was the growing competition from the increasing number of tracks emerging outside of Manhattan. With these courses offering good prize money to attract top notch horses to their meetings, even New York lacked the financial resources to meet the combined competition of these tracks. While New York remained the sport's capital, the virtual monopoly it had of the best horses in former days was undermined. In the years immediately following the Civil War, the proprietors of the turf in Gotham were forced to abandon their policy of arranging purse races throughout the year and adopted a more compact racing season. To guarantee the presence of the best talent, the enlarged market necessitated the creation of some form of systematic scheduling to avoid conflicting engagements.

The subsequent development of the NTA goes beyond the scope of this article. Clearly greater research into this organization, as with all phases of harness racing, is necessary. Nevertheless, the perspective drawn from the experience of New York raises questions concerning the traditional view of the formation of this federation. While New York track operators paid lip service to the need to reform the turf, the desire for order, and thereby profit, motivated them to join the national association. Through collective action they could coordinate the activities of the expanding sport, as well as buttress local authority. While the institutional reform checked some of the persistent problems confronting the turf, they were a product of pragmatic, rather than moral, objectives.

The formation of the NTA symbolized the transformation of harness racing from a premodern to a modern sport. In contrast to the informal road contests which took place in the northeastern section of the country a half century earlier, harness racing evolved into a highly organized sport, with relatively uniform rules and with contests taking place in all sections of the nation. The emergence of a trotting literature (stud books and *Wallace's Monthly Magazine*) and developments in the breeding industry (the formation of the National Association of Trotting Horse Breeders and the creation of a standard breed) in the 1870s further demonstrated the centralizing and modernizing forces at work in the sport. By this decade, one social historian noted, harness racing "had grown to such mammoth proportions and won a greater share of the public attention than any other public pastime which contributed to the enjoyment of the people."

Suggested Readings

Adelman, Melvin L. *A Sporting Time: New York City and the Rise of Modern Athletics*. Urbana, IL: University of Illinois Press, 1986.

Adelman, Melvin L. "Neglected Sports in American History: The Rise of Billiards in New York City, 1850-1871." *Canadian Journal of History of Sport,* 12(1981): 1-28.

Barney, Robert Knight. "Knights of Cause and Exercise: German Forty-Eighters and Turnvereine in the United States During the Ante-Bellum Period." *Canadian Journal of History of Sport,* 13(1982): 62-79.

Berryman, Jack W. "Sport, Health, and the Rural-Urban Conflict: Baltimore and John Stuart Skinner's American Farmer, 1819-1820." *Conspectus of History,* 1(1982): 43-61.

Berryman, Jack W. "The Tenuous Attempts of Americans to 'Catch-up With John Bull': Specialty Magazines and Sporting Journalism, 1800-1835." *Canadian Journal of History of Sport and Physical Education,* 10(1979): 33-61.

Durick, William G. "The Gentlemen's Race: An Examination of the 1868 Harvard-Oxford Boat Race." *Journal of Sport History,* 15(1988): 41-63.

Fielding, Lawrence W. "War and Trifle's: Sport in the Shadows of Civil War Army Life." *Journal of Sport History,* 4(1977): 151-168.

Folsom, Ed. "The Manly and Healthy Game: Walt Whitman and the Development of American Baseball," *Arete: The Journal of Sport Literature.* 2(1984): 43-62.

Goldstein, Warren. *Playing for Keeps: A History of Early Baseball.* Ithaca, NY: Cornell University Press, 1989.

Gorn, Elliott J. "Good-Bye Boys, I Die a True American: Homicide Nativism and Working-Class Culture in Antebellum New York City." *Journal of American History,* 74(1987): 388-410.

Gorn, Elliott J. *The Manly Art: Bareknuckle Prize Fighting in America.* Ithaca, NY: Cornell University Press, 1986.

Green, Harvey. *Fit for America: Health, Fitness, Sport, and American Society.* Baltimore, MD: The Johns Hopkins University Press, 1988.

Jable, J. Thomas. "Social Class and the Sport of Cricket in Philadelphia, 1850-1880." *Journal of Sport History,* 18(1991): 205-223.

Kirsch, George. *The Creation of American Team Sports: Baseball and Cricket, 1838-1872.* Urbana, IL: University of Illinois Press, 1989.

Lewis, Guy. "The Muscular Christianity Movement." *Journal of Health, Physical Education, and Recreation,* 5(1966): 27-42.

Lewis, R.M. "American Croquet in the 1860s: Playing the Game and Winning." *Journal of Sport History,* 18(1991): 365-386.

Lucas, John A. "A Prelude to the Rise of Sport: Ante-bellum America, 1850-1860." *Quest,* 11(1968): 50-57.

Park, Roberta J. "Harmony and Cooperation: Attitudes Toward Physical Education and Recreation in Utopian Social Thought and American Communitarian Experiments, 1825-1865." *Research Quarterly,* 45(1974): 276-292.

Park, Roberta J. "The Attitudes of Leading New England Transcendentalists Toward Healthful Exercise, Active Recreations, and Proper Care of the Body, 1830-1860." *Journal of Sport History,* 4(1977): 34-50.

Rader, Benjamin G. "The Quest for Subcommunities and the Rise of American Sports." *American Quarterly,* 29(1977): 355-369.

Redmond, Gerald. *The Caledonian Games in Nineteenth Century America.* Rutherford, NJ: Fairleigh Dickinson University Press, 1982.

Rosenzweig, Roy, & Blackmar, Elizabeth. *The Park and the People: A History of Central Park.* Ithaca, NY: Cornell University Press, 1992.

Struna, Nancy L. "The North-South Races: American Thoroughbred Racing in Transition, 1823-1850." *Journal of Sport History,* 8(1981): 28-57.

Verbrugge, Martha A. *Able-Bodied Womanhood: Personal Health and Social Change in Nineteenth-Century Boston.* New York: Oxford University Press, 1988.

Vertinsky, Patricia. "Sexual Equality and the Legacy of Catherine Beecher." *Journal of Sport History,* 6(1979): 39-49.

Whorton, James. *Crusaders for Fitness: The History of American Health Reformers.* Princeton, NJ: Princeton University Press, 1982.

Wiggins, David K. "The Play of Slave Children in the Plantation Communities of the Old South, 1820-1860." *Journal of Sport History,* 7(1980): 21-39.

Yates, Norris W. *William T. Porter and the Spirit of the Times.* Baton Rouge: Louisiana State University Press, 1957.

PART 3
❖

SPORT IN THE ERA OF INDUSTRIALIZATION AND REFORM, 1870-1915

Sport evolved from an essentially unorganized activity to a highly structured and organized phenomenon during the latter stages of the 19th century and early years of the 20th century. The rapid rise in industrialization, new technologies, massive tide of immigration, decline of religious opposition to recreation and leisure activities, expanding middle and working classes, and influence of the British and this country's "Nouve Rouche" all played roles in the establishment of governing bodies in collegiate sport, increased organization and control of amateur athletics, and growing stability of professional sport. This period alone witnessed the founding of the American Association for the Advancement of Physical Education; formation of the National Croquet Association; founding of the League of American Wheelmen; staging of the first National Women's singles tennis championship; organization of the Amateur Athletic Union; invention of basketball and volleyball; beginning of Davis Cup tennis competition; formation of the American League of Professional Baseball Clubs; and founding of both the Playground Association of America and the National Collegiate Athletic Association.

One sport that showed rapid growth through the formation of elaborate organizational structures was baseball. It spread quickly across the country during the latter half of the 19th century, evolving into a mass cultural movement involving literally thousands of players organized into teams and leagues from the Eastern seaboard to the coast of California. Baseball, commonly called "The National Pastime" or "America's Game," was embraced by young men in this country with a passion rarely seen in sport.

The reasons for the enormous popularity of baseball has been a source of much debate by historians. Ronald Story is one of the latest in a long line of academicians to speculate as to why Americans fell in love with the game. He argues in his essay, "The Country of the Young: The Meaning of Baseball in Early American Culture," (chapter 7) that the level of involvement and powerful attraction of baseball cannot be accounted for merely by reference to Irish ethnicity, working-class occupations, promotionalism, sponsorship, the masculine subculture, or the railroad-based entertainment industry. Story claims that the love affair with baseball came about because it fulfilled for young males their emotional needs for comradeship, recognition, and order. Although other sports helped fill some of these needs, it was baseball that best served young males and became their salvation during an era characterized by rapid industrialization and destabilizing mobility.

The needs filled by baseball could not have been fully realized without the accompanying sporting goods and equipment produced and marketed in ever-increasing numbers throughout this period. The very nature of sport was being transformed during this era by a new array of sporting goods produced and marketed by such creative enterpreneurs as Michael Phelan, John Brunswick, Al Reach, George Wright, and Albert Spalding. This growth in sporting goods and its role in the institutionalization of sport is the subject of chapter 8, Stephen Hardy's essay " 'Adopted by all the Leading Clubs': Sporting Goods and the Shaping of Leisure." Hardy acknowledges the influence of traditional field sports to the initial growth of specialized sporting equipment, but he concentrates on such highly structured games as baseball and football in his analysis. The result is a fascinating look at the interplay between the producers and consumers of sporting goods and how they contributed to both the shaping of leisure and the transformation of informal pastimes into specialized game forms.

Perhaps nowhere was the institutionalization of sport more visible than in intercollegiate athletics. Like sport in general, college sport during this period was transformed from a largely informal activity to a complex organization characterized by several layers of bureaucratic structures. Initially in the hands of students themselves, intercollegiate athletics at many institutions were taken over by faculty and administrators who came to believe that the promise of college sport could only be realized under their control. This shift from student to faculty governance took place at uneven rates and was marked by each individual institution establishing its own rules and regulations over such matters as player eligibility, paid coaches, and professionalism. The lack of uniform athletic policies resulted in conflicts between individual schools and several early attempts to bring college sport under some form of interinstitutional control. Ronald Smith examines these initial efforts at interinstitutional control in chapter 9, his essay, "Preludes to the NCAA: Early Failures of Faculty Intercollegiate Athletic Control." Smith argues that the early failures at interinstitutional controls resulted largely from the resistance of schools to give up their institutional autonomy and take action that benefited everyone involved in college athletics. It was only with increased social legislation in America around the turn of the century and after a crisis in football that schools finally took collective action and established interinstitutional control of college sport through creation of the National Collegiate Athletic Association in 1905.

The bureaucratization of college athletics was part of both a larger movement toward modernization in sport and development of sport as a popular form of commercialized entertainment, two interrelated processes closely identified with urbanization and political institutions. This evolution of sport and its relationship to political behavior within an urban environment is the theme of chapter 10, Steven Riess's essay, "Sports and Machine Politics in New York City, 1870-1920." Focusing on baseball, boxing, and horse racing, Riess examines the role machine politicians played in the promotion and facilitation of urban recreation in New York City and, conversely, the influence sport had on the city's political culture.

CHAPTER 7

The Country of the Young: The Meaning of Baseball in Early American Culture

Ronald Story

We know we love it above all others. But why do we? Or rather, since it started a long time ago, why *did* we? Why *baseball* and not some other sport? Or *no* sport? And why baseball with such passionate single-mindedness rather than as one sport among many? How did this come to be?

We can find some tentative answers, I believe, by looking closely at the period when baseball truly began to sweep the country: the years from about 1875 to 1895. Because it was the 1880s (as we'll call them for brevity's sake) with their gaudy promotionalism, kaleidoscopic franchise and league formation, spring training and transcontinental and international barnstorming treks, expanded seasons, city and world series, tobacco cards, product endorsements, knothole gangs, booster clubs, flamboyant daredevil players and weekly baseball newspapers—it was in the '80s that baseball became what can only be described as a mass cultural movement, a large-scale, passionate American affair on the scale and intensity of other mass movements such as revivalism or temperance, and capable, therefore, of creating a bedrock of players and "cranks" on which promoters and sponsors would build.

A mass cultural movement of this kind cannot be accounted for, it seems to me, the way most baseball historians have tried to account for it, by reference to, for example, working-class occupations or Irish ethnicity, or to the masculine subculture or railroad-based entertainment industry, or to promotionalism and sponsorship. These were all significant, the Irish factor particularly so. But they do not explain why the groups, the subculture, the entertainment moguls, and the politicians gravitated so powerfully to baseball rather than to something else. Nor, most importantly, do they explain the intensity and passion, the sudden breathless sweep, of the late 19th century's involvement with the game.

From the *Cooperstown Symposium on Baseball,* Alvin Hall (editor), Westport, CT: Meckler, 1991, pp. 324-342. © 1991 Ronald Story. Reprinted by permission.

Baseball became so enormously popular in the 1889s for one reason: men loved it. And they loved it, I would argue, because they played it when they were young. Our concentration on the men's clubs and professional teams has misled us. The fact is that for every club or professional player we can identify from the late 1860s to the early 1880s, there were almost certainly a hundred nonprofessional players on organized teams and a thousand on unorganized ad hoc ones, almost all of them boys or young men between the ages of 10 and 20. It was the coming of age during the late 1870s and '80s of these thousands of youthful players that produced the huge critical mass of players, spectators and followers on which the mass baseball movement rested.

Love and passion—strong but appropriate words. Because these boys and young men not only played baseball but played it in the face of adult disinterest and disapproval. This is one of the most important differences between the 19th and 20th century games. Nineteenth century adults did not really want their adolescent sons playing baseball. Stories abound of 19th century fathers tracking down sons and whipping them off the ball field, of mothers throwing iron pots and boiling water at team organizers, of tempestuous quarrels over ball playing instead of chores and serious work. Nor, except for a handful of colleges, did schools sponsor baseball teams; and when school teams did appear, it was the students themselves who organized the teams.

So baseball was not only a mass movement, it was a youth movement, fomented in the face of disapproving authority. It was not only a counterpart to 19th century revivalism and temperance, it was a precursor to 20th century movies and rock and roll. And it left an equally indelible impression.

Mass movements, and mass youth movements especially, arise because they satisfy deep-seated emotional needs among their adherents. Baseball must have been no different. The question, then, that finally addresses the meaning of baseball in early America, and the reason for its fabulous later popularity, is simply this: What needs did this era's adolescent male population have that baseball seemed able to satisfy so powerfully?

First some basics. Baseball was an outdoor activity for the hot months of the year. Nineteenth century houses were places of work and basic bodily functions with poor ventilation and lighting and, until the mid-1880s, no window screens. In summer, a house was "a place to get out of," as were most school buildings and places of work. And houses were crowded, commonly holding eight or more persons in a few small rooms. Front porches and steps were important living and socializing spaces in hot weather. But many houses had the main porch in the rear, and anyway, step and porch activities had to be fairly restrained. That left the streets and vacant lots and fields. Baseball flourished more than "saloon" games such as cards, darts or billiards partly because it gave exuberant young males something exciting and vigorous to do outdoors at a time when staying indoors was agony.

Early baseball was also aggressively physical. It was simple to learn and unlike, say, cricket, easy enough to play to accommodate a range of ages and skills. But the same thing that made the game relatively easy to play—underhand pitching and lenient ball–strike rules—insured lots of hitting and thus lots of fielding and base

Children in this country played baseball in a variety of settings and not always under optimal circumstances, as evidenced from this turn-of-the-century photograph.
Courtesy of the National Museum of American History, Smithsonian Institution.

running, too. There were, therefore, endless bursts of action and limitless quick sprinting with very little dead time in between. And even though agility, speed and reflexes mattered, so did muscle—the capacity to throw the ball swiftly and hit it powerfully.

Baseball, in other words, was a superb outlet for the energies of boisterous young males in a way that languid pursuits—fishing or the saloon games or backyard games such as horseshoes or marbles—were not. Baseball's intensely competitive nature, even in the most casual contests, also led ball players to develop and hone their skills—to exert, that is, even more physical energy and on a more sustained basis. The sport probably never produced enough exertion to trigger the state of ecstasy reported by modern track stars and mountaineers. But the combination of physical exertion and competitive tension could produce tremendous exhilaration, something that even experienced young players called "joy."

This physical side of baseball, the premium it placed on strength, speed, and agility, is especially significant in view of the conditions in the country during the years when it became popular. Nineteenth century America was nothing if not rough, and although the ball field was not the boxing ring, a reputation for baseball excellence carried over in other areas, lending status to players in a brawling era that held physical prowess and "grit" in high regard.

Ball players' pride in their skill, toughness, and physiques must have been acute in the 1860s and '70s because so many men were visibly unfit—frail, disabled, or both. The frail consisted in great measure of Irish immigrants and their offspring, who bore the twin burdens of the potato famine and its aftermath and the harsh poverty of unskilled laborers. Some Irish were, of course, rugged specimens, but many others were not. Their arrival in America lowered the country's average height and held urban life expectancy to under 45. And with this residue of hunger and poverty went the damage of the Civil War. Limbless veterans inhabited every town and city for years after Appomattox, multiplying prosthesis shops as well as pension relief.

Paul Longmore argues that the disabled have been a negative reference group for other Americans just as blacks have been for whites. We define ourselves by what we are not—disabled, black, feminine, and so forth. Conscious of these frail, damaged men, their haler counterparts reacted typically: to display their health and wholeness, they rushed to play a physically demanding, highly visible sport—baseball.

Lastly but perhaps not least, baseball had some sexual significance. Anthropologists have speculated about the phallic symbolism of the ubiquitous bat. But the bat seems no more suggestive than other sporting implements—guns, fishing poles, cricket bats, lacrosse or hockey sticks—and the sport itself no more sexually freighted than games such as football, basketball, or soccer where players "penetrate" the goal with the ball. Yet baseball must have had a sexual dimension. Its players were almost exclusively young males with high testosterone levels and strong sexual urges that did not simply vanish because the sport was all-male. Promoters, in fact, took great pains to stress the game's "manly" and "masculine" qualities, and journalists took careful note of the number of women among the spectators and whether they were young, attractive, and single.

It was, in fact, not the bat but the player that had sexual import, particularly at higher levels where players wore tight-fitting, sometimes colorful, even red, uniforms. Opportunities for male physical display were rare in this era. Ordinary clothing did not enhance distinctive masculine features—broad shoulders, powerful chest, strong thigh and calf—and few activities gave adolescents and young men an opportunity for aggressively physical, therefore implicitly sexual, behavior that everyone, including women, could see. This may have appealed especially to our young Irishmen. Ireland had a heritage of separation, almost segregation, by gender, and the Famine migrants brought this legacy with them to America strengthened by the Great Hunger and reinforced by same-sex schooling. Irish boys had limited occasions to meet girls and gain facility at courtship, and most native-born Americans had it no easier. All-male sports allowed young Irishmen to send sexual signals while remaining safely apart. In this, baseball was a godsend, and not for the Irish alone.

Unfortunately, the basics, interesting as they are, don't really explain baseball's staggering popularity because there were other physical outdoor alternatives that might have satisfied these needs. Walking contests were leading spectator events in the mid-19th century but never captivated the country's youth as baseball did. Young men would watch walkers but only sporadically walk themselves, so an ardent mass following never developed. Important boxing matches drew throngs well into the 20th century, and boxing clubs attracted immigrant members and political patronage. Every 19th-century boy had to know how to fight with his hands or take a licking at every corner, and boxing as a sport with commonly accepted rules attracted zealous young participants. Yet neither walking nor fighting swept youthful America save on exceptional occasions when hordes would show up to see who was "fastest" and "toughest."

And there were others. The kicking and/or tackling game of football had been known since colonial times, got frequently touted by the mid-century sporting press as a cool weather sport, and had scattered "clubs" of its own. But it made little headway even after important collegiate matches began; "Irish" football, a soccer-like game played in the 1850s, did no better. Lacrosse, introduced here and there in the 1860s, made even fewer waves, while gymnastics, again widely known, remained almost exclusively a German pastime. Even cricket, which had a significant following before the Civil War, ultimately fared badly.

The question thus recurs. What emotional needs did the young males of this era have that were not met so well by these other sports but that baseball could, and did, meet singularly well? There were, let me suggest, three such needs, intertwined but nonetheless distinctive: comradeship, recognition, and order.

Twentieth century studies indicate that young Americans prefer team sports to individual sports while Europeans and Japanese incline to the opposite. This American preference first manifested itself in the 1860s and '70s, when baseball began to outstrip boxing, footracing, gymnastics and other individualistic physical activities. The young men's clubs that sponsored the earliest organized baseball teams were, in fact, highly "clubbish" affairs even off the field, placing great emphasis on dinners and fetes, and while such fraternal clubbishness declined with the spread of professionalism its aura may have lingered into the '70s.

But far more crucial, similar feelings flowed from the field of play. Not only did "teams"—aggregates of individuals—contest for victory, but the victory itself seemed to require actual "teamwork," a constant working together to blend disparate talents. Warren Goldstein suggests that early artisan players brought this stress on "victory through teamwork" with them from the shop floor and thereby imbued the sport with their particular mode of competitive labor excellence. But the game itself generated "team spirit," too. Teams that won with consistency needed several good players, not just one; even though only one player batted at a time, no one player, however talented, could carry a team. Winning was an inherently collective enterprise, inherently engendering solidarity. So, for that matter, was losing.

Far more than today, moreover, 19th-century teams at every level of play used what Bill James calls a "long sequence" offense, scoring by stringing small things together (two singles, two errors, and a single for three runs) rather than by doing fewer, but bigger things (double, single, home run). Historically, long-sequence offenses seem to produce more teamwork and team solidarity than short-sequence offenses because they force players to rely more on one another, thereby producing greater esprit de corps. And this playing-field esprit was intensified by the comradeship of the "bench"—teammates sitting or standing together when their "side" was batting, swapping vulgarities in the summer heat, shouting support in unison, enjoying male closeness.

The collective bonds produced by interdependence, joint contributions, and shared fate were different from the fraternalism of the early baseball clubs. Club members came together on the basis of common interests and attributes to play ball, or at least jointly sponsor ball playing. Teammates, by contrast, felt bound emotionally because they played together. But this esprit then spilled over the boundaries of the ball field to produce an intense camaraderie off it, too—at the adolescent level a tighter neighborhood or ethnic or "street" feeling, at the older level "the boys" singing on the train or in the hotel lobby, seeing new sights together, challenging all comers. The sociability of the club thus fused with the spirit of the team. "We played for love and excitement," they said. "We were a band of brothers, carrying everything before us."

Why did the young males of this era find this dimension of the sport so compelling? Why was the fraternal impulse so powerful among the period's young males? Undoubtedly in part because the rate of urbanization was so high. Urban populations were doubling every 10 years, propelled by a steady migration from country to city. This migration was disorienting under the best of circumstances. Massive war mobilization and demobilization and still more massive immigration, particularly from Famine Ireland, made it especially so. Nor did merely settling in the city mean the moving was over, because the population constantly churned so that boys would often live in three neighborhoods and attend four schools by the age of 15.

Young urbanites of this generation were highly likely, in other words, to have been born elsewhere or to have had parents born elsewhere and therefore to have experienced a dearth of conventional significant others—cousins, grandparents and the like and, even more, familiar faces from their own age cohort. Nineteenth-century boys were perpetual "new kids" in town, "green as the verdant prairies," nervous about going outside lest they "be spoken to by someone not a member of the family." Boys created and recreated their own communities all through the 19th century, forming Tom Sawyerish "gangs," shaping streets and blocks into play areas and turfs, finding school "chums." Young men, encountering unfamiliar social landscapes, did much the same with fire companies, reading groups, political clubs and other voluntary associations. But it was not easy for so "scattered" a people to do. Therefore the opportunity to participate in a sport such as baseball, to "break into those crude games of ball" which seemed to create instantaneous community, was irresistible.

Other sports developed facsimiles of this comradely ethos. Racing and fighting exuded a pungent masculine clubbishness, as did early cricket. But they did so almost exclusively at the adult level, where gambling, drinking, and politics helped create the atmosphere, and almost exclusively as spectacle, the comradely ambience deriving from the shared excitement of observing and celebrating, with the contestants' arena more or less delineated from the spectators. Baseball engendered this clubbish aura, too; but it also generated a sense of solidarity among its participants, drew its players together as they played, in a way that fighting and running could not. Further, the dynamic of "the bench" helped produce a sense of comradeship not only by drawing together the players as they played but, as game pictures show, by blurring the line that separated participants and spectators, and rolling players, bench and crowd together into an emotionally unified whole.

But baseball meant more than comradeship. It also, to a degree unique among team sports, meant individual recognition. Lacrosse, soccer, and later basketball and hockey enabled individual players to stand out, chiefly by handling or scoring with the ball. But these sports did not guarantee every player a chance to gain recognition; and particularly at lower skill levels and among youthful players where baseball took strongest root, a handful of players, even a single player, could not only dominate a game but virtually monopolize the ball, leaving other players few ways to excel or even participate.

One player could influence a baseball game, too, especially pitchers; and some positions—pitcher, catcher, first base—got more action than others. But baseball's entire defensive and offensive configuration had individualistic overtones. Each player bore a title corresponding to a specific position—third baseman, right-fielder, and so on; each player bore responsibility for the area indicated by his title; each player himself defended it—caught balls thrown or hit to or through it—alone, out in the open, without aid or hindrance. Some positions had more action than others, but the ball came to every position sooner or later, usually pretty often in the early, high-scoring games. When it did, a single, visibly isolated player had to handle it.

Similarly on offense: A team's players took the offensive in serial fashion, one at a time in prearranged order, for approximately the same length of time—each batter until he reached base or made an out, each team until it made three outs, the game to last until teams made 27 outs or it got dark. Baseball's fundamental structure, that is, guaranteed that every player would have exactly the same offensive opportunity as every other player; that his opportunity would come automatically, without competition or combat for the opportunity; and that in the course of these high-scoring games, teams would bat through their lineups frequently, so that individual opportunities would recur just as frequently.

The offensive structure had other implications, too. By sending one batter to the plate at a time, baseball made every player the team standard-bearer, a personification of the whole team with all eyes on him, teammates' included—a limelight opportunity that the game guaranteed not just occasionally, but frequently during each game. And the rapidity with which teams wheeled their batters to and from the plate insured that offensive players not hitting or on base would keep focused on the field because their turn would soon come again. The sport's structure, rules, and inherent dynamic gave every player an equal chance to play the role of team champion in the offensive spotlight; and it gave him a captive audience while he was there.

Baseball thus brought recognition to its participants by scattering them defensively and bringing them quickly and serially to bat. Early newspaper coverage and the notational formulas devised to summarize the game accentuated these patterns. Organizing a team in the spring meant, among other things, submitting a roster—nine players plus an extra or two, all with their positions—to the press along with an appeal for opponents and sometimes the address of the club's headquarters or captain. Midwestern papers of the 1870s normally published only the rosters of the better young adult teams, but by 1880 they were publishing the rosters of adolescent teams as well. Playing serious baseball was often the best, if not the only way for boys to see their names in print—visible testimony to their individual as well as group identity. Once the season's games began, the papers sometimes announced impending contests by giving the starting lineups, printing players' positions along with their spot in the batting order, hence doubling the individual recognition. At the professional and semiprofessional levels and for big collegiate and city championship matches, papers would occasionally include a box score consisting of times at bat, runs scored, and some fielding information along with the written account, thereby tripling the recognition factor.

Numbers mean immortality, argues Bill James. Baseball players will live in a way that football or lacrosse players cannot; a player's numbers, compiled from the evidence of the box score, guarantee it. For young players of the 1870s and early '80s, far below the professional level where statistics most mattered, it was not so much the cumulative record of the boxes that counted, although boys may have kept rough track of their own numbers and perceived their games partly through the borrowed lenses of the professional box scores— conceptualized their participation, in other words, according to the portrait of individualized collectivity suggested by the boxes. It was rather that rosters and lineups, and box scores later, publicly acknowledged players' existence not only as *belonging* persons but as *persons.*

Why did the era's young males yearn for recognition? A simple answer is that they resembled young men in most places at most times. The literature of the 18th and 19th centuries is filled with "young men from the provinces" seeking fortune and fame—a little recognition in the world's urban centers. Nineteenth-century Americans were no different, though many already lived in cities. They merely had more immediate models than Robinson Crusoe: the older ball players on display at the nearest grounds of whom they "made heroes" and "dreamed of imitating." They even dreamed of becoming heroes themselves.

For baseball, while a collective endeavor, was collective partly in the sense that the sum of a series of individual actions constitutes a collectivity. A team achievement was a statistical construct, the rolling together of many small components. Recognition was comradeship transposed. You were accepted, wanted, for what you yourself, with your own distinctive strengths and idiosyncrasies, could accomplish for your mates. When you failed, then that, too, the downside of responsibility, was glaringly evident. The inherent properties of the game guaranteed it.

Nineteenth century boys may have felt the need for recognition with a special urgency. As family historians are beginning to show, mid-19th-century fathers, both immigrant and native-born, commonly related to their sons in two ways: by neglect, if farmers or wage workers; by domination and control, if artisans or clerks. Life, after all, was an ordeal. Security and status as well as survival spurred long hours at work or politics. Long hours meant long stretches when the father was not present, leaving children to feel ignored and neglected—not "recognized" as having value. What they got, instead, was regulated—rigidly directed as to daily regimen, as to schooling, as to fealty, behavior, work. Fathers did what they believed necessary under the alternatively tantalizing and ominous circumstances of the 19th-century world. Sons experienced it differently.

Were nineteenth century mothers different? Ball players, like everyone else, remembered their mothers as "friends" and "supporters," full of compassion and concern, and maybe they were. But the typical household was large, with four, five, or more children to make demands on mother's attention and energy. Housework itself was arduous. And consider this: nearly half the total time that a boy might live in his parents' home, his mother was either pregnant or in postpartum recuperation, growing weaker, in many cases, with each pregnancy. Whatever the memories, it hardly seems possible that mothers had much in the way of surplus attention to bestow on a needy son or of surplus energy for meeting the innumerable emotional demands of a bursting household.

A speculation might be in order in this connection with the Irish and baseball. In the "stem" system of Irish families, a single son, usually the eldest, traditionally received what there was by way of patrimony and therefore what existed of concentrated, undivided attention. Favored, usually eldest, sons lived longest at home, got the most advantageous schooling, were introduced earliest to potential patrons or employers. Younger sons—the vast majority of sons—got packed off to work or school. So they sought recognition where they could find it: on the ball field.

Comradeship. Recognition. But also order. Allen Guttmann observes that whereas most team sports—soccer, hockey, rugby, basketball, polo, football, lacrosse—oscillate between the two poles, baseball is circular in its fundamental configuration and flow. This is true because, unlike other sports, where a team scores by moving the ball forward across a line or through a space that the opposing team defends, baseball players score without the ball, which is driven away from the offensive action, thereby enabling an individual player to touch the four points of a square (diamond) for a "run." Guttmann speculates that baseball's rounding of the square perhaps touches fundamental biorhythms related to the transit of the seasons and, by extension, the rhythms of the agricultural world. If so, he reasons, baseball may have served as a mechanism for easing the great transition from rural to urban life that has characterized the U.S.

Guttmann is almost surely right that there was something significant about the geometry and configurations of the game. Before the Civil War, players of ball-and-bat games had three more or less distinct ways to lay out a playing ground. One way was for cricket, with bowler and batsman occupying positions determined by the location of the wicket that the bowler aimed at and the batsman protected; batsmen scored by running along a line to the bowler's area and back. The field itself was oval, extending in every direction to a boundary laid round the outer limits. With "fair" territory defined in this way as anywhere inside the oval, which is to say everywhere, cricket had no fixed defensive posts, and players assumed a sometimes bewildering variety of positions according to their captain's orders.

Another was for baseball New England style, or "town ball," as it was first called. Here the striker stood halfway between home and 1st, then ran to touch markers at the four corners of the square to score before being hit by a thrown ball. The position of the batter meant, however, that there was no good way to demark "fair" from "foul" territory. If lines were drawn along the home–3rd base line and the 1st–2nd line, the field became a rectangle reaching outward from the home–1st line towards the "out" (now left) field, leaving a narrow confining space where crowded fielders jockeyed and jostled for room. As a result, baseball New England style reverted to the cricket mode, a limitless space extending in all directions where players occupied uncertain spots depending on whim, circumstances, or a captain's will. Moreover, with no out-of-bounds there was no particular reason to touch bases in order and, therefore, no need for base paths to control a runner's movement, producing a game that was even more random and willful—disorderly—than cricket. This square-within-an-ovoid New England baseball lasted until the late 1850s when the angular "diamond" New York game supplanted it. When baseball flourished after 1865, it was in this New York form, which then helped it pass cricket in people's affections and thus become *the* model for the sport.

So there was clearly something important about the diamond formed by placing the batter at home plate. In this New York game, three of the right angles formed by lines intersecting the fourth point ("home") were out of bounds. Balls batted there were foul, no good except in a few special instances, and so did not need defending. This definition of "inbounds" as the space inside the single 90-degree arc formed by the diamond thus combined with the four bases of the diamond to determine the logical distribution of defenders—namely, in a double arc, a four-position configuration around the outer limits of the "infield" and a thinner, three-man arc beyond that. And as noted in connection with the recognition factor, from this logical configuration of defenders (fielders), came with equal logic the conventions of fixed and separate positions, each with a name, each name associated with a special space.

Baseball's rules, in other words, and the defensive logic that flowed from the geometry of its diamond-shaped infield, gave its participants fixed defensive positions within discrete spaces. Once the rules and logic became clear, moreover, virtually the same was true for ad hoc contests between odd numbers of players on narrow streets or rooftops or other expanded or smallish areas lacking true squares or a limitless widening of the "fair" angle. The discrete spacing held even under these conditions because of what players had to do to score—touch all bases consecutively without the ball—and how the field was conceived—as a rapidly spreading 90-degree fair territory. Meanwhile, batters who struck the ball had to move along the sides of the square and there only. Baseball, that is, imposed order on its players by sending them to specific areas of the field on defense and down rigidly delimited paths on offense. And it did so automatically by its rules and regulations.

Here is a primary difference between baseball and Guttmann's oscillating sports. In the latter, players' movements were more random and willful, players' paths and spaces less inviolate. There was greater opportunity for conflict, including physical collision, and less clarity of individual opportunity and objective. Sometimes collision was inherent, as with rugby or Irish or collegiate football; or players could perform tasks with little knowledge of how plays developed, again as in football but also sometimes in lacrosse or soccer. Order—the setting of boundaries, trajectories, and responsibilities—could be found in all these sports, but it was a partial order and one largely imposed by a captain's, coach's, or manager's authority. None had baseball's fixity of position, hence inviolability of person, and delineation of pathways, hence clarity of trajectory. Moreover, baseball controlled space and people *automatically*. The rest did so, *if* they did so, by means of external authority.

And observers knew this right away. Baseball was a game "whose regulations are calculated to prevent the ill-feelings engendered by other games." It was a "nonviolent" sport, with "splendid order" and "control," the "most organized of all sports being played." Renderings of 19th-century games commonly show the players separated on the field, fixed in distinct spaces, poised for action yet scattered and detached, moving down the narrow paths of the base lines. They stand forth amid the representations of boisterous and uncontrolled 19th century groups, all but frozen in worlds of their own spaces, detached from the welter of ordinary urban life.

Yet the question, as before, is not only what baseball offered—in this case order—but why young men thirsted for it. And explanations lie readily at hand in the period's disorderly, destabilizing mobility and insubordination, particularly as evinced in the brawling cities and experienced by boys in the city streets. Besides seeing their fathers move from job to job, their families from neighborhood to neighborhood, themselves from school to school and boss to boss, males born in the 1850s and 1860s lived through war mobilization and massive waves of immigration, sharp financial panic and deep economic depression, ravenous fires and bitter labor disputes. And disorder's handmaid was raw violence: crime waves, a raucous saloon culture, political combat, turf battles, gang fights.

These young men were tough, make no mistake. They fought continuously to prove and protect themselves, and for thrills. But even the toughest young men, Robert Coles shows, need respite, "time out," if they can find it without losing face, and the not-so-tough-beneath-the-surface majority need it especially. Lacking adult authority figures to furnish safety and sanctuary, in the 1860s and '70s they found their own: on the ball field.

Richard Sennett argues that in the absence of powerful overarching institutions—a standing army, a national church, a corporate economy, a rigorous system of national schooling—a chief 19th-century refuge from danger and disorder was the family. But this is not wholly persuasive for our period. Consider the household from the standpoint of a boy growing up there: perpetually crowded with little room for consolation or order; the mother distracted, fatigued, "sick" with childbirth; the father remote, often absent, but when at home severe and critical and a conveyor, too, of the angry social and political passions of the world outside, a bearer sometimes of its physical wounds, always of its anxieties.

We may surmise, then, as follows. Young males of this generation needed security and order—breathing space, respite—in a world where violence and chaos seemed the norm. But families, which might have been a refuge, were often microcosms of the outside world, fecund sources of their own forms of unhappiness and insecurity; schools and gangs helped but brought uncertainties of their own. Still needing security, young men sought it where they could, especially in the surrogate family ambience of team sports. And of the available team sports, baseball, after the adoption of New York rules, served best. It constrained willfulness and assault better, and ordered space better, and it did so automatically and spontaneously, without adult aid or intervention.

This was, finally, an encompassing national movement because all of America was in turmoil in the 1860s and '70s. And baseball, which carried the seeds of security and control, of comradeship and recognition, within itself, was there to scatter them in identical ways all across the country. Because adolescent boys of that generation needed them, baseball became their salvation and their love. And they never forgot it. In partial payment, they made it the American game.

CHAPTER 8

Adopted by All the Leading Clubs: Sporting Goods and the Shaping of Leisure

Stephen Hardy

Scholars considering the institutionalization of American sport have correctly focused on the growth of bureaucracies—voluntary associations, corporate businesses, state agencies—and the struggles among them. At the same time, research has looked at the ideological debates and legal battles among sporting elites: the Amateur Athletic Union versus the NCAA, the National League versus the Brotherhood, Yale's Walter Camp versus Harvard's Charles W. Eliot. Historians have vividly described most of the key antagonists and their competing ideas about what sport should mean, but formal opinion offers only limited explanation of why some activities and their sponsors caught the fancy or devotion of a wide range of consumers. Another source of explanation lies in the physical materials that consumers used to participate in leisure. Equipment and uniforms provide important clues about how sports developed. Indeed, an examination of sporting goods takes us out of the realms of high ideology into the store windows, onto the streets, and all over the playgrounds of history, where sports were lived experience and not just written expressions.

This chapter considers the historical influence of sporting goods on America's sporting culture, particularly during the 19th century, when many of the forms developed that we take for granted today. After describing the growth of sporting goods firms and markets, I look at how the industry and its products aligned with other "providers" to institutionalize certain types and styles of games. My focus is on those sports that take the form of rulebound, competitive play such as baseball and football, but it is important to note the influence of fishing and hunting during the early 19th century. These traditional field sports provided the basis for the earliest periodicals devoted to promoting outdoor activities; they were the source of the initial markets for specialized sporting equipment; and it was frequently the journalists and merchants of field sports who became product

From *For Fun and Profit*, Richard Butsch (Editor), Philadelphia: Temple University Press, 1990, pp. 71-101. © 1990 by Temple University Press. Reprinted by permission of Temple University Press.

champions for the "new" varieties of games that emerged during the middle third of the century.

Sports Market Foundations, 1800–1860

American colonists brought traditional sports to the New World as part of their cultural baggage. These activities were integral to life styles that could be patrician or plebeian, segregated or communal, urban or rural. Rules, records, and reputations were basically *local* accords, although 18th-century elites did begin to nurture and formalize wider understandings about behavior and attitudes appropriate to such activities as horse racing. Even so, in 1800 there were few published works on sport and leisure. By the mid-19th century, however, ingenious journalists and entrepreneurs had circulated persuasive arguments about the value of fishing, hunting, horse racing, rowing, and other activities assisting Americans to confront the disruption and uncertainty of an emerging urban and industrial order. Their publications—*American Farmer, American Turf Register, Spirit of the Times,* and assorted books and monographs—contributed to a slow expansion of local to regional to national accords about sports and leisure. They represent the beginnings of an industry of providers, even though the production of sporting goods appears to have lagged behind the production of formal ideology. Through the first half of the century, consumers who could *read about* sports in specialty publications tended to *play* sports with goods furnished through homecrafting, merchant importers, or local artisans. Not until the mid-century would they enjoy the products of large-scale, integrated manufacture from American specialty firms.

Homecrafting was the most traditional form of production, for which many 19th-century books provided instructions, suggesting the authors' awareness of the limited production of ready-made goods. Early handbooks for boys often contained such instructions. William Clarke's *Boy's Own Book* (1834) and the *Boy's Treasury* (1847) both explained, for example, how to make a baseball by cutting India rubber bottles into coils that could be wound round a cork, then covered with a tight winding of wool yarn and a handstitched leather cover. In similar fashion, *The Boy's Own Book*—an often praised "bible" for middle-class youth—noted that footballs should be made of "light materials—a blown bladder, cased with leather, is the best." It also advised that the easiest method of making fishing line lay in the use of a "little machine which may be bought at most of the shops where also you purchase your lines, if you think fit." *The American Anglers Book* (1865), aimed at an older audience, contained a chapter on rodmaking that listed the equipment a 19th-century do-it-yourselfer would need—bench, vise, knife, jack plane and fore plane, files, paper—and included a picture of a steel template of notches and gauged holes of various diameters. One can imagine that many anglers found the instructions simpler on paper than in practice.

"The Spalding"

Name or Trade-Mark

Represents the One Standard

of Quality in Athletic Goods.

The Spalding Official Inter-Collegiate Foot Ball.

The most perfect Foot Ball ever produced.   Each ball is thoroughly
tested, packed in a separate box and sealed, and is exclusively
used by all the leading colleges.

EVERY REQUISITE FOR THE GAME.

Spalding's Official Foot Ball Guide for 1899.

EDITED BY WALTER CAMP.   240 PAGES.

Containing new rules; instructions for beginners; review of season of
1898; articles on training; portraits of all leading teams and players.

10 CENTS: POSTPAID.

Handsomely Illustrated Catalogue of All Sports, Free.

A. G. SPALDING & BROS.   NEW YORK, CHICAGO, DENVER.

The interrelationship between sporting goods and the shaping of leisure patterns can be seen in this advertisement for ''The Spalding Official Inter-Collegiate Foot Ball.'' Courtesy of Stephen Hardy.

Homecrafting continued as a popular and necessary art throughout the century, though the mention of ''shops'' indicates that wealthier sportsmen might opt to buy custom or ready-made equipment. In a sample of Maryland estate inventories, Nancy Struna found that the ratios of sporting goods to total inventories rose from under 6 percent in 1770 to over 26 percent in 1810. While the lists do not distinguish homemade from finished goods, they probably do reflect a movement toward the latter, as well as wider sporting interests among wealthy and middling well-to-do Marylanders.

Struna wisely concludes that ''no consumer revolution occurred'' during that period. Nonetheless, even before the Revolutionary War, urban merchants offered stocks of imported goods, mostly from England. One James Rivington advertised shuttlecocks, cricket balls, and tennis rackets in New York. Jeremiah Allen imported bamboo, dogwood, and hazel fishing rods to Boston. Rivington and Brown offered Philadelphians an assortment of sporting goods that included quail nets and cock spurs. English goods would continue to enjoy periods of popularity that coincided with the importation of new activities from Albion's workshop of sport.

Until the mid-nineteenth century, however, most finished sporting goods on both sides of the Atlantic came from the shops of small craftsmen. Struna found that there were numerous such artisans by the late 1700s: Hardress Waller of Norfolk, for example, sold his finished ivory billiard balls for ten shillings a pair. While such equipment was typically a small item among larger areas of craft, such as leather- or woodworking, the evidence does suggest some slight movement toward specialization before the Civil War, particularly for field sports. Two of the oldest specialty firms were located in Philadelphia. George W. Tryon, a gunsmith, bought out his mentor in 1811 and began to develop a special niche with sportsmen. In 1836 son Edward persuaded him to expand the business by importing fishing tackle from England. Under the name of Edward K. Tryon, the firm would become a major wholesaler of sporting goods east of the Mississippi. Tryon nevertheless had competition: in 1826 gunmaker John Krider opened his "Sportsman's Depot" and also began retailing angling apparatus. While he advertised the finest in imported goods for hunting and fishing, he also complained of unnamed "scribblers" of American field sports who spent too much time glorifying British goods. He suspected that these early sports journalists were "paid by London gunmakers to puff their work on this side of the Atlantic." No doubt they were, as the competition became stiffer. The first useful American fishing guide, which appeared in 1845, claimed that American-made rods had overtaken their British counterparts in volume and quality. The compiler was a New York tackle dealer who operated "The Angler's Depot."

Such dealers slowly multiplied during these years. William T. Porter's *Spirit of the Times* ran advertisements for several New York establishments. One was "Hinton's Military and Sportsmen's Warehouse and Manufactory," where one could buy "on reasonable terms" a variety of muskets, pistols, cartridge boxes, trout rods "of all descriptions," single and multiplying reels, sinkers, hooks, files of all types, and even boxing gloves. William Read & Son carried similar goods in Boston, as did Samuel Bradler's store at the "Sign of the Angler." By the 1840s the *Spirit* had notices for cricket bats and stumps, such as those manufactured by Philadelphia's William Bradshaw, reflecting an expanding notion of "sport."

The trend toward specialization represented by these firms was slow to evolve before the Civil War, but one can find clear evidence of public awareness that a separate industry was emerging, one that supplied goods and services for consumption during leisure time. Leisure was a small but special niche for the sharp entrepreneur such as Jonas Chickering, who rationalized the production of pianos in his Boston factory during the 1830s. Perhaps the best example of the markets and the fortunes to be made in sports lies in the career of Michael Phelan, arguably America's first prominent sports hustler. Phelan, an Irish immigrant, began in the 1840s as a "marker" in a New York billiards saloon. After a sojourn to the California gold country, he returned to New York in the early 1850s to make and sell his own billiards equipment. In 1857 a local credit agent could find little in his reputation or his means to warrant a good rating and characterized him in 1860 as a "fast man, betting on horse races or anything that turns up." Yet it was also obvious that the firm of Phelan and Collender was doing a "large business." Phelan's promotions through playing tours and books all paid off. By 1866 his personal worth was estimated to be at least $250,000.

One of Phelan's major competitors was the Cincinnati firm of Swiss immigrant John Brunswick. A carriagemaker by training, Brunswick built his first billiard table in 1845, viewing it as a challenge in woodworking as much as a source of profit. His craftsmanship found an eager market, however, and within two years orders were arriving from cities as distant as New Orleans and Chicago. By the time of the Civil War the "J.M. Brunswick & Brother" company was operating a large factory that employed seventy-five hands and produced $200,000 worth of tables.

Phelan and Brunswick were extraordinary successes in a young sporting goods industry. Although field sports and horse racing (thoroughbred and harness) enjoyed widespread popularity in the antebellum years, there was no real national market for brand-name goods related to those activities. Similarly, while rowing, cricket, and baseball were gaining participants and spectators, their equipment production had not yet developed beyond the limited artisan stage. The 1860 *Census of Manufacturers* reflects the marketplace: federal enumerators recognized discrete categories for billiard cues, billiard and bagatelle tables, pianos, playing cards, toys, and games; there is no mention of cricket or baseball equipment. In the next two decades, however, sporting goods would become a separate segment of manufacture.

Market Recognition, 1860–1880

The next twenty years saw the clear emergence of a sporting goods industry. The conditions—social, economic, and cultural—were ripe for it, despite or perhaps because of the Civil War. The expansion of rail lines, improvements in printing, and advances in production technology combined with anxieties about social dissolution, exhaustion, and degeneracy to provide a most opportune moment for marketing products linked to wholesome recreation. But even fertile ground requires husbandry and cultivation. This was especially true for such "new" sports as baseball, croquet, football, tennis, and bicycling, which most Americans viewed as exotic and frivolous indulgences. It was one thing to write an article or book promoting the value of a new activity; it was quite another to risk capital and credit in the production or sale of sports equipment. Nevertheless, venturesome souls did gamble on opportunity. During this period two types of entrepreneurs emerged, both in manufacturing and in retail. The first were those who diversified into the "new" sports, either from field sports or from a nonsports product. The second, often athletes or former athletes, opened businesses solely devoted to sports. Their combined activities meant that Americans could for the first time enjoy a steady and increasing supply of finished sporting goods.

Baseball offers the clearest example. As early as the 1850s its promoters had proclaimed it the "National Pastime," and growth in participation had been impressive, but there is little evidence of a baseball goods industry until after the Civil War. The 1870 census was the first to list "baseball goods" as a discrete category of manufacture, and even then it showed a paltry five companies—three in New York and two in Massachusetts—employing a total of only 118 workers, with an aggregate capital value of $24,500 and product value of $72,605. This is in sharp contrast to a frequently cited claim in the *Baseball Player's Chronicle* of 17 June 1867 that every city had a "regular bat and ball manufactory . . . turning out bats by the thousands and balls by the hundreds."

The discrepancy may be explained in part by the *Chronicle*'s boosterism and in part by the still-casual nature of the census itself. It is more likely, however, that many a "bat and ball manufactory" was a sidelight enterprise in a larger firm. The credit ledgers of R.G. Dun & Co. show, for instance, that Charles W. Jencks & Brothers in Providence produced paper boxes, particularly those used in the packaging of perfumes. As early as 1875 and into the next decade, however, the firm also operated the "American Base Ball Co." In similar fashion, the Philadelphia firm of J.D. Shibe & Co. was listed as a manufacturer of "fancy leather goods," but in 1882 its credit report notes that it had "been in the manufacture of base balls for a long time." By 1883 about sixty hands were devoted to the baseball side of the business, and a year later the firm's account lists it as a baseball manufacturer—appropriate recognition of its conversion into the expanding industry. Apparently, brother Benjamin Shibe had thought the family too slow in adjusting to the market: three years earlier he had taken his $400 interest and joined the Reach Sporting Goods firm.

The R.G. Dun credit ledgers do not indicate exactly when these firms first diversified to include baseball products, but their doing so appear to represent the sort of gradual activity that baseball promoters recognized and census enumerators missed. As late as 1895 the *Sporting News* reported that the production of uniforms was not far removed from the days of "putting it out" to undisclosed manufacture. Many entrepreneurs were slow to convert to all-sports production. Hillerich and Bradsby, now famous for their baseball bats, began in 1859 as a small wood-turning shop in Louisville, where J. Frederich Hillerich crafted such products as bedposts, handrails, balusters, tenpins, and bowling balls. When his son "Bud" encouraged him in 1884 to expand into the production of baseball bats, the conservative father resisted, seeing greater market potential in the current rage for swinging butter churn booms, and little profit in a "mere game." Only slowly did Bud's persistence succeed in converting the firm.

Other entrepreneurs were more eager. Often athletes themselves, with a feel for the market's potential, they typically began in retail operations, which required less initial capital investment. Their established reputations as athletes doubtless aided their young businesses, but it was aggressive promotion of sport and careful integration into manufacture that enabled some to become giants in the field. Al Reach, celebrated subject of an 1863 bidding war between several supposedly "amateur" baseball teams, wound up in Philadelphia; by 1869 he had opened a retail outlet there for cigars and other goods, including baseball equipment. In 1874 his stock's estimated value was $3,000 to $4,000. Throughout the next decade he expanded his line of sporting goods, probably first selling the "Reach" name brand by farming out manufacture to existing companies such as the Shibe brothers, who made baseballs as a sideline. Benjamin Shibe's defection to Reach may have been the catalyst for expansion; in any case, by the late 1880s Reach had integrated into manufacture and had agents around the country selling his brand.

Another professional ballplayer who turned to the new market was George Wright, who opened his Boston store in 1871 while he was still playing for the local Red Stockings. His salary was the store's only capital in the early years, but in 1879 Wright brought a wealthy partner, H.A. Ditson, into the firm. Despite generous credit the partners were cautious and in 1881 carried a stock worth only about $5,000, yet two years later they were "monopolizing the bulk of the trade" in Boston. Recognizing the value of celebrity status, Wright began to market goods under the name brand Wright and Ditson. For a number of years his fellow star John F. Morrill served as the firm's general manager.

The greatest exemplar of the gamesman turned goodsman was Albert G. Spalding, who started later but would within two decades outstrip and silently acquire both Reach and Wright. In March 1876, however, A.G. and his brother J. Walter opened a modest Chicago retail store, which they claimed to credit agents was capitalized at about $2,500. Spalding's cash sales policy, his prominence and salary as a ballplayer, and his Rockford, Illinois, property clearly bolstered his credit, but it was his shrewdness in marketing and backward integration that ensured rapid growth. Within two years the Spaldings' stock of goods had more than tripled, to about $12,000 in value. Late in 1878 the Spaldings and their wealthy brother-in-law William J. Brown purchased half the stock of Wilkins Manufacturing Co., a firm in Hastings, Michigan, that was already making bats, skates, fishing gear, and croquet equipment. For the first time in America a sporting goods house began on a large scale to sell goods of its own make.

Reach, Wright, and Spalding were noteworthy successes in the sporting goods industry. Hundreds of others had an eye on their marketplace, especially at the retail level: hardware stores, department stores, and the old field sports "depots" diversified their lines to include goods for baseball, croquet, and other sports. A similar expansion occurred in manufacturing. The census of 1880 counted eighty-six firms in the newly defined category of "sporting goods" manufacture—almost double the number found in 1870 for baseball, croquet, and field sports equipment combined (guns were a separate category). And despite the severe economic woes of the 1870s, aggregate capital in sporting goods manufacture had more than doubled, to $1,444,750—the largest rate of increase until the 20th century if one excludes the bicycle industry.

Still, this figure was less than one-fifth the capital value of, for example, the fancy paper box industry, and some credit agents were skeptical about the prospects for sporting goods. Dun's Brooklyn agent noted in 1875 that the new firm of Heege and Kiffee faced a cloudy market; chances for success "in their locality" appeared "somewhat doubtful," since the demand for "this class of goods" was "very limited." As late as 1882 a Boston agent thought it unlikely that there was business enough for Wright and Ditson to make money. The credit agents were wisely cautious, for in the 1870s entrepreneurs were probably hurtling ahead of market demand.

Competition in the Marketplace, 1880–1900

If the 1870s were a period of market recognition, with entrepreneurs becoming aware that sports could provide more than an artisan-level trade, the 1880s saw a mass of capitalists on the make. Product markets became arenas of competition among manufacturers and retailers easily as intense as the rivalries emerging on the diamond or the gridiron. Improved economic conditions doubtless had an encouraging effect. So did the nation's stronger embrace of physical activity. The calls had been issued by reformers for over forty years; the 1880s, however, brought peace, relative prosperity, and expanded public space to go along with a heightened consciousness of the benefits of sport and exercise. Equally important, increased numbers of sporting goods manufacturers and retailers expanded their efforts to attract consumers.

There were few barriers to entry in the 1880s, especially with infant sports like tennis and football. These replicated the cycle of initial dependence on imports and small-scale manufacture. Wright and Ditson, Bancroft of Rhode Island, and D.W. Granbery of New York all prospered through their efforts in the promotion of tennis. Lester C. Dole's small New Haven store, opened in 1880, made a strong name for itself by supplying the prominent college football teams with ''official'' imported English rugby balls.

Around the country, entrepreneurs moved into sporting goods production and distribution. In 1888 the Rawlings Brothers opened in St. Louis, promising a ''full-line emporium'' of all goods, although they also claimed a specialty in baseball uniforms and gloves. Rawlings had strong competition in St. Louis from C. & W. McClean, which diversified into the new lines from the production and sale of field sports equipment. Stronger still was the Meachan Arms Company, which moved beyond guns and powder into baseballs and bicycles. In Philadelphia the Tryon brothers expanded their line of sporting goods. In Covington, Kentucky, Philip Goldsmith was moving out of toy production and into sports, having recognized that cheap baseballs were his hottest product. Through mergers, his firm eventually grew into the giant MacGregor Company.

Firms scrambled for market share. Al Reach sought control through rationalized production, greater volume, and wider price ranges. Under the direction of Benjamin Shibe, the Reach plant in Philadelphia set standards for quality and consistency. While cheap balls could be made by covering a compressed pulp of poor yarn and rubber, the better balls required careful attention to winding layers of yarn around a small rubber center. The outer cover of leather was always hand-stitched. High-grade balls remained a labor-intensive product, although machines developed in the 1890s automated the winding process. In 1899 the Reach plant had machines said to wind upward of 18,000 balls a day, but only four years earlier the *Sporting News* estimated that over a thousand workers toiled inside the building preparing the balls for the final covers, which were stitched on by hundreds of women doing sweatshop labor at home. Writer A. H. Spink marveled at the range of balls the plant could produce, from the $1.50 Association Ball to the nickel ball used all over the country's back fields and side streets. The style names were dazzling: Deadball, Bounding Rock Ball, Out of Sight Ball, Cock of the Walk Ball. Spink was further amazed that Reach could produce a good leather glove selling for as little as twenty-five cents. Even the top-of-the-line Buckskin fielder's glove was priced at only $3.00.

Because such quantities of sporting goods could bring ''clutter'' to the market-place, manufacturers responded by promoting brand recognition. One of their shrewdest practices was the publication of "guidebooks." Of course, introductions to sports activities were nothing new. Treatises on field sports date back at least to Xenophon; Dame Juliana Berners and Sir Izaak Walton carried a long tradition into the modern age. And as noted earlier, there were many "boy's books" and adult guides to sports of all kinds, often providing details about the construction of equipment. What proliferated in the late 1800s, though, were guidebooks published by sporting goods manufacturers who promoted activities in the hope of creating customers for *their brands* of finished products.

Baseball is a good example. As David Voigt has showed, the earliest guidebooks—*Beadles Dime Base Ball Player* (begun 1860) and *Dewitt's Base Ball Guide* (begun 1868)—came from firms outside of baseball. This began to change in 1876, when Spalding got exclusive rights to publish the "official" book of the National League—and at the same time slyly began to produce a separate *Spalding's Official Baseball Guide,* the word "official" clearly intended to convince the consumer that he was purchasing the league book. Ethics aside, the Spalding guide was probably a better purchase; at ten cents it included not only the league rules and constitution but also records, descriptions of the past season's play, instructions, and history. The reader was also introduced to Spalding products. Peter Levine has carefully documented Spalding's efforts to expand both the guide's circulation and its advertising.

Spalding was not alone. In 1883, Reach began publishing his own guide, which was "official" to the American Association and later to the American League. Then George Wright joined the fray, publishing the "official" guide of the Union Association in 1884. In all cases the guides appeared in March and April, their promotional campaigns helping to elicit the annual spring renewal of baseball euphoria.

A major promotion medium was the *Sporting News.* Advertising in the *News* meant advertising largely for market share, since one could assume that readers of this specialty magazine were already hooked on sports in general and baseball in particular. The *News* began publication in 1886 and quickly rivaled the *Clipper* and *Sporting Life* for preeminence in the field of sports papers. Within a year it claimed a circulation approaching 60,000. In 1890 it began a Chicago edition to supplement its home edition in St. Louis. The growing list of advertisers from around the country makes it a useful source for analyzing competition within the industry.

Manufacturers had a compelling interest in advertising. Wherever or however the consumer might purchase an article of sporting goods—through the mail or at a hardware store, general store, department store, or sportsman's "depot"—the manufacturer wanted him to buy a specific brand. Spalding, Reach, Rawlings, Meacham, and McClean continually presented their names to the readers of the *News*, especially in the spring, when athletes and their managers would be in the market for new uniforms and equipment. Smaller firms, too—Keefe and Becannon of New York, Chicago's John Wilkinson and Jenny and Graham—tried to capitalize on the baseball wars of the period. Rawlings ran full-page ads offering large discounts for bulk orders. These seemed to overwhelm the announcements of competitors like H.H. Kiffe of Brooklyn, who promised "no discounts to anyone."

Manufacturers also fought to promote brand recognition by acquiring the rights to supply a top league with the "official" ball. In the late 1870s Spalding wrested this advantage from L.H. Mahn of Boston by agreeing to *pay* the National League a dollar a dozen for the privilege of supplying *free* balls. Reach soon had a similar deal with the American Association; Wright and Ditson became the official ball for the Union Association; and Keefe and Becannon claimed to manufacture the "real" thing for the Brotherhood League.

The struggle did not stop at the major league level, since consumers might be tied emotionally to a local minor or amateur league. By 1884 Spalding had gained recognition from the Northwestern League, the American College Baseball Association, the Louisiana Amateur Baseball Association, and the Iron and Oil Association. Nor did he lose any time in grabbing a share of the expanding football market. Though an 1908 ad noted that the firm was sole agent for the British "Lillywhite Regulation Football," three years later the ball of notice was the Spalding "Official Intercollegiate Foot Ball," which had been "adopted for the second year by the Intercollegiate Association and must be used in Match Games."

Manufacturers were so liberal in their proclamations of "official" status that one must be ever suspicious; the hapless consumer was confronted with "league" balls produced by virtually every baseball manufacturer. Rawlings, which offered a minimum nine-inning guarantee for its top-of-the-line baseball, claimed that it was not only any ball's equal but was made by the same factory that had produced the National League balls for years.

Actual adoption by a recognized league was certainly worth the effort, however, and a related means of product distinction was an ad carrying a personal endorsement: from a satisfied customer ("Every ball player's batting average who uses [these bats] should increase at least fifty percent") or, better yet, a player or manager. In 1889 the young Rawlings Company published an endorsement from "Der Boss," Chris Von der Ahe, who noted his satisfaction and his promise to purchase more Rawlings goods for his St. Louis team. Sometimes the endorser's name could become a generic term. In January 1890 Reach advertised its new "Reach Mit [*sic*] Glove," as "manufactured under the personal supervision of Mr. Harry Decker, catcher of the Philadelphia Baseball Club." Just five months later the Paul Buckley Glove Company of Chicago included "Deckers" among their glove styles, without further reference to the well-known player.

Endorsements presented other problems of timing as well, as Reach discovered. When boxing gloves and Queensbury rules gave boxing a veneer of respectability, especially after 1892 when James Corbett defeated John L. Sullivan in the first gloved heavyweight championship, Reach moved quickly to run ads for his brand-name gloves, which he claimed had been used by the famous pugilists. A year later he began selling "Corbett (Trade-Mark) Boxing Gloves." Unfortunately for Reach, in March 1897 a large endorsement by Gentleman Jim appeared in the same issue of the *Sporting News* that described how Bob Fitzsimmons had pummeled the champion and taken the title. Corbett's promise to "win in a walk and Reach Fitz with Reach Gloves" must have drawn snickers from readers.

While every firm was seeking increased market share, Spalding was perhaps the most aggressive and most successful. By 1892 the company had silently acquired Reach, Wright and Ditson, Peck & Snyder, the St. Lawrence River Skiff, Canoe & Steam Launch Co., and George Barnard & Co., even though for years the subsidiaries continued to offer their own name brands. Spalding was not the only expansionist, however; in 1898 Rawlings acquired the vast manufacturing plant of the Meacham Arms Company, a move that vaulted the firm toward the top of the competition.

Indeed, it is a distortion to think of Spalding as a "monopolist." He might have aspired to monopoly, but no manufacturer controlled channels of distribution that well. Spalding complained bitterly about jobbers and mail-order houses that discounted goods, and in 1899 he began selling directly to retailers on a "one-price" basis. But he could not keep Montgomery Ward or Sears from succeeding in just that strategy. At the "high" end of equipment lines, his products faced competition from such specialists as the Ted Kennedy glove company of Peoria and the Waldo Claflin shoe company in Philadelphia. Moreover, major teams such as the Harvard football club often preferred to place their orders with smaller local firms, where they could exert greater control on design.

Except for the bicycle trade, there were few barriers to entry into sporting goods. The market was expanding, manufacturing was not capital intensive, and distribution was dominated by independent wholesalers and retailers who took on the brands that would sell. By 1900 the census listed 144 sporting goods manufacturers (excluding bicycles and billiards), a 67 percent increase from 1880; aggregate product value had more than doubled to $3,633,396. Given the continued existence of "sidelight" manufacturing, these figures are clearly conservative. Retail outlets expanded as well. In 1899, Spalding and Bros. claimed to have 20,000 accounts on their books. This number—which doubtless included hardware stores, department stores, old sporting goods depots, and younger specialty stores—suggests the extent of a distribution system that also involved direct mail and extended from the posh houses of Fifth Avenue to Bowery pawn shops that did a brisk trade in boxing gloves.

Expanding the Market for Finished Goods and Games

Sporting goods, then, found a competitive marketplace. Manufacturers like Spalding enjoyed a strong presence, but there was plenty of room for more. There was also enough room and enough cooperation to allow trade associations of manufacturers and dealers to develop in the early 1900s. Publishers had already sensed enough industry identity to establish trade journals: the *Sporting Goods Gazette* begin in 1888; eleven years later Charles C. Spink started the *Sporting Goods Dealer,* which continues to this day.

This combination of competitiveness and special identity was reflected in an 1889 advertisement from R.E. Dimick, a St. Louis retailer. Dimick highlighted the prominent name brands he carried—Wright and Ditson tennis goods, Abbey & Imbries fishing tackle, Gray's body protectors. Reach's bats—all testimony to consumer awareness. At the same time, however, he emphasized that "we are not in the gun business and for that reason we only cater to the wants of the athletes and gymnasts." Dimick, I suspect, did not mean to say that guns could not be part of a sport but only that his business was specialized. He wanted to position himself in the distinct area of commerce that I have called the sport industry.

Like Dimick, Albert Spalding was eager to promote the *special* nature of his products. In one series of ads that ran in the spring of 1893, the copy each week offered folksy commentary on the benefits of various Spalding baseball products: balls, bats, chest protectors, shoes. A description of Spalding bats began with a story about the pathetic "crank" who couldn't even hit a ball until his team captain insisted that he throw away the " 'Jonah' Bat that was made for him by a wheelwright up in the country," but with a new Spalding bat, he was soon leading the team. Then there was the hapless runner, staggering between bases in clodhoppers habitually purchased "from some inexperienced cobbler," who might be able to fit the lad but "not with Base Ball shoes." This was the fundamental message of all manufacturers: sporting goods were specialized products, not to be entrusted to the hands of old-style general craftsmen.

Even as they competed with each other, sporting goods entrepreneurs worked to expand the market for all. They were hardly content to leave promotional efforts in the hands of liberal theologians and urban reformers. One method was to sponsor sports contests, as boatbuilders and gunmakers had done for years. In the 1850s Michael Phelan had carried the art to new heights on behalf of billiards, and in 1869 George B. Ellard, who owned a "Baseball Depot" in Cincinnati, was active in the formation of the professional Red Stockings. A.G. Spalding too sought to expand the market for his goods by investing in such promotions. Best known was the "world tour" of 1888-89, in which his Chicago ball club played a series of exhibitions against an "all-star" team in venues as far away as Australia, Ceylon, Egypt, Italy, France, England, Scotland, and Ireland. He also sponsored amateur baseball tournaments in England, the Philippines, and Canada.

Though bold enough to seek a global market, Spalding knew that the foundation for profits lay at home, where he championed sports of all kinds. He donated "Play Ball" trophies to school leagues around the country. Following a successful association with the Paris Olympics of 1900, his firm designed the stadium, organized the athletics competition, and provided equipment for the St. Louis Games of 1904. Although he never failed to nurture sales of his own brands, these promotions were aimed at increasing general activity.

Golf is another sport that the Spalding company promoted in America; it was the first to begin large-scale American manufacture of golf clubs (1894) and golf balls (1898). More important, in 1899 Spalding financed a national tour by Harry Vardon, one of the sport's premier players.

No such tour would have been possible, of course, without the prior existence of a circuit of golf courses around the country. It would have been out of the question as late as 1890, when George Wright imported his first order of golf equipment from England. The game was then virtually unknown in America; the St. Andrews "course" in Yonkers, New York, was only two years old and hardly a landmark. Hence, displaying the logic of an experienced promoter, Wright wrote to the Boston Parks Commissioners requesting a permit for the "privilege to play in Franklin Park the game of Golf." Since the commissioners were known to be protective of the park's tranquillity, Wright assured them that the exhibition "would not draw a crowd, as the interest in the game is only with the players, there is nothing to the playing of the game to cause a noise, or injure the shribery [sic] in the park." On the strength of Wright's reputation and assurances the commissioners granted the request, and Boston had its first public display of the game that rapidly became the hallmark of the country club set. Wright's continued promotion led to the establishment of public links in Franklin Park; more important, the development by 1899 of twenty-nine courses around Boston meant increased sales of golf equipment.

While George Wright was promoting the game of golf, J.M. Raymond of Boston was trying to resurrect interest in roller-skating, which had been in vogue in the 1860s. The Raymond Skate Company was a firm with a sputtering history. Organized in 1884 with a capital stock of $10,000, it manufactured the "Raymond" skate, which enjoyed brisk sales initially. By 1886, however, demand had lagged. Four years later Raymond reopened the "Olympian Skating Club" in the Mechanics Building, and the *Sporting Goods Gazette* credited this move with reviving "the once popular craze of roller skating in this city."

Like Wright and Spalding, Raymond and others realized that the purveyor of goods had to be a promoter of activity. As Albert Pope wrote in 1895, bicycle manufacturers knew "at the outset" in the 1870s that they must "educate the people to the advantage of this invigorating sport"; hence, "with this end in view, the best literature that was to be had on the subject was gratuitously distributed." This was true in all sports. When George David announced the opening of his new store in Worcester, Massachusetts, he added that he wanted to sell sports as well as equipment. He promised that his store would have a gathering spot where "the sporting papers of the country would be kept on file." When the Rawlings Brothers moved to larger quarters in St. Louis, they featured a "wigwam" where sportsmen could congregate and "swap hunting and fishing stories to their hearts content." The provision of meeting rooms, the dissemination of information and instruction, the sponsorship of leagues and contests all became part and parcel of the selling function.

In short, sporting goods manufacturers and dealers did not simply fatten off some vast instinctive demand. As Arjun Appadurai argues generally, demand is neither a "mechanical" response to production nor a "bottomless natural appetite." Nineteenth-century sporting goods firms knew they could not rely on a fickle public which, as Thomas Wentworth Higginson realized, was always hungering for novelty, ever "dissatisfied with last winter's skates, with the old boat, and with the family pony.'' Too many velocipedes, tennis rackets, and roller skates lay in barns and cellars collecting dust, rust, and mold—testimony to fleeting profits.

Few serious entrepreneurs wait around for demand. They create customers. In order to do so, sporting goods firms became the front line of promoters and educators during the great sports surge of the late 19th century. Retailers especially were face-to-face instructors, teaching not only the use of equipment but the value of physical activity. Reformers could pen all sorts of rationales for the benefits of active sports in opposing their favorite menace, ''commercial amusements,'' but dealers saw the enemy up close. If they didn't act, they went out of business. As one dealer wrote in the early 20th century: ''If you don't do something to encourage sports, the nickelodeons are going to win hands down.'' He suggested the promotion of youth leagues.

As they competed, then, dealers and manufacturers expanded demand with aggressive marketing. Their tactics included ingenious mixes of the four P's associated with modern marketing: product, price, place, and promotion. Designs became safer and easier to use. There were inexpensive models of most equipment (inexpensive Japanese sports items started arriving in the early 20th century). Furthermore, the industry's sense of product always emphasized information about the craft and lore of the sport. Always in the forefront, Spalding developed a series of volumes in the 1880s called the Library of American Sports, and his American Sports Publishing Company soon churned out three hundred publications explaining the nuances of different sports, extolling their virtues, and hawking Spalding products.

Smart retailers in turn advertised and sold these and other guides. ''We make a specialty of Sporting Books of every description,'' announced R.E. Dimick of St. Louis. ''They are very good to have when settling disputes.'' For the homebody or the hot-stove leaguer, sports knowledge was increasingly available through a system of distribution that linked goods with game forms. Albert Applin has argued that much of the remarkable spread of basketball in the 1890s may well have been related to the circulation power of Spalding's *Official Basketball Guide,* which immediately gave the young game exposure in thousands of outlets like Dimick's and, along with the YMCA's promotion, resulted in what was arguably the fastest national diffusion of any sport before or since.

Realizing an Industry and Institutionalizing Sport

The marketing efforts of sporting goods firms clearly expanded opportunity and interest in active play among a wide range of Americans; Spalding, Reach, Wright, Dimick, Rawlings, and the rest had a serious interest in democratizing leisure activities. But democratizing should entail more than just the opportunity to participate; it should include an opportunity to determine the nature of participation—and here the industry tended to part company with democracy. Success in the marketplace depended on packaging and selling *preformed* games and goods. Manufacturers and dealers had an interest in innovation, but they had a greater stake in the stable growth of widely understood products. To achieve it, they established ties with other specialists who had similar interests, particularly coaches, players, journalists, and the administrators of leagues and associations. They all shared a vision: to be providers of particular forms of activity, which they would sell to the public. Their alliances resulted in mutual legitimacy and market influence, the foundations of a larger sport industry. Every successful partnership *inside* the industry, however, established firmer boundaries on the range and styles of sports offered to consumers on the *outside*. This was how *some* games became *the* games.

Just as Spalding aggressively promoted standardized goods made by rationalized production, so also did he and his colleagues champion scientific action, crafted by expert coaches, trainers, and managers. What counted most, though, was the circulation of inexpensive, standardized *packages* of expert knowledge that linked sporting goods to game forms. Guidebooks were a perfect medium; so were such specialty booklets as Henry Chadwick's *Technical Terms of Baseball*, published by Spalding in 1897. Another Spalding product, "Professor" William Elmer's *Boxing*, promised in 1903 that "any boy with the aid of this book can become an expert boxer." Catalogues offered ready-made instruction and ready-made goods through the mail. The 1886 Peck & Snyder *Price List of Out & Indoor Sports and Pastimes* offered "Goodyear's Pocket Gymnasium" and "Prof. D. L. Dowd's Home Exerciser," each with accompanying texts written by experts.

Aligning with *scattered* experts and scientists of sport and exercise, however, would not ensure the more stable or *institutionalized* markets that sporting goods firms desired. An expert's endorsement might give a product *legitimacy* but would not necessarily provide *authority* or legitimate domination in the marketplace. Authority depended on what Paul Starr has called effective "gatekeeping," or strategic positioning between technology, expertise, and consumers. Starr has masterfully outlined the gatekeeping of the new medical profession: in the late nineteenth century physicians successfully positioned themselves so that consumers increasingly had to work through them to enjoy the benefits of medical expertise and technology. The concept is valuable also to an understanding of the way sports evolved.

I have shown how Reach and others sought market share by gaining or claiming a product's status as the "official" ball of this or that league. Likewise, when Peck & Snyder introduced its new tennis ball in 1886, the firm happily announced that it had been "adopted by the United States National Lawn Tennis Association and by the Intercollegiate Association, as the Regulation Ball to be used in all match games." There was a similar message on lacrosse balls; since there was no American governing body in lacrosse, however, it could only state that Peck & Snyder published the rules of the Montreal Lacrosse Club and that this ball had been "adopted by all the leading clubs." Spalding aggressively pursued such sanctions, seemingly from every association in existence, claiming more exclusivity than he actually hand—though his influence with the National League, the Intercollegiate Football Association, and the Amateur Athletic Union is obvious.

Endorsements and official sanctions were important credentials for any piece of equipment, but authority worked in two directions. Just as an endorsement helped the tangible goods in the marketplace, so too did "official" goods provide legitimacy and authority to the distant endorsers. Walter Camp understood this very well. His *Book of College Sports* cautioned: "It is best that [football] players should never use anything but the regulation ball" and duly noted that two brands met the standard: The British "J. Lillywhite" and the American "Spalding." At the same time, he added that a regulation ball "should bear the stamp, 'Adopted by the Intercollegiate Foot-ball Association.'" Every Spalding ball repaid Camp's endorsement with interest, for every person who bought an official IFA ball paid homage to Camp's version of the game. A similar process occurred in all competitive sports—for example, track and field, women's basketball, and field hockey, where leagues and governing associations emerged to standardize and regulate competition.

Historians have recognized the importance and power of these organizations but have not examined *how* they achieved control. It appears that much of their authority stemmed from their symbiotic affiliations with sporting goods firms. Tangible goods, then, built up the structure of authority like "coral islands."

I do not mean to suggest that a few moguls had a plan to steal sports from "the people." The relationship between sporting goods and governing bodies shows that in fact the providers were often at odds. While equipment helped to legitimate control by leagues and associations, product innovations could challenge and stretch the boundaries of rules and styles of play. Football is a case in point. In 1902 Rawlings ran advertisements for a new line of football equipment, designed by the company's product genius, William P. Whitley. Aptly named "Whitley's Football Armor," the line included a jacket "reinforced with cane ribs which, when struck, equally distributes the force of the blow, thus preventing injury to the player." Ironically, amid a growing controversy over football violence and governance, protective uniforms doubtless *increased* the levels of aggressive play.

A similar boomerang apparently occurred in ice hockey, where protective equipment developed in tandem with the slashing, hard-checking "Ottawa" style of play. Elliott Gorn notes that the same thing happened in boxing: manufacturers such as Reach and Shibe claimed that their gloves would "preclude the possibility of injury or disfigurement," whereas in fact, gloves allow the slugger to be even more brutal in his attack because he has less fear of hand injury. Leagues and governing bodies, then, may sometimes embrace equipment that ultimately makes their sports less controllable.

Sporting goods can challenge in other ways. As manufacturers worked to "democratize" game forms, they developed equipment that simplified the activity. The safety bicycle was one example. So was Coburn Haskell's rubber-thread-wound golf ball, which turned more golfers into long hitters and caused wholesale changes in course design. Such pressures have led to many jousts between manufacturers and rulemakers; they continue today over specifications on ball dimples, club grooves, graphite bats, and oversized racquets, to name only a few.

Even as they pressed the boundaries of established rules, however, manufacturers did not radically challenge institutionalized sport. If anything, the occasional squabbles have further cemented the gatekeeping status of governing bodies, coaches, and other new experts. Just as the public increasingly bought ready-made equipment designed by product experts like William Whitley, so too they bought ready-made rules and ready-made styles of play crafted by governing bodies and expert coaches or players. As Donald Mrozek has argued, advertisements for training equipment—blocking sleds, tackling dummies, rowing machines—were liberally sprinkled with references to science. No wonder the public worshiped professional coaches and champion athletes: they were masters of a new science. Their knowledge of equipment and technique gave them what Burton Bledstein has called "special power over worldly experience."

Their authority came from their working *within* the structures of the emerging sport industry. They offered what the public seemed to want: mastery, efficiency, and victory within the rules they had helped to write. Yet many critics protested the consequences for sports in the schools and colleges. Their feelings are summarized in a scathing 1929 report on American college sports, published by the Carnegie Foundation for the Advancement of Teaching:

If athletics are to be "educational," the player must be taught to do his own thinking. In every branch of athletics the strategy of the game should not be beyond the capacity of the alertly-minded undergraduate. As matters now stand, no branch owes even a vestige of its strategy to the undergraduates engaged. Such matters are the affair of the coach.

Such an outburst, which typified the profession of physical education, revealed serious marketing myopia. Physical educators and sports reformers were well intended but out of touch. They wrote articles about educational sports, but they could not understand, as Hal Lawson notes, "that not all knowledge is of equal value in the eyes of society's members." Coaches offered what players, college presidents, boosters, and fans wanted: mastery and victory in *preformed* packages.

Moreover, reformers failed to see that school and college sports could not be isolated from the wider marketplace of goods and game forms, flowing in vast circulation among manufacturers, retailers, professional leagues, and their associated experts. If equipment, techniques, and styles of play emanated from *other* providers, they could not be transformed merely by hope. Only women educators realized this, developed their *own* styles of play, and until the last two decades enjoyed a special sphere of authority. Successful reformers, then, had to become active providers of preformed play.

Indeed, this is a peculiar and recurring irony in the history of sport. Reformers do not democratize. For instance, at the turn of the century when some reformers became "play specialists," they developed "play curriculums" and scientific equipment, thus nurturing their own profession of recreation, which sought legitimacy and authority for programming the leisure time of children and adults in playgrounds and community centers around the country. Even the current reformers—proponents of "new games" that are supposedly educational, creative, cooperative, and nondebilitating—market packages of "Earthballs," "stretch-ropes," and "bataca boffers" along with instruction booklets, thus themselves becoming the experts of a new science of creative play.

Has this industry of providers strangled sport as play? Is sport now part of some mass culture of leisure sold along with radios, records, and videotapes to an inert and pliant public? I don't believe so. Players at all levels create their own styles of play, their own rules, and their own meanings. Players and spectators are always at once both producers and consumers of sports and games. In their dual role they may press out the boundaries of structure. What actually occurs on the fields, on the playgrounds, and in the stands may differ from what the providers intended.

Nevertheless, the spread of standardized goods does reflect and support the spread of standardized behaviors and values. Providers do make buying or adopting packaged goods and games easier than "free play." Control in the marketplace does make a difference. A relative handful of rules committees do control the game forms played by most Americans, and relatively few manufacturers do supply the goods used at all levels. For almost a hundred years this network of expert coaches, journalists, administrators, manufacturers, and dealers has largely shaped the boundaries of American sport.

Unfortunately, today's periodic laments about sports—accusations of commercialism, violence, alienation—are typically directed at individual teams, leagues, and associations. These are myopic views. Control and influence are much more complex. Philosophers and critics who seek to change the nature of sport in America must first understand its complex history from the inside out.

CHAPTER 9

Preludes to the NCAA: Early Failures of Faculty Intercollegiate Athletic Control

Ronald A. Smith

When Chancellor MacCracken of New York University in 1905 called for an inter-institutional faculty conference to decide whether intercollegiate football should be banned or reformed, the resulting birth of the National Collegiate Athletic Association was not the first attempt to bring about faculty control of intercollegiate athletics. Neither was the creation of the Intercollegiate Conference of Faculty Representatives (Big Ten) in 1895. The movement toward inter-institutional faculty control of athletics began a generation before the NCAA, when faculties from Princeton and Harvard Universities independently formed faculty athletic committees. Concern about the inability or unwillingness of students to control their own athletic programs initiated the faculty responses. Within a few years a move by faculty to create inter-institutional control of student games was instituted in eastern colleges. Though these faculty reforms were structurally unsuccessful, they were the harbingers of faculty-controlled athletic conferences and a national athletic body.

A theme of rugged individualism on the part of college students in running their own extracurriculum pervades the period before the NCAA was born. Like the industrialists who favored a *laissez faire* policy in the late nineteenth century, students were reluctant to share authority in athletics with their academic superiors in a non-academic area. Similarly there was strong resistance to giving up individual institutional autonomy over college sports in favor of greater control and the collective good. Nevertheless, as America more generally advanced into the Progressive Period of the 1890s and early 1900s with increasing social legislation, American college athletics progressed in a similar direction. By 1905 and the creation of the NCAA, it was apparent to a number of college faculties and administrations that a generation and more of principally *laissez faire* attitudes

This article is reprinted with permission from the *Research Quarterly for Exercise and Sport,* Vol. 54 (1983). The *Research Quarterly for Exercise and Sport* is a publication of the American Alliance for Health, Physical Education, Recreation, and Dance, 1990 Association Drive, Reston, VA 22091.

toward student-controlled intercollegiate athletics had not been successful. By the early 1900s, there was a growing belief that unless some type of collective action above the level of student control were taken, intercollegiate athletics might not survive at some institutions. Only a crisis in football, the dominating college game from the 1890s on, brought to an end the lengthy period of rugged individualism in college athletics.

Faculty Control and the First Athletic Committees

Almost from the beginning of intercollegiate sports, there was a concern for institutional control of athletics. President McCosh in 1874 alerted his Princeton Board of Trustees to the problems of athletics. "It is a nice question," McCosh reported, "whether evils may not arise from sports in no way under control of the College authorities." In due time, by the early 1880s, the Princeton faculty took action by forming the first college faculty athletic committee in an attempt to settle athletic questions. In the remaining two decades of the nineteenth century, nearly all colleges formed autonomous athletic committees of faculty members when problems arose. Yet, by the early twentieth century, despite attempts to do so, leading eastern colleges in athletics had not joined together to create an inter-institutional policy. Said Alexander Meiklejohn of Brown University only days before the NCAA was created at the close of 1905: "The independent Athletic Councils can never solve the problem of athletics. There is no provision for intercollegiate cooperation in the management of athletics." Meiklejohn stressed that there must be "mutual understanding and cooperation between competitors for the keeping of such agreements as are necessary for the welfare of sport." From the 1870s, when McCosh saw the need for institutional control, to the early 1900s, when Meiklejohn recognized the need for inter-institutional action, college authorities wrestled with what became a burning issue by 1905.

College faculties had been caught in a paradoxical situation with regard to extracurricular affairs, including athletics, since the extra-curriculum became important in the nineteenth century. Faculties had been traditionally involved only with the curriculum and with the conduct of students. Emphasis upon the classical curriculum and patriarchal control of student behavior, or "in loco parentis," was traditional. Most faculty members did not relish involvement in sport, which many thought was frivolous. Except when intercollegiate athletics became noticeably disruptive, nineteenth century faculty generally kept a *laissez faire* policy. When the student-controlled games began to disrupt classroom activities in the 1870s, however, college faculties became alarmed. One might ponder the statement of Yale's alumni advisor Walter Camp. The "Father of American Football" in 1885 said that "neither the faculties nor other critics assisted in building the structure of college athletics. In fact, they put some obstacles in the way. It is a structure," added Camp, "which students unaided have builded, and with pride they point to their labor, and love it more dearly for its very difficulties." The paradox was that while college faculties generally did not become involved in college sports, many felt the need to temper the

This *Harvard Lampoon* sketch (1883) helps illustrate the frustration of students with the Harvard faculty who had abandoned their traditional laissez faire approach to intercollegiate athletics and assumed control over the school's sports program.
Courtesy of Ronald A. Smith.

enthusiasm of students for their games. Albert Bushnell Hart, the Harvard historian, knew of what he wrote in 1890, for he had been involved with attempts to control Harvard athletics in the 1880s. "Busy Faculties," claimed Hart, "have neither the time nor the inclination to form and hold a consistent policy in regard to athletics." Hart indicated that often college faculties believed that student-controlled athletics "should be unrestricted or wholly prohibited."

Faculties, nevertheless, became involved in more than banning of student games. Princeton in 1881 and Harvard the next year organized the first two faculty athletic committees. The need for the committees in both cases was prompted by the excessive amount of faculty time which was being spent on intercollegiate athletic concerns in the latter 1870s and early 1880s. Of prime concern was the number of days athletes were spending away from their classes on trips to compete against other colleges. As the faculty would grant one concession to the baseball team, for example, the team would probe further for another out-of-town engagement, or the football team would want privileges similar to concessions given to the baseball team. This time-consuming process in faculty meetings created the need for a special faculty committee to replace the lengthy faculty discussions. It was natural, then, that the athletic committees formed at Princeton and Harvard in 1881 and 1882, created, as their first actions, regulations on when and where students could contest their games. The two athletic committees soon went well beyond questions of time and place as they took a paternalistic attitude in relation to student games. Harvard, for instance, required physical exams for all athletes and swimming competency for all crew members, while banning both contests against professionals and betting by athletes on their own contests. The Harvard committee further usurped authority previously held by the students when it began to veto student choices for trainers or coaches for various teams. Lastly, the faculty committee decided to restrict attendance at contests when it voted to build a fence around Jarvis Field, its main athletic grounds, to exclude "objectionable persons."

Other college faculties followed the path paved by Princeton and Harvard by founding athletic committees in the 1880s and 1890s. By 1900, nearly all colleges had athletic committees in which faculties had sole power to regulate athletics or, more commonly, in which faculties divided the authority with alumni and student representatives. Each institution drew up its own athletic rules. Conflicts arose when the regulations of one college gave it an athletic advantage over another. Individual institutional athletic committees acting without some form of inter-institutional controls led to almost constant arguments over eligibility rules and conditions of competition, such as the choice of officials or the use of professional coaches. As a result of inter-institutional athletic conflicts, calls for cooperative efforts to solve joint athletic problems were heard. Harvard and Princeton again led the way. Yale, the third member of the so-called Big Three which dominated college athletics, for two decades rejected efforts to form inter-institutional athletic rules.

The First Attempts at Inter-Institutional Controls

Charles W. Eliot, Harvard's long-time president, pointed the way toward inter-institutional control in 1882, when he wrote a letter to other New England college presidents. "Our Faculty," Eliot's letter stated, "wishes me to inquire if your Faculty would think it expedient first to prohibit your baseball nine from playing with professionals and secondly to limit the number of matches. . . ." Eliot indicated that his faculty was ready to take action against professionals, but believed that common action would be more effective. The faculty of Harvard's chief rival, Yale, considered Eliot's proposal but took no action. The Yale faculty inaction is believed to be the first of a generation-long series of *laissez faire* actions by Yale faculty and administration with regard to inter-institutional control of athletics. This *laissez faire* policy itself was largely due to Yale's unquestioned athletic supremacy during this period—the administration apparently felt there was little reason to tamper with success. The cooperative effort proposed by Eliot failed, and Harvard took action unilaterally to control professionalism.

The next year, the Harvard Athletic Committee sent a letter to Yale requesting its faculty to call a conference of leading colleges to discuss common intercollegiate athletic problems. When the Yale faculty declined, the Harvard Athletic Committee went ahead and issued a call for a late December, 1883 meeting. The issue of professionalism, especially of professional coaches, was the primary concern. Several weeks before the meeting, Dudley A. Sargent, one of Harvard's three-member athletic committee, visited five other colleges to obtain a cross-section of opinions about the use of professional coaches in colleges. Sargent talked to, among others, Walter Camp of Yale, the athletic committee of Princeton, a professor at Columbia, an Amherst physical educator, Edward Hitchcock and the president of Williams. Sentiment, according to Sargent, was decidedly against professional coaching.

The issue of professionalism was on the minds of the faculty conferees when eight institutions met in New York City on December 28, 1883. This first gathering of faculty predated the Big Ten's first conference by 11 years, and was 22 years to the day before the original meeting of the NCAA. Yale did attend the first meeting, along with Harvard, Princeton and five lesser athletic institutions: Columbia, Penn, Trinity, Wesleyan, and Williams. By the time the conference had developed several resolutions, Yale had withdrawn. Among the eight resolutions passed by the conference were the following:

- No professional athlete should be employed as a coach of any college team.
- No college team should play against a non-college team (including professional teams), and games should only be contested on one of the college's home grounds.
- Athletes were to be limited to four years of athletic participation.
- Each college should set up a faculty athletic committee to approve rules and regulations, and the colleges who accepted the resolutions would only compete against others who accepted them.

The resolutions were sent to 21 eastern institutions with the condition that when five colleges adopted them they would become binding. The Harvard faculty adopted them by a 25-5 vote, and the Princeton faculty and trustees adopted them unanimously. No other colleges voted to support the resolutions. Thus the first attempt at inter-institutional control was unsuccessful. The defeat was to a great extent due to the lack of consensus on various college faculties on individual resolutions. For instance, the Harvard Athletic Committee debated whether colleges should be able to participate against amateur, but non-collegian teams, and whether some athletic contests might be played on neutral grounds rather than on home fields. Dudley Sargent believed that any modification of the eight resolutions would weaken all of their work. "If the rules could not be accepted as they were," Sargent stressed, he "would vote to abandon joint action entirely and let each college fall back upon its own regulations."

While the 21 college faculties debated the issue, students became aware of the resolutions and, in near unanimity, opposed them. The student-controlled Intercollegiate Amateur Athletic Association of America (IC4A) meeting in late February, 1883, was nearly unanimously opposed to the faculty resolutions. From a Lehigh University athlete who claimed that professional coaches were necessary, to Amherst students who only favored the four year rule, to Columbia athletes who felt that it was none of the business of faculty how athletes were governed, students opposed the meddling of faculty. A Harvard senior commented that the resolutions were "objectionable in themselves and objectionable on the grounds that we were not consulted, but mainly objectionable on the principle they violated, that of non-interference." Princeton students passed a satirical circular protesting the athletic action of its faculty, while the Columbia students called for an intercollegiate student convention to oppose faculty interference. At least one faculty member, Yale's E.L. Richards, agreed with the students. He wrote to Princeton's Professor William Milligan Sloan, chairman of the faculty conference, that "the management of athletic sports might wisely be left to the students."

The student-faculty conflict over the nature of intercollegiate contests was to continue for the next generation. Students saw athletics as their own creation and their responsibility to conduct as they saw fit. Faculty generally reacted only to what they saw as the evils of college sports. The 1883-1884 faculty conference represented this conflict clearly.

With the failure of the conference of 1883-84 to ratify the resolutions, individual colleges returned again to their own rules regarding eligibility, participation against professionals, and hiring professional coaches. Complaints continued among faculties. Following the football season of 1886, President James McCosh of Princeton, concerned about the athletic excesses of the period, sent a circular to other eastern college presidents urging once again intercollegiate cooperation to eliminate athletic abuses. McCosh proposed that Harvard, as the oldest American college, should issue the call for another convention. The Harvard faculty replied that Harvard would gladly be present at such a meeting provided that Yale would be represented. Yale, led by Walter Camp, had no such notion. The Yale position had not changed since 1884 when Camp wrote in support of student control, saying that "college athletic organizations if left to themselves would soon work out their own salvation." Following Yale's refusal to be involved in the third attempt at inter-institutional faculty control, President McCosh's proposal died stillborn.

The Brown Conference of 1898

More than a decade would pass, and the birth of the midwestern Big Ten Intercollegiate Conference of Faculty Representatives would occur, before another major effort to institute eastern inter-institutional faculty control would surface. Individual colleges increasingly formed athletic committees, often composed of faculty, alumni, and undergraduates, as professionalism and questionable ethics made inroads into intercollegiate sports. But, because each college tended to set its own standards, there were often acrimonious charges that one institution's rules gave it an advantage over another in the quest for victory. The idea of a permanent organization of colleges working cooperatively to achieve uniform rules was, of course, not new when it was suggested in the mid-1890s by the chairmen of athletic committees of several eastern colleges. Many problems had arisen since the previous 1886 attempt at mutual intercollegiate rules, primarily with football and baseball, which loomed large on most eastern campuses in the 1890s. The question of eligibility in football caused particular problems as "tramp athletes" transferred with impunity from one college to another primarily to participate in athletics. Athletes at many institutions could play more than four years, and often played as graduate students in professional schools. Normal progress toward a degree often was not a condition of participation. Students were commonly paid in one form or another to play football and baseball. Payment of college baseball players to compete for summer resorts was commonplace, and there was no agreed-upon definition of an amateur athlete. Nor was the question of the advisability of hiring professional coaches resolved. In addition, as football grew to be an ever larger spectacle, the questions of preseason, summer practices and commercialization through large gate receipts became prominent concerns. With all these issues, the overriding question of the place of athletics in American higher education was in need of resolution.

On February 18, 1898, four days after the sinking of the battleship *Maine* in Havana Harbor, faculty, alumni, and undergraduate representatives from seven colleges met to do battle in their own way with questions which for colleges were nearly as inflammatory as the question of possible war with Spain. All the colleges of the present-day Ivy League, with the exception of Yale, met in Providence, Rhode Island, with Brown University at host. Each of the seven colleges—Brown, Columbia, Cornell, Dartmouth, Harvard, Penn, and Princeton—sent three representatives—a faculty member, an alumnus, and an undergraduate—to meet in an attempt to find joint answers to vexing athletic questions of the previous decade or so. Yale, it should be emphasized, was conspicuously absent.

The original meeting of the Brown Conference of 1898, which was closed to outsiders and the press, began in the afternoon and continued past midnight. Discussed were all major issues including eligibility of undergraduates and graduate students, athletic scholarships, summer baseball for pay, contests held on grounds other than those of the college, professional coaches, excessive gate receipts, and faculty control of athletics. No decisions were made concerning the principal questions, but a special committee was struck to conclude the work of the Conference.

Wilfred Munro, the Brown University professor who chaired the meeting, was given the responsibility of heading a committee of the Conference, composed of seven members, all of whom were faculty members. No students or alumni were represented. This committee of professors met several times during the spring of 1898. The first drafts of the committee report probably showed truer feelings of the faculty than did the published report. An early draft charged that "many of the abuses which have existed in inter-university athletics were due to [athletics being] vested solely in undergraduates,'' while ''most of the quarrels are due primarily to the actions of graduates.'' The faculty, according to a pre-published outline, desired to ''weed out'' any ''student who has entered the university for athletic purposes solely.'' The inflammatory statements were either eliminated or toned down in the final draft. So too was the negative statement about ''gladiatorial contests'' which was changed to a somewhat more positive ''public spectacles.'' Even with editorial changes, which were probably made to create less anxiety or agitation among students and alumni, the 1898 Report on Intercollegiate Sports was a strongly worded faculty document.

The Brown Conference Committee Report stands out as a potent call from faculty for cooperative action to cure the evils of intercollegiate sports. ''We are not engaged,'' the final report asserted, ''in making athletes. . . .'' What the Committee wanted to do was to prevent college athletes ''from interferring with the mental and moral training of the students.'' The Committee also knew what it did not want in college sports. It did not want college athletes to be tainted with professionalism and commercialism. The Report spoke out for the upper class British sport model found at Oxford and Cambridge, where a gentlemanly game of enjoyable competition transcended victory-at-all-costs.

The attainment of excellence in athletics was not a high priority of the faculty-controlled Brown Conference Committee. ''We should not seek perfection in our games, but, rather, good sport,'' the report read. But seeking perfection, or at least excellence, was exactly what college athletes wanted to do in the 1890s. Because college students desired to beat other college teams, they had already developed an elaborate system of rigid practice schedules and training systems, had hired coaches and recruited athletes, and had developed methods of raising revenue. Historically, American college athletics had been commercialized from the first railroad-sponsored contest between Harvard and Yale in 1852. Athletics had been professionalized by the next decade, when the first professional coach was hired by Yale in 1864 to enable the Yale crew to defeat Harvard.

There is a touch of irony in the issue of excellence and winning, which students and alumni favored, and the concern for gentlemanly participation, advocated in the Brown Conference Report. Harvard's President Charles W. Eliot, the leading exponent of the British model of moderation in sports, had been one of the first college spokesmen for attaining preeminence in athletics at Harvard. Eliot had championed superiority in athletics as early as 1869. In his inaugural address upon assuming the Harvard presidency, Eliot said: ''There is an aristocracy to which sons of Harvard have belonged, and, let us hope, will ever aspire to belong—the aristocracy which excels in manly sports. . . .'' Eliot's inaugural was a challenge to Harvard students to be the best not only in intellectual concerns, but in athletics. The statement was not lost upon the ears of Yale faculty; lovers of Yale athletics quoted Eliot's own inaugural words for many years, saying that Eliot had ''expressed a desire to win in athletics; that Harvard had set the pace for Yale and drawn them in to it.''

Harvard's premier philosopher, George Santayana, apparently knew the spirit of America better in the 1890s than did the Brown Conference Committee when he, too, called for an athletic aristocracy similar to that of Eliot's a generation before. Santayana said that athletics at the highly competitive level was for the few who could excel, was played as a "dire struggle" in a situation analogous to war, and was valued by society because of the degree of perfection reached. Students who played the contests might never have thought about it, but they would likely have agreed with Santayana who said that in athletics as in all performances:

> The value of talent, the beauty and dignity of positive achievements depend on the height reached, and not on the number that reach it. Only the supreme is interesting: the rest has value only as leading to it or reflecting it.

Students would almost certainly have ridiculed an early Brown Conference Committee draft statement which claimed that "there is very little fun in watching a college team which has been so trained and perfected that it can win every game during the season." And Santayana would probably have concurred with the students. Intercollegiate contests in America did not have the tradition of gentlemanly play for recreation and fun—they had been played for more than a generation emphasizing excellence and winning. The Brown Conference Committee Report could not change the thrust of sport in American colleges, though it would attempt to do so.

Neither the Brown Conference philosophy nor its 20 proposed rules were accepted in American college athletics. Neither was its suggestion that a yearly conference be summoned to consider regulation and the proper development of athletics. But both the athletic rules and the suggestion for annual meetings on athletics were not entirely forgotten.

The 20 suggested rules by a group of faculty from prestigious institutions gave colleges throughout the United States athletic guidelines as they worked toward faculty athletic control. To attempt to ensure order in institutional control with significant faculty direction, the Report stated that: (1) each institution should form an athletic committee with faculty representation on it, (2) the athletic committee would approve all coaches, trainers, captains, and team managers, (3) no athletic competition would take place without athletic committee approval, (4) any student participation in more than one sport would require athletic committee approval, and (5) the athletic committee would ensure that all athletes were bona fide members of the university.

To ensure that college athletes would be bona fide students, the Brown Conference would require that: (1) only students in good academic standing could participate, (2) special or part-time students could not participate until they had attended college for one year, (3) students deficient in studies in one university department could not participate in athletics if they transferred to another department in the same university, and (4) no student admitted without passing the university entrance examination, or convincing governing authorities that he was capable of doing a full year's work, would be eligible for athletics.

The Brown Committee also prescribed the length of athletic eligibility. The Report recommended that: (1) students be allowed no more than four years of eligibility, (2) students transferring from one institution to another could not participate in intercollegiate athletics for one year, (3) only freshmen would be allowed to participate on freshmen teams, and (4) no freshman could participate on both the freshmen and varsity teams.

The Brown Conference faculty group hoped to better control the nature of practices and contests. To this end they recommended that: (1) teams were not to practice during college vacations, except 10 days prior to the opening of the Fall term (even then football was given some priority—principally to prevent injuries), (2) all contests were to be held on college grounds, and (3) students of the competing colleges were to be given preference in the allotment of seats to contests.

Finally, the Brown Conference Report placed a stamp of approval on what the faculty members believed would be an amateur code in the fight against encroaching professionalism in college athletics. The proposed amateur code stated that

1. no student could participate in athletics if he had previously played for money, such as a baseball player at a summer resort or an athlete who received financial support to participate on a college team,
2. no student could participate in athletics if he had ever taught sports for financial gain, and
3. no student would be athletically eligible if he received board free at a training table, or if he owed money for training table meals.

In general, the Brown Conference Report of 1898 came out strongly in favor of faculty and athletic committee control of truly amateur contests in which the athletes would be bona fide students within a restricted commercial atmosphere. While the goals of the Report were exemplary for the upper class ideals of nineteenth century, British-like, amateur sport, the attempt to place those ideals into a fiercely competitive, win-oriented, and less class-restrictive American society was to prove unsuccessful. Some individual athletic committees did accept a number of the specific rules as their own, and in so doing moved colleges closer to uniform eligibility rules. Yet colleges chose not to take collective action on the rule proposals. The Brown Conference suggestion for yearly conferences "to consider regulations and the proper development of the athletic sports" did not bear fruit at this time. Colleges were still reluctant to commit the direction of athletic programs to an annual conference in which faculties would have a strong influence. They were likewise reluctant to have the extracurriculum taken away from student control. A dilemma in athletic governance resulted.

The Dilemma of Athletic Governance

The 1898 Brown Conference showed the difficulty of attempting to regulate intercollegiate athletics through nonstudent groups, such as faculty-initiated athletic committees or annual conferences, while at the same time allowing students at the individual campuses to manage the details of athletic practicing, arranging competition, hiring officials, and financing the teams. Yet this is evidently what many institutional leaders desired. A year before the Brown Conference, a committee of the Harvard Corporation dealing with sports recognized that "athletics were apart from the ordinary affairs of the college, and a matter which the Faculty could not well control." Because of this, the Athletic Committee at Harvard had been formed in 1882. Yet, this 1897 Corporation committee concluded that "The undergraduates, under careful general restriction, ought to be given so far as possible, a *free hand* in the management of their sports." Harvard, the leader of faculty control of athletics since the 1880s, recognized the principle of student management of athletics while consistently violating this principle with Athletic Committee actions. Wrote Harvard Athletic Committee Chairman, Ira N. Hollis, in 1900:

> It is at present the settled policy of the Athletic Committee to leave the management of sports and contests in the hands of students so far as it is compatible with good behavior and good scholarship.

According to Hollis, "Contests should have their beginnings among the students, and should be controlled by the Committees." With control in athletic committee hands and management in student hands, a continuous tension and conflict inevitably followed at Harvard and elsewhere.

At Columbia, the chairman of the Athletic Committee, George Kirchwey, attempted to play the middle ground, as did Harvard's Hollis and many other institutional leaders. Kirchwey wrote in the early 1900s that "the failure of the system of unregulated student control does not necessarily involve the adoption of the alternative system of direct control by the university authorities." A major problem, a dilemma, of turn-of-the-century intercollegiate sport was that there were no clearly defined athletic policy makers, nor was it clearly established who would manage athletics.

Yale, among the leading eastern colleges, had a policy which apparently created the least amount of internal conflict, but was the most controversial one externally. Yale was for student and ex-student control and management of athletics. Yale had no athletic committee and saw no need for one. President Arthur T. Hadley of Yale was adamant in his opposition to faculty meddling in athletics, and this opposition at Yale for the last two decades of the nineteenth century kept the premier athletic college from participating actively in faculty or presidentially initiated conferences of the 1880s and 1890s.

Yale was, indeed, in the rear guard, supporting student control of athletics. The travail which other colleges were experiencing in the governance of athletics, as evidenced by the Brown Conference and its predecessors, was not felt strongly at Yale until the twentieth century. Yale's established hands-off athletic policy remained even during the trauma that hit college sports in the early 1900s.

Seven years after the Brown Conference, a crisis of immense dimensions arose in intercollegiate football, the dominating college sport. In response to a profusion of acts of questionable ethics, of brutality and of fatal injuries, college authorities questioned whether football should be reformed or perhaps abolished. Chancellor MacCracken of New York University invited representatives of eastern colleges to meet and to resolve the issue in early December, 1905. Out of this meeting came a call for a national conference of faculty representatives on December 28, 1905. It was from this meeting that the future National Collegiate Athletic Association was formed. As over 60 colleges met, the Brown University Athletic Committee informed the Dean of Brown College, Alexander Meiklejohn, that "for the present it does not seem advisable to join in the call sent to the leading colleges for a Brown conference." The Brown Conference, which had failed in 1898 to solve major athletic problems, was not to be reconvened in 1906 as an eastern attempt to come to grips with vexing questions. The NCAA, though, on a national level would eventually address the issues.

From the 1880s, there had been a change away from *laissez-faire,* student control of intercollegiate athletics toward increased faculty control, both at the local level and between colleges. The formation of faculty athletic committees at institutions was the first step. The inter-institutional athletic conferences of the 1880s and 1890s, though failures, increased the university faculty and administrative governance in the most visible extracurricular activity in colleges. The leading colleges of the east were experiencing great difficulty in breaking down the long tradition of hands-off policy and of student-run games. Not until after the 1905 crisis in football did colleges on a national level join together as they sought order in athletic affairs. Eventually the NCAA addressed the issue of inter-institutional governance of athletics, but the search for order has been an elusive goal throughout the twentieth century.

CHAPTER 10

❖

Sports and Machine Politics in New York City, 1870–1920

Steven A. Riess

American historians since Frederic Paxson and Arthur M. Schlesinger, Sr., have portrayed the city as the primary site for the rise of organized sport in the post-Civil War era. As the urban setting became increasingly complex and organized, sport developed modern characteristics, including specialization of roles, bureaucratic organization, and a degree of equality of opportunity. At the same time, sport became a popular form of commercialized entertainment. The modernization and maturation of sport was largely the product of urbanization. The city also served as the locus of the dynamic social development of sport as that institution became linked with the processes that constituted urbanization—namely, the interaction of physical setting, social organization, and collective behavior. This essay examines the relationship between the development of sport and the evolution of modern political institutions and political behavior. Professional politicians, particularly machine politicians, played an important role in the development of urban recreation. They were among the major promoters and facilitators of commercialized urban spectator sports from 1870 until about 1920, when they began to be supplanted by urban elites and syndicate criminals.

This study focuses on the three major professional sports in New York City at the turn of the century: baseball, boxing, and horse racing. By far the largest city in the United States, New York had a population in 1910 of 4,766,883, greater than the combined total of the next three biggest cities (Chicago, Philadelphia, and St. Louis). More importantly, as the sporting capital of America, New York was emulated by other urban areas. The city was the center of thoroughbred racing supervised by the prestigious Jockey Club, the preeminent racing association in America. It also served as the principal site for boxing, the second city after New Orleans to have legalized prizefights. Finally, in 1903, New York became the only city with three major league baseball teams. Tammany politicians and their cronies played a crucial role in promoting and facilitating professionalized spectator sports. In turn, organized sports had important ramifications for the

From *The Making of Urban America,* Raymond Mohl (editor), Wilmington, DE: Scholarly Resources, 1988, pp. 99-121. © 1988 by Steven A. Riess. Reprinted by permission.

city's political culture and became central to the nexus existing between urban politics and organized crime.

I

Machine politicians generally held a prominent place in New York's largely Irish, male, bachelor subculture. Participants engaged in a wide variety of "manly" recreations such as gambling, drinking, wenching, and athletics, frequently at a saloon where they gathered to gossip, gamble, or attend to business. At a time when an exclusively male culture dominated sport, politicos held a leading place in the sporting fraternity. As youths, Tammany Bosses Richard Croker and Charles F. Murphy gained local reputations as boxer and baseball player, respectively. As adults, they frequented billiard-saloons, ballparks, racetracks, and boxing clubs. They were heroes and role models to newspaper boys and other working-class youths. Machine politicians, gangsters, entertainers, and other members of the sporting fraternity attended sporting events together, bet with each other, and socialized late into the evening after sporting contests. These political figures achieved a celebrity status, and the press always noted their presence at opening-day ball games, major stakes races, and championship fights.

Not just famous sports fans, professional politicians also facilitated the expansion of mass participatory sport, which undoubtedly improved their standing among constituents. On a modest level, political organizations sponsored athletic clubs, baseball teams, and outings that attracted young men to their colors. Tammany-sponsored picnics usually drew from 200 to 800 boys and men for such sports as baseball, football, track and field, even Gaelic football. The grandest and most famous picnics were sponsored by the Timothy D. Sullivan Society of the Lower East Side. Sullivan was the local district leader and the number two man in Tammany Hall. On September 10, 1900, the society sponsored its greatest outing as a memorial to the end of prizefighting, banned just ten days before. Transported by boats to a Long Island resort, some 6,000 people enjoyed a day of sports, drinking, and revelry. They marked their return to Manhattan that evening with a parade through the Bowery. The five-dollar tickets for the outing were paid for by saloon-keepers and other Bowery businessmen trying to stay on good terms with Boss Sullivan.

Urban politicians also encouraged participatory sport by nonenforcement or selective enforcement of penal codes impinging on sport. The most important legal restrictions on sports were Sunday blue laws supported by pietistic, native-born Protestants who believed in preservation of the Sabbath. Advocates of the American Sabbath sought to regulate the moral conduct of the entire community, particularly urban immigrants who needed indoctrination in the traditional American value system. Nearly every state had Sunday blue laws, although enforcement varied from region to region. The Midwest and far West were rather lenient, and cities like Chicago and Denver had professional Sunday baseball in the late nineteenth century. In the South, blue laws were strictly enforced by common consent. In the Northeast, rural-dominated, state legislatures ardently supported

This drawing from the Currier and Ives collection features The Futurity Race at the famous Sheepshead Bay Track in Coney Island. The track was established in 1880 by the Coney Island Jockey Club, an organization that featured such prestigious members as Pierre Lorillard, Jr., William K. Vanderbilt, and August Belmont, II.
Courtesy of the Library of Congress.

the American Sabbath as a real and symbolic means of insulating against immigrant-congested cities regarded as centers of vice, crime, and corruption. In New York City, Tammany's working-class, immigrant constituents preferred a Continental Sabbath on their only day off and vigorously opposed the Sunday blue laws. Resentment built up against elite New Yorkers who played golf and tennis on Sundays at their resorts, while urban youth were being arrested for playing ball. Tammany strongly supported reform of the blue laws. The organization had little success in Albany in repealing the detested penal codes, but Tammany judges usually discharged those arrested for Sabbath-breaking sport. Some Tammany politicians had ulterior motives: they owned semiprofessional teams that regularly played on Sundays and sought protection against police harassment.

The most important contribution by politicians and city government to the rise of mass sport participation was the development of municipal parks. By the mid-nineteenth century, New York was already terribly overcrowded, with limited available open space for sports or healthful outdoor recreation. Even in the era of the walking city, most New Yorkers found sports fields increasingly inaccessible. In 1855 city and state governments, with backing from Mayor Fernando Wood, approved the construction of the 840-acre Central Park in Manhattan. It was expected to be a panacea providing harmony, social uplift, improved health, and an escape valve for hardworking people living in New York's unhealthy environment. However, park planners Frederick Law Olmsted and Calvert Vaux opposed sport activities that injured the natural environment. They advocated a philosophy of receptive recreation, by which parkgoers would receive pleasure without conscious exertion as they enjoyed the beauty of nature. In time, parkgoers began to use the grounds actively for sports. Ponds were being used for ice-skating by the winter of 1859-60, but no ballplaying was allowed until the 1880s.

Central Park and, in the 1890s, Pelham Bay and Van Cortlandt parks were supported by Tammany because their development provided sources of patronage jobs and graft. Indeed, the Republican state government was so worried about Democratic use of Central Park for graft and patronage that it took over the park site in 1857, about the same time the state took control of the city's police department. Construction supervisor Olmsted was under enormous pressure to provide jobs to party workers. During the depression, his house was broken into by job seekers, and a few days later his office was besieged by over 5,000 laborers, led by politicians trying to impress their constituents. When the Democrats captured the state legislature in 1870, a new city charter was quickly approved, thereby returning the park to city control. Olmsted was fired by Boss William M. Tweed's lieutenant, Peter "Brains" Sweeney, but left office proud that he had held out against political pressure. Tammany thereafter milked the park for make-work projects for thousands of laborers at a cost of $8 million. The carefully landscaped beauty of the park was destroyed in the process. The abuse of the park ended in 1871 with the collapse of the Tweed Ring.

Despite the needs of constituents for accessible breathing spaces, Tammany did not have much interest in the small parks movement of the 1890s and early 1900s. Small, inner-city parks offered limited opportunities for graft and patronage, and construction costs were high at a time when New York was in financial distress. One historian has noted, moreover, the considerable community opposition to the neighborhood park concept among Lower East Side Jews. Residents of the Lower East Side feared that knocking down buildings for parks would destroy needed housing in the neighborhood.

This pattern of neglect was not unique to New York, for Chicago's local ward machines also ignored the small park movement. In Boston, however, Democratic machine politicians representing poor Irish districts worked vigorously to secure small parks for their constituents. They opposed distant and inaccessible park sites until city leaders supported small, inner-city parks and playgrounds as well. In the mid-1890s, under the direction of Boss John F. Fitzgerald, pressure from poor sections of Boston succeeded in getting a park built in the North End at Charlestown, as well as improvements for the Charlesbank Gymnasium in the West End. These community breathing spaces came under local control and were used for the active recreation prohibited in the beautiful suburban parks.

II

The close connection between commercialized sport and urban politics was probably first evident in prizefighting. As early as the 1830s and 1840s, gangs of New York youths worked actively with Tammany Hall in seeking the immigrant vote for the Democratic party. Gangs helped bring out the vote, and "shoulder hitters" made sure the electorate voted correctly. The first politician to organize the gang leaders was Captain Isaiah Rynders. Tammany boss of the Sixth Ward, Rynders established the Empire Club in 1843, which served as the focal point of ward political activity and as "the clearing house of all gangster activities which had to do with politics." Other Democratic factions had their own shoulder hitters, as did the Whigs and Nativists. In the antebellum era, all leading New York boxers were aligned with politicized gangs. Perhaps the most famous was Irish-born John Morrissey, the American boxing champion from 1853 to 1858. Later a big New York gambler, Morrissey utilized his fame in getting elected to the U.S. Congress after the Civil War. Ward leaders and public officials in this era often became boxing patrons, arranging bouts for side bets at hangouts like Harry Hill's Dance Hall, a favorite meeting place for the sporting crowd. Politicians often rewarded favored fighters with such jobs as emigrant runners, bouncers, tavern keepers, and policemen.

The need of politicians for shoulder hitters declined after the Civil War. Political parties marshaled their use of supporters by more rational means, including patronage and payoffs. By 1893, Tammany had become virtually omnipotent in New York City, although it suffered some defeats following episodes of outrageous corruption revealed by public investigations. Tammanyites remained interested in boxing, but formal matches were difficult to pull off because the violent and bloody sport was illegal. Contests had to be fought in out-of-the-way sites such as barns, barges, or saloon backrooms. Some of the important exhibitions in the early 1880s were held at Madison Square Garden, a refurbished railroad station. The big attraction was usually John L. Sullivan, the heavyweight champion of the world after 1882, who fought a number of four-round fights there until 1885, when the promoters gave up after repeated police interference.

In the 1880s the center of boxing shifted to New Orleans, where local promoters and politicians used various techniques to circumvent proscriptive laws. In 1890 the city and the state passed laws permitting "glove contests" sponsored by regularly chartered athletic clubs. Athletic clubs began promoting organized boxing matches in indoor arenas, selling tickets for admission. Boxers fought for a specified purse rather than side bets, although betting continued to be important. Contests were increasingly fought under the new Marquis of Queensberry rules, requiring gloves and rounds with time limits. In New Orleans on September 7, 1892, James Corbett defeated Sullivan for the championship in the first heavyweight championship fight under the new rules. Corbett won the $25,000 purse and a $10,000 side bet.

Prizefighting staged a revival in the New York metropolitan area in the early 1890s, and New York regained its preeminence in the sport. The main site of bouts was Coney Island, a wide-open resort that was becoming a major sporting center. Known as "Sodom by the Sea," Coney Island was infamous as an area of low-life amusements. The local political boss was John T. McKane, a former Democratic president of Kings County, who after 1884 served concurrently as president of the local town board, chief of police, and head of the water and health boards. The principal boxing club there was the Coney Island Athletic Club (CIAC), organized in May 1892 by McKane and various machine politicians. McKane owned the arena, provided political protection, and prevented any big bouts at Coney Island unless he had a share of the action. Police Justice Dick Newton was the matchmaker, and Magistrate James T. Tighe handled financial affairs. The club staged a number of important bouts, reputedly earning $150,000 in under five months. But the CIAC was not omnipotent and in 1893 was forced to cancel the Jim Corbett-Charley Mitchell championship bout because of public pressure.

The CIAC was only one of several boxing clubs in the metropolitan area sponsored and protected by local politicians. These clubs operated even though professional boxing was illegal. For example, in 1895 the New Puritan Boxing Club of Long Island City held its matches at a site owned by the town's former mayor, James Gleason. His partners included Big Tim Sullivan and former Justice Dick Newton, recently released from a jail sentence for corrupt electioneering.

Tim Sullivan was first elected to the state assembly in 1886 at the age of twenty-three and moved on to the Senate in 1893. He served in the U.S. Congress from 1902 to 1906, but in 1908 he returned to his power base in the state senate. Sullivan's last victory came in 1912, when he was again elected to Congress, but he was never sworn in because of failing health; he died one year later. Sullivan was associated early in his career with such gangsters as Monk Eastman, Kid Twist, and Paul Kelly, who provided him with intimidators and repeaters at election time. In return, organized crime was allowed to flourish. Big Tim was idolized by his constituents as a friend of the poor. He provided them with patronage, relief, outings, and any other assistance. Sullivan was a great sportsman. He raced horses, gambled heavily, and, after 1895, dominated the New York poolroom business. Furthermore, by 1898 he also monopolized boxing in New York State, except in Brooklyn, where the new CIAC was protected by Democratic Boss Hugh McLaughlin.

In 1896, under Sullivan's guidance, a bill passed the legislature and was approved by the governor legalizing ''sparring'' matches of up to ten rounds at licensed athletic clubs. New York became the only state with legalized boxing because Louisiana had banned the sport after the death of a New Orleans fighter in 1894. New York's 1896 Horton Act seemed, on the surface, to outlaw prizefights (boxing for a purse), contests regarded as brutal and unscientific and where the object was to pummel an opponent into unconsciousness. But in reality the new law legitimized prizefighting. Police thereafter rarely interfered with bouts, especially after New York Police Commissioner Theodore Roosevelt attended a rough contest at Sullivan's Broadway Athletic Club and told the press that the match had complied with the law.

Tammany control of the police department further obviated any fears of harassment at the politically connected athletic clubs. Police Chief Bill Devery rarely interfered with boxing bouts, even well-advertised matches like the heavyweight championship match in 1899 between titleholder Bob Fitzsimmons and challenger

James J. Jeffries at the new CIAC, a club politically allied with Hugh McLaughlin. Devery had joined the police department in 1878 and owed his rise to the sponsorship of Boss Croker and Tim Sullivan. His career was marked by several episodes of incompetence and corruption. In 1894, Devery was fired from his captaincy because of criminal charges resulting from the Lexow Investigation, but he was acquitted on a technicality and regained his post. Five years later the Mazet Investigation documented his corrupt activities as chief. His work was so scandalous that the state legislature abolished his position in 1901 in favor of a commissioner. But the new head of the police simply appointed Devery his deputy and left the department in his care. When Seth Low was elected mayor on a Fusion ticket that year, he fired Devery immediately.

Legalized boxing lasted only until 1900, when the state legislature repealed the Horton Act because of the sport's brutality, the gambling menace, and the Tammany influence in boxing. Approximately 3,500 contests had been staged over five years, mainly in New York City. The cheapest tickets were fifty cents for club fights (equal to the cost of general admission at baseball parks), while tickets to top-flight matches ranged between one and three dollars. Admission to championship bouts went for five to twenty-five dollars. Most of the profits came from box office receipts, but additional revenue came from the sale of movie rights to championship bouts. The single largest gate of the Horton era was Jeffries's title defense in 1900 against former champion Jim Corbett, which brought in $60,000.

The repeal of the Horton Act did not completely stop boxing, since it survived surreptitiously in saloon backrooms and at club smokers. Private clubs circumvented the law by holding three-round exhibitions for the entertainment of "members," who paid a one-dollar "fee" to join the club. The most prestigious of the membership clubs was Tim Sullivan's National Athletic Club, which reputedly had 3,000 members. By 1908 fifteen clubs in New York held weekly bouts. The police generally did not interfere and seldom made arrests. However, if promoters became too audacious, or drew too much public attention by scheduling big-name fighters, the police were pressured to stop the bouts.

Tammany politicians tried in vain for several years to legalize boxing again. Prospects brightened in 1911 when the Democrats gained control of both the state legislature and the governor's mansion for the first time in years. This enabled Senator James J. Frawley, a former president of the Knickerbocker Athletic Club, to pass a bill legalizing ten-round, no-decision boxing contests. The sport was placed under the supervision of an unpaid three-man State Athletic Commission responsible for licensing athletic clubs and fighters. A 5 percent tax was levied on the box office take, which came to nearly $50,000 in 1912. The Frawley Act resulted in a renewed interest in boxing, and by the end of 1912 there were eighty-nine licensed boxing clubs in the state, forty-nine in New York City. The bouts were held in small neighborhood boxing clubs and large downtown arenas like Madison Square Garden.

Prizefighting operated under the Frawley Act until 1917, when the law was repealed by a Republican administration. The prestige of the sport remained low.

Its brutality, the low-life types associated with it, and incessant gambling and rumors of fixes did little to improve the standing of boxing as a sport. The Athletic Commission never fully enforced its guidelines. Its public image further suffered once it had become overtly politicized by the Republicans, who regained control of the state legislature and the governorship in 1915. Governor Charles Whitman's new athletic commissioners were patronage appointees with substantial salaries. That was not enough, apparently, because the commission chairman was fired by the governor in 1917 after an investigation revealed that he extorted money from promoters and fight managers. Shortly thereafter a fatality occurred in the ring at a match attended by two commissioners. This episode convinced Whitman that he had to abolish the sport. Yet despite its many problems, boxing had its friends in the state legislature, and the governor's first efforts at repeal were badly defeated. Whitman called for repeal late in the session as a party measure, getting his bill approved on a strict party vote. Not one Democratic senator voted to abolish boxing. Whitman's battle against boxing was a politically astute move signifying to upstate voters that the Republican party stood for tradition and high moral values, unlike the Democrats who had supported an immoral blood sport with dubious connections to urban political machines and gangsters.

The repeal of the Frawley Act was a major blow to American prizefighting. The sport was legal in twenty-three states in 1917, but it was severely restricted, if not completely outlawed, in the major markets of New York and Chicago. Even in San Francisco, which had temporarily supplanted New York as the boxing capital after the repeal of the Horton Act, the sport was greatly curtailed by a 1914 state law limiting matches to four rounds. The outlook for boxing improved markedly during World War I, however, because the sport was used to help train soldiers for combat. Consequently, boxing's image became much better. Even the reform-minded *New York Times* became an advocate of pugilism. Nevertheless, boxing supporters failed to get a bill through the legislature in 1918 restoring the sport. One year later a measure favoring pugilism passed the Senate but was defeated in the lower chamber by conservative Republicans. Legislators had just approved the legalization of Sunday movies and baseball, and, as one ranking Republican suggested, "We can't afford to be too liberal." Then, in 1920, under the direction of Senate Minority Leader Jimmy Walker, a loyal son of Tammany, the legislature enacted a law permitting twelve-round matches, with judges empowered to choose a victor if the contests went the distance. An unpaid athletic commission was established to supervise the sport and license boxing clubs, trainers, and fighters.

The passage of the Walker Act enabled New York City to regain its position as the national center of boxing. In the 1920s local fight clubs became important sources of top-flight fighters. Most major American bouts were held at Madison Square Garden. The promoter there was Tex Rickard, probably best known for his successful work in pulling off the Jeffries-Johnson championship fight of 1910 in Reno, Nevada. Rickard's first promotion in New York was the Willard-Moran heavyweight championship fight in 1916. An out-of-towner, Rickard generated a lot of jealousy among local promoters and politicians, compelling him to provide passes, favors, and bribes to bring off the match. By 1920, Rickard had learned his lesson and developed important connections in Tammany Hall. His backers included Governor Al Smith, who interceded on Rickard's behalf with owners of Madison Square Garden, helping the promoter get a ten-year lease for $400,000. Smith believed that Rickard was the only man with the imagination and promotional flair to operate the huge arena successfully. Rickard succeeded in making boxing a respectable and profitable sport. Boxing was soon legalized in other important states like Illinois, and the sport's heroes, particularly Jack Dempsey, were among the most admired Americans in the 1920s.

III

Politics dominated not only the "sport of pugs" but also the "sport of kings." Despite the aristocratic image of the sport, horse racing often came under severe moral scrutiny from church leaders and moral reformers because of the gambling, crooked races, and animal abuses associated with the turf. More than any other sport, racing depended upon betting for its appeal and survival. Consequently, thoroughbred racing at the turn of the century was widely forbidden. Where the sport did operate, as in New York, it was heavily influenced by machine politicians and politically active elites, such as William C. Whitney, Thomas Fortune Ryan, and August Belmont II. These men used sport to facilitate cross-class coalitions in the Democratic party to help protect their transit franchises. Streetcar executives out of necessity became intimately involved in urban politics; they needed inside information, long-term leases, and rights of way. Elite sportsmen like Ryan and Belmont owned and operated racetracks. Along with machine politicos like Croker and Tim Sullivan, they owned, bred, and raced thoroughbreds, and they wagered heavily at the track. Sullivan and other professional politicians were also prominent in the business of gambling, usually as organizers and protectors of bookmaking and offtrack poolroom, or betting parlor, syndicates. The elite and plebeian members of the sporting fraternity worked together on issues of mutual concern, such as the facilitation of racetrack operations and the legalization of ontrack betting. They were bitter enemies, however, when it came to offtrack betting.

Thoroughbred racing was a popular elite diversion in the Colonial era. The sport subsequently enjoyed a boom in the 1820s and 1830s but faltered in the North after the depression of 1837. The center of racing then shifted to New Orleans, where it remained a vital institution until the Civil War. The turf did not revive in the North until 1863, when John Morrissey staged races at the resort town of Saratoga Springs to attract elite vacationers. He was supported by wealthy sportsmen Leonard Jerome, William R. Travers, and John Hunter, who apparently were not adverse to working with a former Tammany shoulder hitter.

The Saratoga experiment was such a resounding success that Jerome, Chairman August Belmont of the national Democratic party, and other elite sportsmen organized the American Jockey Club (AJC) in 1866 to sponsor races in the vicinity of New York City. Jerome played a leading role in securing 230 acres in Westchester, where a racetrack was built and named Jerome Park in his honor.

The goals of the AJC were to improve the breed and maintain racing as an elite sport. The jockey club introduced several important innovations, such as holding three meets each year and replacing the traditional long distance heat with the shorter English dash system. This resulted in more races on each card, which meant more betting to attract turf fans. Larger purses, averaging about $13,000 per meet, attracted better horses, particularly annual stakes races like the Belmont, initiated in 1867 in honor of the AJC's first president. Expenses were met by gate receipts, at least $3,000 per day, along with daily fees paid by auction pool-sellers and concessionaires and the entrance fees paid by horsemen for the right to race thoroughbreds.

Not all of the 862 original members of the AJC between 1866 and 1867 were socially elite. Some were horse fanciers of more modest origins. The membership included such politicians as the notorious Tammany Boss William M. Tweed. Boss Tweed was also interested in Monmouth Park, established in 1870 at Long Branch, New Jersey, by gambler Joseph Chamberlain who hoped to turn Monmouth Park into another Saratoga. Chamberlain's other associates included robber barons Jay Gould and Jim Fisk, Jr., who "practically owned the Legislature."

New York horsemen needed considerable political savvy to circumvent the legal barriers to gambling, the backbone of the sport. An antipool law was passed by the state legislature in 1877 in response to the widespread wagering on the Tilden-Hayes election. Despite fears that this law would hurt track attendance, the turf continued to flourish, largely because the auction pool system of betting was replaced by bookmaking. The locus of racing moved to the Coney Island area, a forty-cent, one-hour train ride from mid-town Manhattan. Local politicians were expected to protect the tracks from rigorous enforcement of the penal codes. In June 1879, William A. Engeman, builder of the Brighton Beach Hotel and politically well connected, established a proprietary racetrack at Brighton Beach. The track was quite successful, and, by 1882, Engeman was netting $200,000 per year. Late in 1879, Jerome organized the prestigious Coney Island Jockey Club (CIJC), which included Belmont, William K. Vanderbilt, and Pierre Lorillard, Jr. One year later the CIJC established the important Sheepshead Bay Track in Coney Island. Finally, in 1885, the politically astute Dwyer brothers, plungers who had made their fortune as butchers, opened Gravesend as a proprietary track. These three tracks were tolerated and protected by local politicians under the direction of Boss McKane, who permitted pool-selling to flourish. A political opponent, the Republican Kings Country district attorney, secured fifty-seven indictments for penal code violations but could not obtain one single conviction. His Democratic successor never interfered during the racing season. McKane personally benefited from benign neglect because his construction company was awarded many lucrative contracts, including the building of the betting booths.

In 1887 representatives of the racing interests passed the Ives Anti-Poolroom Law forbidding off-betting but permitting betting at the tracks during the May to October racing season. The state also levied a tax on the race courses to raise money for agricultural societies and county fairs. The new law resulted in a boom in racing and gambling. It led directly to the formation of the Metropolitan Turf Alliance (MTA) in 1888, an association of over sixty well-connected book-makers who sought to monopolize the bookmaking privilege at the tracks and whose secretary was Timothy D. Sullivan. Another result was that, in 1889, John A. Morris constructed Morris Park Racetrack in Westchester to replace Jerome Park, which the city had purchased for a reservoir. Morris came from a wealthy New York family, but his reputation was not of the highest order because he had made his fortune operating the infamous Louisiana Lottery. He was politically influential, however, and his Tammanyite son was the district's assemblyman. Managed by the New York Jockey Club, Morris Park had the largest grandstand and the longest track in the United States. The facility cost several hundred thousand dollars and was regarded as palatial by contemporaries. It immediately became an important resort for the social set who traveled to the track in expensive carriages. Lesser folk had to be satisfied with a half-hour train ride from Grand Central Station.

Poolroom operators learned to adapt and stay in business despite the Ives Anti-Poolroom Law. Poolrooms were mainly located in midtown or the Tenderloin, where clerks took bets on New York and New Jersey races. They attracted a lot of business, primarily from young clerks and artisans who could not afford the ninety-cent roundtrip and the two-dollar admission, much less the time to go to the tracks. Poolrooms not only made it unnecessary for gamblers to travel to the tracks, but they also took small, one-dollar bets that bookmakers at major New York tracks would not accept. Occasional raids were instigated by reformers like Anthony Comstock of the Society for the Suppression of Vice, but the poolrooms usually operated with impunity. The poolroom operators were well protected by Mayor Hugh Grant and other Tammany friends, by their contributions to Governor David B. Hill, and by payoffs to police and local political powers. Machine-appointed jurists were also supportive. In 1890, for instance, the courts ruled that poolrooms could operate as commission agents and transfer clients' money to the tracks. Immediately, all pool-sellers began to represent themselves as betting commissioners. They would accept bets right up to posttime, even though it was physically impossible to get the wagers to the track.

The poolrooms got their race results from Western Union. The telegraph company paid about $1,600 per day to each New York track for the exclusive privilege of transmitting race results. Its racing department, which made $18,000 to $20,000 per week, was the most profitable unit in Western Union. These payments gave the racetracks a vested interest in the poolroom business. Early in the spring of 1893, the police instigated a major attack against local poolrooms, possibly at the instigation of Boss Richard Croker. The Tammany boss had recently purchased the famous Belle Meade stud and wanted New York tracks to prosper so he could race his horses there. In addition, Croker was a good friend of the Dwyers, who had often given him betting tips, and he hoped to protect their interests. With Croker's support, and despite the opposition of Tim Sullivan, the state legislature enacted the Saxton Anti-Poolroom Law making the keeping of a poolroom a felony.

The status of horse racing was seriously threatened one year later by a coalition of social reformers, clergymen, and other Tammany opponents. This group used the September 1894 state constitutional convention as a forum to ban all horse-race gambling. There was widespread sentiment against betting, particularly at illegal poolrooms. Racing fans had become increasingly alienated against the sport by the activities of the Morrises and Dwyers, who seemed more interested in profits than improving the breed. Repeated rumors of fixed races also stimulated public outrage. The elite Jockey Club, organized in the summer of 1894, was expected to supervise carefully all aspects of the sport, but it did not assuage critics. Opponents were bolstered by the closing in December 1893 of New Jersey's tracks, which had been totally controlled by corrupt machine politicians. The New York State constitutional convention adopted a proposal banning horse-race betting completely. When the proposal was approved by voters in fall elections, the end of racing appeared imminent.

Racing interests waged an all-out campaign to save the sport. Calmer minds recognized that the convention might have gone too far. Even the reform-minded *New York Times* sought to save racing, which it believed helped improve the breed. The turf had powerful friends in Albany. Racing advocates flexed their muscle in the passage of the Percy-Gray Act, establishing a state racing commission to supervise the sport. The new law permitted racing associations to race horses for a stake, but without wagering. Yet when the tracks reopened in the spring of 1895, betting was soon resumed by bookmakers, who instituted the English system of credit betting, in which no written records were kept and debts were paid off on an honor system. The courts ruled that the new system was legal, since bets were made on an individual basis and no odds were advertised.

Offtrack betting was also back in business, even though a new law had been passed accompanying Percy-Gray that banned such betting. The enterprise now came under the protection of Big Tim Sullivan, and, under his patronage, offtrack betting soon reached its apogee. Sullivan's operation had Croker's approval. As many as 400 poolrooms belonged to the syndicate, each paying from $60 to $300 per month for the privilege of staying in business. New poolrooms paid Sullivan a $300 initiation fee. The poolroom operations were extraordinarily successful, and in 1902 the syndicate earned $3.6 million.

Poolrooms operated openly in the backrooms of Tenderloin saloons, or under the guise of a bucket shop. Poolrooms were usually forewarned by police head-quarters about occasional raids. Arrested clerks and telegraph operators generally were freed by sympathetic magistrates or fined a minimal amount. The poolrooms became a major issue during the 1901 city elections. Reform fusion candidates castigated Sullivan and the rest of the so-called Gambling Trust, which reputedly included Bill Devery, Frank Farrell, Police Commissioner Joseph Sexton, City Clerk J.F. Carroll, and Mayor Robert A. Van Wyck. Seth Low promised to clean up the gambling menace when elected, but other than firing Devery, he accomplished very little. DeLacey, Farrell, and Mahoney soon set up their own poolroom syndicates in cooperation with Sullivan, later described by journalist

Josiah Flynt as "the most scandalous individual in the pool-room Griff in the United States."

Thoroughbred racing's greatest crisis came in 1908, when Governor Charles Evans Hughes in his annual address to the state legislature called for the end of racetrack gambling. At first, the proposal attracted little public enthusiasm. The turf was popular, and its advocates had considerable political and economic clout. But the progressive governor believed that gambling on races was both a moral outrage and a flagrant violation of the state constitution. Hughes engaged in a major educational campaign to win public support for his views. He used his influence to get Republicans behind a bill to abolish on-site betting. The Agnew-Hart bill easily passed the assembly but failed on a tie vote in the Senate. Tammany and the state's eight jockey clubs seemed to have succeeded in saving the sport. The tracks purportedly raised a $500,000 defense fund, spending $162,000 for publicity and an untold amount for vote buying. Republican Otto Foelker claimed he had been offered $45,000 to vote for the racing interests, and at least one senator later admitted taking a $10,000 bribe.

Disappointed with this defeat, Hughes persevered. He ordered a special election to fill a vacant Senate seat from the traditionally Republican Niagara-Orleans district. The governor put his prestige on the line by campaigning for the Republican candidate, who pledged to vote against racetrack gambling. Republican William C. Wallace won the seat in a surprisingly close contest. Hughes then convened a special session of the legislature, which passed the Agnew-Hart bill by a margin of one vote in the Senate. This victory was described by a Hughes biographer as his "most dramatic venture in the area of moral reform."

The new law severely hampered the racing industry, a $75-million business nationwide. The major tracks tried to remain open by allowing oral betting, which the courts ruled was legal, but attendance declined by two-thirds. In 1910 the legislature passed the Agnew-Perkins Act, making racetrack owners liable for any gambling violations at their facilities. The result was that tracks still operating immediately went out of business. In 1911 and 1912 there was no thoroughbred racing in New York. However, in 1913, Judge Townsend Scudder ruled in the *Shane* case that track managers were liable only if they had wittingly permitted bookmakers to operate. As a consequence, Belmont Park and two minor tracks, Jamaica and Aqueduct, reopened. But such historic racetracks as Gravesend and Sheepshead Bay, each worth about $2.5 million, never reopened.

IV

Unlike boxing and horse racing, which operated under severe legal restriction and social opprobrium, baseball was the national pastime. A clean, exciting sport, baseball epitomized the finest traditional American values like rugged individualism, hard work, and courage, as well as teamwork. Baseball owners were regarded as selfless, civic-minded men who sponsored teams out of a concern for the public welfare. But in reality, owners were not drawn from the "best people." New York baseball magnates included a heavy representation of machine politicians. They used their clout to benefit their teams, which provided patronage, financial and psychic rewards, and good public relations.

Baseball in New York from its earliest days was closely tied to local politics. Tammany was an early sponsor of amateur baseball teams, the most important being the Mutuals, established in 1857. By the 1860s, when Tweed had become involved with the club, it was already one of the leading amateur nines. Players were subsidized with patronage jobs in the sanitation department and the coroner's office. In 1871, when the Mutuals joined the first professional league, the National Association of Professional Baseball Players (NA), its board of directors included the sheriff, several aldermen, two judges, and six state legislators. One of only three teams that played in all five NA campaigns, the Mutuals in 1876 joined the new National League (NL). But late in the 1876 season, after refusing to make a costly western trip, the Mutuals were expelled by the NL.

New York City was without major league baseball until 1883, when Tammanyites John B. Day and Joseph Gordon and former minor leaguer John Mutrie were awarded franchises in both the NL and the year-old American Association (AA). They devoted most of their attention to the Giants (NL), because the senior circuit charged fifty cents for tickets and the AA only twenty-five cents. In 1885, Day and his partners sold the AA team to Erastus Wiman, a Staten Island traction magnate who hoped to enrich his ferry business with fans traveling from Manhattan to Staten Island for ball games. His ball club, however, was a failure and lasted only two seasons. The Giants played at the old Polo Grounds at 110th Street until 1889, when political pressure forced them to move north to a new site at 157th Street. A competitor was established across the street in 1890 in the new Players' League, a cooperative venture of capitalists and players revolting against the reserve clause. The financial backers were prominent Republicans, who bought out the Giants in 1891 after the collapse of the Players' League. Tammany regained the Giants at the end of 1894, when Andrew Freedman, an intimate friend and business partner of Boss Croker, purchased the club for $48,000. Freedman held no elective office but wielded great influence through Croker and in his own right as a member of Tammany's powerful Finance Committee. In 1897, Freeman became treasurer of the national Democratic party.

Brooklyn baseball was also heavily dominated by politicians. In 1884 the city got an AA franchise that played in the Red Hook section. The owners were gamblers Ferdinand Abell and Joseph J. Doyle (the latter a close friend of Tammany Boss John Kelly), realtor Charles Byrne, and editor George J. Taylor of the *Herald*—all typical members of the sporting fraternity. In 1890 the franchise was transferred to the NL and replaced in the AA by a club run by James C. Kennedy, a prominent sports promoter with important political connections. Brooklyn also had a team in the new Players' League owned by Brownsville boosters, including Wendell Goodwin, a politician who worked for a local traction line. But one year later, only the NL team remained, which Goodwin and his associates bought and moved to Brownsville. This shift did not work out well because of high rent, poor transportation, and the lack of neighborhood interest in the sport. In 1898 the Trolley Dodgers returned to South Brooklyn under a new president, Charles Ebbets, a former state assemblyman and future alderman. The switch was financed by Red Hook traction magnates who expected the presence of a baseball team to increase traffic along their routes.

Freedman of the Giants used his clout to cower other owners, and sportswriters claimed that he ran his team as a Tammany appendage. The object of considerable abuse from fans, the press, and fellow owners for mismanagement and encouraging rowdy baseball, and disappointed with his profits, Freedman decided to sell out after the 1902 season. Besides, he had more important matters to attend to, principally the construction of the New York subway system. He sold most of his stock for $125,000 to John T. Brush, an Indianapolis clothier. Brush had just sold his Cincinnati Reds baseball team to a local syndicate consisting of Mayor Julius Fleischmann, Republican Boss George B. Cox, and Water Commissioner August Herrmann, Cox's right-hand man. According to one journalist, Brush had been forced to sell out to the machine, which threatened to cut a street through the ballpark.

Despite the sale, the Giants remained the Tammany team. Still a minority stockholder, Freedman was more than willing to use his clout for the club. Brush died in 1912, and his heirs sold the team in 1919 for $1 million to Tammanyite Charles Stoneham, a curb-market broker of limited integrity. Other partners included baseball manager John J. McGraw, and Magistrate Francis X. McQuade, who was best known for his liberal handling of Sunday baseball cases. Stoneham's powerful political friends included Governor Al Smith and former sheriff Tom Foley, one of the machine's most powerful district leaders. Another important friend, along with McGraw, was the notorious Arnold Rothstein, partner in a rum-running deal and a Havana racetrack. Rothstein reputedly had been the middleman in Stoneham's purchase of the Giants.

The Giants were enormously successful on the diamond in the early 1900s under McGraw's management. They won six pennants from 1904 to 1917 and became the most profitable team in organized baseball. From 1906 to 1910 the club annually earned over $100,000, and by 1913 earnings surpassed $150,000. After World War I, baseball experienced an enormous boom in the city, largely because of the legalization of Sunday baseball. In 1920 the Giants established a league record $296,803 in profits. Most of the revenue came from ticket sales, but profits also came from concessions, Western Union fees, and rents from such events as boxing matches, operas, and Yankee games played at the Polo Grounds from 1913 to 1922.

The Giants had Manhattan to themselves until 1903, when the rival American League (AL) secured a New York franchise. The junior circuit had failed to organize a New York team earlier because Freedman controlled virtually all the potential playing sites through his political power and real estate interests. Even after Croker was exiled to England on the heels of Seth Low's election as mayor in 1901, Freedman and his Tammany friends still had enough power to stymie any interlopers. Late in 1902, AL President Ban Johnson convinced August Belmont II that the Interborough Rapid Transit Company (IRT) should purchase land at 142d Street on the East Side and lease it back to the league. However, the plan was vetoed by IRT Director Andrew Freedman.

Johnson could not avoid dealing with Tammany Hall. In March 1903 the AL granted a franchise to a syndicate headed by Joseph Gordon, a figurehead for the real owners—poolroom king Frank Farrell and former Police Chief William Devery. They soon constructed a field on a rock pile at 165th Street that Freedman apparently had ruled out as unsuitable for baseball. Devery and Farrell paid the local district leader $200,000 for excavation and another $75,000 to build a grandstand. The site was inaccessible from downtown, but a subway with a nearby station was scheduled for completion one year later.

The Highlanders (later known as the Yankees) failed to prosper, either on or off the field. After coming in second in 1904, they finished in the first division just twice between 1905 and 1914 and made a substantial profit only in 1910. By comparison, the Giants were first in the hearts of New Yorkers. They won four pennants and one world championship during the same period. Disappointed in the team's performance and estranged from each other, Devery and Farrell sold out in 1915 for $460,000 to brewer Jacob Ruppert, Jr., and C. Tillinghast Huston, a rich civil engineer. Ruppert was a prominent member of the sporting fraternity who bred and raced dogs and horses. A great fan of the Giants, he was a notable member of Tammany Hall, served on its Finance Committee, and had been selected personally by Croker in 1897 to run for president of the city council. But Ruppert's nomination raised jealousies among other brewers and Germans, and was withdrawn. One year later he was chosen to run for Congress from a Republican district, was elected in an upset, and went on to serve four undistinguished terms. The Yankees struggled at first under new ownership but by 1920 had become the most profitable franchise in baseball, earning a record $373,862. Sunday baseball contributed to this, but the main reason was the new Yankee right fielder, Babe Ruth, who hit an astounding fifty-four home runs, nearly double the record twenty-nine he had hit one year before with the Red Sox. The team's attendance doubled from 1919 to 1920, a league record 1,289,422, which stood until 1946.

New York owners took advantage of their political connections to enhance their baseball operations in valuable ways. Clout was used to deter interlopers from invading the metropolitan area. Influence at city hall provided access to the best possible information about property values, land uses, and mass transit, all essential matters when teams built new ballparks. This was especially crucial once teams began constructing permanent, fire-resistant ballparks that cost in excess of $500,000. In 1911 the Giants built their new Polo Grounds in Washington Heights on the site of the old field that had burned down. Two years later the Dodgers built Ebbets Field in an underdeveloped section of Flatbush known as "Ginney Flats," derided by most experts as a poor location far from the fans. But Charles Ebbets knew what he was doing, having purchased land cheaply in what would soon become a lovely and accessible residential community. A decade later the Yankees moved into their own ballpark in the Bronx, at a spot years before rejected for a ballpark as too distant. But when completed in 1923, Yankee

Stadium was just sixteen minutes from downtown Manhattan via the Jerome Avenue extension of the East Side subway.

Political connections facilitated various mundane but necessary business operations. Teams without such protection could find themselves vulnerable to political pressure and high license fees. Cities also provided teams with a variety of municipal services, including preseason inspections to check for structural defects in the ballparks. Baseball men without influence might end up with an unusual number of expensive code violations. The most important ongoing service was police protection. Officers were needed to maintain order among those waiting to get into the park, keep traffic moving, and prevent ticket scalping. Inside the grounds, police prevented gambling and kept order among unruly spectators who fought with other fans, umpires, and even players. All cities provided protection outside the park, and in New York, teams got free police protection inside the grounds until 1907 when the reform commissioner Thomas A. Bingham stopped it. In Chicago that practice continued for years, saving the White Sox and Cubs thousands of dollars.

New York was the center of the fight for professional Sunday baseball. Tammany led a long fight against the American Sabbath. The club owners wanted Sunday ball because they expected it to be popular with working-class fans who could not attend any other day. At the start of each season from 1904 to 1906, either the Giants or the Dodgers tried to use their political clout to stage Sunday games. They sought to circumvent the law by selling scorecards or magazines, or by asking for "donations" instead of selling tickets, which was against the law. However, each year the courts ruled against the ball clubs, and the Sunday experiments were halted.

In 1907 the scene of the battle shifted to Albany, but Tammany was unable to defeat upstate sentiment in favor of the American Sabbath. Support for Sunday recreation broadened during World War I. Many Americans believed that the doughboys fighting overseas for freedom should not have to return home to find their own liberty diminished by strict blue laws. Ebbets played a leading role in a reform coalition that included organized labor, progressives, journalists, veterans' organizations, women's groups, and Tammany. A local option measure nearly succeeded in 1918 but was blocked by Governor Whitman, who feared antagonizing conservative upstate voters. In 1919, however, a coalition of urban Republicans and Democrats passed, and Governor Smith signed, the Walker Bill permitting Sunday baseball on a local option basis. The city council promptly approved Sunday baseball, and it became a huge success, drawing crowds in excess of 20,000 to Ebbets Field and the Polo Grounds.

V

Urban machine politicians and their closest associates played a crucial role in the rise of commercialized sports in New York. They were mainly Irish-American sports fans who seized the opportunity to promote spectator sports as a financial investment that might improve their political standing and social status. Professional sport was a business open to white men of ability, regardless of social background, much like the contemporary new movie industry shunned by old wealth and dominated by risk-taking Jewish entrepreneurs. Unlike amateur sports, dominated by distinctly old-stock Americans, commercialized sports had a prominent non-WASP composition. It was a field of enterprise in which professional politicians could utilize their clout to considerable advantage, much as they did in businesses like construction or real estate.

Sports promoters used inside information to build their structures at the cheapest, most accessible sites. They employed political clout to protect their ballparks, racetracks, and boxing clubs from competition or police interference. This was especially crucial for betting parlors of the gambling syndicate, whose connections at police precincts and magistrate courts normally prevented strict enforcement of antigambling statutes. Political ties not only provided protection but also meant preferential treatment from municipal agencies. The machine's influence extended to Albany, but the legislature and governorship were usually in Republican hands. Nevertheless, the Democrats tried and occasionally succeeded in protecting urban sportsmen against new legal restrictions demanded by rural upstate constituents. They ultimately secured the legitimization of prizefighting and horse racing. Thus, politically connected sportsmen who promoted athletic contests, managed fighters, raced thoroughbreds, and owned or operated sports arenas, baseball franchises, and poolrooms profitably organized diversions for urban folk. Yet the politicians were not omnipotent and did not have the power to operate completely as they pleased. Pugilism was illegal until 1896 and then permitted only intermittently until 1920 when the Walker Bill was passed. Horse racing, and particularly turf betting, was always under severe scrutiny, and the sport actually was discontinued in 1911. Even in baseball, restrictions against Sunday games were not lifted until 1919.

The manifest function of sponsoring commercialized sports was to make money, and politicians had considerable opportunity to profit handsomely from sporting enterprises. In addition, sponsorship had important latent functions, such as providing new sources of patronage and greater popularity with constituents, both of which could be translated into votes. Sporting activities gained politicians a leading position among the community of manly Americans, members of the bachelor subculture. Celebrity status enabled politicians to mix with sports heroes and social leaders. Sport, like politics, was a largely male preserve. It was perceived widely as a means of combatting the growing feminization of American culture. The politicians' sporting ventures proved that they were ''one of the boys,'' offering vivid demonstration of their role in the neighborhood. They provided protection for local bookies and gave community youth a chance for fame, heroism, and wealth through boxing and baseball. Participation in sports raised self-esteem and provided an opportunity for individual accomplishment that working in a political machine might not bring. Sport also provided a nexus through which certain machine politicians became involved with syndicate crime. Politicians needed underworld money, power, and access to election workers, in return for which they provided protection for betting and other illicit operations.

The politician-sportsmen discovered that leadership in sports did not guarantee instant respectability, even though they mingled with segments of the elite. Bosses like Richard Croker and other machine politicos like John Morrissey desperately sought acceptance and recognition by the social elite and tried to emulate their behavior. While the Belmonts, Lorillards, and Jeromes might race with the Crokers and gamble with the Morrisseys, they would never bring them home for dinner with the family. Unlike participation in boxing or horse racing, ownership of a baseball team was regarded as a civic contribution. Frank Farrell's image was markedly improved by his operation of the Highlanders, but that alone did not assure social acceptance. Baseball owners at the turn of the century seldom came from the social elite. Generally men of new wealth, they sought financial profits and social acceptance through a business largely shunned by old money.

The prominence of professional politicians, particularly urban bosses, as promoters and facilitators of professional sports was not limited to New York. It was a nationwide pattern common to urban areas with a citywide machine and cities where the local ward machine model prevailed. In such major sporting centers as Chicago, Cincinnati, New Orleans, Philadelphia, and San Francisco, machine politicians were leading members of the sporting subculture. As political scientist Harold Zink reported in his classic *City Bosses in the United States* (1930), thirteen of his twenty subjects were well-known sportsmen.

As befitted their venal reputations, the machine politicians were especially prominent in prizefighting and horse racing, sports that operated under severe moral disapproval and widespread legal restrictions. In New Orleans, the leading fan was probably John Fitzgerald, referee of the seventy-five-round bare-knuckle championship fight in 1889 between John L. Sullivan and Jake Kilrain. Fitzgerald was elected mayor in 1892 but was later impeached. After the sport was banned in New York in 1900, San Francisco became the major site of pugilism. Its leading promoters all were affiliated with Boss Abe Ruef, who received payoffs to guarantee licenses for staging bouts.

In horse racing, it was commonplace for proprietary tracks to be affiliated with political machines. Offtrack betting operations were always closely allied to urban bosses for the necessary protection. In New Jersey, for instance, racing in the early 1890s at the state's six major tracks was nearly always illegal, notorious outlaw tracks like Guttenberg and Gloucester operated with impunity, servicing the sporting fraternity from New York and Philadelphia. Gloucester was owned by Bill Thompson, the local political boss, while Guttenberg received its protection from the notorious Hudson County machine that enabled it to operate year-round. In Chicago, the racing center of the Midwest, certain track officials were so closely allied to the local machines that the sporting press claimed its horsemen were outdoing Tammany. The most flagrant example in the early 1890s was Garfield Park, a proprietary track owned by West Side bookmakers. Their political clout emanated from Mike McDonald, reputed head of syndicate crime; Bathhouse John Coughlin, boss of the infamous Levee District;

and Johnny Powers, "Prince of Boodlers" in the city council and boss of the Nineteenth Ward. These political connections were also important in Chicago's bookmaking circles, since nearly all the handbook operators were tied to local ward machines.

The national pastime was not as tightly controlled by machine politicians as either prizefighting or horse racing, but nonetheless, professional baseball was dominated by notable politicos. Historian Ted Vincent has found that politicians made up nearly half of the 1,262 officials and stockholders of the nineteenth-century ball clubs he studied. Most teams outside New York were not organized and controlled by local political bosses. Several important teams did have such connections, most notably the Philadelphia Athletics, which until its demise in 1892 had always been run by members of the local Republican machine. Fifteen percent of the businessmen involved in baseball teams were also involved in traction, a highly politicized enterprise. The pattern established in the nineteenth century continued until 1920. Between 1900 and 1920 every American and National League team's ownership included professional politicians, traction magnates, or friends or relatives of prominent power brokers. A similar situation existed in the minor leagues, where traction executives often subsidized or sponsored baseball franchises to increase streetcar traffic. All the teams welcomed political connections as a means to protect the franchise against interlopers, to secure vital inside information from city hall, and to obtain preferential treatment from the municipal government.

Baseball best exemplified the pastoral world that white Anglo-Saxon Americans sought to maintain and protect in the face of industrialization, immigration, and urbanization. The sport helped to certify the continuing relevance of traditional values. But, paradoxically, baseball was in large measure controlled by men who typified all that mainstream America detested in the immigrant-dominated cities.

Suggested Readings

Berryman, Jack W. "Early Black Leadership in Collegiate Football: Massachusetts as a Pioneer." *Historical Journal of Massachusetts,* 9(1981): 17-28.

Captain, Gwendolyn. "Enter Ladies and Gentlemen of Color: Gender, Sport and the Ideal of African American Manhood and Womanhood During the Late Nineteenth and Early Twentieth Century." *Journal of Sport History,* 18(1991): 81-102.

Cavallo, Dominick. *Muscles and Morals: Organized Playgrounds and Urban Reform, 1880-1920.* Philadelphia: University of Pennsylvania Press, 1981.

Eisen, George. "Sport, Recreation and Gender: Jewish Immigrant Women in Turn-of-the-Century America." *Journal of Sport History,* 18(1991): 103-120.

Eisenberg, Michael T. *John L. Sullivan and His America*. Urbana, IL: University of Illinois Press, 1988.

Fielding, Lawrence W., & Pitts, Brenda G. "The Battle Over Athletic Priorities in Louisville YMCA, 1892-1916." *Canadian Journal of History of Sport,* 20(1989): 64-78.

Gelber, Steven M. "Their Hands Are All Out Playing: Business and Amateur Baseball, 1845-1917." *Journal of Sport History,* 11(1984): 5-27.

Grover, Kathryn. (Ed.) *Fitness in American Culture: Images of Health, Sport, and the Body, 1830-1940*. Rochester, NY: The Margaret Woodbury Strong Museum, 1989.

Grover, Kathryn. (Ed.) *Hard at Play: Leisure in America, 1840-1940*. Rochester, NY: The Margaret Woodbury Strong Museum, 1992.

Hardy, Stephen. *How Boston Played: Sport, Recreation, and Community, 1865-1915*. Boston: Northeastern University Press, 1982.

Hardy, Stephen, & Ingham, Alan G. "Games, Structures and Agencies: Historians on the American Play Movement." *Journal of Social History,* 17(1983): 285-301.

Harmond, Richard. "Progress and Flight: An Interpretation of the American Cycle Craze of the 1890s." *Journal of Social History,* 5(1971): 235-257.

LeCompte, Mary Lou. "Cowgirls at the Crossroads: Women in Professional Rodeo, 1885-1992." *Canadian Journal of History of Sport,* 20(1989): 27-48.

Levine, Peter. *A.G. Spalding and the Rise of Baseball: The Promise of American Sport*. New York: Oxford University Press, 1985.

MacAloon, John J. *This Great Symbol: Pierre de Coubertin and the Origins of the Modern Olympic Games*. Chicago: University of Chicago Press, 1981.

Oriard, Michael. *Reading Football: Sport, Popular Journalism, and American Culture*. Chapel Hill: University of North Carolina Press, 1993.

Park, Roberta J. "From Football to Rugby—and Back, 1906-1919: The University of California-Stanford University Response to the Football Crisis of 1905." *Journal of Sport History,* 11(1984): 5-40.

Paul, Joan. "The Health Reformers: George Barker Windship and Boston's Strength Seekers." *Journal of Sport History,* 10(1983): 41-57.

Pesavento, Wilma J. "Sport and Recreation in the Pullman Experiment, 1880-1900." *Journal of Sport History,* 9(1982): 38-62.

Riess, Steven A. *Touching Base: Professional Baseball and American Culture in the Progressive Era*. Westport, CT: Greenwood Press, 1980.

Roberts, Randy. *Papa Jack: Jack Johnson and the Era of White Hopes*. New York: The Free Press, 1983.

Shattuck, Debra S. "Bats, Balls, and Books: Baseball and Higher Education for Women at Three Eastern Women's Colleges, 1866-1900." *Journal of Sport History,* 19(1992): 91-109.

Smith, Ronald A. *Sports and Freedom: The Rise of Big-Time College Athletics*. New York: Oxford University Press, 1988.

Somers, Dale A. *The Rise of Sports in New Orleans, 1850-1900*. Baton Rouge: Louisiana State University Press, 1972.

Sumner, Jim L. "John Franklin Crowell, Methodism, and the Football Controversy at Trinity College, 1887-1894." *Journal of Sport History,* 17(1990):
5-20.

Uminowicz, Glenn. "Sport in a Middle-Class Utopia: Asbury Park, New Jersey,
1871-1895." *Journal of Sport History,* 11(1984): 51-73.

Vertinsky, Patricia A. *The Eternally Wounded Woman: Women, Exercise and
Doctors in the Late Nineteenth Century.* Manchester, England: Manchester
University Press, 1990.

Whorton, James C. "Athlete's Heart: The Medical Debate Over Athleticism,
1870-1920." *Journal of Sport History,* 9(1982): 30-52.

Wiggins, David K. "Isaac Murphy: Black Hero in Nineteenth Century American
Sport, 1861-1896." *Canadian Journal of History of Sport and Physical
Education,* 19(1979): 15-32.

PART 4

SPORT, CONSUMER CULTURE, AND TWO WORLD WARS, 1915-1945

American sport was greatly affected during the middle years of this century by new-found prosperity, domestic crisis, and international conflicts. The two World Wars, women's suffrage, development of a consumer culture, northern migration of southern blacks, and the ''New Deal'' legislation would all influence sport as it became increasingly woven into the fabric of American life. These events had substantial impact on the rise of sport heroes; increased involvement of women in sport; growth of less expensive mass sport; expansion of all-black sporting organizations; passage of state legislation requiring physical education in the public school systems; increase in public recreation programs; and building of elaborate athletic facilities and sports arenas.

World War I played an important role in the development of sport in this country. As many scholars have pointed out, the war helped foster the growth of boxing and served as the impetus for state physical education requirements, school athletics, and the development of sport-related programs sponsored by such organizations as the American Legion and the Knights of Columbus. In chapter 11, Timothy O'Hanlon sheds light on the philosophical rationale for sport participation and the place of school athletics in the war effort in his essay titled ''School Sports as Social Training: The Case of Athletics and the Crisis of World War I.'' O'Hanlon contends that the integration of sports into physical education curriculums, the debates within secondary schools over military preparedness, and the use of sports during the war combined to reinforce the interrelationship between athletics and the notion of effective citizenship. Educators in the public schools during this period organized varsity sports as a means to cultivate the virtues of the team player in students destined for unequal work roles and to duplicate the institutional forms of competition and cooperation found in schools. Just as in the military, educators in the public schools envisioned mass athletics as an instrument to offset the divisiveness of ranking, sorting, and testing.

The mass athletics that emerged around the time of the first World War would remain intact during the decade of the 1920s. The ideology of sport in the Twenties, however, would be markedly different from the preceding era. As Mark Dyreson makes clear in his essay, "The Emergence of Consumer Culture and the Transformation of Physical Culture: American Sport in the 1920s" (chapter 12) the conception of athleticism that emerged in the Twenties was a significant departure from the ideology of sport evident during the progressive era. Whereas the Progressives used sport as a means to preserve traditional values and as a tool to help citizens adapt to the new human environment, Americans during the 1920s increasingly viewed sport as a form of entertainment—one of the many forms of amusement available in a culture that glorified consumption. The declining spirit of reform, the rejection of physical culture by American intellectuals, and the full development of a consumer-driven economy combined in the Twenties to transform sport into a consumable item and an escape from social realities. In short, sport was now seen as one of life's central purposes and as an end rather than a means.

The changing ideology of sport in the Twenties helped make heroes out of such people as Jack Dempsey, Gene Tunney, Red Grange, and Babe Ruth. Hidden from the view of many people, however, were the sports organizations established by the various racial and ethnic groups that helped make up American society. Perhaps the most noteworthy (or at least the most written about of these organizations) were the all-black teams and leagues that sprang up across the country in baseball and other sports at various levels of competition. Unable to transcend racial barriers and compete against the best players in white-controlled sport, African-Americans increasingly turned to their own resources and established sporting organizations that contributed to their sense of community as a distinct racial group and helped them cope with life behind segregated walls.

The sporting organizations found in America's black community had their counterparts among this country's white ethnic groups. Immigrants from Eastern Europe and other places around the world established sporting organizations that assisted them in both forging cohesive ethnic communities and assimilating into American society. In St. Louis, as Gary Ross Mormino explains in chapter 13, "The Playing Fields of St. Louis: Italian Immigrants and Sports, 1925-1941," Italian immigrants fashioned a sporting life that helped them preserve their ethnic subculture while at the same time acculturating them into a large urban environment. Involvement in sport, in other words, served as an important symbol of ethnic group identity as well as a powerful assimilating agent for Italian-Americans living in St. Louis.

Sport played just as powerful a role among Japanese-Americans in central California as it did in the Italian neighborhoods of St. Louis. As Sam Regalado points out in chapter 14, ''Sport and Community in California's Japanese American 'Yamato Colony,' 1930-1945,'' the Japanese families who established the agricultural community in central California known as the Yamato Colony created different sport forms that served as both a means of acculturation and a way to maintain a sense of cultural heritage. Members of the Yamato Colony nurtured a sense of group pride and social cohesion through the creation of teams and leagues in baseball and other sports popular in American society. The nurturing of social cohesion through sport served the Japanese of the Yamato Colony particularly well during their confinement in internment camps following the United States' entry into World War II. Sport allowed them to maintain a sense of morale and provided an important outlet for the anxiety and frustration of camp life.

CHAPTER 11

School Sports as Social Training: The Case of Athletics and the Crisis of World War I

Timothy P. O'Hanlon

In 1915, Europe was engulfed in war. The question of the secondary school's role in preparing young men for the eventuality of America's entrance into the conflict became a controversial issue. Leading school and college administrators along with prominent physical educators argued strenuously that physical education programs (with a prominent place for sports) offered a means of fostering preparedness without encouraging militarism. Physical education and sports, they claimed, offered lessons in social discipline and cooperation no less valuable for citizens in an industrial society than for future soldiers.

Interestingly, their opponents who favored the introduction of military training into the high schools also evoked the goal of efficient citizenship. The conception of citizenship put forth by individuals on both sides of the military training debate was consistent in significant respects with that voiced by educators before preparedness became such a burning issue. The image of the productive citizen was consistent with the orientation of the reorganized public school. It was an image that endured, retaining essential features after the War, maintaining a strong association with schoolboy sports during the 1920s and 1930s.

The widespread use of athletic programs during the War sheds additional light on the social and psychological aims of athletics. When statements in behalf of school athletics are analyzed alongside those attesting the aims of sports in the military, the attributes associated with good citizenship bear an important resemblance to the qualities associated with becoming a good soldier.

The controversy over preparedness and the actual employment of athletics in the war effort strengthened the drive for physical education programs in the schools. The prominence of sports during the crisis period also reinforced the move to make sports the centerpiece of the high school P.E. curriculum. Finally, the intercamp 'championship' competition and mass athletics supported by the

From the *Journal of Sport History,* 9:1 (Spring, 1982). © 1982 The North American Society for Sport History. Reprinted by permission.

military resembled the distinction between varsity sports and sports conducted through physical education and intramural programs, as those activities developed in the two decades after the War.

The following paper will examine the debate over the place of sports in fostering military preparedness, the use of organized athletics during the War, and the emergence of high school sports programs after the War. The social role of sports, however, cannot be successfully analyzed apart from the larger context of public education. Therefore, before taking up the case of school athletics and World War I, the paper will trace the development of athletics as part of the history of twentieth century public schooling. This overview will encompass not only the years immediately preceding the war but also the two decades following the conflict. In it we will consider the uses of sports as envisioned by leading educators as well as points of divergence between the rhetoric of athletics and the reality.

School Reform and the Labor Market

At the turn of the century, leading educationists and their allies in business, civic, and professional organizations were engaged in the process of restructuring education to accommodate the increasingly diverse population flocking to the doors of the public high school. High school enrollments increased a dramatic 711% between 1890 and 1918. Despite these impressive figures, however, most children dropped out after grade school, and the majority of those who went to high school left before graduation. In 1918, the influential Commission on the Reorganization of Secondary Education reported that only one-third of all grade school students entered high school and only about one out of nine ever graduated.

Educators frequently blamed the high dropout rate on the schools' failure to meet the educational needs of their more heterogeneous clientele. Elite reformers agreed that the schools needed to assume a more extensive role in meeting the requirements of the industrial labor market, that is, in selecting and training students for different kinds of occupational roles. This vision of schooling was supported by the widespread acceptance of the modern corporation and the accompanying fragmentation of work roles into a steeply graded division of labor as necessary features of social and economic life.

Claiming that student bodies had been "modified by the entrance of large numbers of pupils of widely varying capacities, aptitudes, social heredity and destinies in life," educators moved to diversify the secondary school curriculum by adding alternative courses and programs of study. *The Cardinal Principles of Secondary Education* report issued by the Commission on the Reorganization of Secondary Education in 1918 expressed a firm commitment to a differentiated curriculum as a hallmark of the American comprehensive high school. In the words of that report,

A variety of sports was used by the armed services during World War I, as evidenced by this army ski training at Camp Grant, Illinois.
Courtesy of the National Archives.

The growing recognition that progress in our American democracy depends in no small measure upon adequate provision for specialization in many fields is the chief cause leading to the present reorganization of secondary education. Only through attention to the needs of various groups of individuals as shown by aptitudes, abilities and aspirations can the secondary school secure from each pupil his best efforts.

The practice of offering some choice of coursework in high schools was not new. The Cardinal Principles document's endorsement of differentiation, however, reflected the increasingly vocational orientation of American schooling. During the early years of the twentieth century, sorting for the labor market usually took place before the high school years. Some urban school districts established industrial training or vocational programs in the upper elementary grades in order to reach youth before they went to work. As the average years of school attendance increased, differentiation centered on the high school. But with the persistence of high dropout rates, the schools not only shaped the aspirations of their charges, but continued to sort in a more passive sense by reflecting the economic constraints imposed on students and their families.

By 1918, educational needs had become more closely identified with the capacity to perform various kinds of occupational roles. In the process, all schooling, both the academic courses and the less academic alternatives, had become more vocationalized in the sense of having become more strongly associated with labor market outcomes. Succeeding decades witnessed differentiation in a variety of forms. Some high schools offered alternative courses and patterns of courses. Others set up alternative curriculums or some form of tracking. There were offerings in vocational, commercial, industrial, domestic, and agricultural subjects as well as academic courses with a more practical focus for the less scholarly.

Programmatic expressions of differentiation varied, but the commitment to rationalizing access to positions in society through schooling remained well established. This commitment was buttressed by the continuing belief that schools had to accommodate widely divergent aptitudes which included, among other things, the idea that many students were not academically inclined. Academic subjects were assuming an added significance as screening devices which determined one's qualifications for higher white collar positions. Aided by the development of vocational guidance programs, reformers reorganized schools to accommodate the separation of planning from execution so characteristic of the twentieth century workplace. Academic programs came to signify training for "thinking" rather than "doing" jobs.

The routinization of work roles placed constraints on human judgment, initiative, control, and skill. Lower level jobs subjected individuals to close supervision and relatively low status and pay. Educators acknowledged the unequal conditions and rewards of the workplace to some extent, but focused their attention on the divergent interests and aptitudes which they presumed to exist among the American population. Ellwood Cubberly of Stanford University, a powerful voice in school reform, urged that the schools needed to "give up the exceedingly democratic idea that all are equal, and that society is devoid of classes." Charles Prosser, an influential figure in the industrial training movement, observed that "we are swinging around to the idea that it is to be the mission of the schools in the future to select by testing and training—to adjust boys and girls for life by having them undergo varied experiences in order to uncover their varied traits and aptitudes and to direct and to train them in the avenues for which they display the most capacity."

In practice, this meant channeling a portion of the student body into jobs which required little skill, save perhaps enormous toleration for boredom or frustration. The educational implication of uncovering "traits and capacities" was captured by the president of the school board in the famous *Middletown* study. Casting a retrospective glance at the role of the high school in his town from the vantage point of the 1920s, he noted that "for a long time all boys were trained to be president. Then for a while we trained them all to be professional men. Now we are training our boys to get jobs."

The language of intellectual and psychological differences made schooling seem less like a high stakes competition for a limited number of desirable jobs or an institutional means of rationalizing social and economic inequality, and more like a process of guiding students into work roles commensurate with their real talents. With the organization of production taken for granted, problems in the workplace were perceived as problems of testing, training, intelligence, and socialization. Although there was widespread recognition that many jobs were joyless and stultifying, it was up to the student to demonstrate his fitness for a dignified occupation.

Athletics and Socialization, A Blueprint for Citizenship

A second prominent feature of early twentieth century educational reform concerned the school's role in cultivating common values and allegiances among students from different social classes and ethnic backgrounds, students who would be funneled into different occupations. Extracurricular activities including school sports were touted as potentially powerful agencies for inculcating the kinds of attitudes and behaviors associated with effective citizenship. According to leading educationists and physical educators, athletics could provide the kind of practical lessons in cooperation and social discipline required for participation in an industrial society. "The times," agreed Luther Halsey Gulick, a founder of the New York Public Schools' Athletic League, "demand men with high corporate morality and it cannot be learned from books or lectures." Gulick believed that athletics offered the schools a means of providing a genuine social education. Above all, sports "awakened" a wholesome sense of group consciousness that enveloped player and nonplayer alike. "There is," he concluded,

> no other avenue open to us by means of which it is possible to develop the idea of corporate, of inter-institutional morality—that which represents the individuals but includes them as a whole—than inter-institutional athletics. No other agency can be so effective, for nothing else begins to have grip on the imagination and emotional life of our young men as do these athletics.

Gulick's remarks, penned in 1911, captured some already popular themes concerning the benefits of properly supervised sports, themes which would be reiterated again and again over the next thirty years. Athletics could be an effective source of influence because sports were so popular. And athletics, particularly in the form of team sports, emphasized the kinds of values and forms of interaction compatible with participation in an industrial state.

Criticisms of laissez-faire principles were a characteristic feature of the rhetoric of school reform from early in the century to the second World War. In disparaging rugged individualism as an anachronistic vestige of the nineteenth century, however, educators were not really rejecting the value of competition, but seeking to rationalize it. Social cooperation was to be forged in the competitive atmosphere of the public school. The acceptance of common values meant, among other things, the acceptance of common notions of fairness, merit, and opportunity.

The task of unifying the student body involved getting them to accept the procedures and criteria through which one was thought to earn, or fail to earn, a prestigious role in society. Cooperating in school became associated with a willingness to compete in approved terms and to accept the consequences.

Athletics emerges from the educational literature as a means of tempering individualistic qualities and superimposing on them the ethos of the team player. Addressing an annual convention of the National Education Association, Charles Whitten boasted that no other activity came close to athletics in offering students the opportunity for the "actual practice" of the ideals learned in the classroom. Whitten, an educator and long-time Secretary of the Illinois State High School Athletic Association, maintained that "in addition to the personal qualities of alertness, determination, persistence and courage, the successful team must practice the virtues of self-control, teamwork and cooperation, the submergence of self in the interest of the group and unselfish devotion and loyalty to a social unit, virtues of which all society stands so much in need." Educators' concern with establishing a sense of community in a society beset with the centrifugal forces of class, ethnicity, and fragmented work roles helps to explain the consistent endorsement of the idea of mass athletic participation in the schools.

Interscholastic athletics, however, posed a particular set of problems for educators. Inter-school competition was well under way by the first decade of the twentieth century. As was the case with college sports such as football, high school teams frequently came into existence as the result of student initiative. The story of varsity athletics involved not only the proliferation of new programs under the guidance of faculty and administration, but also the attempt to wrest control from student administered teams. A 1907 study found that in more than one out of six cases surveyed (37 out of 192), school teams remained under student domination. The tide, however, was turning. The campaign for school control was successful, and by 1924, state high school athletic associations operated in all but three states.

Although varsity sports prospered, they came under consistent attack for placing too much emphasis on winning. Charges of commercialism, bad sportsmanship, and bending the rules were as commonplace and predictable as the enduring popularity of games. Over the first four decades of the twentieth century, educators never stopped raising questions about the educational and social value of interscholastic athletics, but neither of the two main currents of athletic reform threatened their demise. The dominant view throughout the '20s and '30s, no doubt heavily supported by community sentiment, was that varsity sports could promote sound values if they were properly regulated. This position provided the rationale for the leagues and state associations which strove to regulate and standardize competition between schools. The maintenance of eligibility requirements and other rules governing athletic relations between schools constituted the heart of the campaign to reform the excesses of interschool contests.

Interscholastic athletics not only drew fire for encouraging a "winning is everything" attitude but for failure to involve the average student. Efforts to promote mass participation made up the second major strand of reform. While schoolmen struggled in the early years of the century to gain control of athletics, physical educators were seeking to replace the older curriculum of formal exercises with one more oriented toward sports and games. Belief in the social benefits of mass participation in sport for boys not only gained considerable currency among leading physical educators, but also garnered support from a more general movement for organized play and recreation. Such "modern" programs of physical education, however, had apparently not been implemented on a very extensive scale in American high schools before the War. Spurred on by the preparedness crisis, the drive to establish sports-centered P.E. programs picked up steam after the conflict. By the 1930s, intramural athletics had won widespread recognition as an important means of cultivating mass participation and developing wholesome leisure habits. But, even though critics continued to tout the relative merits of intramural programs over varsity sports throughout the decade, the latter continued to dominate the high school sports scene.

Ironically, the organization and conduct of varsity athletics came to resemble that of schooling much more closely than intramurals. Shaping the school into a more efficient instrument for allocating places in society, as noted earlier, constituted a major thrust of early twentieth century school reform. The introduction of differentiated curricula, vocational guidance, and the widespread employment of I.Q. testing after World War I reflected the effort to rationalize competition for work roles and establish schooling as a legitimate basis for determining one's vocational aptitude.

The relationship between schooling and the labor market was a dynamic one effected by patterns of school enrollment which in turn were tied to social class, race, urban-rural, and regional variations. Using the school to gain access to jobs meant different things to different people. Despite impressive upward trends in years of formal education, many students still did not graduate from high school in the 1920s and '30s. Undoubtedly, teachers often encouraged promising working class students to pursue further academic training. For many, however, the prospects of finishing high school or preparing for college presented themselves as unrealistic expectations rather than foregone conclusions. Similarly, enrollments in vocationally oriented curriculums not only reflected assessments of academic potential but also projections of life chances made by counsellors, parents, and the students themselves. The programs and procedures instituted by educational reformers facilitated the long term development of schooling as the primary source of competition for jobs. Gaining higher level work roles, however, involved not only school performance, but the economic, social, and psychological resources to persist in the right kind of school program.

Access to the labor market through schooling was not the same as competing for positions on the football team. The influences of social class were different and more pervasive in schooling than in sports. Varsity athletics, of course, were not immune from racial discrimination. Leading educators openly opposed interschool programs for women. On the other hand, for those boys who got a chance to try out, interscholastic athletics may have been conducted on a more clearly meritocratic basis with respect to social class differences than schooling was. Despite these and other possible differences, however, the parallels between schooling and sports are worth exploring.

Schooling, whatever the shortcomings of its meritocratic pretensions, was becoming associated with occupational success, both in perception and in fact. It was increasingly recognized as the place where youngsters proved their fitness or lack thereof for better kinds of jobs. By the 1920s, the institutional mechanisms for guiding students into different levels of the labor market were well established. Cries of overemphasis in varsity football and basketball during the '20s and '30s obscured the interesting ways in which these team sports had adapted organizational procedures similar to those employed in schooling. Candidates for the team competed with one another for a limited number of starting and starring roles. In sports as in schools, individuals were subject to continuous evaluation and ranking in accordance with standards developed and administered by professional experts. By placing youngsters in similar situations and exposing them to similar institutional demands, interscholastic athletics supported a major ideological component of schooling. The structured competition of schooling helped to legitimatize social stratification and a stratified workplace. Varsity athletics contributed by reinforcing the idea that unequal rewards were the fair result of unequal ability determined through standardized competition. Just as schooling reinforced the premise that relatively unsuccessful students did not deserve the better jobs, sports practiced the idea that less able athletes did not deserve to play. Playing time was a matter of coaching strategy, not an inherent right of team membership. Athletes were continually called upon to demonstrate their abilities and usefulness to the team in order to maintain their positions.

The coach's teaching role was constrained by the overriding goal of organizational proficiency. His problem of developing team spirit in athletics resembled the problem of cultivating cooperative citizenship in schools. In team sports, jealousy and resignation loomed as twin stumbling blocks to team efficiency. If players accepted the idea that they had to demonstrate their abilities to the satisfaction of the coach, then he stood a good chance of enlisting their whole-hearted cooperation in carrying out their assignments for the good of the team.

School personnel confronted the task of fostering common values and a spirit of cooperation among students heading for unequal work roles. Coaches encountered the task of forging a spirit of teamwork among competitors who held positions of unequal rank and prestige. In both settings, successful management depended on maintaining the legitimacy of the reward system. For those who worked hard, there was the promise of promotion. But hard work, after all, often was not a sufficient condition for advancement. Some would not rise, no matter how hard they tried.

Through civics classes, guidance counselling, and a variety of curricular and extracurricular activities, schools attempted to instill the idea that the well being of the nation and individual enterprises depended upon each person performing his allotted task to the best of his abilities. For unsuccessful students or those otherwise unable to acquire the right kind or amount of schooling, the blueprint for cooperative citizenship often included training for a subordinate role in the labor market. Coaches sought to reconcile their charges to the unequal conse-quences of competition by emphasizing that the team's success depended on the effort of each member. Each athlete was exhorted to contribute his talents to the fullest and to play his designated role with enthusiasm, no matter how humble it turned out to be. "The key to team spirit," wrote Coleman R. Griffith, author of *The Psychology of Coaching,* "lies in making every man feel that his contribu-tion to team-play is an important contribution and a matter of personal satisfaction to the coach." According to Griffith, the coach was "responsible for helping his men to see that real greatness lies in placing a generous value upon *any* contribution made by any man."

Varsity team sports were organized and conducted in ways that reinforced patterns of socialization in schools. The popularity of such sports also indicated that the influence of interscholastic athletics in molding conceptions of fairness and cooperation, however effective, extended to the majority of nonparticipants.

One more point is worth noting here. The attempt to cultivate allegiance and cooperation in contentious situations was not confined to schools and to the athletic field. Corporate managers also struggled with this problem as a crucial issue of control. Welfare schemes, employee-representation plans, pension plans, work incentive programs, and promotions policies all involved the attempt to enlist loyalty and unity in a hierarchical situation. Managing students, athletes, and employees shared some common ground.

The Preparedness Controversy

As the clouds of war loomed menacingly on the horizon, most educators agreed that schools should contribute to keeping America mentally and physically pre-pared for whatever challenges lay ahead, but they disagreed, sometimes rather heatedly, over the means. Critics of military training for schoolboys focused on forms of military drill which were thought to be characteristic of high school programs. Educators frequently offered physical education as an alternative to military drill. They argued that a sound program of physical education (which would in most cases include a prominent role for sports) offered a means of preparedness training in that it developed soldierly attributes without encouraging a lockstep military mentality. On the contrary, according to many supporters, athletics helped to cultivate the physical and, most particularly, the psychological traits essential for both war and peace.

Military training programs were in existence in some American high schools at the outset of the War in Europe. High schools in Boston had apparently required drill since Reconstruction. The New York Public Schools' Athletic League offered competition in rifle marksmanship for high school boys as part of its massive sports and recreation program. Military training, however, was not a systemic component of American secondary education. One source counted only 113 high schools "giving military drill of any kind" in 1915 and reaching an estimated total of 14,500 boys.

In 1916, the New York state legislature in an otherwise undistinguished session passed two companion laws designed to implement preparedness. The Welsh Bill prescribed mandatory physical training for all students above the age of eight, beginning with the 1916 school year. The law specified 20 minutes a day as minimum and included private as well as public schools.

The Slater Bill was more controversial. It set up a Military Training Commission whose purpose was to establish and oversee military training for young men between the ages of 16 and 19. In accordance with the provisions of the bill, the Commission could legally compel military training for a maximum of three hours per week in addition to the regular physical education provided by the Welsh Bill. Only those boys who were regularly engaged in working for a living were exempt. The law also permitted the Commission to create summer military camps which would last from four to six weeks. The legislature appropriated only $10,000, however, which forced the Commission to establish priorities among various eligible groups. According to one magazine account, secondary school-boys were at the top of the list.

The laws generated a great deal of discussion, most of it critical. Besides objections registered against the principle of compulsion, critics charged that the training was inadequate. The *School Review* joined this second group of naysayers in attacking the New York scheme, even though elsewhere the journal had published a series of editorials favorable to the idea of military training in the schools. Casting a retrospective glance at the program in April 1918, the *Review* observed that attendance in many high school drills had dwindled from a beginning figure of three or four hundred to 30 or 40. In the next issue, the journal produced additional figures to substantiate its indictment:

Acting Superintendent Straubenmiller, of the New York City Schools, reports that military training is being sadly neglected. Only four high schools have an average attendance of 50 percent of the boys enrolled for the training. Attendance in various schools ranged from 2 to 89 percent. One report shows that of 10,898 boys enrolled for drill, 4,489 were present, 3,575 absent.

The journal pointed to boredom as a prime cause of the depressing statistics, noting that the training consisted almost entirely of close order drill. Furthermore, it noted, the boys received no academic credit for their after-school efforts.

The "Wyoming Plan" constituted another controversial yet apparently more popular alternative to the New York experiment. The Wyoming idea was conceived by Lieutenant Edgar Z. Steever, while serving a tour of duty as Inspector-Instructor of the state National Guard. Steever's plan called for the division of student cadets into units which remained the same throughout the school year. The units engaged one another in a series of competitions beginning with wall scaling and calisthenics during the fall. The second semester featured competitions in drill, troop leadership, and field firing. Beginning in May, there was an increased emphasis on interschool contests. The program attempted to recreate the flavor of military life by ending the year with 14 days of summer camp.

The Wyoming plan soon spread beyond the confines of its rather isolated birthplace. Late in 1916, *Everybody's* magazine began a concerted campaign to promote Steever's brainchild. The publication set itself up as the official headquarters of the High School Volunteers of the United States, a confederation of cadet organizations which had adopted the Wyoming Plan. The Wyoming scheme received approval from the U.S. Army War College and some support in Congress. Secretary of War Newton Baker also came out in support. As a result, schools which put together cadet brigades of 100 or more were entitled to an instructor and equipment provided by the Federal Government.

The majority position in the educational press seemed to favor physical education over military drill or the Wyoming Program as a desirable means of building preparedness. Many attacked military drill as a useless and obsolete form of preparedness. In 1915, the Massachusetts Commission on Military Education issued a report which opposed military training for boys between the ages of 14 and 21. The Massachusetts study was widely cited by critical schoolmen.

> The overwhelming weight of opinion from school teachers, military experts, officers of both the regular army and the military and the general public is against military drill. . . . It is generally agreed that the military drill which a boy receives in school is of little or no advantage to him from the point of view of practical soldiering. As far as available evidence goes, drill in the schools has had no beneficial effect in promoting enlistments in the military except in a few isolated localities.

In fact, stated the report, drill had the opposite effect. It created an aversion to military life.

Other critics, speaking individually and in association with peace groups, raised the ominous spectre of militarism. To the venerable Charles W. Eliot of Harvard, military training in the schools smacked of despotism. "I have heard a great deal of talk lately about the importance of a boy's acquiring the habit of implicit obedience," he noted; "that is the worst habit a boy can acquire after he ceases to be an infant, because it implies the subjection of the boy's own will."

David Starr Jordan, Chancellor of Stanford University, maintained that mandatory drill in the schools constituted an entering wedge for compulsory training under state control. He argued that in order for training programs to be effective, they would have to include the majority of boys who either dropped out or failed to attend high school. At that point the state would take authority out of the hands of the school boards because military drill would no longer be an educational activity in a strict sense.

Jordan cited Australia as a living example of his fears. He pointed out that some 22,143 had been prosecuted in less than three years under Australia's compulsory service laws. "In general," he concluded, "no nation with compulsory military service can long retain its sanity or its freedom. The first purpose of compulsory service is to make subservient industrial as well as military units of the young men of the country.'' In adopting a policy of militarization, a nation flirted with totalitarianism. ''The docile army is the right arm of privilege,'' argued Jordan, ''and the reliance of the industrial exploiter. Military drill accustoms men to blind obedience. They are taught to regard frightfulness in terms of exalted patriotism.''

Friends of the Wyoming idea attempted to counter the charges that military training killed initiative and fostered lock step obedience. Steever defended his program as an alternative to old style military drill. He contended that the Wyoming Plan was modelled on nothing more sinister than competitive sports. ''Our military instruction has been adopted to the game notion,'' declared Steever in the 1917 symposium in the *School Review*. ''We have taken the old lock-step, routine work out of military instruction and we have adapted it to the game.'' By pitting high school cadet units against one another, he claimed, ''we get all the dash and all the efficiency of the football team in our national-defense games.''

Regarding the question of individual initiative, Steever attempted to turn the tables by taking a critical glance at the authority structure of varsity sports. In a statement cited by journalist George Creel, Steever invited the reader to observe typical baseball and football teams. He expressed confidence that the observer would soon be disabused of the notion that varsity athletics developed initiative. ''You rake the school or college for the strongest and most skillful and put these chosen few in the hands of specialists who demand the blindest sort of obedience.'' The Wyoming idea not only placed more of a premium on initiative, according to Steever, but provided a chance for all boys to participate.

From the outset, the Wyoming approach was sold as a means of fostering preparedness by inculcating the qualities of effective citizenship. The laudatory piece by George Creel, which was read into the *Congressional Record* in February 1916, emphasized Steever's statement that the Wyoming Plan would create citizens instead of soldiers. ''Your boys,'' Steever reportedly told parents at the outset of his efforts in Wyoming, ''will be taught the advantages of a strong body and a clean mind, the value of self-control and decent restraints, civic duties and responsibilities.'' The goals then were in line with the social orientation of the public school. His program aimed at ''full development of the fraternal instinct, the community-of-interest spirit, so that every youngster will grow up in the understanding that no group, whether it be a cadet company, city, state, or nation, is stronger than its weakest member.''

The United States Army War College, in a published description of the Wyoming Plan, accepted the claims made in its behalf and recommended its adoption by local school boards as a citizenship training program. Statements in *The Outlook* and *Everybody's* also advanced this view and presented the Wyoming idea as a means of avoiding militarism. The slogan of the High School Volunteers even during the war years as ''For Better Citizenship.''

Concern with personal fitness, national unity, and individual and social discipline may have intensified as the war drew closer. Similarities in the rhetoric of educators across the first seventeen years of the century may underestimate the sense of crisis after 1915 and its possible effects on ideas of citizenship. Conceptions of democratic citizenship may well have differed in important respects, not only among those who supported physical education but also between the proponents and opponents of military training schemes. Similarities in the rhetoric of preparedness and citizenship may have masked significant social and political disagreements regarding such vital questions as civil liberties.

Nevertheless, with the proponents of military training stressing the role of those programs in developing good citizenship, the controversy took an interesting turn. The emphasis on social discipline and cooperation advanced by apologists for the Wyoming idea and opponents of military training was not new. This suggests that both sides were invoking conceptions of citizenship which were rooted in the response to social and economic changes in American life at the turn of the century. Disagreements over the adequacy of different training programs for high school boys were on one hand a response to a burning issue of the day, the possibility of war. In a larger sense, however, the preparedness issue also reflected well established aims of schooling and citizenship training.

Both critics and defenders of the Wyoming Plan named a competitive games approach as an alternative to military drill. Steever and others for their part presented the Wyoming idea as a kind of intramural program combined with Boy Scouts, where group games were modified to meet the general needs of national strength and vigilance. Those who opposed both military drill and the Wyoming Plan threw their support behind systematic physical education, which called for the liberal employment of athletics. Schoolmen may have feared militarism but they had few scruples about using organized play as a means of social conditioning. They continued to express the hope that sports programs could help the schools shape a more disciplined and cooperative social order. Individuals would continue to contest one another for individual rewards, but they would compete according to well defined rules and be willing to abide by the consequences.

In 1917, the National Education Association's Committee on Military Training in the Public Schools issued a report recommending that schools institute compulsory physical education as part of a comprehensive drive for national unity and security. The Committee stood foursquare against the introduction of "any form of instruction which is distinctly or specifically military into the elementary or secondary schools." The document, sprinkled liberally with the statements of authorities, argued that early military drill was at best ineffective and at worst deleterious to health, peace, and freedom of thought. One such negative comment was provided by Captain H.J. Koehler of West Point.

> The use of the musket as a means of physical development for anyone, be he man or boy, is more than worthless. It is, in my opinion, positively injurious. I deny absolutely that military drill contains one worthy feature which cannot be duplicated in every well regulated gymnasium in the country today. A thorough physical training develops all the necessary

soldierly qualities to the greatest degree and it does it without injury. If we have athletics, we shall never be without soldiers.

Though fearful of injecting a spirit of militarism into the public schools, the authors recommended marching as one of several activities within a physical training regimen including sports, gymnastics, and calisthenics. The report also made a point of urging school systems to "develop and intensify" their efforts to instill loyalty and patriotism, particularly among immigrant children. Committee members, like many educators who adamantly opposed military training in high schools, held no such reservations for older men. Accordingly, the report advocated universal compulsory training for young men beyond the age of 19.

Those critical of military training often pressed a line of argument similar to that of proponents of the Wyoming Plan. They contended that physical education built the kind of toughness and discipline that made good soldiers, but without encouraging either the belligerent or the servile attitudes identified with militarism. Thus, went the reasoning, physical education prepared youngsters for peace every bit as much as for the eventuality of war.

The opposition to military training on democratic grounds did not prevent many educators from equating the requirements for citizenship in modern America with the qualities that went into making a good soldier. Descriptions of these qualities remained virtually the same as those ascribed to athletics and physical education some years earlier. Charles Eliot, for example, preferred physical education because it "would give the boy the best preparation he could receive at that time of his life for a soldier's future and it would also give the boys the best preparation the schools can give for service in the industrial army." In a quote appearing in the *School Review's* symposium on military training, Eliot came out in favor of voluntary enlistment. He attacked both conscription and the discipline of the professional soldier as infringements of personal liberties. "What we want in the form of discipline in the army," he argued, "is just what we want in industries; it is the cooperative work; it is the sense of comradeship, fellowship, which in sports we call 'team-play'."

What Eliot missed was that schools, industries, and varsity sports teams, like the Army, attempted to elicit cooperation from individuals slotted into roles of unequal prestige and reward. Educators' concern with "team play" whether involving capital and labor or members of an intramural team did not reflect a commitment to egalitarian goals. On the contrary, "team spirit" referred to the problem of developing a sense of unity among members of a hierarchical society, a society which leading educators took for granted as the necessary outgrowth of "industrialization."

The attributes necessary for an industrial society and for military preparedness often turned out to be remarkably similar. New Jersey school superintendent D. C. Bliss launched a blistering attack on military training programs in the pages of the *School Review*. But, on the other hand, he argued that any school which did not take as its "fundamental aim" the development of those attributes "which shall be possessed by every upright, useful citizen'' was derelict in its responsibility. ''The moral virtues of obedience, patriotism and self-sacrifice,'' he asserted, ''are no more desirable for the soldier than for anyone else.''

Many individuals who desired to substitute physical education for military training in the schools subscribed to the views of Harvard's Dudley A. Sargent. Sargent, already a leading light in physical education, took an active role in opposing military training in the Massachusetts schools. His testimony before the Special State Board of Military Preparedness was frequently cited and used to buttress the cases of such groups as the School Peace League and the Women's Peace Party of New York. In 1916, the American Physical Education Association gave Sargent's views its official stamp of approval at its annual convention.

Sargent claimed that ''the same qualities that are of most value for war are of most value for peace'' and that military drill was inadequate on both counts. Military drill did not offer the ''opportunity for struggle'' afforded by the playground or athletic field. It was in the rigor of competitive games, not in the ''tin soldierism'' of the drill field, where boys developed courage and a spirit of competition and self-sacrifice. The problem, as always, was that the schools offered the vital lessons of athletics only to an elite. ''What America needs,'' concluded Sargent, ''is some way of providing more athletic students and fewer student athletes, some way of providing more soldierly schoolboys, instead of schoolboy soldiers.''

Jesse Feiring Williams of Columbia, who would emerge as a leading spokesman for the role of athletics in physical education during the 1920s and '30s spoke out against military drill at the same 1916 gathering which endorsed Sargent's views. In an address entitled, ''Proposals for Preparedness in Physical Education,'' Williams proclaimed the superior capacity of athletics to arouse an emotional commitment to the group. In fostering preparedness without militarism, said Williams, athletics played a vital role in the creation of socially responsible citizens which was ''the growing task of physical education'' and indeed of schooling in general.

The arguments of Williams and others bore an interesting relationship to broader educational concerns. The idea that authoritarian forms of control were undemocratic and ineffectual was becoming a common theme in discussions of school discipline and citizenship training before 1910. The nominal rejection of more overt methods of control and socialization, however, did not mean that educators were abandoning the predetermined goals of citizenship training. Old fashioned methods may have seemed unduly restrictive to individual freedom, but shaping attitudes and behavior through group activities such as sports evoked little moral outrage in the councils of education.

A parallel situation seemed to exist in the preparedness debates. Military forms of training and discipline were condemned but little heed was paid to the possibility that athletics also might constitute a coercive, albeit more appealing method of training. Athletics, like other student activities, relied on peer group pressure, emotional involvement, and conditioning more than rational reflection, to achieve its residual social objectives such as loyalty and cooperation.

Athletics for the Armed Forces

The military made extensive use of sports during World War I. Sports were used to distract the troops from less wholesome forms of amusement. In addition to serving as a weapon in the war against vice, athletic games also became a part of the military training program itself. A competitive games concept was employed on several levels. Taking a page from the Wyoming Plan, the military incorporated a group games approach to training exercises. Squads of trainees competed against one another in relays, equipment races, and trench exercises. Team competition, according to the athletic officer at Camp Pike, encourage the kind of competitive *esprit de corps* which was essential to any efficient fighting unit. Joseph Raycroft, a professor of physical education at Princeton and the Director of the Army athletic programs in the training camps, counted "group games" a part of the educational phase of training. In games, a young recruit learned to react quickly under competitive pressure, to adapt to changing circumstances, and to keep his emotions in check.

The military also encouraged widespread participation in a variety of sports. The Army and Navy both set up extensive boxing programs. Movements in boxing were thought to parallel those in bayonet fighting. As was the case in schools, athletics were not merely considered a source of physical training, but an important agency for developing dispositions and attitudes.

Sports like boxing and football allegedly built confidence and aggressiveness. They taught young recruits, as one observer put it, "to get bumped and not to mind it." Preparing for war was a grimmer business than going to school and one should be wary of carrying the similarities between citizens, soldiers, and athletes too far. With that caution duly registered, however, it is important to note the resemblance between the role of athletics articulated by men involved in administering activities for the military and the "educational aims" of school sports. In both cases teamwork involved the efficient coordination of men in specialized ranks and roles carrying out orders from the top.

In addition to incorporating games-oriented training exercises and mass athletics as integral parts of basic training, the armed forces also encouraged inter-camp competition. The latter was the equivalent of school varsity competition as individual encampments sought to put their best teams on the field. As a means of boosting morale after the War, the American Expeditionary Forces staged a far-ranging series of elimination tournaments in several sports. The tournament winners participated in the Inter-Allied Games, a kind of Olympics held in Paris during July, 1919. John Griffith, an athletic officer during World War I and later Commissioner of the Big Ten Athletic Conference, argued that championship play complemented the goals of mass participation by encouraging interest in sports. Prominent men such as James McCurdy, Physical Director for the A.E.F., and Raycroft shared Griffith's views concerning the complementary relationship between mass athletics and championship competition. Raycroft and Griffith both held prominent positions in the National Collegiate Athletic Association after the War. In 1921, Griffith became the first editor of the *Athletic*

Journal and for over two decades ardently proclaimed the educational and social value of interschool sports.

The preparedness issue did not go away immediately after the conflict. Commentators expressed horror over the large numbers of American youth who had been rejected by the armed forces as physically unfit. There were still those who advocated military training as a solution to the problem. *Everybody's*, as of 1919, was still engaged in an effort to promote the High School Volunteers.

Educators continued their support for physical education as an alternative to military training. A National Committee on Physical Education drafted a model bill and agitated for its passage among the various states. The Committee also lobbied within both major political parties prior to the general election of 1920. Their efforts paid off as both the Republicans and the Democrats adopted physical education planks in their respective platforms.

States moved rapidly to adopt physical education laws after 1919. Prior to 1915, only Idaho, Ohio, and North Dakota had physical education laws on the books. In the next three years, eight more states passed physical training laws of one sort or another. Between 1919 and 1925, however, the movement for physical education gained momentum as 22 states passed enabling legislation. Before the end of the decade, 36 states had passed laws pertaining to P.E. in the schools. Apparently not all of these statutes made instruction compulsory, however. A 1927-28 nationwide survey, for example, revealed that only 254 out of 464 high schools required physical education.

The growth of physical education programs ushered in an increased emphasis on athletics. Historian Guy Lewis was substantially correct when he argued that the 1920s witnessed the triumph of the movement to make sports the focal point of P.E., a movement which began shortly after the turn of the century. By the early 1930s, there was substantial support for intramural athletics, fueled by indignation over varsity contests and concern with the cultivation of leisure interests. Intramurals, however, were an addition to, not a replacement for, interscholastic athletics.

The use of sports by the military boosted the drive for mass participation programs after the War, but their influence on the subsequent relationship among varsity athletics, physical education, and intramurals is harder to assess. The relative prestige and the predominance of interscholastic sports were bound up with patterns of popular culture which are too complicated to explore here. Nevertheless, it is worth noting that the establishment of inter-camp competition supported the notion that the more elite forms of participation were compatible with mass play. Through some combination of conviction and expedience, this was the viewpoint which won the day in American public high schools.

The debate over military preparedness, the use of sports during the War, and the successful effort to integrate sports into the physical education curriculum all had the effect to solidifying and reinforcing the association between athletics and the conception of effective citizenship which was emerging during the early years of the twentieth century. Concern with efficiency, organization, order, and unity marked the efforts to transform the public school during the Progressive

Era. By the end of the War, educators had succeeded in reconstituting the school as a more effective instrument for meeting the needs of the industrial labor market. In the process, they set out to cultivate, to impose if necessary, the virtues of the team player on a student populace headed for unequal work roles. Athletics promised not only to cultivate competition, but more importantly to discipline it. As was the case in the military, educators sought in mass athletics an agency for counterbalancing the divisive effects of ranking, sorting, and testing. Varsity team sports, whether educators fully realized it or not, were organized to socialize by replicating the rationalized competition and institutional forms of cooperation found in schooling.

The critical period surrounding the War served to invest the task of building social discipline and cooperation with a greater sense of urgency, but the goals themselves were not new. The frequent claims that athletics prepared men for peace or war reveal as much about the consistent commitment of the schools to the goal of social efficiency as they do about the concern with national security brought on by the war in Europe and its aftermath. Educators, while eschewing militarism, proclaimed sports as the medium for the soldierly qualities of loyalty, self-sacrifice, and group spirit. The point then is not that the crisis of the War years militarized the concept of citizenship, but that the whole military training issue served to illuminate the strong emphasis upon organization, regimentation, and social discipline which was already present and would linger long after the War.

CHAPTER 12

The Emergence of Consumer Culture and the Transformation of Physical Culture: American Sport in the 1920s

Mark Dyreson

The decade of the 1920s witnessed a fundamental reshaping of the ideology of sport in American civilization. During the birth of an "Age of Play," as essayist Robert L. Duffus labeled the Twenties, Americans increasingly understood sport as a vehicle for entertainment—one of the many items available for amusement in a culture which glorified consumption. Duffus declared that Americans had discovered that "the right to play is the final clause in the charter of democracy." But, despite Duffus' claim, the connection of sport to a definition of leisure which made play an end-in-itself obscured the relationship between physical and political culture, and raised new questions about the role of sport in modern society.

The conception of athleticism as an important element in the new "natural right" of leisure, or as a dangerous social narcotic, which emerged in the 1920s through observations of the sporting life by social critics and the mass media marked a sharp departure from the athletic ideology created in the late nineteenth and early twentieth centuries—an ideology which championed athletics as a key element in the plans of social and political reformers to construct their version of liberal modern civilization. The new cultural and social realities of the 1920s, the rapid emergence of a consumer-driven economy, a fully developed mass society, the waning of the spirit of reform, and the rejection of physical culture by the self-described intellectual class, altered the expectations which many Americans held of the role of sport in the evolution of modern society.

The Twenties have often been referred to as a "golden age" of sport. A fascination with athletic spectacles gripped the nation during the decade. In his impressionistic and insightful survey of the period from 1919 to 1929, *Only Yesterday,* the journalist Frederick Lewis Allen asserted that sport "had become an obsession." In Allen's account the multi-million dollar bouts in professional

From the *Journal of Sport History,* 16:3 (Winter, 1989). © 1989 The North American Society for Sport History. Reprinted by permission.

pugilism, Babe Ruth's prodigious exploits on the baseball diamond, the college football craze, the rise of professional golf and tennis, and a host of other athletic activities captured the nation's attention. Anyone in the United States, through newspaper accounts and nationwide radio broadcasts, could participate in the sporting craze. Spectatorship marked one of the new sets of behaviors which knit the nation together into a mass society.

Sport, particularly in the eyes of the American intellectual class, seemed to play a different role in the "Big Society" of the Twenties from that which it had played in the previous industrial epoch. Modern American sport had been "invented" to preserve the concepts and institutions of liberal republicanism and to form a unified national culture in a world transformed by the forces of industrialism, urbanization, rapid and massive immigration, increasingly complex and interconnected markets, and the nationalization of social and political relations.

"Athletism is one of the distinctive forces of the nineteenth century," an American observer of social change had written in 1888, adding physical culture to the list of energies which many commentators declared were forging a "modern" world. "And of all the forces, acting upon the social, moral and physical life of the century, it is probably destined to be the most permanent in its effects." An odd comment perhaps, considering what the techno-industrial economy and the rise the modern nation-state wrought on the history of the nineteenth century. But not quite so odd as one might at first think. Making athletics one of the modern "isms"—like industrialism and nationalism—indicated the belief held by Americans who occupied important positions in "progressive" political culture that the "force" of sport could be used to order modernity.

During a period of rapid social change American "ministers of reform" claimed that "athletism" offered the nation a tool for preserving their "traditional" values—a cosmology which sprang from a combination of the Protestant ethos, the ideology of liberal republicanism, and a competitive but socially beneficial individualism—in an institution which they promised would promote efficiency and support progress under the conditions imposed by the national industrial state. The reformers who invented "athletism" for those purposes, a diverse group of journalists, politicians, educators, settlement house workers, academicians, social critics, scientists, writers, and professional soldiers, preached the value of sport to the emerging industrial state's "new middle class."

Crusading under the progressive banner, the athletic reformers found an audience eager to hear their claims that sport could integrate liberal republicanism and genteel standards into a context which stressed the primacy of the gospel of scientific progress and commanded the rational application of knowledge to social processes. The inventors of the ideology of "athletism" pitched it to the new middle class as a crucial component in a political culture which promised to help realize the dream of an American civilization unified by ideology and ethos—in spite of the fact that vigorous debate consistently raged among the advocates of consensus about just what kind of ideology and ethos ought to prevail.

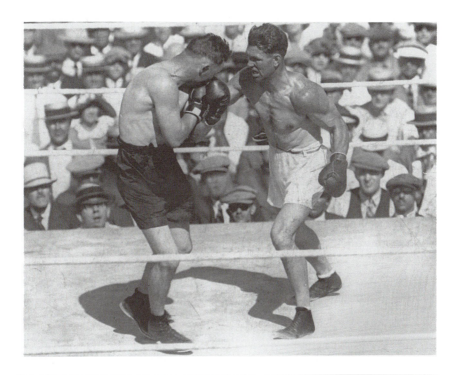

Jack Dempsey, shown here in his well-known title bout against Tommy Gibbons in Shelby, Montana, on July 4, 1923, was one of those athletes who epitomized the transformation of physical culture during the 1920s.
Courtesy of the Amateur Athletic Foundation of Los Angeles.

The self-styled Progressives conceived of modern sport as a social "technology," designed to adapt people to the new human environment. Progressives attempted to utilize sport as an instrument for directing modern energies in efficient directions, inculcating the democratic ethos, teaching respect for law and constitutionalism, assimilating immigrants into American culture, assuaging the evils associated with cities and factories, and insuring the vigor of the nation. The Progressive historian Frederic L. Paxson, remarking in 1917 on the "rise" of modern athletics, wrote that "between the first race for the America's cup in 1851 and the first American aeroplane show of February last, the safety valve of sport was designed, built and applied." *Designed, built* and *applied*; Paxson fully understood that "athletism" was a technology. He believed that it was a "safety valve," engineered to steer the enormous energies of American civilization in productive directions in the years after the New World's "natural" safety valve—the frontier—had disappeared.

The American architects of "athletism" thought that modern sport would contribute to the creation of a national culture, binding the diverse interests of the industrializing country into a unified, coherent entity. They hoped that through athletics they could forge a link between activity and contemplation, between material necessity and moral principle. Playgrounds, YMCAs, public school athletic leagues, and collegiate sport programs were constructed to prepare individuals for citizenship in an industrialized, urbanized America. Perhaps the most popular and certainly the most politically successful American minister of reform, Theodore Roosevelt, epitomized in the popularized versions of his doctrine of the strenuous life the American belief in "athletism" as a necessary ingredient of modern nationhood. Roosevelt preached that the playing field provided the new age with a forum for moral education, an arena for building "character," and a vital testing ground of national will.

Certainly the Progressive idea of "athletism" was not the only ideology of sport which existed in the industrializing United States. The "manly art" of bare-knuckle boxing offered working-class males dramatic depictions of a social reality which differed greatly from the realities expressed through "athletism." Prize fighting symbolized the triumph of "manly" skill in a brutal, primal world. The rowdy bouts in saloons, dance halls and mining camps underscored a working class ethos which rejected the middle-class creed of genteel athleticism. In many industrial towns and cities working-class men and women, having lost much of their power over their vocations to machines, corporations and new techniques of production, resisted the reformers' attempts to create a hegemonic national culture and created leisure-time "alternative cultures" shaped by a variety of ethnic, class and political agendas. Interestingly, working-class groups sought to employ modern sport for reasons similar to the rationales espoused by Progressives. Both groups viewed sport as a technology for ordering communities confronted with the dislocations fostered by industrialism and urbanization.

The Progressives waged battle against not only the working class "amusements" but also against what they considered the idle recreations of the "leisure class." They condemned rich and poor alike for indulging in leisure solely to seek pleasure. Progressive sporting enthusiasts declared that entertainment was a by-product of, and not the purpose for, physical culture. *Outing* insisted that leisure time activities which only the wealthy could afford, like yachting, were not really in accord with the American notion of sport. On the other hand, *Outing*'s editors argued that devices which were within the economic reach of the "common man," like the bicycle and the canoe, should be incorporated into the Progressive definition of sport.

Advocates of social reform through athletics also found enemies among businessmen whom they accused of "commercializing" sport. The intriguing possibilities of new amusement and entertainment technologies, like the great "playground" constructed at Coney Island in the 1890s for the residents of New York City, attracted the attention of both the middle and working classes. Condemned by the true believers in the gospel of Progressive athleticism as a false idol which sucked away energies from their constructive and uplifting pursuits, the entrepreneurs who ran amusement parks nevertheless drew many customers and encouraged revolts against the genteel creed of leisure.

The contest to define the role of sport and recreation in the social life and political culture of the United States spawned a host of Progressive attacks on what they defined as the unhealthy and immoral "amusements" created by the working class counter-cultures and the new commercial enterprises which sold leisure-time diversions. Of course the companies who manufactured bicycles, canoes and other athletic implements profited from their commerce in equipping the nation for the "strenuous life," but boosters of "athletism" sanctioned their sales in much the same fashion as Theodore Roosevelt drew lines between "good trusts" and "bad trusts." The central issue in defining "athletism" against competing ideologies rested in the belief that certain sporting practices would produce the kind of national culture the Progressives desired. The reformers adamantly refused to accept compromises in the battle to control and shape physical culture. Indeed, even Progressives who like the University of Wisconsin sociologist Edward Alsworth Ross admitted that the "labor question" posed by industrialism precipitated "class struggle" which could only be solved by an effort to "balance the claims and interests of contending groups," refused to perceive the struggle to define sport in the same terms. "The disposition of leisure time is preeminently a conscience matter," claimed Professor Ross. "A youth submits perforce to the conditions of his work, but he chooses his recreations in freedom."

If, according to Progressives, the patterns of work under industrial conditions did not conform as neatly as they might have hoped to the blueprints of liberalism sketched by Adam Smith and Thomas Jefferson, they asserted that the realm of recreation was still connected to an ideologically-charged realm of "freedom" untainted by the forces which had diminished liberty in the urban-industrial order. Progressive minds connected sport directly to the ideals of the political culture which they championed. "Athletism" served as one of their most important arenas of freedom and they invested a great deal of effort in defending it against alternative definitions of leisure.

"Athletism" enjoyed an enormous advantage over its rivals in the contest to define the nature and practice of physical culture in modern America. The nation-wide community of discourse created by the revolution in communication and journalism techniques played a central role in reform efforts. Both the "high brow" and the mass market media overwhelmingly endorsed the Progressive ideology of sport against competing claims. "Athletism" was presented to the reading public as an acceptable and necessary modern institution, while editors and sportswriters railed against the decadence of "leisure class" pursuits and the brutality, backwardness and immorality of the working class athletic ideology.

During the late nineteenth and early twentieth centuries the inventors of "athletism" defined the mainstream idea of modern sport. They shunned games which they believed were escapist, aristocratic, commercial, or "uncivilized." For the supporters of "athletism," sport had little to do with either play or leisure. The games and exercises which they favored were supposed to have a direct influence on political and social life. Theodore Roosevelt succinctly identified the central premise of the Progressive athletic code when he proclaimed that "athletic sports are a means and not an end, and he who puts them out of their proper place and diverts them from their proper and wholesome purpose is their enemy.'' There was some debate in Progressive circles over just what kind of exercises and sports should constitute ''athletism.'' But there was general agreement on the role that sport should play in society. Roosevelt and Dudley Sargent, Harvard's pioneering physical educator, certainly disagreed over which games comprised ''athletism,'' and in what spirit those games should be undertaken. But they both insisted that sport was a means and not an end, a preparation for life but not life's purpose.

The Progressive boosters of the ''athletism,'' proclaimed that sport prepared nations and individuals to meet the challenges of modern life. In one cogent anecdote, the *Ladies Home Journal* captured the essence of the Progressive vision of sport in American life. The popular magazine related a tale in which a lad, ''divided between the love of books and love of sports,'' got a chance to meet President Roosevelt. The President, despite the fact that he had urgent business with his cabinet, took the time to ask the boy what was his favorite sport. When the boy replied that he preferred baseball, the President lamented that he himself had never been proficient in that game owing to his miserable eyesight. ''What an awful pity, Mr. President,'' replied the lad, while a roomful of anxious power-brokers restlessly waited for the pleasantries to end so that the business of the nation could be taken up. The President smiled, and revealed that if baseball was not his forte, when ''it comes to riding or shooting or tennis, I can hold my own, I think; and do you know jiu-jitsu?'' The boy related he did indeed. And then, in the presence of the rich and powerful, the President and the American youth shared their knowledge of the finer points of that strenuous activity.

A few months later the lad undertook, at considerable risk to himself, a mission to save a valuable government launch befouled by its own anchor. Emerging with a few bumps and bruises, he was confronted by his mother. '' 'Why did you do it?' his horrified mother asked. 'What did I learn to dive for?' he asked. 'The President made me feel, when I saw him, that sports were intended to make men.' '' The *Ladies Home Journal* averred that ''the President's ideas of sports were fitly expressed in these words of the boy.''

The mass circulation monthly's fable underscored the Progressive belief in the moral and political power of sport. The social reformers had designed ''athletism'' to ''make'' modern men—and women. The Progressive mind linked sport directly to political culture. ''Athletism'' was supposed to produce good citizens and able leaders, inculcate liberal tenets and convert immigrants into ''Americans.'' Progressives believed that modern sport, political reform, and rational social action could be used to construct a harmonious national culture. But the ''end of American innocence,'' the revolt of the intellectual class against political activism and social engineering, and the catastrophe of the Great War, combined to doom their optimistic visions. In the ''Big Society'' which emerged after the First World War, sport lost much of its association with politics and social reform. ''Athletism'' took on new roles.

In 1927 the historians Charles and Mary Beard commented on the shape of the new national culture. They asserted that the "machine process" had stamped every facet of American life with a rigid standardization. Mass production and mass consumption had created a new reality, joining the nation together in a myriad of interlocking lifeways. Mass culture meant that "within the week of their announcement the modes of New York, Boston, and Chicago became the modes of Winesburg, Gopher Prairie, and Centerville and swept on without delay into remote mountain fastnesses." In the nation which took shape during the Twenties, the Beards reported that the "technology of interchangeable parts was reflected in the clothing, sports, amusements, literature, architecture, manners, and speech of the multitude."

Sport, from the Beards' vantage, had become a manifestation of Big Society, an item which the masses consumed with an insatiable appetite. In the new order the relentless hammerings of the machine process pounded every aspect of life, "material and spiritual," into the routes which the utilitarian commandment that governed the system prescribed. Nothing was exempt from the machine's maw. Education, the arts, social reform, and every other human activity fell under the sway of mass culture. "All these tendencies, springing naturally out of the whirl of business, were encouraged by the conscious struggle for efficiency in every domain, by the discovery and application of the most economical apparatus for the accomplishment of given ends."

In the world which the Beards sketched sport offered only a temporary, and illusory, escape from the rigid routine of the machine process. The escape allowed the process to continue by providing a momentary respite from the inhuman conditions of mass culture. Social critics who had found something of value in more traditional conceptions of sport, like Johan Huizinga, Lewis Mumford and Arnold Toynbee, were horrified by the change in physical culture. As the Beards described it, Americans "sat on the bleachers at games, in vicarious playing, to cheer their favorite teams," free for a moment from hard realities. In the eyes of the Beards, and a great many of their intellectual contemporaries, sport had become an opiate which allowed the average person to cope with Big Society. It offered an arena in which the masses could turn their eyes away, if only briefly, from the grim political and economic realities of the modern world. The Beards themselves were hopeful that mankind could rise to the challenge of the machine age—although they described no transcendent role for "athletism" in the process. But much of the intellectual class, in the wake of the Great War and new criticisms of human rationalism, abandoned the optimism of the Beards and their Progressive forebears. The social critics of the 1920s detested sport because they felt that it hid the true nature of modern civilization.

Frederick Lewis Allen disliked the sporting craze for precisely those reasons. "More Americans could identify Knute Rockne as the Notre Dame coach than could tell who was the presiding officer of the United States Senate," groused Allen. He found all the "ballyhoo" a befuddling commentary on an America out of touch with the important issues of life. Allen pictured the 1920s as an era in which a nation tired of reform and social change seized on a bunch of "new toys," sport among them, and ignored the larger political and economic issues of the age. Of course, sport was not a "new" manifestation of the Twenties, but it did take on new and "spectacular" forms during the decade. Clearly Allen understood sport in different terms than had the ministers of reform who invented "athletism."

That athletic spectacles seemed more popular with the masses than the great questions of political life greatly annoyed intellectuals. Radicals detested sport because it prevented the masses from recognizing their plight and thus blocked a true revolution. More traditional thinkers were upset that what they deemed a frivolous orgy consumed attention better directed toward more important issues.

"More profound blah has been scribbled and spoken about the significance of our national vogue for sports than upon almost any topic, including Fundamentalism, Freud, the League of Nations, and the hot weather," fumed George S. Brooks in an article which epitomized the intellectual disdain for the new version of the "athletism." He equated the Roman descent into an orgy of "bread and the circus" with the current American fascination with "gas and the games." " 'Gas and the games' has become the motto of these United States," Brooks protested. "Contrary to the opinions of professional and amateur sport-promoters," he surmised that it was "doubtful the tremendous furor over motors and sports proves anything—except that our civilization has reached a highly artificial state, and that most of our citizens are bored with their jobs." Brooks, like the Beards and most of American intellectuals, blamed the sporting craze on the rise of mass society. "As the cities fill with routine workers, whose each day is a monotony of repetition, so fast does the desire for motor, movies, and sports increase," he observed. "Business and occupation become duller as the central control increases. Motoring, motion-pictures, camping out, playing or watching games are merely an escape from the circumscribed routine of factory, store, or office." Clearly, Brooks linked the sporting culture of the 1920s with the other amusements available to consumers. His criticisms indicated that important shifts were taking place in the role which sport played in American life.

But it was not only academically-inclined critics like Brooks who regarded the escapist ideology of athletics with disdain. Commentators in the mass media reacted in a similar manner. Even a few sportswriters found all the attention paid to athletics a little too much to stomach. W.O. McGeehan, the sports editor of the *New York Herald,* coined the term "ballyhoo" to refer to the excessive attention on the trivial. McGeehan, and others, often used the term to refer to sporting style of the Twenties. McGeehan insisted that publicity agents and the press had manufactured a star system in athletics which rivaled that of Hollywood. "How much of their fame is pure metal and how much of it is mere ballyhoo does not matter as long as they add to the gaiety and credulity of nations," observed the *Literary Digest* of the new sporting stars. In mass culture sport belonged to the sphere of leisure.

Even some of the sport stars wondered about the intensity of the adulation which they received from a fervently devoted public. In an article in *Success,* three-time American tennis champion Mary K. Brown complained that Americans were "sports-mad idiots." "Why should I have become elevated to a position of first-page importance merely because I am somewhat more dexterous than most in manipulating a contrivance of catgut and wood which is commonly called a tennis racquet?" she wondered. "It will be for the future to find the answer to the present sports hysteria that is gripping America to the exclusion of other and greater matters."

Perhaps the harshest critic of American sporting habits in the 1920s, John R. Tunis, was himself a practicing sportswriter. Tunis loved the beauty of informal athletic games, and the escape from the daily grind which sport could provide. He thought that play was the true essence of modern sport. Tunis reveled in the existential moments in which one drove a golf ball well and truly, or executed a perfect groundstroke on the tennis court. "All that is best in sport can be found—and what is more, is found—in these friendly encounters upon the golf links and tennis courts of the country," he wrote. But the rise of the highly organized spectacles which garnered so much attention during the 1920s bothered Tunis immensely.

Tunis rejected the notion that organized sport was a morally edifying institution. He blamed the press for blowing up the importance of athletics to the point where "there has grown up in the public mind an exaggerated and sentimental notion of the moral value of these great competitive spectacles of sport, a fiction which may be termed The Great Sports Myth." He complained that "the sporting heroes of the nation are our gods" and worried that the amount of energy devoted to athletics would have detrimental effects on society. "Man has always, I suppose, been a hero worshipper," Tunis admitted grudgingly. The United States had no religious prophets to exalt, nor a royalty to admire, nor even a Mussolini to erect as a national icon. "Consequently we turn hopefully to the world of sports," he theorized. People in mass society needed to identify with individuals who had risen above the bleak routines which marked modern life. Sports stars became the heroes and heroines of consumer culture.

The national culture which the Progressives had labored to bring into existence had in fact become a reality during the 1920s. But it did not take the shape which Progressives had hoped for. Instead of a nation united by liberal ideology and a commitment to social reform through rational methodologies, the national culture which emerged during the Twenties was bound together by Madison Avenue, marketing techniques, new consumer goods, and the machine process. Beneath the surface of "Business Civilization" lurked enormous tensions. The United States was divided by numerous political and cultural conflicts. Abandoned by the intellectuals and the reform-minded politicians and professionals who during the Progressive era had sought to engineer progress, "athletism" mutated into new forms.

The consumer culture of the Twenties had its roots in the social and economic transformations of the previous epoch. The national market, the new communication and transportation systems, the assembly line technologies which produced consumer items, had all been pioneered in the years before the First World War. Scientific management, time-and-motion study designed factories, and the gigantic corporate dimensions of the big businesses designed to serve a consuming public had also begun to take shape before the war. In 1907 Henry Ford had announced his dream of manufacturing a motor car for the "common man." Ford's efforts revolutionized the relationship between the mode of production and the masses. But it was not until the 1920s that the full impact of those changes became readily apparent to Americans, and that consumer culture emerged fully developed in American life. It was only after the war that American civilization became aware of the cultural transformations which decades of industrial innovation and social engineering had produced.

The appearance in quick succession during the Twenties of mass-produced and mass-marketed motor cars and home appliances, radio networks, a thriving motion picture industry, revolutionary advertising techniques, chain store empires, credit and installment purchase plans, and numerous other technological and business innovations designed to spur consumer purchasing produced the impression of the sudden birth of a new social order. The relentless pitchings of professional sales agents who promised the members of mass society the ever-multiplying fruits of the machine process served as the battle-cry of the consumer revolution. New technologies and new forms of production fundamentally altered society. Sears-Roebuck had provided goods to the masses in the late nineteenth century. But much of their inventory consisted of implements to improve the productive capacity of farmers, artisans and homemakers. The consumer culture of the 1920s made consumption, rather than production, the fundamental motif of economic action.

The new America took a far different form than its predecessor. Society began to abandon much of the Protestant ethos that had served it for so long and assumed the ethics of affluence. In his studies of popular biographies Leo Lowenthal charted the change in ideals, as they shifted from the worship of the idols of production to the idols of consumption. In mass culture the baton of fame and fortune passed from the Horatio Algers of the world to those individuals who happened to be in the right place at the right time. He noted that the biographies of the Progressive era "are written—at least ideologically—for someone who the next day may try to emulate the man whom he has just envied." In the Twenties a new type of life history replaced those of the characters whom Lowenthal labeled productive—politicians, the captains of industry, serious artists. The new stories concerned people whom, "almost every one of them is directly, or indirectly, related to the sphere of leisure time." Lowenthal discovered that the ideology of the newer biographies celebrated the lives of "the heroes of the world of entertainment and sport."

The new glimpses into the who was who of consumption culture revealed individuals conditioned from childhood by a sort of "vulgarian behaviorism" for success if, and only if, the persons were lucky enough to get a break. Lowenthal discovered that the newer biographies portrayed a universe in which the work ethic no longer held sway. People no longer believed that they controlled their social and economic destinies. The focus of the success stories turned from examinations of will and motivation to superficial observations of an individual's connection to mass society. The biographies reveled in minute descriptions of mundane personal habits and preferences. "The real battlefield of history recedes from view or becomes a stock backdrop while society disintegrates into an amorphous crowd of consumers," wrote Lowenthal. He drew a frightening picture of an America in which the machine process had triumphed with totalitarian results. "Our people could occupy an imaginary world of technocracy; everybody seems to reflect a rigid code of flexible qualities: the rigid and mechanized set-up of a variety of useful mechanical institutions." In the new order, the individual could only identify, socially and psychologically, with the community. The primacy of individual will and action in the pattern of American culture had been replaced by an "other-directed" code of behavior.

Lowenthal surmised that "it is some comfort for the little man who has become expelled from the Horatio Alger dream, who despairs of penetrating the thicket of grand strategy in politics and business, to see his heroes as a lot of guys who like or dislike highballs, cigarettes, tomato juice, golf, and social gatherings—just like himself." The public could purchase products which made them feel like sports stars and helped them to transcend the mundane grind of modern existence. "A Spalding Swimming Suit won't teach you to swim," admitted one piece of advertising copy. "But it will make you *feel* like an Olympic champion." Spalding also peddled "official Olympic" discuses, throwing hammers, shot puts, hurdles, and a line of "Olympic championship" running shoes. Anyone could *feel* like an Olympic champion; all they had to do was buy Spalding's products.

Of course A.G. Spalding and his company had made a great deal of money selling sporting goods in the decades before the consumer culture of the Twenties had emerged. Despite the disdain for commercialism which "athletism" preached, profits were made through Progressive era exhibitions of "wholesome" sport. But in the Twenties, as never before, entrepreneurs began to recognize the possibilities of marketing athletics to the new breed of American consumers. The mass culture of the Twenties created new categories and definitions of leisure and amusement, climaxing as historian John Kasson noted, the long revolt against genteel standards of civilization and reordering the relationship between sport and political culture in American life.

The public began to understand, and to consume, sport in different ways than they had in the past. The increasing popularity of professional baseball in the 1920s furnishes some instructive insights into the changing role of sport in consumer culture. On one level baseball continued to be identified with liberalism and traditional values. The press, the baseball establishment and the fans perceived the "national pastime" as a realm of democracy and opportunity in which the ideals of individualism and competition were still cherished. But in other areas baseball was undergoing tremendous changes in both its structure and its cultural role. During the Twenties the "home run" was enshrined as the centerpiece of the national pastime's appeal. The press commented that the growing importance of the "long ball" represented the craving for excitement which permeated the "Jazz Age." Some baseball scribes worried about the growing commercialism and sensationalism, and complained that overpaid players and spoiled fans would ruin the game. Their greatest fear was that baseball would degenerate into "mere amusement."

The structure of the teams began to change as well. The Twenties witnessed the beginnings of the farm-system and the application of corporate management techniques to major league franchises. Baseball experienced the growth of a white-collar mentality, in which conformity and predictability were stressed and a "chain store" system of producing and marketing players was developed. Entrepreneurs, advertisers and press agents began to sell the national pastime as a form of entertainment and an avenue for escape. Showmanship, radio broadcasting and hoopla, particularly during the World Series, increased profits and tied baseball to the thriving show business industry of the 1920s.

The biggest symbol of change, and of continuity, in baseball was Babe Ruth. Cultural historian Warren Susman labeled Ruth the "ideal hero for the world of consumption." Ruth was the "home run king" who provided the sensational feats that fans increasingly demanded. As an "idol of consumption" Ruth served mass culture magnificently. The public never tired of hearing the details of his personal life, and they worshipped his expansive, exaggerated public persona. He merged an unlettered, fun-loving image with his fantastic baseball skills to form the archetype of consumer culture's brand of celebrity. And he made sure to treat himself as a commodity, hiring an agent to take financial advantage of his massive popularity.

Ruth was the biggest name, and baseball the most important game, in the sporting craze of the Twenties. But he was certainly not the only figure from the playing field who was lionized during the decade. The cultural heroes and heroines created during the Twenties symbolized a new understanding of the role of athletics in American life. Where "athletism" had been a political tool for making citizens and rationalizing social relations, the sporting ideology of the Twenties increasingly represented the escape from social realities which athletics could provide. The idea of sport was changing, and so was the relationship between sport and political culture.

The changes manifested themselves clearly in professional prizefighting. The "manly art" had begun a slow journey away from a total identification with working class hooliganism and the blue collar saloon to a more mainstream appeal as early as the 1890s. But it was not until the 1920s that boxing attracted serious attention from the mass public. The rise of Jack Dempsey to heavyweight champion of the world in the early years of the decade coincided with a revolution in sports marketing techniques which transformed professional fighting into one of the major cultural dramas of the Twenties. Dempsey's bouts with Georges Carpentier, Luis Firpo, and especially with Gene Tunney, were transformed by skillful promoters and the national press into morality plays which highlighted many of the conflicts that rent American civilization during the decade. The boxers themselves became symbols of the age. Tunney stood for the uneasy marriage between the traditions of liberal individualism, scientific efficiency and the corporate ethos which so many Americans in the Twenties desperately hoped could be consummated. Dempsey symbolized the untamed energy of the frontier and the desire to smash through the new structures and strictures of mass society. He became a new version of the old American love affair with images of anti-civilization.

Dempsey and Tunney created popular athletic dramas which were very different from anything which the inventors of "athletism" had espoused—or would have condoned. Their fights sold millions of tickets and newspapers, and large blocks of radio advertisements. The entertainment industry had seized on sport after the social reformers had abandoned it. But that did not mean that the Twenties' version of "athletism" was completely divorced from political ideology and discourse. Lowenthal's thesis needs revision. The biographies of Dempsey, Tunney, Ruth and other Twenties sports stars, could be every bit as didactic as a tale about Horatio Alger. A favorite theme of the sports biographies described the triumph of individuals who succeeded against the odds, not simply because they got the breaks, but because of their adherence to the traditional values of perseverance, hard work and clean living.

As idols of consumption, sports heroes and heroines sold lifestyles and values. In that way the role of athletics in the mass culture of the Twenties retained a certain kinship with the Progressive ideology of sport. But the association of athletics in the 1920s with leisure, entertainment and big business, greatly altered the political and social expectations which both the intellectual elite and the middle-class press placed on sport. A different relationship with the culture of athleticism had evolved. Progressive sporting ideology had been concerned with the production of a vital citizenry and the adjustment of liberalism to industrial reality. The "idols of consumption" offered escape from mass social relations and an easy and shallow identification with political and cultural symbols. Where "athletism" had been an active component in an ideology or liberal political reform and a technology for effecting social change, sport in the Twenties was increasingly disassociated from the production of a "progressive" civilization.

A combination of factors—the intellectual revolt, the waning of the spirit of reform, and the social transformations engendered by an economy geared toward mass consumption—dragged "athletism" away from its origins as an active agent of social reform. The very groups which propagated and internalized the Progressive ideas of athletics, the "professional" intellectuals, social reformers and the middle-class public, no longer utilized their invention in the traditional fashion. Sport no longer seemed to provide an effective avenue for the construction of political and social relations. In "the Age of Play" athletics were described as an end and not a means. In consumer culture sport had come to be viewed as one of modern life's central purposes.

Robert L. Duffus, who had dubbed the Twenties "the Age of Play," summed up the new mores in a 1924 article for *The Independent*. "The most significant aspect of the Age of Play," he wrote, "is not in its inventions, good and bad, but in an alteration of an ancient attitude—a veritable change in one of the most fundamental of folk ways." Duffus surmised that "for uncounted generations man has survived and made progress . . . only by unceasing industry." But the machine age "struck a fatal blow at the ancestral faith in mere hard work."

Duffus did not believe that the mechanization of work was without danger, nor that all the amusements of leisure were wholesome. But he warned that "these evils are not to be curbed by curbing the spirit of play. Reformers and educators must accept this spirit as more sacred than anything they have to give; they can help by guiding, not by restraining." The intellectual class did not fully comprehend Duffus' wisdom. Madison Avenue treated it as the new gospel.

The 1920s witnessed the emergence of mass advertising. The same escapist and entertainment qualities which were changing sport had an enormous impact on the consumer economy. The bards of consumption sold lifestyles and values packaged as products. A brand of toothpaste could make someone into a sex-pot, the right cut of suit created a corporate mover and shaker, and an automobile could turn an urban family into summertime pioneers. Consumption became the national religion—and it profoundly altered the composition of the American mind. A 1925 article in *The New Republic* highlighted advertising's role in modern cognition. "When all is said and done, advertising does give a certain illusion, a certain sense of escape in a machine age," noted the author. "It creates a dream world: smiling faces, shining teeth, school girl complexions, cornless feet, perfect fitting union suits, distinguished collars, wrinkleless collars, odorless breaths, regularized bowels, happy homes in New Jersey. . . , charging motors, punctureless tires, perfect busts, shimmering shanks, self-washing dishes—backs behind which the moon was meant to rise."

Advertising did more than provide escapism. It helped shape a new reality. It gave new meaning to that hallowed American phrase, "the pursuit of happiness." Madison Avenue thrust visions of the fruits of the machine process into every home in the land, creating a rising tide of affluent expectations which have affected American culture enormously in the decades since the Twenties. The sales pitch contained subtle ideological messages. The advertisers marketed the American dream and promised material plenty without social alienation, new technology without the destruction of traditional values, and "cost-free progress" in the march toward modernity.

Madison Avenue also remade political culture. The shift away from the "idols of production" into an era in which industrial progress seemed to usher in an "age of play" restructured perceptions of the relationship between individuals and the community—or, in current rhetoric, "the system." As new definitions of the importance of entertainment and amusement in modern civilization reshaped American sporting ideology, they also influenced political life and brought into question the ability of republicanism to cope with the realities of mass society. The new forms of persuasion, in conjunction with the intellectuals' abandonment of politics, restructured the roles of the bestowers of power and those who sought it. The new electorate began to look at politicians in the same way in which they looked at consumer goods. Walter Lippmann had realized that ideas and political platforms could be sold as easily as automobiles and razor blades. As the politicians began to recognize the new realities, American democracy changed forever.

During the twenties the change manifested itself visibly in presidential politics. George Harvey, commenting on the election of 1924, remarked that Calvin

Coolidge would not be elected "for what he said or did, but for what he was." That was a revolutionary thought, a sentiment that could never be used to describe Thomas Jefferson or Abraham Lincoln, let alone Theodore Roosevelt or Woodrow Wilson. For if candidates were not what they said and did then they were only the images they represented in the public's perception. In the new culture you picked a president the same way you picked a brand of toothpaste.

The campaigns of the Republican electees in 1920 and 1924, Warren G. Harding and Coolidge, offered the public no coherent platform beyond a hazy vision of "normalcy," an amorphous idea which meant many things to many people at a very superficial level. Although the administrations of Harding and Coolidge did effect a revolutionary restructuring of federal bureaucracies which made the executive branch a much more effective manager of national policies, the public image of the Republican stewardship was characterized by media visions of Harding as a bungling incompetent surrounded by greedy cronies, and Coolidge as somnolently indifferent to the course of history. The "white-collar" revolution in federal management aroused very little passion in a populace titillated by sensationalistic accounts of sex, crime and sporting spectacles, and inundated by a host of exciting new gadgets and services. A few of the numerous scandals which plagued the Harding administration captured the front pages and the radio waves for a brief span, but the bumbling public images of the ascendant Republicans bored a generation which had lost faith in the connection between the political process and personal power. Big Society dwarfed the individual. In the United States it seemed that not even big government could control the awesome energies of the machine process.

It came as no surprise then, that the nation turned to other forms of communal solidarity. If Harding and Coolidge appeared to have no control over the processes of history, at least Gehrig and Ruth, Grange and the Four Horsemen, Dempsey and Tunney, and America's Olympians could control their athletic destinies. Sports stars seemed to be masters, not victims, of fate.

In September, 1924, Democrat John W. Davis, Republican Calvin Coolidge, and the Progressive Party's Robert La Follette were contesting for the presidency of the United States. But *The Nation,* then under the editorship of Oswald Garrison Villard who proved much more sympathetic to sport than E.L. Godkin ever had, commented that the World Series between the Washington Senators and the New York Giants fascinated the public more than the presidential race. *The Nation's* editors mused that election day would sort out the futures of Coolidge, Davis and La Follette, "but whatever happens to them, we may say already—and with entire confidence—that the popular vote has been cast in favor of sport." Sport pushed the presidential election to the back of American minds. "It has been seated on the American throne," opined the editors. "It has been clothed with almost dictatorial powers." The editors asserted that "this absorption in sports—already so great and apparently on the increase—is both a good and a bad sign of the times." *The Nation* thought that professional games and spectator sports were frivolous. "Yet if these great spectacular events sometimes seemed like an opiate for the people—or the 'bread and circus' of the Roman Empire—one should recognize that they develop and encourage a great growth of amateur sport, of no import whatever to the newspapers but of supreme consequence to the health and spirits of the people,'' concluded *The Nation*.

The Nation's editorial demonstrated the paradoxical conjunction of traditional and modern patterns in American culture. The editors wanted to preserve the traditions of ''athletism.'' And yet they feared the rising narcotic power of spectator sport. Such was the constant paradox of the Twenties, an overwhelming nostalgia combined with a headlong gallop toward new horizons. The decade brought into sharp relief the changing shape of a new America.

But nostalgia could not bring back the old Progressive ideology of sport. The idea of athletics as a social technology designed to effect reform had depended on the belief that sport and political culture were intimately connected. The transformations engendered by the recognition of consumer culture and the realities of mass society had altered both sport and politics. The explicit links between sport and liberal versions of republicanism became murky and imprecise as mass society increasingly consumed athletic spectacles as a respite from the demands of modern industrialism.

Alongside the increasingly popular definition of sport in the 1920s as entertainment and amusement, an institution without any direct connection to politics, a few athletic experts and public figures still clung to the older sporting ideology. One can find many resonances of ''athletism'' in the writings of YMCA leader Elwood Brown and in General Douglas MacArthur's official report from the 1928 Olympic Games. Odes to the ''Americanizing'' influence of the playing field still appeared in the professional journals of physical education and recreation science. In classrooms and pep talks coaches and teachers still celebrated an emotional affinity between the lessons learned through athletic competition and vague conceptions of democracy and patriotism. Sportswriters still paid homage to the connection between sport as an ''American way of life.'' But the linkages between sport and politics made in the Twenties were not the clear and calculated explanations of sport as a dynamic tool for social control and the creation of a national culture which the Progressives had espoused.

As the insights of Charles and Mary Beard, Mary Brown, George Brooks, Robert Duffus and John Tunis demonstrated, social criticism in the mass media increasingly interpreted sport in the context of ''play,'' casting it as a symptom of social alienation or an idealized arena separated from the complexities of ''real'' life. Indeed, two of the more insightful observers of the social shifts in American life between the 1890s and the 1920s, Robert and Helen Lynd, lamented that high school basketball rather than some more politically charged and socially conscious institution was the glue that held together ''Middletown''—their cipher for the American ''everytown.'' The Lynds clearly felt that sport obscured efforts to discuss and solve the important social questions which confronted modern mass societies.

The consumer culture of the Twenties changed the nature and structure of both sport and politics. The new dynamics reshaped the cultural perception and role of each institution. In the 1920s sport no longer seemed to offer American civilization the prospect of balancing rational contemplation with the dynamic energies of the modern age. The Progressives invented ''athletism'' to build a national community. They identified sport with the production of rational social systems. But the ''age of play'' created a different relationship between sport and political culture.

CHAPTER 13

The Playing Fields of St. Louis: Italian Immigrants and Sports, 1925–1941

Gary Ross Mormino

The following essay, "The Playing Fields of St. Louis," examines the interrelationships between immigrants and urbanization upon two generations of Italian-Americans between the 1920s and World War Two. The article contends that sport played a galvanic role in the acculturation of Italian-American youth, and that athletic voluntary associations became major factors in the evolution of the neighborhood in the 1920s and 1930s. Sport channeled forces that had historically divided Italian immigrants in St. Louis and harnessed these divisive energies into creative participation. Finally, the emergence of a neighborhood athletic federation provided a powerful symbol of ethnic group identity. Recreational enterprise performed a dual purpose. It accentuated the Italianate character of the colony, helping to retard assimilation. But sport also allowed athletes to become Americanized and acculturated them into a larger urban society through the participation of intra-city teams. Indeed, sport encouraged not only the preservation of an ethnic subculture, but the preservation of the community itself.

Several forces helped solidify the Italian-Americans gathered in St. Louis into a cohesive ethnic community. These factors—geographic isolation, the local economy, the Roman Catholic Church, the neighborhood school, the urban gangs, and the many voluntary associations—also contributed to, and were affected by, the phenomenon of sport.

"Six-hundred Italians, a community saloon, the North of Italy tongue, and a $500 Italian flag," constituted the basics of "Dago Hill," which according to a 1901 journalist was "unique among the communities of St. Louis." Attracted by economic opportunities in the clay mines and brick factories of Fairmount Heights, northern Italians from Lombardy and southern Italians from Sicily began arriving in the 1880s and by the turn-of-the-century, the district in southwest St. Louis was dubbed by immigrants as "*la Montagna*,"—the Hill. Natives derisively called the colony "Dago Hill."

From the *Journal of Sport History*, 9:2 (Summer, 1982). © 1982 The North American Society for Sport History. Reprinted by permission.

Geographically and culturally, the Hill remained an isolated and insulated colony for the several thousand Lombards and Sicilians who had arrived by 1910. The colony's cultural homogeneity reinforced the insularity; well over 90% of its residents hailed from Italy. Typically, immigrant colonies were situated in inner-city districts. Not so for the Hill, which was located miles from the congested St. Louis downtown. Not until the 1920s would bus service provide intra-city transportation for area residents. Most first-generation Italians preferred the seclusion of the self-sufficient community. "When I was growing up in the 1920s," recollected Lou Cerutti, a life-long resident, "the Hill was like a little country town." The bus ride to Sportsman's Park widened the social vistas of second-generation Italian-Americans like Joe Garagiola, but his immigrant parents clung securely to their geographic isolation. "Downtown," Garagiola reminisced, "as far as Hill mothers and fathers were concerned, was the place you went to take your citizenship test. Otherwise, downtown was as far away as the Duomo in Milan [Lombardy]."

By 1920, more than 3,000 first and second generation Italians had settled on the Hill. Given the local industrial character of the area and the lack of urban transportation, it was natural that nearly all the residents worked in the local brickyards, clay mines, and foundries. Pay was low and mobility limited. Hill Italians were drastically over-represented at the bottom of the St. Louis occupational ladder; nearly four times as many workers were classified as "unskilled laborers" as in the city (35% vs. 9%).

No-nonsense Italian immigrants had come to St. Louis to work. No work, no dignity. The demands of work and the challenges of building a community exacted harsh sacrifices from these immigrants. Having emigrated from a rigid social-economy which treated peasants like slaves, Lombards and Sicilians viewed leisure as a plaything for the *prominenti* (the elite). "A cane, work, and bread make for beautiful children," counseled a Sicilian proverb. Giovanni Schiavo, a pioneering historian writing about the St. Louis Italian community, observed in 1929:

It is well known that as a whole the Italian immigrant has not brought with him any traditions of national games . . . the only pastime for which the immigrant is noted is apparently *bocce* [an Italian game resembling lawn bowling]. National American games do not appeal to the average Italian.

However, Schiavo pointed out that the sons of these immigrants were attracted by the lure of sport. "Their leisure," he wrote, "is more a sign of their own particular environment, rather than the influence of national trends." Yet precisely at the moment Schiavo penned those words (1929), Hill Italian-Americans were poised at a pivotal crossroads, as national and local forces were reshaping the values and institutions of ethnic America.

The 1920s witnessed the transformation of American sport and the rise of the athlete as hero. The proliferation of radio and the urban tabloid penetrated ethnic America—even once isolated colonies such as the Hill. Italian-Americans were

One of the greatest Italian-American athletes from the "Hill" in St. Louis was Yogi
Berra, the frequently quoted Hall of Fame catcher of the New York Yankees.
Courtesy of the Amateur Athletic Foundation of Los Angeles.

swept into the sporting vortex both as spectators and participants. Whereas no
Italians were represented in the major leagues between 1901-1906, and where
only two Italian rookies broke into the circuit in 1920 (out of 133), by 1941
fully eight percent of big league rosters counted Italians, more than double
their share of the white population. Individual exploits of Tony Lazzeri, Ernie
Lombardi, and Joe DiMaggio popularized the sport in Italian communities. In
the boxing ring, Italian-Americans were even more prominent, to the point that
by the 1930s, that group boasted more champions than any other ethnic cohort.
These idols became important role models for second-generation ethnics, who
importantly, now had the leisure time to indulge in recreation.

The first waves of Italian immigrants possessed neither the time nor inclination
to play soccer or join an athletic club. By the mid-1920s, industrial laborers were
receiving one and a half-days' rest per week and some paid holidays. Moreover,

the young remained in school longer and began work at a later age than their immigrant fathers.

Youth would be served. Italian parents, unconcerned with birth control, produced large families, thus supporting the swelling ranks of the second-generation who were susceptible to the lure of athletics. During the decade of the 1920s, more than 700 men aged fifteen to thirty matured on the Hill. A thousand more joined the demographic ranks in the 1930s, making the youth cohort a majority of the population.

Significantly, these young men were second-generation Italian-Americans, aggressively "new world" in social outlook. In sociological terms, this group was becoming acculturated, acquiring America's language, aspirations, and ideas. Young boys were rebelling against the patriarchal domination of old world fathers, reported social worker Elmer Wood in 1936. Many, he noted, "were ashamed of their parents."

The neighborhood school, another powerful Americanizing and organizing influence, served both as a laboratory for democracy and a cauldron of socioeconomic conflict. Italian parents looked upon the American school with suspicion and distrust. Unlettered immigrants (in 1930, illiteracy rates for foreign-born adults on the Hill approached 40 percent) saw the institution as a threat to parental influence. Compounded by the growing needs of the family, Hill Italo-Americans made limited educational gains. "A fourteenth birthday means a work certificate and a farewell to studies," lamented Ruth Crawford in 1916. Little had changed two decades later when a student observed that few Hill students finished the eighth grade and even fewer finished high school. "Most of the Italian children have difficulty in school because of their language handicaps and poor home training," wrote Wood. Appallingly, in 1940 only eleven Italian-American males over age twenty-five claimed a high school diploma, making that cohort the least-educated group in metropolitan St. Louis. Blue collars predominated.

Inside PS 101, children learned world geography; outside the cloistered halls, they quickly assimilated the essentials of ethnophysical geography. "Well, let's give you a little geography," chuckled Lou Berra (no relation to "Yogi"), obviously delighted in his role as teacher:

Kings Highway . . . the creek . . . railroad tracks . . . that was *our* boundary!
. . . Up the Hill we had the Blue Ridge Gang—Irish. To the northwest we had the Cheltenham Gang—a mixture of Germans and more or less natives. East of Kings Highway was the Tower Grove Gang, what most of us refer to as Hoosiers, people up from small towns . . . then the Dog Town Gang to the west. . . . You go beyond that and you get your ass kicked around so you stayed within your limits.

The rude confrontation with a hostile outside world presented a difficult transition to some, a challenging proposition to others. "In school they taught me all about democracy," remembered Sam Chinicci, a Sicilian immigrant. "Then you would come outside and find these antagonisms and would have to fight for all the things they taught you in school. We used to have these fights.'' To outsiders, there was no mistaking the Hill's ethnic boundaries; to insiders, once Italo-Americans left the colony, ''Krauts,'' ''Micks,'' and ''Hoosiers'' lurked in the shadows. ''If you got caught on the other side of Southwest Avenue,'' reminisced Lou Cerutti, ''you got the heck kicked out of you!''

Like urban teenagers across the country, Hill Italo-Americans clustered into their street corner societies. ''Every kid on the Hill belonged to a gang or club,'' remembered Joe Garagiola. ''You either belonged or were out of the action.'' Called the Hawks, Falcons, Ravens, Little Caesars, and Stags, gangs proliferated throughout the 1920s and 1930s, climaxing in 1941 when nearly fifty neighborhood clubs boasted a thousand neighborhood members. Whereas the spirit of *campanilismo* (old-world localism) governed the selection and membership of the mutual aid societies among the first-generation arrivals, second-generation club members relied on block-territorial imperatives, regardless of the parent's old-world ties. ''All the kids around my age who lived on Elizabeth Avenue made up a sports club,'' recollected ''Yogi'' Berra.

In urban enclaves across the nation, gang members coalesced around territorial loyalties. ''There is a definite geographical basis for the play group . . .'' contended Frederick Thrasher in his classic study of the gang:

> The gang . . . is characterized by the following types of behavior: meeting face-to-face, milling, movement through space as a unit, conflict and planning. The results of this collective behavior is the development of tradition, unreflective internal structure, *esprit de corps,* morale, group awareness and attachment to local territory.

In his classic study, *Street Corner Society,* the participant-observer William Foote Whyte reported the raucous and colorful lifestyle of Cornerville. Like Cornerville's gangs, Hill athletic clubs mapped out territories, sponsored club houses, respected intricate internal hierarchies, participated in local politics, and bootlegged moonshine.

The Hill also had its William Foote Whyte, in the character of Elmer Shorb Wood. A social worker and graduate student, Wood became a confidant to the colony, reflecting later that ''I doubt if there was another person who had been in more homes and had the pleasure of knowing and observing family life on the Hill to a greater degree than I [1930s].'' The young sociology student was particularly fascinated by the gang phenomenon, whose characteristics bore great similarity to other working-class, bachelor subcultures:

> Boys and young men between ages 16-25 have . . . established gangs, or what they term athletic clubs, where they spend their unoccupied time. . . . A few years ago when the easy money was available (prohibition era) and the community gave them a free rein, the activities of these gangs became anything but moral. One or more prostitutes from outside the Hill would be imported.

Wood further reported that at one school teachers complained that "Italian boys are not trustworthy, especially on the playgrounds, and always have to be watched, as they delight in hurting someone." The teacher's lament was a familiar complaint on the Hill. In 1915, a local teacher complained of "continual indulgence in alcoholics," by the youth, as well as the lack of "legitimate amusements."

Clearly, Italian "toughs" threatened the future direction of the community. Organized sport would help channel the raw, undisciplined energies of young Italian-Americans into constructive outlets for societally-approved violence. In sports as in life, there exists a fine edge between a keen and healthy rivalry and rancorous, self-destructive competition. Sport had polarized the clubs in the early 1920s. "We had soccer teams nobody could beat," boasted a proud Roland De Gregorio. "But then," he said, his voice slipping noticeably, "we used to fight among ourselves."

The man who helped transform the Hill's athletic direction arrived in 1925. Joseph Causino, son of Italian immigrants, walked into St. Ambrose Church in 1925, eager to proselytize the gospel of sport and brotherhood. Causino, a new breed of social worker, had been formally trained as a recreation director and was employed by the St. Louis Southside YMCA.

Joseph Causino, despite the Italianate sound of the name, was a third-generation Bohemian whose family (originally named Kacena) had prospered in St. Louis. Raised a Catholic, he later converted to Lutheranism. Having graduated in Fine Arts from Washington University, Causino was forced to cut short a promising artistic career when his family suffered a severe economic setback. Causino found a career with the St. Louis Young Men's Christian Association.

Nationally, the YMCA had made an extensive effort to counsel America's burgeoning youth population. By 1920 the organization had erected over 1000 buildings, valued at ninety-six million dollars. Locally, the YMCA had begun in St. Louis in the 1850s and by the 1920s had established a Southside branch to serve the distant Hill.

Causino discovered an enclave in need of formal direction. The Hill contained no recreational center, not even a playing field. Causino represented the ethos of the YMCA—an appeal for citizenship, the Protestant work/play ethic, the creed of Americanization—and he appealed to the youth on their grounds. "He kept us out of jail," volunteered one of his many converts, adding,

Because, like I said, we had cousins and big brothers who were gangsters, with knives and guns. It took a guy like Joe Causino to see that we were headed for trouble. . . . We let off steam that way (with sports). And that's why a lot of guys will tell you that, by the grace of God and Uncle Joe Causino, we were all cleancut kids.

"You call me Uncle Joe," he admonished gang members. "Don't ever call me Mr. Causino." He recollected his thoughts a quarter of a century later. "Like a lot of people, I had the idea that there was something unfriendly about this place. But they treated me wonderfully.''

Causino—who learned to speak Italian—fully expected opposition from immigrant parents. ''My father never liked my playing ball,'' remembered Yogi Berra. ''He always got sore if I came home dirty and he would smack me for sure if my pants were torn!'' Soon after Causino's arrival, an angry parent cornered the youthworker and demanded that he state his intentions. ''I want to bring in an organized recreational program,'' the undaunted Causino replied—in fluent Italian. ''I want to make them better citizens, good Americans.'' The immigrant smiled, satisfied with the answer. ''That's what we want,'' he said, ''we want our boys to be good Americans.'' Sport became a handmaiden for Americanization.

Countless huddles, rap sessions and confrontations later, plenty of good Americans had graduated from Uncle Joe's school. Grown men forcefully swear to Causino's decisive impact upon their lives and the Hill's future. ''The greatest who ever lived. Dynamite!'' extolled Phil Verga. ''If you needed dough, he gave you money. If you needed a job, he'd help you find a job.'' Les Garanzini concurred:

He was concerned with us young kids on the Hill. . . . He was for clean living, good people. . . . He got us sponsors for each club . . . ours was the Fawns . . . then he had this clubhouse—he'd let us use the clubhouse for the whole weekend—30, 40 boys. Go camping, hiking. A clean life. Lead a clean life. Be active in sports to raise a good, clean body. He was very concerned with the young people.

''It finally got to the point,'' exclaimed Lou Berra, ''where Uncle Joe got us working together. One of the things that welded us together was sports.''

Causino packaged pride, character, unity, and the strenuous life through the appeal of baseball and soccer. Few denied that Causino's techniques and programs were less than a roaring success. His recreational programs, dovetailed with the extensive St. Ambrose Church youth movement, created an effective hold on the colony's young, leaving little room or inclination for deviation.

Causino was aided in his efforts by the parish church—indeed it is difficult to judge who aided whom. In 1926 the colony built at immense collective sacrifice, St. Ambrose Church. Immediately the Church became the most important social complex in the community. ''The Church at that time,'' recalled lifelong resident Fr. Anthony Palumbo, ''was the center of not only the spiritual activities of the colony, but the social activities gravitated around the church . . . it made for a very closely known community and closely knit parish.''

The Church, aware of the gang problem, set out in the 1930s on an extensive youth program, part of which was the invitation to Causino to help organize athletics. Prior to 1930, the parish had been administered to by native Italian priests, all of whom were in advance of fifty years. In order to appeal to the colony's young men, St. Ambrose recruited four young priests in the 1930s, two of whom were the first non-Italians to serve the parish.

Fathers Anthony Palumbo and Peter Barabino were exemplary of the new priests; the former appealed to the young with his airplane, the latter with a soccer ball and baseball glove. ''No one did more to start it [soccer] on the Hill than Father Anthony Palumbo,'' observed long-time sports editor of the St. Louis *Globe-Democrat,* Robert Burns. Fathers Charles Koester and John Wieberg also worked actively with the youth-sport movement. ''We priests were the sparkplugs of the community . . .'' reminisced Koester, today a bishop. ''Sports were very important to the Hill. You must remember, the Hill was very poor then and soccer and baseball provided entertainment for the people. It also built character and provided an outlet for our young men.''

Soccer and baseball served as a recreational antidote for the Depression-strapped Hill. And beyond the colony, Americans continued to indulge in leisure activities with even greater enthusiasm than before. For St. Louisans, free entertainment was offered each Sunday throughout the 1920s and 1930s, as millions of soccer, baseball and softball fans crowded into urban parks. In 1927-28, for example, over a million St. Louisans attended soccer matches at a cost to the city of only $1,985, or $.0018 per capita. Sports received a federal boost in the 1930s as New Deal programs sought to involve urban youth. ''I was thirteen years old [in 1939] and just as juvenile as our juvenile delinquents of today,'' reminisced Joe Garagiola. ''That was the reason for this league, a project undertaken by the WPA to keep us juveniles off the streets.''

The blistering competitiveness, channeled into a community-wide spirit, proved unbeatable on diamond and turf. The Hill's athletic *risorgimento* upset the balance of power in St. Louis soccer, heretofore dominated by the German Sports Club, the Spanish Society, and the Irish Catholic League. ''The Hill had some of the city's most fantastic kickers,'' contended Bill Kerch, veteran reporter for the *Globe-Democrat.* ''They were simply outstanding . . . very well disciplined . . . not vicious . . . the best in the city.'' Trouncing Germans and Irishmen added a new dimension to ethnic rivalry, proving far more popular than belting the *paesano* next door.

Sports offered an acceptable outlet for the free-spirited Italo-Americans. Soccer matches in particular were impassioned affairs. During the 1929-30 Municipal Soccer League season, 51 players were suspended for roughness and fighting. A typical match in 1934 involving Southside rivals Dog Town and Dago Hill nearly ended in a riot before 3,500 not-so-sedate fans. ''The game was tough all the way through,'' complained Coach Norman of Carlstrom's Dog Town. ''This is nothing new with our games with St. Ambrose,'' he continued, scowling. ''I couldn't stand such conduct so I took my team off the field.'' But the violence and ill feelings were short-lived. Soccer collisions were a mild form of cathartic release, an acceptable outlet for societally approved violence. ''To individuals too ready to follow some subversive drummer,'' suggested Eugen Weber, ''games offered opportunities for self-assertion and sometimes for indulging in competitive violence.''

The spirited play exhibited in the 1930s made St. Louis the capital of American soccer, with the Hill shining as one of its brightest jewels. ''The Hill was an important breeding ground for soccer players," wrote sports historian James Robinson. "Since 1929 the Hill has been an outstanding center for soccer activity in the St. Louis area." The 1928-29 season was the first in which Hill athletes competed under one banner. That year, soccer players rallied under the banner of Calcaterra Undertakers, winning the title in the city's Foundry League.

In a remarkably brief period, Hill Italians had successfully perfected the team demands of soccer. In 1924, Louis Jean Gualdoni, a Democratic politician, could find no local Italian youths to play on his Fairmount Soccer Team. "No one. None," laughed Gualdoni, today a ninety-year-old observer. "There was none of 'em who could qualify. This was before Joe Causino and Father Palumbo. What I wanted was a winner . . . eventually we got lots of Italians on the team."

The popularity of soccer on the Hill must be explained in terms of the St. Louis environment. German immigrants had introduced the *turnverein* and soccer in the nineteenth century, and the popularity of the game has persisted through today. Moreover, since the Hill's geographic and ethnic neighbors, the Irish and German, played soccer, it was only natural that the community's youth would embrace the sport. Soccer remained a second and third-generation phenomenon; Italian immigrants had neither played nor understood *calcio* in the old country.

After 1930, Hill athletes vied for supremacy in nearly every sport. In the early 1930s, the gangs were formally organized into an overarching federation, calling themselves the Royal Knights of Italy (later changed to Fairmount Athletic Union because of anti-fascist publicity). The federation, brainchild of Sam Chinicci, a volunteer, promoted tournaments and intramural competition. "I used to organize parades to motivate the boys," said Chinicci, then a filling station operator. "I organized the federation with the help of the National Youth Administration."

Like everything else, sports after 1930 tended to revolve around St. Ambrose, keeping the parish the unquestionable social center of the community. "On Sunday morning, everybody in our neighborhood went to church," reminisced Yogi Berra:

> There was never any question about it if you were going. We went unless we were flat on our backs . . . and it didn't pay to fake. If you were too sick to go to Mass in the morning, you can bet your life you were going to be too sick to go out and play ball in the afternoon.

When Yogi quit school after the eighth grade, a concerned Papa Berra asked Joe Causino and Fr. Charles Koester of St. Ambrose to guide the errant young man.

Sports, like politics and the brown derby, flourished in urban Catholic America. Sons of Irishmen, Poles, and Italians took to baseball and basketball, football, and soccer. Frank Deford writes:

> In the palmy days of yore, when order reigned over innocent games, sport was uplifting, and a glorious celebration, like the Mass. Sport and the church both stood for authority. . . . Heroes were larger than life, canonized as athletic saints, a comforting adjunct to the church's own hagiology.

The Roman Church has always been perturbed by sex, and for its male adolescents, joining a team was considered the next best thing to a vow of celibacy.

Deford's portrayal of the Catholic Church as the bastion of conservatism and the nexus between church and sports fits the well-ordered Hill. Berra claimed:

Another thing that helped in our neighborhood was the church. St. Ambrose's was the big institution on the Hill, and we could count on catching it from the old man if we forgot to go to confession on Saturday afternoon on our way to take a shower at the 'Y.' So we didn't dare do anything too bad during the week because we knew we'd have to tell the priest about it in the confessional on Saturday.

"No problem was so big that Father Palumbo couldn't figure it out," reminisced the inimitable Garagiola. When Garagiola was asked to try out for the St. Louis Cardinals, he began to search for a catcher's mitt. "None of our guys had one," he wrote. "The only one we knew of belonged to Louis Cassani. He wasn't one of the boys, but Father Palumbo said that our Johnny Colombo knew Gino Pariani who knew Louie Cassani. The network began operation and we got our mitt."

The Hill had completed a remarkable athletic transformation in a span of less than 20 years. When in the early 1920s local politicians attempted to organize a soccer team, they could find no qualified Italians with which to man the team and thereby attract Democratic voters. By 1929, the first organized Hill soccer team had won the divisional championship, and by 1940 St. Ambrose climaxed the pre-war successes with the Missouri Ozark Amateur Championship. The fiery center from that team, Joe Numi, would return after the war to lead area soccer teams to new heights. Coach Numi was guaranteed quality players, since his farm team, St. Ambrose, won the Sublette Park Parish School League title eleven consecutive years, 1934 through 1945.

Sports had a catalytic impact upon the Hill, an effect measured far beyond tarnished trophies. Potentially the greatest threat to community stability had been the gang, for if the Hill could not win the affections of its young, the neighborhood was doomed. "If the gang does not become conventionalized in some way into the structure of the community as its members grow older," Frederick Thrasher ominously warned readers in 1927, "it often drifts into habitual crime and becomes completely delinquent." The assorted gangs on Dago Hill were harnessed by Joe Causino, the Catholic Church, and immigrant fathers. So great a transformation had occurred by 1934 that Causino's colleague, Harold Keltner, published a YMCA guide ironically entitled *Gangs: An Asset to the City of St. Louis.* Keltner described an encounter on the Hill:

Good sportsmanship is one result of the direction of athletics. The Little Caesars, for instance, last year played several ineligible men on their baseball team. This they did unwittingly and, when they discovered it, wrote a special letter of apology to all the clubs and voluntarily forfeited all of the games.

Sports became a handmaiden for solidarity, a vehicle which helped transform factional conflict into creative competition. By 1941, the Hill had become, partly through the medium of sports, an ethnic phalanx. Young and old, Lombard and Sicilian, old-world mustachioed Petes and New world, Yogis passionately identified themselves with the Hill, with St. Ambrose, with neighborhood teams. "What impressed me the most about the kids from the Hill," insisted Fr. Anthony Palumbo, priest and soccer coach at St. Ambrose (1932-1948), "was that they were willing to make a lot of sacrifices to play on the team . . . they were willing to sacrifice for the Hill."

That sport played such a critical role amongst Hill youth can be attributed to the ecological characteristics of the locale. These structural factors also reinforced the ethnic dimension of the sport network. Historically, ethnic identification is likely to become intertwined with territorial commonality whenever ethnic residential patterns converge with a working-class population. The Hill presents a striking case of this. Boston's Italian West End—a much studied neighborhood—also exhibited similar characteristics: a strong identification with territorial space, high investments in inter-personal relationships, and strong personal association rather than achievement orientation.

Sports not only crystallized Italo-American feelings internally within the colony, but also provided a public forum from which St. Louisans, and in a broader sense Americans, judged the neighborhood from a different perspective other than busted stills and ethnic caricatures. A St. Louis columnist rhapsodized in 1949:

All is not spaghetti, macaroni and choice wine on the Hill, that famed neighborhood in Southwest St. Louis. The principal occupation is sports and the main export nationally is known athletes. Many people think that it is baseball . . . but almost every other sport has produced a similar quota of great stars.

Observed a reporter from the prestigious *Post-Dispatch* in 1941:

The Hill is a neighborhood of some 10,000 first, second and third generation Italians. It boasts its own factories and stores, its schools and churches. But best of all, it boasts of being a neighborhood with the lowest juvenile delinquency rate of the city.

Organized athletics had distinctly altered local perception of the Italian Hill. But what role had sports played in retarding or encouraging the acculturation of Italian-Americans? Had athletes promoted assimilation into a greater urban society?

Sports played a complex, often conflicting role in the formation of urban-ethnic values. On the one hand, athletics fostered acculturation to American ways of life by mixing nationalities in team play. "Sports was a tremendous thing for us Italians," exclaimed Joe Correnti, a dry cleaner who helped organize local soccer teams. "You must remember we were almost a closed community. Sports was an outlet for us." Athletic competition forced Hill players outside the sheltered neighborhood.

Local athletic successes also enabled several dozen soccer and baseball players to attend area colleges on scholarships. According to sociologist Richard Rehberg, participation in sport has the most effect on boys least disposed to attend college by raising their educational expectations to attend college. These successful athletes also served as role models for area youth. In 1940, only one Hill resident had obtained a college degree; following the war, college became more attractive, owing to the successes of the GI Bill and athletes. By 1955, the Hill had spawned a half-dozen professional baseball players, twice that number of professional soccer players, and several national soccer club championships. "It is doubtful," wrote historian Richard Sorrell in describing Woonsocket, Rhode Island, "if any city of comparable size [50,000] produced as many major leaguers [three, including Napoleon Lajoie], let alone from one ethnic group [French]." One neighborhood, the Hill, comprised of only 5,000 Italian-Americans, easily eclipsed Woonsocket's enviable record.

On the other hand, organized recreation promoted ethno-religious identity through competition and the preservation of parish-colony teams. Ironically, the high water mark of Hill athletic competition occurred during a period in which two forces, the mass media and the automobile, were making important inroads into the colony. But the Ford Coupe and Gateway Trolley, the *Post-Dispatch* and Zenith radio, while widening the social vistas of the community, also served to make Hill Italians more conscious of their uniqueness. Urban journalists, eager for unusual copy made a sport of accentuating the Italian character of the Hill and the Latin flavor of its athletes.

The Hill's enthusiasm for soccer accentuated the ethnic dimension of the neighborhood, especially outside St. Louis. John Pooley argues in "Ethnic Clubs in Milwaukee" that soccer fostered ethnoculturalism:

> Since the sport of soccer is alien to the core society; and since soccer is the major game of the countries origin of the ethnic groups; and since members of the ethnic groups in question were involved in the activities of soccer clubs . . . it is thereby hypothesized that ethnic soccer clubs in Milwaukee inhibit structural assimilation.

In one of the greatest mass movements in modern history, three million Italians immigrated to the United States in the half-century after 1880. Into the maelstrom of an emerging urban-industrial economy sailed the immigrants, most of whom came poorly prepared for the rigors of modern society. They survived, and in their quest to find a better life in the United States adapted to and adopted the values and institutions of the host society. Historians have made great strides in studying the sensitive issues of *pane e lavoro*—bread and work—but have reluctantly ventured beyond the traditional topics and chronology of the great wave of immigration, 1880-1924. The complex matrix of relationships between immigrant parents and sons, and between second-generation peer groups—a familiar theme in novels—has been largely ignored by immigration historians. One such issue which affected immigrants and sons was the question of recreation. Future ethnic scholars might well address themselves to the unexplored seams of sport history and the immigrant community, for the study of athletic voluntary associations provides a microcosmic portrait of the immigrant group.

CHAPTER 14

Sport and Community in California's Japanese American Yamato Colony, 1930–1945

Samuel O. Regalado

Hot windswept summers commonly blanketed southeastern Colorado. "There were nothing but sand dunes in the whole area," recalled Yuk Yatsuya, who spent the war years in the region. Indeed, the arid land held little personality. Miles of desolation served as a constant reminder of one's isolation. But, during the summer of 1943, the crack of a bat against a ball intruded the serenity of the barren land. Amidst the Colorado hinterlands, hundreds of people gathered around a makeshift diamond set inside a barbed wire enclosure as two teams prepared to do battle against one another. In the direction of center field, the fences and lookout posts, manned by machine guns, decorated the scenery beyond the outfield fences. The encampment at Amache, Colorado, was not a pleasant place to live, but it is where the Dodgers of Livingston, California, began play that year. They, like other Japanese Americans, were in the midst of their second year of confinement in one of ten internment camps strewn across the United States during World War II. Their freedom impaired, baseball and other recreational activities were major factors in maintaining community cohesion. Through sport, the Japanese American faction from Livingston, and others like it, nurtured cultural camaraderie, competitiveness, and pride. These activities, of course, were vital throughout their years of internment. But their importance and development, to be sure, preceded the evacuation period.

During the first decade of the twentieth century, several first generation Japanese families, Issei, came to Livingston, California, a farming community which lies in the center of California's rich agricultural San Joaquin Valley. Led by Kyutaro Abiko, a San Francisco newspaper publisher and businessman, in 1904, they formed an agricultural settlement known as the Yamato Colony. Like so many of their contemporaries from other countries, these agrarians came with high hopes and an eagerness to do well in the "land of opportunity." However,

From the *Journal of Sport History,* 19:2 (Summer, 1992). © 1992 The North American Society for Sport History. Reprinted by permission.

anti-Asian legislation, which included the 1907 Gentlemen's Agreement, created difficulties for the Issei in their quest to succeed. The 1913 Alien Land Act, for instance, which prohibited Japanese land ownership, "underlined their alienness and encouraged other kinds of discrimination and unpleasantness." Indeed, in California such organizations as the American Legion, Native Sons of the Golden West, and the California State Grange fueled xenophobic splinter groups such as the California Oriental Exclusion League and the Americanization League of San Joaquin Valley. By 1924, another barrier, the National Origins Act, not only curbed immigration from each country to two percent of its proportion of resident aliens based on the census of 1890, but also effectively barred the Issei from attaining citizenship. Prevented by law both from owning land and earning citizenship, many Issei farmers, it seemed, would have little recourse but to leave the United States. Nativists were clearly delighted at the prospect. James D. Phelan, a former senator, expressed the sentiments of many of his fellow Californians when he declared, "The Japs are routed."

But the determined Japanese found loopholes in the law. Members of the Yamato Colony, for example, offset the impact of the Alien Land Act and, later, the National Origins Act, by forming farm co-ops, called *Nogyo Kumiai*. Title to the co-ops was placed in the name of American-born offspring—Nisei—while the parents acted as guardians. In fact, long before the Alien Land Act became law, Kyutaro Abiko and his business contacts had purchased ample plots for the colony. Despite the blatant hostility, Abiko's labor contracting firm, the *Nichibei Kangyosha,* confidently promoted the project in their homeland: "We believe that the colony will become a paradise—a place of welcome for those wishing to move to the United States." Wives, children and "picture brides," many who began their long trek from Japan to the colony since the period of the Gentlemen's Agreement, to be sure, also were vital to the community. "Wives and children," according to Yamato chronicler Kesa Noda, "would give the settlement an assurance of stability and continuity that could not be achieved by the mere ownership of land. Each marriage was seen as a triumph for the man and the community—a building block toward the future."

As the Japanese American community developed, so, too, did organizations such as the Japanese Association of America which, founded in 1909, was designed to promote the general welfare of its constituents. At the local level, Buddhist and Christian church assemblies such as the Seinenkai or Young Men's Group, together with the Educational Society known as the Gakuen, and the Kendo Club (the Japanese art of bamboo-stave fighting) sponsored many activities such as talent shows, picnics, and concerts. Such communal events as these, provided "emotional support," claimed historian Valerie Matsumoto. Furthermore, they served to maintain "as much as they could of the Issei's cultural heritage."

Sport, of course, was also directly tied to highly valued samurai principles: courage and honor. "Stern visage, resoluteness in action [and] physical toughness," claimed writer John Whitney Hall, ". . . were the qualities most admired by the samurai class." More importantly, the warrior "remained true to his

The Cortez Wildcats, shown here in a photograph taken about 1937, were one of the many Japanese-American baseball teams in central California's Yamato Colony.
Courtesy of Yuk Yatsuya.

calling and his sense of cultural identity as a Japanese." This approach was not uncommon among many old line immigrants who, according to historian Steven A. Riess in *City Games,* believed that "the maintenance of historic old-world sporting organizations or the creation of new ones which emphasized the 'ancient and honorable games' " was of great importance. Issei in the Yamato Colony followed a similar pattern: the adoption of sport as a means to acculturate at no expense to cultural heritage.

One Issei, Koko Kaji, spearheaded competitive sports, particularly baseball, in the Yamato Colony. Baseball, of course, was not unfamiliar to many of the Japanese migrants. Indeed, America's national pastime planted its seeds in Japan during the late nineteenth century. Robert Whiting, in his book *The Chrysanthemum and the Bat: Baseball Samurai Style,* credits Horace Wilson, an American professor in Japan, for having introduced baseball to that country in 1893. The game, Whiting claimed, was initially "played by kimono-clad youths in sandals. . . ." However, Donald Roden, in his article "Baseball and the Quest for National Dignity in Meiji Japan," argues that, in 1883, Wilson's colleague, F.W. Strange, in his quest to introduce Western sport to the Japanese, included baseball in his own special handbook entitled *Outdoor Games.* In either case, it is unclear if Kaji's adoption of baseball came from his native country or the United States. What is clear is that by the middle 1920s, "Smiling" Koko Kaji formed and managed the Livingston Peppers baseball team which received attention in the town's local newspaper, the Livingston *Chronicle.*

Many Nisei inherited their love for baseball from their elders. As the Yamato Colony grew, second generation Americans of Japanese ancestry continued Kaji's legacy by forming community-based teams. By the middle 1930s, many of Kaji's "Peppers" were past thirty and the club dissolved. However, as young adults, Nisei athletes in the Yamato Colony organized another community team, the Livingston Dodgers. "By the time we got out of high school we developed our own sports activities," recalled Fred Kishi, a local sports star in the region. Indeed, throughout the San Joaquin Valley Nisei athletes formed amateur adult teams and eventually established baseball leagues. From 1934 to 1941, the Central Valley Japanese League consisted of eight teams. Sponsorship of most clubs came from churches and local merchants. "We played against Walnut Grove, Lodi," remembered Kishi. "These were all Nisei leagues and we played for probably about three or four years actively in this league. Most of the Nisei players developed their expertise playing in [these] leagues." So great was their love of sport that team members often assisted their mates on the farms to make time for baseball. "Every weekend we had the Livingston Dodgers," said pitcher Gilbert Tanji, "so every Sunday when I had a hard time getting away all the boys used to come and help me with certain work so I could take off Sunday early." Fred Kishi emphasized that a special chemistry brought the team together. "The players on this team knew each other practically from the day we were born; we went to church together, we played on Saturdays together, and we went to high school together, so it just fell into place," he pointed out. Coach Masao Hoshimo, an Issei, stressed unity both on and off the field. Kishi remembered that Hoshimo "had good psychological methods of getting us together. He made us to go Sunday school before we went to any games, so it was a very close-knit group that we had." Former player, Robert Ohki added, "the manager always used to say, 'you guys got to go to church or we're not going to play on Sunday.' "

By the middle 1930s, sport activities throughout the Yamato Colony had expanded beyond baseball. While the Dodgers competed in an all-Valley League on Sundays, a number of Japanese American softball clubs formed throughout Central California and participated during weekday evenings. The participants on the softball diamonds ranged from high school age to elderly Issei players. At times, they also competed against Caucasian teams from Livingston. During the winter, basketball replaced baseball as the area's most popular sport; both male and female teams were in abundance.

Rivalries, of course, emerged to liven the competition. Among the most intense was the baseball competition between Livingston and nearby Cortez. Like its counterpart in Livingston, the Cortez Young People's Club (CYPC), was sponsored by a branch of the Gakuen. The CYPC sponsored cultural events, but by the late 1930s its primary interest turned to sports. Baseball was so popular that the Cortez players proudly carved out their own baseball diamond amidst the vegetable fields. "We had a great big ballpark," Yuk Yatsuya, former pitcher for the Cortez Wildcats, proudly claimed. "We were the only ones that had our own ballpark." Yatsuya was a standout pitcher, who, in one 1939 contest, came within one hit of pitching a perfect game against Lodi. Like the Livingston team, Cortez players also designed their work schedules so as to provide ample time for baseball. "We used to pick berries in the morning, then run to the game, and then we'd come back and finish the work," remembered Yatsuya. Yatsuya's teammate, Yeichi Sakaguchi asserted, "We were obligated to the team . . . so we tried like heck to make [the games]." The Cortez team, in fact, was unique because its coach, Hilmar Blaine, was a Caucasian, a Shell Oil Company distributor, who delivered gas to farmers in the Yamato Colony. Blaine was a baseball advocate and "helped us get started and then he helped us get uniforms," remembered Yatsuya.

The fact that Cortez and Livingston were neighboring communities intensified the rivalry between many of the players who attended the same schools. "We didn't care who we won from [sic], just so we won from Cortez. We went to school with the Cortez boys and beat them, maybe seventy or eighty percent of the time," claimed Gilbert Tanji. Yuk Yatsuya's competitive spirit still burned brightly a half century later as he reflected on the domination of the Livingston club. The Dodgers were able to "practice more than we did," he claimed. "They [also] had a lot more material to pick from." Indeed, between 1939 and 1941, the Livingston Dodgers compiled an impressive record of thirty-four wins and four losses.

Community sport, of course, was not uncommon within America's ethnic enclaves. In Pittsburgh's black community between 1920 and 1940, for instance, athletics, according to writer Rob Ruck in *Sandlot Seasons: Sport in Black Pittsburgh*, offered residents there "a cultural counterpoint to its collective lot, one that promoted internal cohesion. . . ." In addition, Ruck claimed that, through sports, black residents there gained "a sense of [themselves] as part of a national black community." Baseball, in particular, offered millions of foreign-born citizens the opportunity to "Americanize" their communities. According to historian Harold Seymour in *Baseball: The People's Game,* "One way children of foreign birth or parentage could fit into the new culture was to take part in baseball, and early on, many of them perceived in it their badge as Americans." Rudimentary teams, some formed from street gangs, appeared in the German and Italian neighborhoods of the eastern seaboard. Seymour also pointed out that in Chicago's Slavic community, in 1927 "the American Bohemian Alliance there was sponsoring a fifteen-team [baseball] league of nine senior and eight junior teams, furnishing their equipment, and charging an admission fee to the games." Mexican American teams in the southwest also utilized baseball as a means of fomenting and cementing family ties and tradition. There, mariachi bands and Mexican cuisine provided entertainment and refreshment in the stands. The Negro leagues were, of course, the most obvious example of ethnic-based teams. They, too, utilized baseball as a means to enter the mainstream. Author Donn Rogosin aptly pointed out, in *Invisible Men: Life in Baseball's Negro Leagues,* that the "black players realized an essential goal of black culture, namely, to prove that blacks and whites were equal, and they proved it in a way that common people understood.'' Racial discrimination notwithstanding, however, many generations of blacks had adopted and contributed to American culture. Newly arrived aliens, on the other hand, needed to acculturate.

Whether the Nisei used sport as a means to enter the American mainstream, however, remains open to interpretation. Like other ethnics, their ambition and drive stemmed in part from the need for acceptance. Academics, for instance, was an area in which they excelled. Noting that Japanese parents often drove their children to maintain high standards, Robert Wilson and Bill Hosokawa observed in *East to America* that ''[the Nisei] seemed to sense that in a competitive society in which they operated at a disadvantage, they would need to be superior to compete even equally.'' Sociologist Harry Kitano also saw sport as another means of adaptation to American culture. ''The basketball teams served as vehicles for acculturation,'' he argued, '' . . . the Nisei were free to develop in the American pattern. The play, the rules, the goals and values, were all American; only the players were Japanese.'' The teams, leagues, and all of the athletic activities, however, consisted almost exclusively of Nisei. In California's Central Valley, Nisei cultural interaction outside their respective communities was limited. With respect to sport, Nisei competitors were all but insulated from the ''outside.''

Nisei athletes, to be sure, often found inspiration from their fathers. ''I can remember as a child going to church and watching some of the Issei play tennis,'' claimed Fred Kishi. ''In fact, they built the tennis court at our local church site.'' Kishi's introduction to baseball also came when he was probably eight or nine years old: ''Two of my Issei neighbors got involved with a semi-pro baseball team. In fact, Mr. Kaji was their manager.'' In these, and other ways, Issei parents sought to maintain control of their offspring. In fact, sports associations created throughout America by the Issei and other immigrants, ''fostered athletic participation by the second generation . . . in hopes of maintaining an ethnic identity for the American-born and reared,'' claimed Steven Riess. Most social activities, hence, revolved around the Japanese community and, often stemmed from the local Buddhist or Christian churches. At the same time, however, it remained imperative that the Nisei acculturate in order to compete in the larger societal framework. ''[The Issei] knew [that] their children must absorb the American culture, must be Americans, to make their way in the land of their birth,'' claimed Hosokawa in *Nisei: The Quiet Americans*. ''But they were disturbed that the Nisei were ignoring, and in some cases rejecting, their Japanese heritage.'' Through baseball and basketball, however, Japanese and American culture was bridged with seemingly no threat to traditional values.

While teams competed throughout the decade, changes occurred within the Japanese American community. By the dawn of World War II, a generation gap between the Nisei and their elders came of age. The Issei, for instance, identified in most aspects with Japan. They incorporated old folkways into their churches, press, and civic groups. Moreover, Japanese remained their primary language. ''They remembered . . . the Japan of their youth,'' claimed Roger Daniels.

Moreover, because of the rigid anti-Oriental laws of earlier periods "the Issei were probably better insulated against Americanization than were contemporary immigrant groups from Europe." The Nisei, on the other hand, "had," according to historian John Modell, "inherited from [their] parents a remarkable desire to succeed in the face of hardship, but had also learned the American definition of success, [whereby the] standard . . . made by his parents could not be considered satisfactory." The creation of the Japanese American Citizen's League (JACL) in 1930 best exemplified their generation gap. Among its mandates, this Nisei organization barred Issei from membership and sought to minimize the cultural ties with Japan. Therefore, given the growing polarization, recreational events helped to bridge some gaps.

By the late 1930s, many Issei were too old to participate in athletic activities. Recreational leagues and elaborate sport programs were dominated by male and female Nisei. Basketball, kendo, sumo wrestling and volleyball drew great attention. The Issei, for their part, most of whom might have otherwise disagreed with Nisei goals, encouraged their children's athletic endeavors because of their own interest in sports. By the end of the decade many, it appeared, recognized and appreciated the competitive spirit as part of their own heritage. In December of 1941, however, both generational conflict and all athletic activities came to an abrupt halt.

Japan's surprise attack on the American naval base at Pearl Harbor on December 7, 1941, plunged the United States into World War II. It also provided powerful ammunition for West Coast nativists who, for several decades, had warned of a perceived "yellow peril." Even before the "day of infamy," some Japanese had already predicted their fate. "Our properties would be confiscated and most likely [we would] be herded into prison camps," predicted one Nisei student attending the University of California at Berkeley as relations between Japan and the United States soured. In the weeks following the attack, government agents saturated Japanese neighborhoods in search of evidence that suggested sabotage. Major newspaper columnists fueled the hysteria when many claimed that a "fifth-column"—espionage activity—operated in their region. Chief among the paranoid was General John L. DeWitt, who headed the west coast command forces at the San Francisco presidio where ". . . confusion rather than calm reigned," for, claimed historian Roger Daniels, "the confusion was greatest at the very top." In February 1942, partly in an effort to pacify western xenophobes, President Franklin D. Roosevelt signed into action Executive Order 9066, which gave DeWitt the power to evacuate all suspected "enemy aliens" and other perceived threats to national security from areas deemed "militarily sensitive"—that is, the entire West Coast. The president's order led to the eventual internment of Japanese Americans throughout the Western states. During the spring of 1942, hundreds of Issei and Nisei families were ordered to regional assembly "holding" centers to await further relocation. By the middle of the year, over 110,000 people of Japanese ancestry entered one of ten internment camps in some of the most desolate regions in America.

Prior to the announcement of Executive Order 9066, Nisei farmers working in Stanislaus and Merced counties were understandably uncomfortable. "We were ready for the worst, but hoped that there would be no evacuation," recalled Robert Ohki. "[Then] all of a sudden they put out the order. They never warned anybody. We didn't know how long we were going to be gone." From December 1941 to February 1942, Livingston farmers utilized the local chapter of the JACL to act as mediators with the local authorities. In nearby Cortez, Nisei residents found similar circumstances. In fact, social gatherings were strongly discouraged by Caucasian officials. "We didn't know what the future was going to hold for us," said Yeichi Sakaguchi. During this "interim" period, fear and harrassment of Japanese Americans grew. Governor Culbert L. Olson of California, for example, contributed to the uneasiness with a radio broadcast which claimed, among other things, that a "fifth-column operated in his state." Local papers, like the Modesto *Bee,* described the arrest of Japanese American residents for traveling from Stockton to Merced without a permit. One article reported vigilante-type raids on Issei farmers in nearby counties, while others described the confiscation of radios from various Japanese homes. Though the *Bee* cautioned its readers not to overreact, incidents aimed at Japanese residents continued during the first few months of 1942. Further south, the Merced *Sun-Star* ominously tallied the number of "enemy aliens" that resided in that county as if to warn its readers of a possible threat. Japanese Issei, in particular, attempted to curb the sweeping fear by writing letters to the local papers. One such response came from the president of the Cortez Grower's Association, who claimed, "I own land in America, and I never expect to return to Japan. My children have been educated here and I want them to be good Americans. The association pledges its fullest cooperation with the United States in this emergency."

By the middle of the spring, Japanese American communities throughout the San Joaquin Valley received relocation orders. In May, those in the Stanislaus and Merced counties left their beloved Yamato Colony and took up residence at the nearby and hastily built assembly center at the Merced County fairgrounds. "As they entered Merced Assembly Center," stated Yamato chronicler Kesa Noda, "the Japanese began a life that held an odd mixture of restrictions, humiliations, and 'freedom.' " In a show of dignity, sports writer Mack Yamaguchi wrote, "We will go without hate or fear, thankful for your unceasing love and understanding. . . ." In a more poignant farewell, Fusaye Obata, in a poem entitled "We Shall Meet Again," penned:

Some inland points to settle may roam
As leave they must their coastal home
The rest of us in turn will enter
The barracks at some reception center.

Assembly Centers, sixteen in all, were mostly located along the West Coast. In addition to county fairgrounds, athletic stadiums and racetracks were used to house the Japanese Americans while more permanent internment facilities were

under construction elsewhere. Once at the Assembly Centers, however, the evacuees immediately embarked upon improving the conditions there. In less than two
weeks, not only did an assembly center newspaper appear, the *Mercedian,* but
"incarcerated" sport also commenced.

Internment, of course, was among America's darkest chapters. While some
Nisei characterized their situation as a distinct sign of loyalty, under no circumstances did the evacuees believe their incarceration to be just. Sport helped them
endure their trauma and contributed to their sense of dignity. Consequently,
athletic activities were embraced in an upbeat tone. Indeed, through sport, the
Nisei came together during a period when cohesion was vital. Traditional Japanese
activities, such as Go and Shogi tournaments were soon organized. But it was
baseball that took center stage.

Along with the Livingston Dodgers and Cortez Wildcats, many players from
communities well beyond the Stanislaus-Merced areas, such as Sebastopol, Walnut Grove, and Petaluma, for example, all ended up in the Merced Assembly
Center which eventually contained 4,453 residents. The organization of teams,
therefore, proved to be no problem. "Once we got into camp, everything fell
into place," remembered Fred Kishi. "We had to get something going," added
Yeichi Sakaguchi. In fact, prior to their entry into the evacuation center, Masao
Hoshimo reminded his Livingston Dodgers to bring their uniforms and equipment
with their other belongings. "We took our uniforms along with us and we played
at the Merced County Fairgrounds which had a nice [baseball] stadium there,"
claimed Kishi. "I'm telling you the intensity of competition was very great and
well organized." In an attempt to temper the trauma of incarceration, Gilbert
Tanji optimistically viewed the evacuation site as an opportunity to face greater
challenges on the baseball diamond. "We'd win so many games [at Livingston]
that pretty soon nobody came to watch us play," he recalled. "So when we got
into camp there was more competition—it was more fun." "They had [games]
going everyday and we had a nice ballpark," said Yuk Yatsuya. The grandstand
was an attraction to both players and fans, particularly the elderly Issei who
enjoyed sitting in the shade. "They didn't care who was playing as long as they
could watch the games," stated Yatsuya. Games were constantly played at the
fairgrounds and one player remembered the competition was so intense that
"several times we almost came to blows."

Other sports also appeared at the Center. Sumo wrestling matches, described
by the *Mercedian* as "a paradise for the girls' admiration," were part of the
daily schedule. Girls' volleyball and softball leagues also formed. Finally, as
early as July, men and women's basketball leagues began play. Their facilities,
however, left much to be desired. Both basketball and volleyball players competed
on dirt courts, often playing in 100 degree heat. The recreational program at the
Merced Assembly Center was paralleled by similar activities at other evacuation
sites. At the Fresno, California site, for instance, the *Vignette* enthusiastically
kept close watch on that center's six-team baseball league. The entire sports
program, in fact, "[provided] the Center residents with maximum recreation
facilities and entertainment . . ." Farther north, journalists for the Stockton

Assembly Center, *El Joaquin,* lauded its constituents for having "a well-rounded recreational program that was rated as one of the best of the wartime civil control administration's centers."

At the Merced site, baseball captured much of the attention as ten clubs vied for assembly center "honors." In addition, most of the players participated in the various softball programs that took place daily. The Livingston Dodgers, for example, filled the rosters of both sports while those of the Cortez community mixed in with other "block" teams which lacked enough players. The baseball squads managed to complete up to thirteen contests before relocation preparations forced them to postpone their "season." In the fall of 1942, the Wartime Civil Control Administration (WCCA) received orders to prepare the evacuees to move to more permanent sites. Within a short time, the residents learned the whereabouts of their new "homes." The 1943 baseball season, for the Livingston players and others at the center, would commence in southeastern Colorado. As they prepared to depart eastward, one writer for the *Mercedian* summed up the recreational experience there. "Our good ship 'Merced' soon will anchor its three and a half month voyage with a chapter of progress in the realm of sports unsurpassed," wrote Kaneni Ono. "During this short time, the enthusiasm and accomplishments rendered by the athletic supervisors have greatly relieved the possibility of a low morale in this camp."

Over 7,000 evacuees from the San Joaquin Valley and the Los Angeles area crowded into the Granada, Colorado, camp known as Amache. As an enhancement to their discomfort, most of those who arrived in August of 1942 discovered that the compound had a shortage of barracks. Many of the new residents slept in laundry rooms and recreation halls. Other problems existed, such as poor plumbing and the scarcity of lumber and other building materials which testified to the War Relocation's Administration's (WRA) poor and hasty preparation for a "humane" internment. The terrain was not much better. "It was the sand dune of Colorado," stated Yuk Yatsuya. "Nobody lived there until they put the camp up." Amache was not unlike other camps around the nation. According to historian Roger Daniels, "All ten sites can only be called godforsaken. They were in places where nobody had lived before and no one has lived since." The camp sites were primitive at best. Upon arrival evacuees found cramped quarters, a wooden stove, a mop, a bucket, and a broom. "Block" facilities, much like those found in the assembly centers, became homes to entire communities. Finally, schools, dining facilities, and washrooms needed much improvement. Among the major concerns of the evacuees, however, were the issues of recreation and athletics.

Amache had relatively little in the way of sports facilities. There were no gymnasiums, baseball or softball diamonds, and a grassless football field. Basketball and volleyball players again endured dirt courts. "We had to make the baseball diamond and there were no stands, no seats, no nothing—so the crowd just stood around the field and watched the games," remembered Fred Kishi. Gilbert Tanji recollected the fierce sandstorms that sometimes intruded on the action. ". . . A lot of times we had sandstorms and sometimes we had to stop playing," he said. While basketball players also faced less than ideal conditions, relocation officials were at least able to secure the use of the Granada High School gymnasium which stood less than a mile from the compound. In fact, other camps envied the basketball facilities found at the Colorado center. The evacuee newspaper at the Rowher, Arkansas camp, the *Outpost*, determined that the Amache people had "the most fabulous basketball program" because of its access to a gymnasium. By 1943, the Amache camp had its own gymnasium.

Securing players for recreational activities was no problem. In addition to the athletes from the Stanislaus, San Joaquin, and Merced county areas, Amache also held a large number of evacuees from the Los Angeles basin. The competition, of course, was far more intense than at prior sites. Indeed, during the inaugural football season, a group from Southern California, simply known as the "Santa Anita bunch," brawled with their Sebastopol opponents in one contest. Relocation authorities were brought in to restore order. "Their faces were lopsided for a couple of days," recalled Yuk Yatsuya. Like its counterpart on the "outside," camp sports journalism could also be hazardous. On more than a few occasions, Mack Yamaguchi, who reported for the Granada *Pioneer,* was the recipient of criticism from players who bristled at his portrayals of their efforts.

Primitive facilities notwithstanding, football and basketball generated much enthusiasm during the autumn and winter seasons. In April, when softball sign-ups were announced, among the signees were the Livingston Dodgers, complete with their original uniforms. Softball was popular at the outset, if only because baseball programs had not yet organized. In all, sixteen adult male teams—many participants in their mid-twenties—formed and participated in two different divisions. The Dodgers, with their extensive experience in the San Joaquin Nisei leagues during the 1930s, as well as in the abbreviated Merced Assembly Center league, proved to be worthy opponents when they competed on the Amache softball diamonds during the 1943 season. Playing in what they called the "National League," the Livingston club captured the title. Shortstop Fred Kishi, who batted a healthy .714, not only was selected to the first team all-star squad, but also was named as the league's most valuable player. Like other talented athletes, Kishi also participated in sports such as football and basketball. Indeed, his basketball prowess earned him the title of the Livingston Rockets' "points-getter-in-chief," in the Granada *Pioneer.*

While the Dodgers excelled in the Amache camp softball circuit, they did not fare as well in the baseball league. Both the increase of talented opposition and the loss of key members due to work leaves or military obligations took a toll on the Livingston club. Playing as one of five teams in the baseball league, the Dodgers finished the 1943 season with a two and six record. Baseball, however, remained popular with the Amache residents at-large. All-Star teams were regularly chosen and, at times, competed against clubs from outside the camp. In 1944, an All-Star squad was picked to represent Amache in contests against a team at the Gila River, Arizona camp. Confident that wartime hysteria had passed, the WRA, after several weeks of debate, granted permission for the games to proceed. In August the Amache baseball club spent one week competing in Gila

River then stopped off at the Poston, Arizona camp for eight games before returning to their home camp. Writer Mack Yamaguchi indicated that Amache reciprocated by enthusiastically playing host to visiting Nisei baseball teams from other camps. "We looked forward to [competing against] other Nisei players whom, during prewar days, the Japanese papers had made famous," he recalled.

While relocation officials apparently viewed inter-camp athletic rivalries merely as recreational outlets, competition on the ball diamond remained intense. As late as July 1944, two years after having arrived at Amache, one columnist scolded his readers for unsportsmanlike conduct; he lamented that when Nisei compete, "things get somewhat out of hand and usually end up with fists flying."

In 1944, players from the Livingston region did not participate in athletic competition on a regular basis. A year earlier Fred Kishi reported to military intelligence school. Others either joined the service, pursued educational opportunities, or worked in labor outfits. Throughout 1944 and the following year, the Livingston club no longer appeared in the league standings.

By the end of 1945, the internment period came to a close. As the former evacuees slowly returned to the Livingston area, their homecoming was, at times, tainted by viscious attacks that included drive-by shootings on their properties. These and other problems, such as re-establishing their farms, hindered a return to the routine community activities they engaged in prior to the war—sports among them. Hence, while Sansei—third generation—athletes later emerged to resurrect the athletic competitive spirit seen in earlier years, for all intents and purposes, an era had come to an end.

The Livingston Dodgers and other Japanese American athletic teams, however, had made their mark. Ethnic and civic pride sustained them through ordeals unmatched by other Americans. Like other Nisei, they exhibited what historian Valerie Matsumoto termed "a fierce competitive streak which found outlets in sports and scholarship." The Central Valley Japanese League, for its part, served as both an arena of competition and a tool of cultural unity. Together with other communal factors, the Niseis' sporting spirit helped maintain community morale during the evacuation crisis. Indeed, the remarkable quickness with which the Nisei formed athletic leagues once in camps testified not only to their love of athletics, but to the strength of their society as well. Their participation in baseball and other sports, both reflected and contributed to their bonding and morale. "I think our sport activities prevented a lot of mental anguish," claimed Fred Kishi. "We expressed ourselves through sports." To be sure, without the availability of athletics, life in camp, "would have been terrible," stated Gilbert Tanji. Mack Yamaguchi said with pride, "We just picked up the pieces, picked up the ball, and started playing." Without the ball teams, "it would have [driven] you crazy living in a place like [Amache]," said Yeichi Sakaguchi. Sports provided important outlets for anxiety and frustration; organized athletics helped the Nisei maintain their competitive spirit under duress. Hence, the Livingston Dodgers and other such clubs not only carried the banner of pride for their community, but also provided a unique episode in sport and ethnic history.

Suggested Readings

Altherr, Thomas L. "Mallards and Messerschmitts: American Hunting Magazines and the Image of American Hunting During World War II." *Journal of Sport History,* 14(1987): 151-163.

Bennett, Bruce L. "Physical Education and Sport at Its Best—The Naval Aviation V-5 Pre-Flight Program." *Canadian Journal of History of Sport,* 21(1990): 57-69.

Brooks, Dana, & Althouse, Ronald. (Eds.) *Racism in College Athletics: The African-American Athlete's Experience.* Morgantown, WV: Fitness Information Technology, 1993.

Capeci, Dominic J., & Wilkerson, Martha. "Multifarious Hero: Joe Louis, American Society and Race Relations During World Crisis, 1935-1945." *Journal of Sport History,* 10(1983): 5-25.

Carroll, John M. *Fritz Pollard: Pioneer in Racial Advancement.* Urbana, IL: University of Illinois Press, 1992.

Cavello, Dominick. "Social Reform and the Movement to Organize Children's Play During the Progressive Era." *History of Childhood Quarterly,* 3(1976): 509-522.

Chadwick, Bruce. *When the Game Was Black and White: The Illustrated History of Baseball's Negro Leagues.* New York: Abbeville Press, 1992.

Crepeau, Richard. *Baseball: America's Diamond Mind, 1919-1941.* Gainesville: University Press of Florida, 1980.

Davidson, Judith. "Sport for the People: New York State and Work Relief 1930s Style." *Canadian Journal of History of Sport,* 19(1988): 40-51.

Engelmann, Larry. *The Goddess and the American Girl: The Story of Suzanne Lenglen and Helen Wills.* New York: Oxford University Press, 1988.

Gerber, Ellen. "The Controlled Development of Collegiate Sport for Women, 1923-1936." *Journal of Sport History,* 2(1975): 1-28.

Gorn, Elliott J. "The Manassa Mauler and the Fighting Marine; An Interpretation of the Dempsey-Tunney Fights." *Journal of American Studies,* 19(1985): 27-47.

Lewis, Guy. "World War I and the Emergence of Sport for the Masses." *Maryland Historian,* 4(1973): 109-122.

Lucas, John A. "The Unholy Experiment—Professional Baseball's Struggle Against Pennsylvania Sunday Blue Laws, 1926-1934." *Pennsylvania History,* 38(1971): 163-175.

Marvin, Carolyn. "Avery Brundage and American Participation in the 1936 Olympic Games." *Journal of American Studies,* 16(1982): 81-105.

Mennell, James. "The Service Football Program of World War I: Its Impact on the Popularity of the Game." *Journal of Sport History,* 16(1989): 248-260.

Osbourne, John. "To Keep the Life of the Nation on the Old Lines: The Athletic News and the First World War." *Journal of Sport History,* 14(1987): 137-150.

Riess, Steven A. "Professional Baseball and Social Mobility." *Journal of Interdisciplinary History,* 11(1980): 235-250.

Roberts, Randy. *Jack Dempsey, The Manassa Mauler.* Baton Rouge: Louisiana State University Press, 1979.

Rominger, Donald, Jr. "From Playing Field to Battleground: The United States Navy V-5 Pre-Flight Program in World War II." *Journal of Sport History,* 12(1985): 252-264.

Ruck, Rob. *Sandlot Seasons: Sport in Black Pittsburgh.* Urbana, IL: University of Illinois Press, 1987.

Smith, Thomas G. "Outside the Pale: The Exclusion of Blacks from the National Football League, 1934-1946." *Journal of Sport History,* 15(1988): 255-281.

Wenn, Stephen R. "A Suitable Policy of Neutrality? FDR and the Question of American Participation in the 1936 Olympics." *The International Journal of the History of Sport,* 8(1991): 319-335.

Wenn, Stephen R. "George S. Messermith and Charles H. Sherrill on Proposed American Participation in the Berlin Olympics." *Journal of Sport History,* 16(1989): 27-43.

Wiggins, David K. "Wendell Smith, the Pittsburgh Courier-Journal and the Campaign to Include Blacks in Organized Baseball, 1933-1945." *Journal of Sport History,* 12(1983): 5-29.

Wiggins, William H. "Boxing's Sambo Twins: Racial Stereotypes in Jack Johnson and Joe Louis Newspaper Cartoons, 1908 to 1938." *Journal of Sport History,* 15(1988): 242-254.

Zingg, Paul. "The Phoenix at Fenway: The 1915 World Series and the Collegiate Connection to the Major League." *Journal of Sport History,* 17(1990): 21-43.

PART 5

❖

TRANSFORMATION OF SPORT IN THE AGE OF TELEVISION, DISCORD, AND PERSONAL FULFILLMENT, 1945–PRESENT

Sport has grown in America at an unprecedented rate since World War II. An expansion of teams, leagues, and bureaucratic organizations has taken place at various levels of sport competition. Postwar technological advancements, civil rights legislation, the Women's Movement, and a host of other factors have made sport more accessible to everyone and contributed to its rise as a multibillion dollar industry that influences, in one way or another, all of America's social institutions. The last half-century has witnessed the reintegration of both amateur and professional sport; increased involvement of women in organized sport; creation of lucrative television sports contracts; establishment of players' unions; unfolding of gambling scandals and player strikes; conflict between the East and West in international sport; and increased interest in health and fitness through promotion of physical activity and sport.

The growing emphasis on exercise and physical fitness in Cold War America has received an increasing amount of attention from historians. The rationale behind the promotion of physical fitness during this period, however, continues to be a source of debate among academicians. Donald Mrozek offers one of the most convincing interpretations as to the rationale behind the emphasis on physical fitness in chapter 15, "The Cult and Ritual of Toughness in Cold War America." Mrozek argues that individuals from various walks of life in American society used sport and physical training in ritualized forms to bring about a tough and winning attitude during the Cold War. Although an emphasis on toughness was evident in the 1940s, it became increasingly more formalized in the following 2 decades through the promotion of sport and physical training regimens intended to help maintain traditional values and contribute to a sense of personal fulfillment as well as moral stamina in a world teetering on the brink of disaster.

The emphasis on toughness coincided with tremendous growth and revolutionary changes in the television sports industry. Sports had been telecast with some regularity in the immediate post-World War II period, but it was in the 1960s and 1970s that sports television evolved into a multimillion dollar industry and significant cultural force in America. The person most responsible for the revolutionary changes in sports television was Roone Arledge, a Columbia University-trained executive who became head of sports programming at the American Broadcasting Company (ABC). As Randy Roberts and James Olson point out in chapter 16, "The Roone Revolution," Arledge was a media genius who almost single-handedly transformed the nature of sports television through the introduction of new programs and technological innovations. He was responsible for the development of such shows as the "Wide World of Sports," "The Superstars," "The American Sportsman," and "Monday Night Football." In terms of technological advancements, Arledge helped introduce hand-held cameras, rifle-mikes, and instant replay to television sports coverage.

While television has altered our perception of sport, anabolic steroids have altered the performances of many athletes. Since the 1960s, more and more athletes are seemingly turning to anabolic steroids to enhance their performances and improve their chances for victory in the highly competitive world of organized sport. The use of steroids has caused worldwide debate, much finger-pointing, and an endless number of questions concerning the emotional and physiological effects of performance-enhancing drugs on athletes. Terry Todd provides insights into the use of performance-enhancing drugs throughout history in chapter 17, "Anabolic Steroids: The Gremlins of Sport." Todd explains that since the beginning of competitive sport athletes have used various substances to gain advantages over their opponents. The creation of Dianabol and other pharmaceuticals, however, has caused an explosion in drug taking among athletes that may never be completely curtailed in a society that stresses winning at all costs and victory by any means.

The increasing use of performance-enhancing drugs in competitive sport is one of the sadder stories in America's recent past. A counterpoint to this has been the increased involvement of women in sport. Realizing newfound freedom as a result of societal changes and governmental legislation, women have found their way into sport over the last 2 decades in vastly greater numbers than ever before. This growth in women's sport, while offering unprecedented opportunities and competitive experiences for countless participants, has been accompanied by continual struggles for equality and characterized by differing philosophies, often within which women's programs are regarded differently from men's.

Insights into the differing conceptions of men's and women's sport is provided in chapter 18, Joan Hult's essay, "The Philosophical Conflicts in Men's and Women's Collegiate Athletics." Hult, who was involved in women's athletics as both a coach and administrator, describes the philosophical differences between men's and women's athletics through a comparative analysis of the policies and administrative structures of the National Collegiate Athletic Association (NCAA) and Association for Intercollegiate Athletics for Women (AIAW) shortly before the dissolution of the latter organization in 1981. She also discusses the immediate impact that the Educational Amendment Act of 1972 (Title IX) had on women's athletic programs. As it turns out, Hult was prophetic in much of her analysis, suggesting, among other things, that the AIAW could lose the struggle for reform and that control of athletics seemed likely to remain in the hands of men.

The struggle for full equality in sport has also been evident among African-Americans. Since the shattering of the color barrier in major league baseball by Jackie Robinson in 1947, African-Americans have fought to gain entry into sport and realize the adulation as well as material benefits that accompany successful participation in sport.

The quest for full participation in sport has not been in vain, as many African-Americans have found their way into sport and achieved worldwide fame for their athletic accomplishments. Success in sport, however, has not always guaranteed equal treatment for African-American athletes or eliminated racial discrimination in American society. Nor has it erased the deep-seeded stereotypes and need for racial identification on the part of Americans. This need for racial identification is the thrust of chapter 19, Gerald Early's essay, "Hot Spicks Versus Cool Spades: Three Notes Toward a Cultural Definition of Prizefighting." Early argues that boxing in America has always been of symbolic importance, fulfilling people's emotional needs for "completion" through racial contrasts. The interracial boxing matches of yesteryear pitting a black and white fighter in the ring, and more recently, the Roberto Duran and Sugar Ray Leonard matches, have elicited intense emotional responses because they reinforce the belief that people of various races are different both physically and psychologically. Although the scientific evidence does not confirm such a notion, people continue to insist that skin color defines their very being, and nowhere is this reflected more graphically than in boxing, a cultural event fraught with patterns of symbolism and meaning.

CHAPTER 15

The Cult and Ritual of Toughness in Cold War America

Donald J. Mrozek

During World War II millions of Americans in and out of military service experienced physical training and participated in sports that the federal government had organized to raise the national quotient of physical fitness and to impart "combative" values to individual citizens. Many affected by this program, including prominent coaches and athletic managers, slipped beyond the practical purposes of the federal programs in countering the Axis threat and carried a general enthusiasm for physical and moral toughness into the post-war period. To the large extent that political and spiritual struggles assumed a concrete, physical symbology, the conflict between the Soviet Union and the United States to win converts around the world and to stand as the champion of world society's future encouraged the development of a cult of toughness, built on ritual, in America, the seeds of which had already been scattered in the war years. As distinct from fitness, toughness explicitly characterized an aggressive, action-oriented attitude—one that turned abruptly away from the rather dilatory spirit that many Americans read back into the 1930s. Heartened by the experience of World War II, which seemed to prove that Americans were capable of decisive action on an unparalleled scale, various figures in government, organized athletics and physical education used sport and physical training in increasingly ritualized forms to generate a tough and winning attitude in the Cold War.

A comparable error developed with respect to the use of a military draft which gradually became confused with American tradition, despite the fact that it had not previously been a standard measure even in time of war. This kind of misinterpretation fostered alarmist visions of decay and decadence within American culture. Kinkead himself concluded that, in the case of the American POWs in Korea, "it was not just our young soldiers who faced the antagonists, but more importantly the entire cultural pattern which produced these young soldiers."

Tellingly, Albert D. Biderman has pointed out that "we can learn less about pathologies of our society from the behavior of the Americans captured in Korea

From *Rituals and Ceremonies in Popular Culture,* Ray B. Browne (editor), Bowling Green, OH: Bowling Green University Popular Press, 1980, pp. 178-191. © 1980 Bowling Green University Popular Press. Reprinted by permission.

than we can by attempting to understand the reasons for the complaints that have been made against them.'' Much of the lesson to which Biderman directs us rests in the growing belief that political ideas and moral values depended on physical toughness. Thus Kinkead could write with unconcealed satisfaction that the Army had embarked on survival training programs that simulated the environments and practices that soldiers might encounter if separated from their units or taken as POWs. Kinkead clearly agreed with the Army which, he noted, ''now realizes that a man's prior knowledge of a situation'' might be critical to his survival if he should fall into that situation. Then, however, he showed that ''knowledge'' had a special meaning: ''If captured, they are subjected to treatment, which, although not as severe as the real thing, approximates Communist handling.'' Knowledge and learning now assumed so specifically physical a meaning that torture, in the general manner of a Korean POW camp, became accepted procedure. The American would learn not with his imagination but with his body.

Although the cult of toughness had roots in the 1940s, its ritualistic practice grew strong and spread most impressively in the following two decades, stimulated by a debate over the physical and spiritual implications of American performance in the Korean War. The early reports of ''brain-washing'' left many Americans unwilling to believe that extreme physical conditions—the imposition of pain and torture—were effective means of altering value and behavior. The discrimination that Americans in the safety of their home territory made between collaborators and victims helped to define the contours of this belief. Those prisoners of war who had not been subjected to overt physical torture might be the source of some embarrassment; yet, in these cases, some degree of cooperation could be understood, if not accepted. It was specifically the physical nature of the conditioning that Americans identified as central in altering behavior.

This emphasis on the effectiveness of physical stress in ritualistically shaping values and behavior had precedent in the American past, and it enjoyed new attention during the Cold War in the two decades following World War II. Particularly after the reports of collaboration by Americans in Korea began to arouse concern about the physical and ethical toughness of the average citizen, there was renewed interest in taking ''corrective measures.'' Among them was the use of painful physical stress to train or to condition Americans either to achieve or to resist. The desire for physical toughness for its assumed uses as a conservator of values hastened the movement of using pain in a practical, creative ritual. Painful and stressful experience was integrated into sporting events, enhancing their ritual and ceremonial importance.

Not that Americans of the late 1930s and early 1940s were unconcerned with the durability and resolve of the young. In the early stages of World War II, newspaper editors and illustrators promoted a new and tougher image of American youth. A Joseph Parrish cartoon for the *Chicago Tribune* of May 3, 1942, for example, expressed the hope that Axis sneers at American youth as a ''hothouse plant'' made fragile by the American standard of living are misguided. Parrish answered the charge with a sketch of ''fighting American youth'' ensconced in

Bud Wilkinson, who achieved lasting fame as football coach at the University of Oklahoma, was John Kennedy's adviser on fitness.
Courtesy of the Library of Congress.

"The Greenhouse," the gunner's station in a U.S. bomber. So, too, both the young American fighter and Uncle Sam himself were presented as strapping, muscular, powerful men. Uncle Sam lost a good many of his years and most of his paternal reserve and distance; the young American shed frivolity and self-indulgence. All reacted strongly against the sensation of weakness so deeply rooted in the experiences of the Depression, and the sense of challenge and of fulfillment that the war afforded was commanding. Yet, if there was a touch of toughness in the self-image of the American in those years, it was without the complicating touch of pain which can temper inclination into total dedication. Even in cartoons that would imply objective suffering, such as one in which a "fiendish enemy" Japanese is bayoneting a prisoner tied to a post, the principal emphasis rested on outrage, not on suffering. The agony was of the spirit, not of the body—an agony of purpose, and not of experience.

But for critics of the performance of Americans taken as POWs, the realms of spirit and body commingled. In this respect, the attitude of Cold War America toward physical toughening deviated from that of Americans in the interwar years. In addition, the growing vogue of behavioralism itself jeopardized confidence in the priority or primacy of ethical values or in the belief that they were spiritually generated and sustained. In this regard, perhaps behavioralism just proved to be an extreme variant of American pragmatism.

Yet it is important to observe that many problems with this new emphasis on stress and pain were simple and practical. The erroneous assertions of critics such as Eugene Kinkead that the Code of Conduct (1955) for the military represented traditional American policies reflects the tendency, after World War II, to mistake the exceptional and abnormal for the customary and the ordinary. Americans had, for example, accepted parole and favors from captors from the War of American Independence on; and prisoners of war had talked with interrogators well beyond the limits of "name, rank, and serial number only." Kinkead's misunderstanding of history, however, is itself revealing, in that it reflects a wider willingness in the 1950s to accept extreme interpretations of American tradition and behavior.

A far more elaborate program, and one that soon received broad publicity, was the Air Force's survival program at Stead Air Force Base in Nevada. During the last days of the training cycle, after schooling in evasive maneuver and living off the land was complete, the "captive" Air Force personnel were taken to a simulation of a Prisoner of War camp. Here, according to the most prominent and perhaps most sensational report, at the discretion of the training personnel, they could be forced into boxes about 18 inches wide, with a slanted bottom, and set too short to allow the confined person to stand straight. In some cases, interrogators used electric shock from low-powered generators. In yet others, those persons being shocked knelt on broomsticks so that their reflexes, when stimulated by electricity, drew them painfully off the sticks to the floor. Still others were confined in pits filled with water, left there for long hours. During the public discussion of the program in 1955 and afterwards Air Force representatives did not dispute the facts as reported. However, they emphasized that participation should be considered voluntary. Indeed, their cooperation had been essential in making possible *Life* magazine's extensive photo-essay of the program. Moreover, the preponderance of those reporting about the program at Stead concluded that it was tough but necessary.

Dispute developed as to the nature and scope of the program. But the coverage in *Life* magazine left strange implications about the directions of the flying service. The Air Force's torture program reflected an extreme conversion to behavioralism and an embracing of the primacy of material phenomena. Knowledge would rise through experience, and future behavior would be shaped by controlling current physical experience. Thus, to enable flight crews to resist or survive torture in POW camps, the service would torture them now to prepare for the later unpleasant possibility. The logic was both grim and faulty. After all, to "learn" to accept death, one need not be killed. Nor need everyone be raped in order to learn of ways to respond in such extreme conditions. The logic behind the Air Force program failed to distinguish realms in which creative imagination might be a more effective as well as humane mode of learning from those in which actual physical experience proved best.

Since one can hardly presume that all Air Force personnel had rejected in theory all forms of learning other than physical experience, this Air Force program suggests at least that some missions were considered too sensitive to be left merely to searching minds and loyal sentiment. Such a notion, suggesting the dominance of the material world, pointed toward philosophical nihilism. The genealogy of both belief and action was becoming a genealogy of force.

It is striking that by late 1955, 29,000 men would have gone through this program with so little indication (none reported, in fact) of objection. Despite the repetition of Stead's scheduled activities, the staff members appear never to have conceived of them as mere routine. The values to be imparted loomed so large that repeated actions likely assumed the quality of rite rather than rote. For the participants in the Stead program, unfamiliarity and the unknown further strengthened this tendency to see special value in the experience of stress and pain. One senses an authentic acceptance of the program, and in a sense an enjoyment of it. Not only was it something to pull through, something to tough out; it suggested that values were developed in this peculiar crucible. It was, in short, a rite of passage in which pain and suffering were the avenue to distinctive and higher identity. This traditional use of suffering, however, raises relatively few problems of interpretation or understanding. It is the far more arbitrary direction of suffering to a political and military function that requires more sensitive evaluation. For the former hastens acculturation, while the latter aims at specific achievement. Rituals also may be mild or savage, pacific or bellicose. Hence their specific content reveals much in the character of the culture that practices them.

In large part, the Air Force's survival program—even the phase that dealt with the experience of torture—was designed to encourage imagination and ingenuity in evading the worst impact of interrogation, if capture itself could not be avoided. The survival program did encourage wit, although it also made most graphic the physical stress in which that wit would have to be exercised. In covering the story, on the other hand, magazines and newspapers—even when they acknowledged this concern for wit and ingenuity—concentrated on the extreme physical treatment, in this way illustrating the values that they believed were represented by the program. In short, as an indicator of values, the nature of the public attention to the Stead program was even more broadly revealing than the program itself.

Such public sentiment began to gain institutional support. The interest that the Kennedy Administration showed in promoting physical fitness has been widely acknowledged. But the rationale behind that interest has received less attention. It is difficult to ignore the advantages to health and vitality that many have gained from this emphasis, but it is correspondingly easy to note the somewhat self-indulgent quality of the fitness and sporting culture since John Kennedy.

For the leaders of the fitness culture of the Kennedy era, however—including the president himself and his adviser on fitness, "Bud" Wilkinson—physical training and sport were aspects of the Cold War, as well as avenues toward personal fulfillment. Indeed, the promotion of physical education and athletics was couched in a highly Social Darwinist language of competition with possible international rivals, especially the Soviet Union. Increasingly, combative games and sports became the special rites of a Cold War political culture that rested on the premise of struggle and competition. Consistent with this impulse, publicists—such as magazine writers and editors—railed against the alleged "softness" of American youth and became adherents to a cult of toughness. The very word toughness itself, so richly freighted with social implications, soon virtually replaced the more neutral term fitness.

President Kennedy himself addressed the issue in articles for national magazines including "Our Unfit Youth" and "Vigor We Need." In the latter article, published in *Sports Illustrated* in July 1962, Kennedy wrote of colonial and early national history and the stamina of the Americans who carved out the national domain. Then he emphasized that "physical hardihood" enabled Americans to overcome "tenacious foes" in World Wars I and II. Physical fitness was a valuable asset in military action in particular and in international confrontation more broadly. Moreover, he thus sought to place new ritual practices within the sanction of history. Then he associated the improvement of the physical condition of American youth in his presidency with meeting military demands in Europe and in the "jungles of Asia." Physical fitness was the price to pay for guaranteeing peace and the continuation of American civilization and celebrations of physical culture were even more convincingly the components of nationalistic ritual.

The dire implications of Kennedy's articles ran as an *idee fixe* through the pronouncements of appropriate personnel, from Secretary of Health, Education and Welfare Abraham Ribicoff through special consultant on physical fitness Wilkinson. Wilkinson, in an interview-article in *U.S. News and World Report* in August 1961, had agreed with the magazine staff that the Soviet youth were probably "far, far ahead of us" in physical condition. The reason for concern, at least for the magazine's responsible editors, became clear in the headline warning: "At a time when the world is full of dangers, a number of authorities say American youngsters lack muscle." The title question, quite consistently, asked whether American youth was "too soft" in the perilous world around them.

It is important to attend to the logical leaps in these statements. First, they presume a rather precise correlation between physical condition and what one may fairly call "moral stamina" in a convoluted world conflict. If there is a real causal link, it has hardly been conclusively demonstrated; and so the periodic enthusiasm for such views itself assumes historical consequence. The proposition that muscle equals fitness is equally tenuous; and the reigning bias that fitness is, in fact, toughness is all but impossible to sustain objectively. The reason for this last assertion is simple: fitness describes a medical phenomenon; toughness defines an attitude toward personal and social conduct.

As a group the Kennedy Administration gained a reputation for being fitness-oriented—an impression boosted by coverage of specific measures undertaken to enhance the physical condition of American personnel. Typical was the coverage of Marine Corps Commandant David M. Shoup's effort to reinstate the standards of fitness demanded by President Theodore Roosevelt. Described in *Time* magazine as a "physical fitness bug," Shoup was given photographic space in the article reporting his demand that company grade officers be capable of marching 50 miles within 20 hours, with the last 700 yards at double-time. President Kennedy gave his encouragement to Shoup, who was pegged in a caption as "tough to the Corps."

The choice of such a word as tough, with remarkable frequency in the Kennedy years,was assuredly not conspiratorial. But it reflected a combative attitude toward life that many not connected with the Administration itself also shared.

For example, in June 1962, about the time that John Kennedy was featured in *Sports Illustrated, Saturday Evening Post* heralded an article told to W. Gill by R.M. Marshall entitled "Toughening Our Soft Generation." In touting a Pennsylvania Boy Scout program and railing against "coddling" of the young, Marshall couched his sternest warnings in international terms. Marshall observed that 40% of men called under the military draft between 1948 and 1962 had been declared ineligible, most for physical defects. Inadequate fitness meant military weakness. So, too, he cited reports suggesting that nearly 60% of American children showed failure in tests of physical performance that only 8.7% of European children failed. Americans might well, then, be losing physical supremacy to other peoples. Perhaps most tellingly, Marshall then pointed to the Soviet Union's "trouncing" of Americans in the Summer Olympics of 1956 and 1960. Be it understood that the article made measured recommendations on the whole, and its author evidenced a strong concern to avoid "regimentation." Yet there appears here—in explicitly international terms—a sense of the need to compete for survival and to prepare for the competition by becoming personally tough. Marshall underscores this by referring to rough treatment he received in his own conditioning program before World War I which he regards as an indisputable enhancement of his personal security. It is also suggestive that strength for international conflict was to come from a program in the Boy Scouts, traditionally an agency of passage for young males.

The cult of toughness ranged widely through American culture; and, in the early 1960s, it became something of a fad—associated with the glamour of action and youthful vitality. For all the intrinsic merits of such programs, as Outward Bound then, it is relatively easy to see them as reflections of the "strange enthusiasms" of the Kennedy days. After describing some of Outward Bound's strenuous and exciting mountain-region activities for *Reader's Digest,* author Lydia Lawrence then hastened to associate them with other of the nation's heroic images, saying that the events did not occur at "a Marine training site." Outward Bound's director, Joshua Miner, spoke of the thrill and excitement available to young people who, until then, had lived "in a cult of comfort and safety. . . ." Miner may indeed have had in mind only a cult of confidence and thrill to replace the cult of comfort and safety, yet there remains a probably unintended kinship with many of the drives that motivated Kennedy's statements and policy.

The fusion of toughness and pain (or at least the impression that pain is a part of societal progress) was a significant ancillary aspect of the Kennedy era's cult of toughness; and this sentiment spread widely beyond official Washington. In April 1964, *Life* magazine portrayed a new style of swim training as "All-Out Agony at Indiana U." and prominently featured an Indiana swimmer in his exercises so as to emphasize his "achievement" of agony in isometric contraction. Such effort was justifiable as part of a team effort and also because its method of attainment smacked of current technologies and a bit of pseudo-science.

Isometric exercise was rather *chic* and voguish, after all. For a new generation of Americans purportedly willing to "pay any price, bear any burden" for the policies of their nation, swimmer Lary Schulhof served as a photographic example that the road to victory could wind through stages of hurt, pain and agony. A caption for a photograph showing this achievement described it as "Training by Torture." To appreciate the distinctiveness of the characterization of training provided in that article, one may contrast it with a 1939 article concerning a swimming team from Mercersberg, Pennsylvania.

The Mercersberg swimmers showed effort, exertion and determination. But the photographer did not present them in pain, literally agonizing in their training to sweat out the last beads of decadence and softness. Indeed, the coach himself emerged as a warm and decent man, parental and kindly in his attention to his charges. In one photograph, the coach bicycled among the members of the team as they ran, poking them good-humoredly with a pole to encourage the occasional slacker. No one shows much self-consciousness at the coach's actions, and smiles are all but universal. In another scene, the coach gives advice to a swimmer at poolside in a manner that might easily be styled "fatherly." In yet another, the coach personally administers doses of honey to the team. In short, human kindness and consideration closely accompany physical effort. If there is an overriding philosophy in such a training program, it conforms best to *Kraft durch freude,* the achievement of strength and effective performance through the joy—not the pain—of training and competition.

That the Mercersberg swimmers of 1939 had times when, in the casual sense, they were in pain would be difficult to doubt. A photographer with a mind to do so could certainly have found opportunities to catch them in grimaces no less agonizing than those of the Indiana swimmer. What is significant, then, is that the editors, writers and photographers of 1962 did choose those relatively few moments of intense reaction to physical stress and accorded them centrality in their treatment of the training program. Pain was portrayed not as an accident of training but as its very core. Surely swimmer Schulhof experienced stress—whether hurt, pain or agony—in his training exercises. But the article itself has a life of its own. In the portrayal of the less extreme degrees of hurt and pain, for example, Schulhof's facial expression could just as easily have been the grimace of someone having a hard time opening a jar of pickles—it is not a photographic trick, but an act of editorial selection. Not only had Coach Jim Counsilman changed a training program; the magazine staff had redefined the essence of training and identified in it a spirit different from that shown by the Mercersberg team of 1939.

The reassessment of the utility and desirability of pain that appears in the magazine coverage of swim-training was by no means unique. In 1937 *Life* showed its displeasure with professional wrestling in an article headed "Cruel Crowds Demand Mat Torture." The author took the wrestlers' ring antics at face value and deplored the brutality of the performers and the spectators alike. Yet in 1958 *Look* could speak of the "Wrestlers—the New Heroes." Although this article described the rise of wrestling in the schools, its author did not ignore professional wrestling, noting that even its lack of respectability could no longer deter young boys from committing themselves to this tough, combative sport that promised popularity and status as sports heroes. In a day when greater emphasis was being placed on the physical condition and "toughness" of all boys regardless of size and body-type, wrestling's weight-divisions allowed even-handed and more intense competition to all comers. The tone of decrial of 1937 had long since yielded to adulation by 1958. For maturity had as one of its key components the stoic acceptance of the painful effects of violent behavior.

The emphasis had not always been nor need always be on the suffering associated with achievement. For example, *Look*'s 1958 coverage of high school wrestling strongly underscored the supposed ease with which schoolboy wrestlers won admiring fans (and dates) among the females in the student body. Yet popular coverage of the President himself attended periodically to his physical ailments (associated with war injuries) and so all the more emphasized his stoic, Spartan toughness in overcoming the weakness that might putatively have constricted his presidency or even precluded it in the first place.

Yet another article extolled the values of strenuous athletic competitions for boys, even if they included the risks of suffering and injury. The August 18, 1962 issue of *Look* reminded its readers that, even for high school boys, "Football Is Violence"; and so it included the risk of pain and injury, even "an occasional fatality. There were ten last year." But these dangers paled before the advantage that the young athletes were believed to gain in their competition. Risk of pain and suffering, the authors asserted, was often inseparable from life. Hence it was all the more important that football "demonstrates the value of work, sacrifice, courage and perseverance." For the authors, football provided the moral equivalent of on-the-job training, allowing boys to experience the risk and suffering of life while still within the moderating confines of the school system. Photographs accompanying the article included portrayals of young players in pain from injuries sustained in games. The captions emphasize both pain and its value. One injured player, from a team designated the "Knights," is shown as he "grimaces in pain." A photograph that does not show a player suffering an injury nonetheless illustrates that "tackling confronts tackler and runner with the challenge of bodily risks and teaches them to meet it." The cooperative relationship that players appear to enjoy with their coaches and doctors implies that these painful experiences build ritualized links to the adult world of order, dedication and purpose. Nor is this taken to be a minor benefit. When the authors aver that football develops the characteristics of sacrifice and courage, they cannot resist noting that "these lessons are especially salutary in our modern society with its delinquency problem, lack of discipline and physical softness." At once the writers assert the ability of physical activity to control spiritual vision and reveal their horror of "softness" and decadence.

The values extolled in "Football Is Violence" lingered from an older, more traditionalist America, whose heirs now praised work in a culture that generated proportionately fewer meaningful jobs each year. They praised sacrifice when their own cultural experience became increasingly decadent. They lauded courage in an age at least rhetorically made timid by the "shadow of the Bomb." They called for perseverance from a culture increasingly eager for immediate gratification. In a political sense, such views were conservative; and those who harbored them confounded them with physical and sexual biases as well. Decadence, then, became moral, political and physical so that liberals could best be labelled "panty-waists" and communists could be associated with homosexuals in what their detractors regarded as the liaisons of distastefully appropriate bedfellows, literally and figuratively. The politically perverse must be morally and physically so, and *vice versa*.

When *Look* magazine chose to provide a corrective for the physical deficiencies it perceived in American youth, it spotlighted Carmichael, California's La Sierra High School for showing "How America Can Get Physically Touch." The La Sierra program, designed by the school's football coach and physical education director, Stan Le Protti, centered on a system of compulsory exercise for boys which encouraged them to move from group to higher group defined by the level of physical skills demonstrated. Each group had its own emblematic colors, sharpening the adjustment of identity. The article's authors seemed pleased that "A normal or even underdeveloped boy can become a superior physical type." They recorded the opinion of Bud Wilkinson, football coach at the University of Oklahoma and special adviser to President Kennedy on physical fitness, that the La Sierra program would "help make America's youth as agile and physically tough as any in the world." (*Look*'s words, Wilkinson's opinion.) Reflecting its relatively conservative and utilitarian bias, *Look*'s authors asserted that graduates of Le Protti's programs would more than meet the physical demands of military service. Moreover, since the program included requirements of "neatness, good grooming and citizenship," the authors concluded that it produced not only "physical fitness, but . . . good Americans." By close implication, the authors had associated good grooming with patriotism and toughness with the citizenship appropriate for good Americans. The direction of behavior in matters such as grooming would preclude the emergence of alien political and social views. Physical effort in the "rites of autumn" on the gridiron would produce proper, traditionally American views; and perhaps even carefully orchestrated mass physical training could work to the same end.

In a small way at least, the article's authors hinted that the program worked effectively even over the short term. All nine photographs in the article showed boys in their exercises. The authors recorded that girls accepted the program enthusiastically; they "admired the boys for their achievements and sometimes tried to emulate them in the easier tests." La Sierra's system was envisioned in a man's world, in which strain and striving showed in the faces of the male photographic subjects pictured in the article. The quality of these youth was portrayed specifically in the effort that marked their faces and tensed their muscles. Muscular extension and contraction served both as the sign and the source of the boys' dedication and as the badge of their achievement. Toughness had become the virtue Americans at large required, and La Sierra's youth served as ritual models for its achievement.

When John Kennedy died in 1963 there were many who were available to insure that the political value of the cult of toughness would not come to an abrupt end. Not the least prominent was the President's brother Robert. Writing for *Sports Illustrated*'s July 27, 1964 issue, Robert Kennedy began with as clear a statement of the place of sport and physical education in world affairs that the opinion-makers of the Kennedy era could offer. "Part of a nation's prestige in the cold war," he avowed, "is won in the Olympic Games." So, then, the United States owed it to itself in its international responsibilities to make major improvements in its system of physical culture. Excellence in the international celebration of sport would ratify the renewed aggressiveness of Americans. The advantage Kennedy foresaw for Americans at home was the intensifying of their "inner glow of pride." Abroad there would once again be projected "the picture . . . of a young America bursting with enthusiasm." The self-conscious imitation of the days of Teddy Roosevelt carried the Kennedy era "cold warriors" into yet another realm of competition. Physical culture would give Americans the chance to achieve a Social Darwinist *succes de prestige*.

Americans have by no means been unique in being interested in the physical performance of the citizenry. Yet though not unique, Americans have had a deep and special relationship to the material world and to physical experience. Indeed it is difficult to conceive in American culture of an idea existing apart from and independent of physical experience. Formalist and idealist systems have fared none too well among this people. So, then, the nation tends to express its ideas through ritualized actions. In its preparation to meet the challenges of the cold war, then, it is perhaps the more understandable that some in the Kennedy Administration should have equated individual physical "toughness" with the ability of a nation to win its way in international affairs. The fitness, or "toughness," measures that the Administration proposed and that others supported may have offered the individual the benefits of health and conditioning. But they also assumed an important role as cultural rites. For the advocate of "toughness" the appeal of these measures ranged beyond the individual realm to a ritualized social and international confrontation with all that the term means. Personal experience in ritualistic activities accumulated in a ritualized stance of the nation in world affairs.

CHAPTER 16

❖

The Roone Revolution

Randy Roberts
James Olson

The real revolution in sports television came in the 1960s and 1970s, and the moving force behind the change was Roone Arledge, head of sports programming at ABC. A multifaceted man, Arledge had a curious relationship with Richard Nixon. Their first meeting took place in the fall of 1969 during the Texas-Arkansas football game that decided the national championship. Arledge planned to fly to Hawaii that weekend in order to save—or at least attempt to save—his shaky marriage. At the last moment Nixon, a great college football fan, decided to attend the game, and Arledge felt he should produce the contest personally. It cost Arledge his marriage, but as he later remembered, if there had been an assassination, he wanted to cover it. The game was played, Nixon wasn't assassinated, and Texas won. When the contest ended, President Nixon visited both dressing rooms, dispensing the usual clichés. His talk to the Arkansas players moved rapidly from clichés to heartfelt emotions. Arledge recalled, ''Nixon began discussing defeat in the most intensely personal terms. It was extremely moving, since, as we all realized, he was actually talking about himself.''

Four days later, Arledge met Nixon again, this time for a talk at the president's suite in the Waldorf Towers in New York City. It was not the most relaxed atmosphere: ''The room was empty; just an American flag, the Presidential flag, and one man: the President of the United States.'' Nixon tried to put the television sports executive at ease. For a half hour they talked about sports—Arledge's business. Eventually Roone attempted to move the topic away from sports toward his other interests—music, theater, the problems of America's cities. Each time Nixon brought the conversation back to sports. Finally Arledge realized that Nixon ''wasn't trying to put me at ease, he was trying to impress me with his knowledge of sports trivia. While he was rattling off the times of quarter-milers in the 1936 Olympics, I remember saying to myself, I can't believe it. The President of the United States is trying to impress *me*.''

From *Winning Is the Only Thing: Sports in America Since 1945* by Randy Roberts and James Olson, Baltimore, MD: The Johns Hopkins University Press, 1989, pp. 113-131. © 1989 The Johns Hopkins University Press, Baltimore/London. Reprinted by permission.

There was a third meeting, and it was the strangest of all. Nixon agreed to appear on ABC's "Wide World of Sports" and be interviewed by former New York Giants football great Frank Gifford. During a break in taping, the president took Arledge aside for another chat. He explained that when Gifford was a Giant and he was living in New York, he often attended Giff's parties. "I know Frank Gifford," Nixon boasted. "He remembers me." Arledge was amazed: "Here was the President of the United States trying to impress people, first, because he remembered some Olympic records, and second, because he knew Frank Gifford. And because Frank Gifford knew *him*!"

And odd set of events, certainly. But not totally beyond belief. In fact, the Richard Nixon who loved to talk about sports was in part a Roone Arledge creation. Probably the most important single individual in modern sports, Arledge not only changed the manner in which athletic events were watched and understood, but he also dramatically increased interest in sports. In a complex society, divided along economic, social, and racial lines and often sadly impersonal, sports became a currency which all races and classes dealt in. Rich and poor, black and white, young and old—if they could communicate on no other level, they could always talk about sports. They all had television sets, they watched the same sporting events, they were familiar with the same sports heroes, and they all had opinions about what they saw and what they liked. And a man like Nixon, a president who was oddly uncomfortable around most people, used sports to avoid real social interactions. It was an escape—or perhaps benefit—he shared with millions of other Americans who were influenced by the Roone Revolution.

In 1960 Roone Pinckney Arledge did not look like a revolutionary. Slightly pudgy, heavily freckled, and red-haired, Arledge resembled an Irish version of the Pillsbury doughboy. Nor did his earlier career denote a revolutionary nature. Born in Forest Hills, raised in upper-middle-class affluence on Long Island, and educated at Columbia University, Arledge's background prepared him for the New York business world. During the late 1950s he produced Shari Lewis' puppet show "Hi, Mom." He won an Emmy Award for his work, and his future with NBC seemed bright. In 1960 the 29-year-old Arledge moved to ABC. About a month before the 1960-61 football season, he gave Tom Moore and Ed Sherick, the network's programming and sports directors, a revolutionary document. It contained a bold new plan for covering football games. He recommended the use of directional and remote microphones, the use of hand-held and "isolated" cameras, the employment of split screen, and other technical innovations. In addition, he called for a more dynamic halftime show, replacing marching-band performances with in-depth analysis and highlights from the first two quarters. In essence, Arledge wanted to bring the sporting experience into America's living rooms. He believed sports and athletes should be examined "up close and personal." The Roone Revolution had begun.

Impressed by Arledge's plan, Moore and Sherick made Roone producer of ABC's college football programs, thereby giving him an electronic pulpit from which he could preach his new philosophy. Behind his every move rested a central belief: the marriage of sports and innovative entertainment techniques

Pete Rozelle, the former Commissioner of the National Football League, recognized the profits that could be made from televised sport and worked closely with Roone Arledge and the American Broadcasting Company.
Courtesy of the Library of Congress.

would produce higher ratings. Arledge was convinced that he could use sports to entertain people who were not really sports fans. "What we set out to do," he said, "was to get the audience involved emotionally. If they didn't give a damn about the game, they still might enjoy the program." Through hype and technology he would create a large new audience for ABC's sports programming.

In addition, Arledge had near-perfect program judgment. It was his "principal genius," noted former senior vice-president of ABC Sports Jim Spence. As Spence observed in *Up Close and Personal,* Arledge "had an almost infallible sense of such critical factors as how long segments should last, what interviews should be aired, the sequence of presentation for various segments in order to build audience attention, and particularly about the importance of the human element in sports. He realized early on that the *people* participating in the events were the essence of sports."

Arledge's first task was to improve televised college football. As Arledge saw it, his job became "taking the fan to the game, not the game to the fan." The idea was simple and revolutionary, and to execute it Arledge and his staff employed sophisticated technology. He wanted the viewer sitting in his living room to see, hear, and experience the game as if he were actually in the football stadium. Before Arledge, television executives had been content simply to bring the viewer the game. Using three or four situated cameras they were able to document the game. For those who loved football, it was enough, but it was not very attractive for the casual viewer.

Arledge, of course, coveted that casual viewer, the person with one eye on the screen and one hand on the dial. Discussing his philosophy in 1966, Arledge wrote: "What we set out to do was to get the audience involved emotionally. If they didn't give a damn about the game, they still might enjoy the program." To do this Arledge used more cameras. He put cameras on cranes and blimps and helicopters to provide a better view of the stadium, the campus, and the town. His technicians developed hand-held cameras for close-ups. In the stadium he employed seven cameras, three just for capturing the environment. "We asked ourselves: If you were sitting in the stadium, what would you be looking at? The coach on the sideline, the substitute quarterback warming up, the pretty girl in the next section. So our cameras wandered as your eyes would."

Often what Arledge decided would interest his mostly male viewers were young and beautiful women. One of Arledge's most successful directors, Andy Sidaris, became famous in the industry for his "T and A shots." Commenting on his specialty, Sidaris noted, "I'd rather see a great-looking body than a touchdown anytime. You can see thousands of touchdowns every weekend, but a great-looking woman is something to behold." Sidaris's philosophy, like Arledge's, emphasized entertainment, even titillation, over sport. The game was only one part of the sporting experience.

Arledge also brought the sounds of football to the television viewer. Before Arledge, producers would hang a mike out the window to get the sound of the crowd. Normally the television viewer would hear a damp, muffled roar, similar to hearing the sea from a half mile away. Occasionally a few sharp, clear expletives might break the solemnity of the announcers' voices. Arledge's technicians developed the rifle-mike to pinpoint sound. Now the viewer could hear the clash of shoulder pads and helmets, the bark of a quarterback calling signals, and the thump of a well-struck punt.

Analysis and play-by-play announcing were not immune to the genius of Arledge and his technicians. The instant replay was one of Arledge's innovations. In 1960 he asked ABC engineer Bob Trachinger "if it would be possible to replay something in slow motion so you could tell if a guy was safe or out or stepped out of bounds." Trachinger designed the device. Arledge remembered using the instant replay during the 1960 Boston College-Syracuse game: "That was a terrific game and, at one point, Jack Concannon, a sophomore quarterback, was trapped in the pocket but ended up running 70 yards for a touchdown. Six or eight people had a shot of him and we replayed the whole thing in slow motion with Paul Christman analyzing the entire play as it unfolded. Nobody had ever seen anything like that before and the impact was unbelievable. That moment changed television sports forever."

From the very beginning Arledge's approach to sports was successful. As he suspected, he could satisfy sports fans and still entertain casual viewers. His college football broadcasts featured heretofore unseen angles both of football players and cheerleaders. For ABC, which in 1960 was running a distant third in the ratings race, Arledge's innovations meant better ratings, higher rates for advertising, and corporate growth. Before long ABC replaced NBC as the leader in sports programming. By the 1970s ABC was the top-rated network. Arledge played a considerable role in ABC's rise, and between 1960 and 1975 his salary rose from $10,000 to approximately $1 million a year.

For Arledge, college football was only the beginning. If sports programming was to have a significant impact on the television industry, he needed important events to televise twelve months a year. Aggressively, sometimes ruthlessly, Arledge went after the television rights for major sports events. "When it comes to acquiring rights," an executive at another network remarked, "the man is totally unscrupulous. A jackal. He'd rip my heart out for a shot at the World Series." Arledge was less dramatic, but as usual perfectly correct: "If you don't have the rights, you can't do the show." Over the years Arledge's list of acquisitions would put most conglomerates to shame. In addition to college and professional football and professional baseball, Arledge and ABC have acquired the rights for major golf tournaments, horse races, summer and winter Olympics, All-Star games, and a host of other events.

Arledge's impact upon American sports and entertainment can be seen in several of the sports shows he launched. "Wide World of Sports" was an idea he inherited from Ed Sherick but gave his own distinctive stamp. He oversaw every aspect of its production and even wrote "the thrill of victory, the agony of defeat" opening. In April 1961, after a difficult search for sponsors, "Wide World of Sports" made its debut. It fit perfectly into Arledge's definition of sports as entertainment. The program allowed ABC film crews to roam around the world and televise what they thought was interesting, even if it were only tangentially involved in athletics. The production emphasis was concerned as much with the location and personalities as with the sporting event.

Most importantly, "Wide World of Sports" allowed Arledge to control time, the crucial element for programming. The shows did not have to be televised live and were not contained by seasonal schedules. It realized Arledge's vision of "a year-round sports show that could fill the void [between sports seasons] and not have to worry about blackouts." In addition, prerecorded shows could be edited to increase suspense and eliminate dead time. A three-hour downhill skiing event could be edited into two 8-minute segments; an all-day mountain climb could be fit into a half-hour slot. "Wide World of Sports" was, in short, tailored to the average viewer's attention span. "In sports they aren't that familiar with, or in events that aren't important," Arledge noted, "people do enjoy the knowledge that something different will be coming every ten minutes."

To keep "something different coming" continually, "Wide World of Sports" used the broadest possible definition of what constituted sporting activity. Between 1960 and 1966 Arledge presented eighty-seven different sports, ranging from international track and field meets and world championship boxing contests to demolition derbies and an Eiffel Tower climb. And he used sophisticated technology to make each event as interesting—as entertaining—as possible.

Of course, critics carped. Sports purists claimed that "sports" was the last important word in the "Wide World of Sports" title. Programs containing the demolition derby contests particularly drew hostile comments. Again, however, the critics misunderstood Arledge's job. He was in a commercial entertainment business. His duty was to produce shows that attracted high audience ratings, not rave critical reviews. By the 1970s the demolition derby drew up to 25 million viewers to "Wide World of Sports." That number pleased ABC executives and "Wide World of Sports" sponsors.

As far as Arledge was concerned, if an event was visually exciting and had colorful personalities it would "work" on "Wide World of Sports." And if a little creative editing could improve the excitement and color, so much the better. For example, during the Le Mans automobile race there was a major accident in a section of the course where ABC had no cameras to record the wreck. Viewing and editing the film footage back in New York, producer Robert Riger sensed that the "missing crash robbed the story of some of its excitement and drama." To correct this problem, he put several miniature cars into a flowerpot, set them on fire, and filmed the result. He then edited the footage into his Le Mans coverage, where, according to Jim Spence, "it looked pretty good." Again, it was bad, even dishonest, sports coverage but good entertainment.

As a good business executive, Arledge gave the people what they wanted, or at least what they would have wanted if they knew it existed. Arledge used the same business acumen to find and to acquire broadcast rights for little-known events. "Wide World of Sports," for example, introduced the Acapulco cliff divers to the American audiences. Arledge negotiated personally with the head of the Acapulco divers' union. The senior diver told Arledge that the going rate for a special was $100,000. As Arledge recalled the episode, "We told him the price was a little out of line, and that he'd have to reduce it some or we'd forget about it. 'I'll talk to the boys,' he said. A few minutes later he returned, 'We'll take $10 a dive,' he said. He held us to it. He made us pay for all three dives."

Just as "Wide World of Sports" broadened the definition of sport, it also created sports heroes out of marginally athletic individuals. A case in point was the "athletic career" of Robert Craig "Evel" Knievel. Beginning in 1967, he appeared sixteen times on "Wide World of Sports." His motorcycle stunts became sports pseudoevents. Millions of people watched Knievel not to witness the "thrill of victory" but on the chance of seeing the ultimate "agony of defeat." Knievel didn't die for ratings, but he came close on several occasions. In 1967 he broke his back and his pelvis when he attempted to jump the fountains in front of Caesar's Palace in Las Vegas. It was a spectacular crash, and "Wide World of Sports" showed it and other Knievel failures repeatedly in painful slow motion. Knievel might have been bad sports, but he was great television, and as such an Arledge success.

"Wide World of Sports" is the longest-running sports show ever televised, and like most successful series, it has produced a number of spinoffs. Oftentimes the spinoffs have had less to do with sports than the parent show. "The American

Sportsman" teamed announcer Curt Gowdy with a series of celebrity "sportsmen." Together they went after wild animals and untamed fish. The show had all the attraction of "Wide World of Sports": famous personalities, exotic locations, and prerecorded, easily edited events. It could be used to fill empty weekend programming, and if it had to be delayed or even cancelled for a week, there was no real problem. In short, it was, from a business point of view, perfect television sports.

A second successful spinoff of "Wide World of Sports" was "The Superstars." Again, Arledge employed the same formula. Major athletic personalities were pitted against each other in such events as tennis, bowling, swimming, rowing, running, golf, bicycling, and an obstacle course race. The events or the rules of the events were subject to yearly change. "The Superstars" became a huge success, and it fathered its own spinoffs. True it was a "trash sport," an ersatz sport created and packaged by television, but it was also successful television programming. It showed that the viewing audience was as intrigued by incompetence and failure as by success. Like Evel Knievel's grand failures, the memories of Joe Frazier and Johnny Unitas floundering in a swimming pool lingered longer in the public mind than Lynn Swan's graceful speed.

By 1970 Arledge was ready for his next bold move. Encouraged by the commissioner of the National Football League, Pete Rozelle, Arledge decided to invade prime time with "Monday Night Football." If it was not an entirely new game, success would certainly be measured by different standards. On Sunday afternoon, any NFL game that attracted 20 million viewers gave cause for network celebration. The same number during prime time would lead to cancellation. Success during prime time entailed an audience of between 40 to 50 million. To reach that level, Arledge had to attract a wide variety of viewers. The casual viewer suddenly became far more important than the dedicated football fan. And sport took a back seat to entertainment.

How to attract the new viewers? One way was to use more and better technology. Arledge employed a two-unit production team. Chet Forte coordinated play-by-play, and Don Ohlmeyer handled isolated coverage. ABC used more cameras, more technicians, and more videotape than had ever been used before in a football game. The result was tantamount to a perfectly filmed and produced documentary. Every aspect of the game was filmed, and the best footage was rerun, discussed, and analyzed. The result was to make the game larger than life, to give each contest an epic quality. The use of sophisticated technology made even an average game seem exciting.

Technology, however, had always been a staple of an Arledge telecast. The team of announcers he chose for "Monday Night Football" made the show. His casting was designed to create an entertaining balance of humor, controversy, and tension. Instead of two men in the broadcast booth, Arledge employed three. He chose Keith Jackson to do the play-by-play. Jackson's role was clearly defined. As Howard Cosell wrote in *Cosell by Cosell*: "It was impressed on [Jackson] time and again that he was to think of himself as a public-address announcer, slipping in and out, factually, accurately, with the vital information—who made the tackle, who threw the ball, who caught the ball, how many yards were gained, what down it was.''

Arledge picked Don Meredith for his country charm and humor. A former Dallas Cowboy quarterback, Meredith knew the game and looked good on camera. This was his advantage, for Arledge intended Meredith to be the darling of Middle America. Meredith was, in short, cast to play the untutored hayseed from Mount Vernon, Texas, come to the big city to talk on TV.

Howard Cosell rounded out the team. Cosell had been with ABC since 1956, when his radio show ''Sports Focus'' became the summer replacement for ''Kukla, Fran, and Ollie.'' In 1961 he was put on the ABC-TV New York nightly news. The show that brought national attention to Cosell, however, was ''Wide World of Sports.'' Cosell regularly covered boxing for the show, and his outspoken support of Muhammad Ali drew strong critical reactions. ''Get that nigger-loving Jew bastard off the air,'' ran a typical letter to ABC. Cosell's brash, conceited, obnoxious style bothered viewers, but it did not make them turn the dial to another station. In fact, ''Wide World of Sports'' telecasts featuring Cosell scored high ratings. Cosell was and would remain for several decades ''good TV.''

For ''Monday Night Football'' Arledge cast Cosell as the man America loves to hate. Cosell was supposed to irritate, to get under people's skin, to arouse controversy. ABC research predicted that the majority of viewers of ''Monday Night Football'' would come from the young-adult population, people, noted Cosell in *Like It Is,* ''who had been growing up in swiftly changing, severely trying, turbulent, even tormented times. Such people would not be likely . . . to be responsive to a studiedly serious transmission of a football contest placed in the context of an event solemn enough to be originating from St. Patrick's Cathedral.'' What they wanted was irreverence, humor, and controversy. It was Cosell's and Meredith's job to give it to them. From the first, then, ''Monday Night Football'' was a television casting success. It is easier to compare it with CBS's ''All in the Family'' than with any other sports telecast.

Reactions to the show were predictably strong. Cosell's performance drew hate mail and death threats. On several occasions, FBI agents filled the broadcast booth. As Arledge had hoped, Cosell had touched a nerve. Meredith's irreverent humor also attracted attention and viewers. When he said, ''There's got to be more to life than what's going on down there,'' he captured the essence of ABC's attitude toward prime-time football. ''Monday Night Football'' treated the sport like the game it was. To Arledge football was entertainment, not a religion. And successful entertainment was a matter of good casting.

Arledge altered the cast for the second season. He replaced Keith Jackson with former New York Giant star Frank Gifford. Like Meredith, Gifford was a handsome, articulate explayer who was popular with Middle America. Even more important, ABC research indicated that Gifford was the most popular sportscaster in New York City, the nation's largest market. Promptly hired, Gifford was given more freedom than Jackson had enjoyed. Now Arledge had a near-perfect cast—Cosell, Meredith, and Gifford. Ratings shot up. By the time Cosell left the show in 1983, "Monday Night Football" had become the longest-running prime-time hit on television, outlasting such blockbusters as "I Love Lucy," "M*A*S*H," "Rhoda," and "All in the Family."

In his most recent book, *I Never Played the Game,* Cosell modestly claims, "Who the hell made *Monday Night Football* unlike any other sports program on the air? If you want the plain truth, I did." He notes that his ability of "humanizing the players" and entertainingly communicating to a large prime-time audience insured the show's success. Actually, Cosell simply filled a role in a cast. Arledge made "Monday Night Football." He demonstrated how sports could become successful prime-time entertainment.

Just as Arledge "created" prime-time football, he changed the way Americans saw the Olympic Games. Before ABC acquired the rights to televise the Games in 1968, no major network had attempted any sort of comprehensive coverage of the Olympics. In 1964, for example, NBC's coverage of the Tokyo Olympics was minimal. Because of the time difference, NBC covered the Games with fifteen-minute shows televised late at night. Most Americans found it easier to follow the Olympics in their newspapers than on their televisions.

Arledge rightly saw the entertainment possibilities of the Olympics. And he knew how to negotiate for the rights. He promised the host city what it wanted—publicity and exposure. As "Wide World of Sports" had demonstrated, part of Arledge's formula was extensive coverage of the exotic places where sports were played. ABC's coverage of alpine skiing had provided great tourist publicity for such towns as Garmisch, St. Moritz, and Innsbruck. Arledge used this approach to win the rights to televise the 1968 Winter Olympics in Grenoble, France. After the conclusion of the negotiations, a French committeeman told Arledge, "I must tell you that NBC was here, too, and told us about the very impressive list of events they carry. In this connection, there is one question I would like to ask you. What are all these Bowel Games they have the best of?" The committeeman felt such contests were of questionable taste. It was a case of athletic culture shock. Garmisch the French understood. Roses and oranges were only flowers and fruit.

Heroic technology and extended coverage best describes ABC and Arledge's approach to the televising of the Olympic Games. Arledge sent a 250-man crew to cover the Grenoble Games, and he beamed the result home via the Early Bird satellite. At the 1972 summer Games in Munich, Arledge's team exceeded 330 men and women. As the number of technicians increased, so did the hours of coverage. ABC squeezed 27 hours of television from the Grenoble Games. Eight years later, in Innsbruck, ABC extended its coverage to 43 1/2 hours. The increased technology and coverage returned handsome dividends. The reviews and ratings were tremendous. Both winter and summer Games became prime-time successes.

By the mid-1970s ABC executives had found a way to capitalize on their Olympic telecasts. Instead of selling all of the commercial time to outside sponsors, they decided to hold back large blocs to promote their own television shows. This tactic worked especially well during the 1976 summer Games. While the other networks were televising summer reruns, ABC ran over a hundred hours of Olympic coverage from Montreal. In addition, the network devoted hundreds of commercial minutes to their forthcoming fall lineup of shows. As a result, in the fall of 1976 ABC passed CBS in the Nielsen ratings for all shows.

By the mid-1970s Arledge's string of uninterrupted successes had made him one of the top executives in the industry. Few challenges remained for him in the field of televised sports. In 1975 he decided to attempt a bold move. In "Saturday Night Live with Howard Cosell," Arledge tried to parlay Cosell's success on a prime-time sports show into even greater triumph on a prime-time variety show. Cosell believed fully in the idea. Since the start of "Monday Night Football" Cosell had become a genuine telecelebrity. Millions of Americans tuned in to hear what new outrageous things Howard would say. As David Halberstam noted in "The Mouth that Roared," Cosell "became the issue: What would Howard do? Whom would he assault? Would he self-destruct? Would someone finally turn on him? He became in the process what television wants more than anything else, an event." "A legend in his own mind," Johnny Carson called him, and indeed he was. Cosell assured Arledge that the planned variety show would be a success. "I have a lot of due bills out," Cosell announced. It was Howard's gentle way of assuring everyone that he could bring in the real talent.

Howard said he was only telling it like it is. But as Jimmy Cannon commented, "Can a man who wears a hairpiece and changes his name be trusted to tell it like it is?" Cosell's influence was not up to his vision. Perhaps some indication of the pull he believed he exerted came when he proposed to John Lennon that the Beatles reunite on "Saturday Night Live with Howard Cosell." NBC's "Saturday Night Live" had made the same proposal to George Harrison as a joke. Cosell was quite serious. Lennon listened to Cosell's idea and then politely declined the offer.

"Saturday Night Live with Howard Cosell" was an unqualified failure. In *I Never Played the Game,* Cosell blamed Arledge: "As soon as Arledge realized the show was doomed, he quit on me. He became remote and inaccessible. Chaos set in." Arledge blamed the show's time slot: "At eight o'clock Saturday night, none of the people Howard appeals to are home—the audience consists mostly of children and old people. . . . There is ample evidence that even if Elizabeth Taylor did a strip tease at eight P.M. Saturday on ABC, it wouldn't get more than a 15 percent share." In truth the show's real problem was the premise that celebrity status is transferable. Famous athletes and sports personalities are rarely able to achieve equal success in other areas of the entertainment industry.

The ill-fated show, however, did not hurt either Cosell's or Arledge's careers. Inside the insular sports world, Cosell was still a celebrity. As for Arledge, in 1977 he began his move out of sports, a slow process that would take eight years. In that year he became president of ABC News. Although he also remained president of ABC Sports, he devoted most of his energy to the news division.

ABC's spectacular rise forced the other networks to reevaluate their coverage of sports. Ousted by ABC from its first place in the Nielsen ratings, CBS was particularly swift to respond. Head of CBS Sports Robert Wussler and CBS chairman of the board William Paley decided that they had to beat ABC at their own game—Olympic coverage. Although CBS had long taken a cavalier attitude toward sports coverage, its chief executives were now determined to win the rights to televise the 1980 Moscow Games.

Suddenly the Russians had something American capitalism very much wanted. More than a touch of humor and irony colored the courting of the Kremlin apparatchiks by the leading executives of CBS and ABC. For a few months Mouton Rothschild and vodka mixed agreeably. Both ABC and CBS programming took a new attitude toward the Soviet Union. As Benjamin Rader described the search for détente, ''ABC's morning show *A.M. America,* presented a week of reports on life in the Soviet Union. 'We made Moscow look like Cypress Gardens without the water skiers,' admitted one embarrassed ABC man. CBS followed with a prime-time bomb in 1976 featuring a shivering Mary Tyler Moore standing on a street corner in Moscow where she hosted a show about the Bolshoi Ballet.''

The Russian negotiators adapted well to the free enterprise mode of television. ABC, CBS, and late-arriving NBC bid against each other. In the end, NBC won the battle, agreeing to pay the Soviet Union $85 million for television rights to the Olympics. Of course, the eventual United States boycott of the Moscow Games cost NBC dearly.

The Moscow Olympic battle was the first engagement of an eight-year war between the three major networks over the control of television sports. NBC and CBS had taken note of ABC's spectacular rise. Clearly, network executives reasoned, outstanding sports programming was essential to their corporate growth. Not only did sports programming please the affiliates, but it also provided a solid platform for launching the network's fall season. Good sports promoted good ratings, and the sum total of both equalled increased corporate profits.

Such reasoning inevitably created a highly competitive atmosphere. The big-time sports industry became a sellers market, a fact that the men who controlled that industry quickly realized. Giving little consideration to the future problem of overexposure, they sold television executives all the programming the networks desired. Of course, the price was high. Pete Rozelle, commissioner of the NFL, was probably the best—and the greediest—negotiator. After becoming commissioner in 1960, this former public relations man demonstrated his ability to negotiate with network executives. In 1964 CBS agreed to pay $14 million a year for the rights to televise professional football. At the time, owners considered that amount to be staggering. In 1966 CBS raised its annual payments to $18.5 million. By the 1970s such numbers would provide only laughter at the negotiating table. Starting in 1970 Rozelle allowed all three networks to televise professional games. In 1977 the networks agreed to pay the NFL $656 million over a four-year period. In 1982 the networks upped the amount to $2 billion over five years. In 1985 each team in the NFL received $65 million from the television package. As Arthur Rooney, Jr., had said years before, ''Pete Rozelle is a gift from the hand of Providence.''

College football and professional baseball and basketball similarly profited from the networks' increased interest in sports. In 1970 the National Basketball Association received $1 million from television revenues; by 1986 that amount had been raised to over $40 million. During roughly the same period (1970-85) professional baseball's annual television revenues rose from under $20 million to $160 million. Finally, college football's revenues made the phrase "amateur sport" seem somehow empty. In 1977 the NCAA signed a four-year deal with ABC for $120 million. In 1981 the NCAA agreed to allow CBS and the Turner Broadcasting System as well as ABC to televise games. The new price was $74.3 million per year.

By the late 1970s and the early 1980s the networks seemed sports mad. With the exception of hockey, all the major professional and amateur sports profited. Behind Sugar Ray Leonard, its new hero, boxing made a strong comeback on television. Ruled by two separate organizations—the World Boxing Association and World Boxing Council—the sport offered television networks almost weekly championship fights. Television coverage of tennis and college basketball also increased dramatically. Aided by new cable stations and such all-sports networks as Entertainment and Sports Programming Network (ESPN), Americans watched more sports on television than ever before.

The major networks even turned to trash sports to augment their sports programming. Once again Arledge and ABC led the way. In 1973 "The Superstars" made its debut. The show was rooted more in vindictiveness than in imaginative programming, but it captured considerable viewer interest. In part, the NBA was responsible for the show. Between 1965 and 1973 ABC televised NBA games on Sundays. Although the ratings were never great, it captured enough of an audience to satisfy Arledge. Then in what Arledge considered a breach of faith, the NBA dumped ABC for CBS. Arguing unsuccessfully against the switch, Boston Celtics coach Red Auerbach warned, "You don't really think a man like Roone Arledge is going to take this lying down, do you?" Arledge didn't. Furious and feeling betrayed, he moved to destroy the NBA on television. He put a Sunday version of "Wide World of Sports" opposite the NBA games, publicizing the show as if it were the jewel of ABC Sports. The show was a great success. Its ratings quickly moved past those of professional basketball. During that season, Arledge filled one Sunday show with a program called "The Superstars." It was so successful that Arledge expanded the single program into a series of programs the following year. Roone had his revenge and television had a new concept in sports.

The success of "The Superstars" encouraged the networks to create their own athletic contests. Out of "The Superstars" emerged several sequels. "The Women Superstars" gave the show more sex appeal. "The World Superstars" added a touch of the exotic. "The Superteams" pitted teams from different sports against each other. Using essentially the same themes created by ABC, NBC and CBS aired their own trash sports—"US Against the World," "Dynamic Duos," "The Challenge of the Sexes," and "Celebrity Challenge of the Sexes."

Soon anything went. There were buffalo-chip-throwing contests and Bazooka Bubble Gum blowing contests. Championships were staged to discover who was the strongest man and who was the strongest bartender. The most popular contests, however, featured women in tank-top bathing suits. Particularly anxious to display the best features of their performers, the networks joined together in "Battle of the Network Stars." Although men as well as women competed, the real "stars" were the physically blessed women in form-fitting bathing suits. The show's format provided ample opportunity to allow the bathing suits to be saturated with water. Often the difference between "Battle of the Network Stars" and a wet T-shirt contest amounted to the difference between a tank top and a T-shirt. "Saturday Night Live's" parody of the show, "Battle of the T and A's," certainly provided a more accurate name for the friendly network championship.

Mercifully, by the early 1980s the Golden Age of trash sports had passed. More important, by that time there were signs that the Golden Age of television sports might also be ending. The industry was changing in fundamental ways. Communication satellites and the end of the legal restriction on cable television allowed local "superstations" and cable networks to compete head-to-head with the major networks. Ted Turner's WTBS in Atlanta epitomized the aggressive mood of the superstations. WTBS televised professional baseball and basketball and college basketball, and it charged its sponsors less than the major networks did for similar programming. ESPN and USA, the two major sports cable networks, similarly offered sponsors outstanding sports programming for less money. By the mid-1980s the three major networks faced a real crisis.

Increasingly traditional sports sponsors began moving their advertising dollars into other areas. For years Madison Avenue had talked about the sports package, which included sponsors from the beer, shaving cream, life insurance, and automobile industries. Advertising experts believed that most of the selling done on prime time was to women. They regarded sports programming as the last place where advertisers could reach men, and they believed that the male still decided what kind of beer he would drink, shaving cream he would use, car he would drive, and life insurance he would purchase. Since ultimately the advertisers paid most of the bills for televised sports, any change in their thinking and spending would send shock waves throughout the television and sports industries.

The first tremors were felt in the late 1970s. In December 1979, General Motors decided to pull out of CBS's NBA package. The decision—based largely on poor ratings for the NBA and the desire to move into college basketball, which attracted a younger, more affluent viewer—staggered CBS Sports and the NBA. After several hastily arranged conferences, Subaru joined the package, "delighted," wrote David Halberstam in *The Breaks of the Game,* "to sell Japanese products by means of American sports." But Subaru paid far less than the going $18,000 for a thirty-second spot.

By the mid-1980s the tremors were registering high on the Richter scale. They affected every major sport. In part, it was a result of a change in family purchasing patterns. Car-buying decisions, for example, are made more and more by women. Thus advertisers can reach their target audiences more efficiently on "Murder,

She Wrote'' or ''Dallas.'' In addition, beer-drinking men can be reached much more cheaply on such cable networks as MTV. In 1980 the Miller Brewing Company spent 95 percent of its advertising dollars on televised sports; by 1985 that figure had dropped to 70 percent. A Miller spokesman noted: ''Sports programming used to be a bargain compared with prime-time. Now it's as expensive or more. With that, other types of programming become just as important. We are using MTV, late-night shows like David Letterman, and some comedy programming to reach our target audience.''

Television networks found themselves caught between rising costs for television rights and falling advertising prices. In 1985 the major networks lost $45 million on the NFL. Although all three networks have been hurt, ABC has suffered the most. In 1984 Olympic coverage helped ABC Sports to achieve a record $70 million profit. In 1985 ABC Sports lost between $30 and $50 million. William Taaffe for *Sports Illustrated* dubbed it ''a $100 million-plus Wrong War Corrigan.''

Although the full effect of the earthquake is not yet known, the major networks are starting to assess the damages and beginning their clean-up. ABC has made the most dramatic move. In 1985 Capital City Communications, a media conglomerate, bought ABC for $3.7 billion. Howard Cosell called it ''a friendly takeover by the smaller company.'' Not everyone at ABC, particularly the Sports division, believed the takeover was so benign. One of Cap City's first major moves after the takeover was to replace Roone Arledge in Sports with Dennis Swanson, a no-nonsense, bottom-line ex-Marine. Swanson immediately let it be known that ABC Sports' free-spending days had ended. With Arledge as boss, ABC Sports had taken on an expensive country club air: ''Six-block limo rides to executive lunches, hotel suites on the road, helicopters at event sites, and lavish parties were part of the fun,'' wrote Taaffe. Swanson is not cut from Arledge cloth. Said one insider of Cap City, ''Their idea of a good party is pretzels, potato chips, and sodas from the machine in the hallway.''

Less subtly, NBC and CBS have moved along the same path as the new ABC. Undoubtedly in the future, professional and college sports executives will not be able to extract as much money from the networks for sports rights. The signs are clear. NBC purchased the rights for the 1988 Seoul Summer Olympics for an unexpectedly low $300 million; ABC cancelled the award-winning, money-losing ''SportsBeat'' and perhaps gave Cosell reason to rethink his ''friendly takeover'' thesis; CBS dropped its coverage of the Belmont Stakes, and ABC decided not to renew its contract with the Gator Bowl. The end result might well mean less sports for less money on the major networks. Looking into the future, CBS's sports head Peter Lund commented: ''The impact hasn't been felt yet, at least not entirely, by the leagues. The reason is that the [new] baseball and football contracts haven't come up yet. That's where the rubber is going to meet the road—where there is either a leveling off or a diminution in the rights paid to those leagues.''

Perhaps the free-spending era ended with ABC's acquisition of the 1988 Winter Olympics in Calgary, Canada. After a brutal bidding war, ABC ''won'' the rights at a cost of $309 million, an increase of $217.5 million, or 337 percent, over the cost of the 1984 Winter Olympics in Sarajevo, Yugoslavia. From the first, ABC realized that they had bid too high, that pride or vanity or competitiveness had overcome common sense. In fact, the network lost over $50 million on the event. Mae West said that ''too much of a good thing is wonderful,'' but by 1989 the major networks were beginning to reevaluate her sage advice, at least regarding televised sports.

The Roone Revolution, then, is nearing its end, or at least network competition for sports is slackening. But sports will never be the same as they were before Arledge. Nor will television's coverage of sports return to the flat days before Arledge took over ABC Sports. More than any other person, Arledge changed the economic and aesthetic foundations of sports.

CHAPTER 17

❖

Anabolic Steroids:
The Gremlins of Sport

Terry Todd

Throughout history, athletes have used a variety of substances in an attempt to get a competitive "edge." The ancient Greeks, for instance, who were idolized for their athletic purity by such *fin de siècle* sports promoters as Pierre de Coubertin, the self-styled founder of the modern Olympic Games, were well paid professionals who also tried a variety of "medical" measures to enhance their performances at Olympia. The probable originators of the "high protein diet," for instance, were wrestlers from the classical period who often consumed as much as 10 pounds of lamb a day, and there are reports from the third century A.D. that Greek athletes used certain types of hallucinogenic mushrooms to mentally prepare themselves. Other reports indicate that Greek long distance runners ate sesame seeds during races in the belief that the seeds would increase endurance. It is also known that Nordic "Berserkers" thought they could increase their fighting strength 12-fold by eating *amanita muscaria,* a type of psychoactive mushroom.

In the nineteenth century, as sports rose in importance, there were many known reports of drug use. The first surfaced in Amsterdam in 1865, when several swimmers in a canal race were charged with "taking dope." And as bicycle races swept into prominence in both Europe and America, experimentation with a variety of stimulants became common. Goldman reports that by 1869 cyclists were known to use "speed balls" of heroin and cocaine to increase endurance. And in 1886, as a result of such practices, a cyclist died, the first known drug related death of an athlete. Thomas Burks has also pointed out that the use of caffeine, alcohol, nitroglycerine, ethyl ether, strychnine and opium was common among athletes in the late nineteenth century.

The most famous early case of drug enhancement, however, occurred in the 1904 Olympic Games in St. Louis. The case is well known because at the conclusion of the marathon, the winner, America's Thomas Hicks, collapsed. During the investigation, Hicks' handlers, who had been allowed to accompany

From the *Journal of Sport History,* 14:1 (Spring 1987). © 1987 The North American Society for Sport History. Reprinted by permission.

him throughout the course of the race in a motor-car, admitted they had given him repeated doses of strychnine and brandy to keep him on his feet. Even so, Hicks' medal was not taken away, and his joy at winning was expressed to reporters in a telling way when he finally revived, "I would rather have won this race than be president of the United States."

Most of these early cases deal, of course, with stimulants, not muscle-building drugs such as anabolic steroids; but what these early reports do suggest, and why they are important to understanding the rapid growth of the use by athletes of anabolic steroids in the second half of the twentieth century, is that even in the so-called golden age of amateur sport, ethical considerations were often overridden by the desire for attainment. Pierre de Coubertin was just one of many in the nineteenth century to argue that sport should consist of contests between gentlemen and be untainted by any hint of "professionalism," but what Coubertin and other sporting officials failed to fully understand was that money was not the only "dangerous" incentive for athletes. For some—for most athletes, in fact—the recognition and feelings of personal satisfaction they received from winning an event were sufficient in themselves to drive these athletes to extraordinary, often perilous, means. And as the twentieth century progressed, the old adage that, "It matters not whether you win or lose, but how you play the game," was less and less germane to what actually occurred on the playing fields. The attitude that now prevails is well summed up by Lou Simmons, a powerlifter and coach who opposes any controls on drug use in sport: "The psychology of a champion lifter is to reach the top *no matter what* . . . if he doesn't take full advantage of everything at his (or her) grasp, it is his own fault."

In any case, the record seems clear that had steroids, or testosterone, been available in the late nineteenth century, athletes and others would have used them. It was not until 1927, however, that Fred Koch, an organic chemist at the University of Chicago, and his graduate assistant, Lemuel Clyde McGee, were finally able to isolate a highly impure but nonetheless potent form of testosterone. Koch and McGee extracted the hormone by pulverizing several tons of bull testicles and then treating what was left with benzene and acetone to obtain their essence, an essence that had nearly miraculous properties. Capons, for instance, demonstrated masculine characteristics when administered the drug and later studies on hens and female calves confirmed the capacity of the extract to produce aggressive behavior. But the expense and difficulty of the extraction process prohibited any widespread use of the substance and this precluded serious interest by the medical community. By 1935, however, several European physicians were also studying the hormone, and one of them, Yugoslavian chemist Leopold Ruzicka, came up with a process to alter the molecular structure of cholesterol and thus produce synthetic testosterone.

According to science writer Paul de Kruif, there was a great interest in the new hormone throughout the remainder of the thirties since many people saw it as a potential fountain of youth. In *The Male Hormone*, (1945), de Kruif describes many studies which used human subjects. He reports that scientists found that this new synthetic testosterone "did more than give [the subjects] more energy

Harold Connolly, a hammer thrower from Boston who was involved in a famous love affair with fellow Olympian Olga Fikotova of Czechoslovakia, admitted to the U.S. Senate that he became addicted to steroids in 1964.
Courtesy of the Amateur Athletic Foundation of Los Angeles.

and a gain in weight . . . It changed them, and fundamentally . . . after many months on testosterone, their chest and shoulder muscles grew much heavier and stronger . . . in some mysterious manner, testosterone caused the human body to synthesize protein, it caused the human body to be able to build the very stuff of its own life.''

Much of the research involving testosterone and human subjects was done in Germany, before World War II. Heinz Arandt recorded 17 case studies of testosterone use, all of which showed positive results. There is also evidence that the Germans continued their experimentation during the war, and even administered testosterone to some storm troopers to increase their aggressiveness. Dr. William Taylor has speculated that since Hitler had used the drug, it might have accounted for some of the mood swings and aggressiveness of the German fuhrer.

In any case, *The Male Hormone* is full of praise for testosterone, since de Kruif saw in this new hormone a way to extend man's sexual life and increase his productivity. De Kruif himself experimented with the drug and argued that its use was no different than injections of insulin for diabetics. "I'm not ashamed that it's no longer made to its old degree by my own, aging body," he wrote. "It's chemical crutches. It's borrowed manhood. It's borrowed time. But just the same," he added, "it's what makes bulls bulls." And in an observation made chilling by the passage of time, de Kruif speculates on the possible effects of testosterone on athletes.

> We know how both the St. Louis Cardinals and the St. Louis Browns have won championships supercharged by vitamins. It would be interesting to watch the productive power of [a] . . . professional group [of athletes] that would try a systematic supercharge with testosterone . . .

De Kruif would not have long to wait. At the 1952 Olympic Games in Helsinki, the Soviet Union did exceptionally well in the weightlifting competition, despite having been ravaged by World War II, garnering seven medals—three gold, three silver and one bronze. And in what may well have been the first public charge regarding the Soviets and drugs, the U.S. Olympic weightlifting coach, Bob Hoffman, told the Associated Press, "I know they're taking the hormone stuff to increase their strength."

As it turned out, Hoffman was right, and he soon had the proof. At the 1954 World Weightlifting Championships in Vienna, Hoffman was the U.S. team coach and the team physician was Dr. John Ziegler. Ziegler carefully observed the Soviet team and suspected they were using testosterone, a suspicion that was later corroborated at a tavern by one of the Russian team physicians. Armed with this knowledge, Ziegler returned to the United States, acquired some testosterone and tested it on himself, on Bob Hoffman, and on several east coast weightlifters, including Jim Park and Yaz Kuzahara. Concerned about the side-effects of testosterone, including prostatic problems and libido increase, Ziegler wanted a drug which would have the "anabolic" or muscle building effects of testosterone without the "androgenic" effects (heightened aggression, hirsutism, increased libido, etc.). Then, in 1958, the Ciba pharmaceutical company released Dianabol (methandrostenalone), the first U.S. "anabolic steroid." The drug was not intended for use by athletes, of course, but was developed for burn patients and certain postoperative and geriatric cases.

Dr. Ziegler, however, had another agenda and what he did with Dianabol was critical in the spread of anabolic drugs in sport. With Hoffman's blessing, he convinced three members of Hoffman's York Barbell Club team to begin using Dianabol. In addition, Ziegler persuaded them to begin using—in secret—a new, little-known training program called "isometric contraction," which involves pulling or pushing against immovable resistance. Almost immediately, the three lifters began making unprecedented progress in strength and muscle size, and other lifters clamored to know why and how this progress had been effected.

Then, as the lifters approached the world record level, Hoffman published a hyperbolic article in his widely read magazine, *Strength and Health,* entitled "The Most Important Article I Ever Wrote." And in a way it was, as it outlined the new training routine the three lifters were using but failed to mention the little pink pills. But the article only led to further speculation concerning the reason for the continued success of the three lifters, since the use of isometric contraction by his readers generally failed to produce significant improvement. Soon, however, the secret began to leak and it became known that the reason for the meteoric rise of the three York lifters, by now all national champions, was their use of Dianabol.

And so, in a number of predictable ways, the news of steroids spread. The combination of a radically different exercise routine, an evangelical physician, an aggressive promoter with access to a national fitness magazine and the startling progress being made by a few elite lifters, produced a climate of rising expectations in which strength athletes began a big arms race, fueled by an ever expanding array of pharmaceuticals. This is not to say that any one of these four components was individually responsible for the increased use of drugs in sport—only that these components happened to exist at the same time and to interact in such a way as to produce the critical mass necessary for the strength-building drug scene to explode. Ziegler and Hoffman are now dead, the pace-setting lifters have all long since retired, and isometric contraction has acquired a patina similar to that of the bunny-hop and the Hula-Hoop, yet the many and various ergogenic kin of Dianabol continue to thrive.

Evidence of this spread comes from the hammer thrower Harold Connolly, who testified in 1973, at the U.S. Senate subcommittee hearings on drugs and athletics, that he had become "hooked" on steroids in 1964. By the Mexico City Games, in 1968, things had advanced to the point that Dr. Tom Waddell, who placed sixth in the decathlon that year, told the *New York Times* that he estimated a full third of the U.S. track and field team—not just the field event specialists—had used steroids at the pre-Olympic training camp held at Lake Tahoe. This did not, of course, occur in a social and cultural vacuum.

The 1960s were a period of innovation and experimentation in nearly every aspect of American life. As a people we became fascinated with change and technology; science and progress received a special reverence in our lives yet, at the same time, millions of young Americans turned to mood-altering drugs such as LSD and marijuana because they felt increasingly alienated from and dehumanized by our technological society. It now seems clear that it was the combination of these seemingly contradictory phenomena that helped further the drug revolution in athletics. The first phenomenon instilled in athletes who grew up in the sixties the belief that science could make their lives—their athletic quests—easier; the second phenomenon created a significant subculture within our society in which the use of illegal substances was not only permissible, but a hip badge of honor. As Ken Kesey said, you were either on the bus or off the bus. Furthermore, as James Wright pointed out in *Anabolic Steroids and Sports,* by the Sixties the average American home contained more than 30 different drugs, vitamins and nostrums.

Even so, most athletes in the Sixties and early Seventies were secretive about their use of anabolic steroids. But in 1971, American superheavyweight weight-lifting champion Ken Patera shattered the code of silence when he told reporters that he was anxious to meet the famous Russian super-heavy, Vasily Alexeev, in the 1972 Olympic Games. The previous year, at the World Championships, Alexeev had barely beaten Patera, but Patera now felt they were on a more equal footing:

> Last year, the only difference between me and him was that I couldn't afford his pharmacy bill. Now I can. When I hit Munich next year, I'll weight in about 340, maybe 350. Then we'll see which are better—his steroids or mine.

Patera's comments sent shock waves throughout the sporting media, although he maintained in a recent interview that he "didn't hear a peep out of anyone from the U.S. Olympic Committee."

In the 1960s most of the attention on the question of drugs in athletics focused on the use of "hard drugs" such as amphetamines and heroin. A series of drug-related incidents had kept those particular drugs in the forefront of the public's consciousness as the Rome Olympics was marred by the death of Danish cyclist Knut Jensen, who had taken a "blood circulation stimulant." There were other problems throughout the decade. Boxer Billy Bello died in 1963 of a heroin overdose while Britain's Tommy Simpson died in an amphetamine-related death in the 1967 *Tour de France*. Also in 1967, Dick Howard, a bronze medal winner at the Rome Olympics, died from an overdose of heroin. And then, in 1968, another cyclist, Yves Mottin, succumbed to amphetamine complications.

Because of such problems, the IOC established a medical commission in 1967 and banned certain drugs. At the 1968 Games, however, drug testing was done only for research purposes and even then the "research" did not include anabolic steroids, since they were not yet on the IOC's banned substances list. The only meaningful testing done in the 1968 Games was, in fact, a chromosome check to determine whether all the female competitors were biologically women. The chromosome check was prompted in part by the fact that many female athletes had begun training with weights and thus projecting a more "masculine" image, an image which caused some officials to suspect that some of the competitors were not, in fact, women. And so in 1967, at the European Cup, the chromosome test or "sex test" was used for the first time, and one athlete, the Polish sprinter Eva Klubokowska, failed the screening. And then, at the 1968 Olympics, the famous Russian sisters, Tamara and Irina Press, were noticeably absent. Olympian Pat Connally reflected on this in 1981:

> The current situation [regarding steroids] in women's athletics is very disturbing. When I competed against the Press sisters from the Soviet

Union, there were problems with sex tests and talk of men disguised as women. Now there are problems with steroids and we're back to the question of who's really a woman.

Gender disputes aside, however, there were several reasons why the IOC failed to include anabolic steroids and testosterone among the banned substances at their 1967 meeting. The first was that throughout most of the sixties the use of anabolic steroids was still little known to most sports officials. The second, and perhaps more telling reason, was that there was then no way to test for the presence of such drugs. The IOC was also influenced by prevailing medical opinion, which maintained that these hormonal substances provided no athletic advantage. This opinion now seems astonishing, especially in light of the already-widespread anecdotal evidence of the potency of anabolic steroids. In fairness, however, it should be added that little research attention had been given to the question of the use of the substances by athletes, since the drugs were not developed *for* athletes. The research that *was* done, such as a frequently cited UCLA study, found "that steroid administration in normal therapeutic doses is unlikely to increase muscle size or strength in healthy young men . . ." And even though subsequent research sometimes found otherwise and thus supported the overwhelming endorsements of the athletes, it was not until the early 1980s that the opinion of the medical community began to significantly change. A thorough discussion of the medical community's unwillingness to recognize the potential benefits of these drugs to athletes is beyond the scope of this study, but the feeling persists among athletes that one reason the medical community was so unwilling to admit the gains steroids could produce was that physicians hoped this non-admission would cause athletes to avoid such potentially harmful substances. This suspected strategy backfired, however, as it only caused athletes to distrust doctors and to turn, instead, to the black market for drugs and information.

Fed by the powerful sports grapevine, the use of steroids burgeoned as more and more athletes began to train with weights and thus come into range of the siren song sung by competitive lifters and bodybuilders. So rapidly did the usage of anabolic steroids increase that in 1969, they moved squarely into the mainstream of America's sporting consciousness when *Sports Illustrated* writer Bil Gilbert published a three part expose entitled "Drugs in Sport." Gilbert charged that there were "some players on almost every NFL and AFL team that have taken the drugs." He quoted Ken Ferguson of Utah State, who went on to play pro football in Canada, as saying, ". . . anybody who has graduated from college to professional football in the last four years has used them." Gilbert also pointed out that although rumors of both male and female use abounded, nothing was being done to stop the spread of such drugs. He correctly argued that the delaying of the decision to ban the drugs from sport was helping to promote their usage. As Dave Maggard, a high school coach and a former Olympic competitor said, "I'd like to see the NCAA, the AAU and the U.S. Olympic Committee . . . go ahead and put us straight—tell us to either use the drugs, or don't . . . It's this halfway stuff, the rumors, the idea that maybe you *have* to use them to be competitive that has made it such a mess.''

But still the use increased. At the 1972 Olympic Games in Munich, for instance, Jay Sylvester, then a member of the U.S. track and field team and now a faculty member at Brigham Young University, unofficially polled all the track and field contestants in Munich. He found that 68% had used some form of anabolic steroid in their preparation for the Games.

In order for the drugs to be effectively banned, however, a viable test had to be found. Finally, in 1973, two reports in the *British Journal of Sports Medicine* suggested solutions to the problem of steroid testing. The first described a detection procedure utilizing radioimmunoassay, while the second advocated the use of gas chromatography and mass spectrometry. The IOC decided to adopt both procedures in order to guarantee absolute accuracy. The only drawback to the new testing—a significant one—was that few laboratories in the world possessed all the equipment and computer data to do IOC level testing. Even now, in 1987, there are only eight labs throughout the world with IOC approval. This shortage has made testing both expensive and administratively cumbersome.

The new testing procedure was first used on a trial run basis at the Commonwealth Games in Auckland, New Zealand, in February 1974. No sanctions were imposed and the participating athletes were not identified, but nine of the 55 samples tested contained steroids. But in 1975, at the European Cup (track and field), sanctions were included and two athletes tested positive for steroids and were disqualified from the competition and subsequently suspended by the international federation. The first Olympic use of the new test came in 1976 at the Montreal Games, and only eight athletes out of 275 tested were found positive for anabolic steroids—seven weightlifters and one woman discus thrower.

It would be easy to assume from such a low percentage of steroid positives that the athletes had simply decided to come ''clean'' to the European Cup and the Games. Sadly, this was not the case. Despite the IOC's best intentions, they had left a way to get around the test because there were still some substances that enhanced athletic performance but for which the IOC had not developed a test. Ironically, the drug to which the athletes turned at the 1976 Games was the male hormone, itself—testosterone—with all its potent side effects; it was the drug Dr. John Ziegler had abandoned in 1958 in favor of Dianabol. The most striking of those side effects are extreme aggressiveness and mood swings. Although such side effects appear to be to some extent both individually variable and dose dependent, they can have devastating personal consequences, as the following set of separate, paired interviews makes clear. The man interviewed was a former All-Pro lineman in the NFL.

Wife: He's so impatient when he's on steroids, so easily annoyed. He becomes vocal and hostile real fast and he was never that way before.

Husband: It definitely makes a person mean and aggressive. And I was always so easygoing. On the field I've tried to hurt people in ways I never did before.

Wife: His sexual habits really changed. On the testosterone he not only wanted to have sex more often, he was also much rougher. And his sleep patterns were completely different on the testosterone. The Dianabol changed him some, but on the testosterone he was always ready to start the day by five-thirty or six, no matter how late he'd turned in. In the old days he'd sleep till noon.

Husband: One of the bad things about the testosterone is that you never get much sleep. It just drives you so. With amphetamines the effects wear off after a game, but with the testosterone it's almost as if you're on speed all the time.

Wife: I don't think he'll ever be able to give it up. It cost him a wife who loved him and the chance to watch his two children grow up. There've been times when I felt he was almost suicidal. Sometimes, late at night, he'd tell me that he just couldn't help himself and that he couldn't stop using it because of the football, and then he'd cry.

Husband: A lot of guys can't handle it. I'm not sure I can. I remember a while back five of the guys on our team went on the juice at the same time. A year later four of them were divorced and one was separated. I've lost a lot of hair from using it, but I have to admit it's great for football. People in the game know that 50 percent of football is mental, and that's why the testosterone helps you so much. I lost my family, but I think I'm a better player now. Isn't that a hell of a trade-off.

As for the original motivation amateur athletes had to use testosterone, further insight was provided in a 1982 interview with Professor Manfred Donike, head of the IOC-approved drug testing laboratory in Cologne, West Germany.

The increase in testosterone use is a direct consequence of the doping control for anabolic steroids. In former times, athletes . . . have to stop the use of the anabolic steroids at least three weeks before the event. So they have to substitute. And the agent of choice is testosterone—testosterone injections.

Donike, perhaps more than any other member of the IOC medical committee, was concerned about testosterone and its effect on sport. And so, as had been done earlier for anabolic steroids, Donike found a way to determine whether an athlete was using "exogenous" testosterone—testosterone from outside the body. It is important to note that the screening procedure for testosterone involves the use of a ratio of 6:1. In other words, for either a man or a woman to test positive for testosterone, he or she must possess, at the time of the testing, six times more testosterone than is considered "normal" for their respective sex. The 6:1 ratio was arbitrary, though one of the reasons given for its adoption was that it removed any possibility of a false positive. A negative aspect of the 6:1 ratio is that it leaves considerable room for cheating. In any case, after the US-boycotted 1980

Olympics in Moscow, Donike performed unofficial testosterone screens on the urine samples which had been collected and although not one positive test had turned up for anabolic steroids in the Games he found that 20% of *all* the athletes—male and female—would have failed the 6:1 testosterone screen. This 20% included 16 gold medalists. Armed with this evidence, Donike was able to convince the IOC in 1982 to add testosterone to its list of banned substances.

The first official use of Donike's testosterone screen did not come about until the 1983 Pan American Games in Caracas, Venezuela. There, 15 male athletes were found to be drug positive. Included in that 15 were 11 weightlifters (some of whom were using testosterone), one cyclist, one fencer, one sprinter and one shotputter. While those figures are high, what raised the media's and the public's concern to even greater levels was the fact that 12 members of the U.S. track and field team simply packed their bags and flew home after the weightlifting positives were announced. It was apparent by this time that the testing procedures Donike implemented in Caracas were more sophisticated than any ever administered to athletes. Not only could he test for testosterone, but he could detect further back in time the presence of anabolic substances. Several of the U.S. athletes, in fact, openly complained that they were being set up by the IOC as guinea pigs for the new procedures. Adding to the controversy as the Games continued was the fact that a large number of other athletes either withdrew with sudden "muscle pulls and injuries" or performed well below their previous bests in order to finish low and thus avoid being tested.

The resulting furor further elevated the question of drugs and athletics. But Caracas was simply the largest in a series of major steroid scandals following Montreal. In 1979, for instance, the International Amateur Athletic Federation banned seven women track athletes: three Romanians, two Bulgarians and two Soviets; and as a report in *Sports Illustrated* said, "Now even athletes with slight builds, such as middle-distance runners, believe steroids provide explosive power . . ." Though the women were supposed to be "banned for life," subsequent appeals allowed several of them to be back in action by the time of the Moscow Olympics. The earlier (1977) banning and early reinstatement of East German shot putter Ilona Slupianek had aroused similar controversy, and this controversy intensified in 1980, when, after Slupianek won a gold medal in the Moscow Olympics, she was elected by a panel of international track and field experts as sportswoman of the year.

Even with all these precedents, when the Pan American Games fiasco erupted, many U.S. journalists and commentators seemed shocked, and they focused on the fact that 12 members of the American team thought it best to leave Caracas without competing and being tested. Journalists also speculated about why the USOC had done virtually nothing up to that time to control the use of these substances. Furthermore, as the media's analysis continued over the next several weeks, Americans discovered that steroids and testosterone were not used only by Olympic athletes and weightlifters but by athletes in nearly every branch of professional sport. And as the journalists probed more deeply into America's sporting wound, they found that the USOC was not the only group of sports administrators who had chosen the "see no evil, hear no evil, speak no evil" approach to the problem. The NCAA was doing nothing about it either—nor were the NFL, the NBA, pro baseball, pro hockey, or even professional bodybuilding, a sport nearly synonymous with steroid use. And the journalists wondered why this was so. Why, they asked, had many European countries adopted rigorous testing programs while in America nothing was being done.

Finally, after repeated questions from the press regarding drug testing, F. Donn Miller, then head of the USOC, announced that there would be testing at all the upcoming 1984 Olympic Trials in various sports. According to a later report from Miller, however—issued *after* the Games—86 of the tests performed during the pre-Olympic season in 1984 were positive. No sanctions were levied against any of the athletes, with the exception of two track athletes who were removed from the official U.S. team. This after-the-fact disclosure was apparently motivated at least in part by a desire on the part of the USOC not to lose face *before* the Los Angeles Games. Even so, the penalty-free testing and the threat of real testing at the Games led many of the athletes, in their never ending game of cat and mouse with the drug testers, to another way to beat the test—human Growth Hormone [hGH], a hormone manufactured by the pituitary.

HGH apparently made its debut in athletic circles around 1970 when an intrepid bodybuilder began experimenting with it. As this bodybuilder was unable to get *human* Growth Hormone, he used GH from rhesus monkeys, which he hoped would also work on him, since it came from a fellow primate. The primary reasons hGH was not used earlier by athletes seem to be that athletes either did not know about it or couldn't get their hands on it. Until very recently hGH was produced only by extraction from the pituitaries of cadavers, and what was produced was limited in supply and very expensive. Now, however, a synthetic version of hGH is on the market and many people fear it may have an impact on the future of athletics as no test now exists which can effectively discover its use.

Even though it is undetectable, however, it is doubtful that Growth Hormone would have achieved its recent popularity had it not been for Dr. Robert Kerr, a physician from San Gabriel, California, one of the few physicians to openly admit prescribing anabolic steroids and other drugs for athletes. In his book, *The Practical Use of Anabolic Steroids with Athletes,* Kerr equates this drug use to cosmetic surgery such as breast implants. He writes:

It really doesn't matter, the important factor is that they [the athletes] are going to take them anyway. If they are taking them anyway, then at least I can play a role in guiding them in the right direction . . . If I should stop performing this work right now, who would my few thousand . . . patients go to for help, understanding and guidance?

But Kerr was not the drug's only publicist. The authors of *The Underground Steroid Handbook,* in fact, wrote in a special issue on growth hormone:

Just why is it a desired drug? Not only does it make muscle cells grow bigger, but it makes the body grow *more* muscle cells. Tendons and ligaments get thicker, as do bones. Also, GH mobilizes stored fat, and if your body has plateaued on steroids, it can still respond to Growth Hormone. And, lastly, it is not detectable in drug tests used in international Olympic and powerlifting competitions.

In the first edition of the Handbook, the authors had concluded that hGH was the only drug that could "overcome bad genetics . . . We LOVE the stuff."

Such articles and interviews helped to create the attitude that pervades many of the books and pamphlets about steroids and hGH that are usually for sale at most bodybuilding and lifting contests. Essentially recipe books for drug users, these books explain how and when to use steroids, and what the latest wisdom is on beating the drug tests. At a recent powerlifting meet in Austin, Texas, for instance, a neophyte on the drug issue could have purchased, in addition to the above-mentioned publications, Fred Hatfield's *Anabolic Steroids: What Kind and How Many*; Boyer Coe's *Steroids: An Adjunctive Aid to Training*; Dan Duchaine's *Ultimate Muscle Mass*; Stan Morey's *Steroids: A Comprehensive and Factual Report*, or three publications put out by "L & S Research": *Human Growth Hormone: Bodybuilding's Perfect Drug; Anabolic Steroids and Bodybuilding,* and *In Quest of Size: Anabolics and Other Ergogenic Aids.* Besides telling the secrets of "proper" steroid use, some of these books contain another message; they argue for what Fred Hatfield has called a "new ethic."

Many who hold to this [new] ethic recognize that science is ever advancing in technology and knowledge . . . New ethic athletes are pioneers . . . implicit in their philosophy is the notion that no amount of legislation has ever been able to halt the progress of science. As pioneers, these athletes carefully weigh the risk-to-benefit ratio and proceed with caution and with open minds. Can there be much wrong with getting bigger and/or stronger?

And, in a further discussion of his "new ethic," Hatfield states, ". . . [drug use is unethical] by your moral code, but not by OURS!"

Nor is Hatfield alone. In an anonymous interview in a leading bodybuilding magazine, one of the largest steroid dealers in the country explained his reasons for selling steroids:

Steroids are needed by people who wish to set themselves apart from the rest of our weakling society . . . Steroid users aren't suicidal; they're adventurers who think for themselves and who want to accomplish something noble before they are buried and become worm food.

As can be imagined, such attitudes bode well for the continuation of a flourishing trade in black market steroids. No one really knows, of course, how large the black market is, but well-informed insiders know it is very large indeed.

An Ohio drug dealer who was arrested by FDA officials in 1985 consented to talk about the extent of the drug network in the United States. A former world champion with a good job, he began dealing steroids on the side during the late seventies. At first, it was simply a way for him to cover the expense of his own drug use; he saw himself as helping his fellow lifters. His insights into the extent of the drug traffic in athletics are important in understanding the size of the industry.

I can't be sure, of course, but I think there may be as many as 10 dealers in the U.S. who grossed at least $1,000,000 last year, and they'll net at least half of that. And some do more.

The way it works with the domestic stuff is that the big dealers either get it from drug manufacturing companies, from drug wholesale houses, from pharmacists, or from other big dealers and then sell it either to users or to local distributors . . . Most of the main dealers have two or three hungry pharmacists in their pocket. You've got to realize that pharmacists can make more by spending a few hours a month ordering steroids for a big dealer than they can all the rest of the month running a drug store. Figure it out. They can get Dianabol, for instance, for around $7 a bottle, and it will sell on the street for $20 or $30 or even as much as $40 and $50 on the West Coast. I can get it for $11 a bottle, so you can see there's a lot of money made as it changes hands. I believe there must be at least 200 pharmacists in the U.S. dealing steroids on the black market.

Another way the stuff gets on the market is through Mexico. My guess is that at least 100 guys go down regularly to buy drugs and then smuggle them across the Texas or California border. The Mexican connection is really valuable because of the devaluation of the peso. You can buy Primabolin down there for maybe 30 to 40 cents a unit and sell it up here for four dollars.

Most people don't understand how easy it is to buy steroids. All you have to do is to go into almost any gym in the U.S. and inside of a day you can score. Every gym has at least one dealer, and those thousands of small dealers usually get it from the big boys. The largest group of users would be bodybuilders, of course, and I don't mean competitive bodybuilders. I mean average guys who just wanted to be bigger and stronger as fast as they can. The last three or four years, the use of the stuff has just exploded and I'd bet there are over a million guys in the U.S. using steroids.

One reason for the rapid growth of the black market during the early 1980s was the virtual impunity with which dealers could act. Tony Fitton, for instance, who was released in the fall of 1986 after serving nine months in the federal penal system for attempting to smuggle steroids across the Mexico-California border, was stopped by customs agents on at least two previous occasions and subsequently released without serving any jail time. In 1981, for example, he was stopped by the customs police at Atlanta International Airport with more than 200,000 doses of anabolic steroids in his luggage. He received a suspended sentence.

Over the past two years, however, the attitude of state and federal officials has undergone a substantial change. Aware at last of the size and seriousness of the problem, various agencies have begun to act, as Fitton and others have learned to their sorrow. The mail order steroid business has been hit especially hard as the following passage makes clear. It is from a current order form of a California concern known, with wonderful irony, as the John Ziegler Fan Club.

These ordering instructions are current as of 2/2/86. Please follow these instructions exactly for your safety and ours. Do not write or speak on the phone the full name of the product, use only its assigned number code. Method of payment should be either cash or a totally blank POSTAL money order.

You may or may not know that the federal government, particularly the FBI, has instigated a serious effort to WIPE OUT the black market steroid business. In the last month, major suppliers on both the east and west coasts have been put out of business. Why are we doing all this? The government can legally open mail. The FBI can legally, without a court order, tap a phone for 48 hours. We want to stay in business, and you won't believe how hard it's going to be to find anabolics in the future.

Another way in which the federal government is cracking down on the indiscriminate use of anabolic steroids involves the FDA, as the following passage from an article in the *Medical Advertising News* explains.

In its attempts to curtail the black market for anabolic steroids, the FDA recently tightened the approved uses of steroids. The regulatory agency removed all "possibly" or "probably" effective indications for which manufacturers could not provide efficacy proof. In March, the agency pulled off the market two anabolic steroids, methandrostenalone and methandriol, manufactured by 29 companies—most of them generic—because of the lack of proof of efficacy.

Many people who observe the larger sporting world worry that such actions are too little and too late, that anabolic drugs have ruined sport. The main problem with these drugs is that not only do they vitiate fairness and pose potential harm to the health of athletes, but they rob the spectator as well. They require us to bring to the stadiums a new cynicism, a new rationale for the watching of sport. No longer is it possible to simply witness a world record and thrill at the marvelous achievement an athlete can produce through the combination of talent and will. Spectators now also ask, "Yes, but did he or she use drugs to set this record?" Ultimately, such speculation may turn spectators away from sport. The attraction of sport has always resided largely in the simple clarity of the struggle of man against man, woman against woman, actual against potential. Some sport scholars, such as John Hoberman, author of *Sport and Political Ideology,* fear that the most dramatic symbol of the technologizing of sport is a future in which hand-picked, chemically manipulated athletes will compete against other hand-picked, chemically manipulated athletes. Whether we can find a mythology which allows us to be interested in such activity—let alone honor it—remains to be seen.

If the last several years are any indication, however, Hoberman and others have good reason to be concerned about the continuing spread of drugs—the continuing technologizing of sport. Consider these facts: (1) San Diego State University suspended its track and field program pending the investigation of steroid use among its athletes and coaching staff; (2) Baylor's head basketball coach resigned after a player went public with a tape he made while discussing steroids with the coach; (3) Vanderbilt University's strength coach and a local pharmacist were indicted for providing steroids to the Vandy players and for participating in a "steroid ring" that involved numerous other East Coast colleges; (4) a survey by a *Waco Times Herald* reporter revealed that steroid use existed at every school in the Southwestern conference; (5) Michael David Williams, a Maryland bodybuilder, went on a crime binge while on the top end of a long cycle of steroids, robbing six homes and burning three, yet was only required to undergo outpatient counseling after his attorney successfully argued that the steroids and testosterone had altered his personality and made him unable to fully understand the consequence of his actions; (6) five Canadian weightlifters returning from the world championships in Moscow were stopped at the Montreal airport and found to be in possession of tens of thousands of doses of steroids purchased from the Soviet athletes for resale over here; (7) the two top superheavy-weight lifters in the world—Anatoly Pisarenko and Alexander Kurlovich—were stopped a year or so later in the same airport on their way to a Canadian competition and found to have over $10,000 worth of steroids in their luggage; (8) Dr. Walter Jekot, a physician who treats athletes on the West Coast, distributed printed announcements in at least one of his three offices offering free injections of steroids in exchange for the referral of new patients; and (9) Brian Bosworth and 20 other collegiate football players were banned by the NCAA from participation in post-season bowls after testing positive for anabolic steroids. The problem is clearly not going away.

What can be done? For one thing, testing, when properly administered, and with appropriate sanctions in place, makes a difference. Studies have shown that when testing is done, performance levels drop, thus making the competition fairer for nonusers. It is, however, no secret that just as Donike and the testers are searching for greater accuracy, the athletes are searching for loopholes. Growth Hormone, for instance, will remain a problem until a test is developed for it. Some experts recommend that all of these substances—testosterone and its synthetic derivatives as well as hGH—be reclassified by the Food and Drug Administration. Were these drugs to become "controlled" substances, it would be much harder for pharmacists to sell them indiscriminately and black marketeers would face stiffer penalties when caught. Legislation such as that recently passed by the California and Florida Legislatures will also have an impact as it makes the illicit sale of steroids a felony and prevents the prescription of steroids for anything other than medically approved therapy.

But even if all fifty states were to pass such legislation, and all sporting bodies were to test with regularity, it is unlikely that athletics would return to relatively drug-free times. The new wave, the athletic avant-garde, is already looking into other techniques, such as the possible use of implants—electrodes and computer chips—inside the body. One researcher has already succeeded in producing an excess of natural testosterone in animals by implanting and stimulating electrodes in their brains. He told a reporter for *Women's Sports,* "If you're trying to develop superfolk, I can tell you for a fact that the way to do it is through substances in the brain. There are many proteins that can absolutely turn someone into a raging superstar if tapped appropriately."

Finally, consider the fact that the same bodybuilder who first experimented with rhesus monkey Growth Hormone is now working with a team of Japanese scientists on the possibility of a computer chip implant that will control his hormonal secretions. He estimates that the project may cost him as much as two million dollars, but he is now a rather wealthy man and he intends to go ahead with the project. He began his bodybuilding career as most young men do—with the simple desire to become a little stronger, a little healthier. But, as the philosopher George Santayana said, "Fanaticism consists in redoubling your efforts when you have forgotten your aim."

CHAPTER 18

The Philosophical Conflicts in Men's and Women's Collegiate Athletics

Joan S. Hult

After the SNOWBOWL, things went on as usual. The snowball had grown bigger than ever and was dangerously close to the cliff's edge. However, if the snowball was to support itself it had to continue to grow. The only noticeable change other than the increased danger of the snowball falling off the cliff was the small friendly snowball being pushed down an adjacent hill by the Women's Snowball Team.

The Athletic Snowball by Charles Corbin (1977) is a satire that effectively describes the commercialized aspects of men's intercollegiate athletics. Although Corbin's snowball team analogy recognizes the emergence of women on the athletic scene, it fails to take into account the many women leaders of intercollegiate athletics who truly wish to build a graceful ice sculpture of their own design rather than play upon that miniature adjacent hill. The decision to avoid a carbon copy of the men's program with all the excesses and misplaced emphases which commercialism has brought about, has resulted from philosophical differences between the men and the women now shaping the destiny of the next generation of student athletes.

This is an analysis of the major philosophical conflicts which have arisen out of the differing fundamental beliefs of the men and women who provide the leadership for the National Collegiate Athletic Association (NCAA) and the Association for Intercollegiate Athletics for Women (AIAW). The major philosophical conflicts include

1. the use of an educational or a commercial model for intercollegiate athletics;
2. the nature of intercollegiate athletics as program-centered or student-centered;
3. the governance and administrative decision-making authority;

From *Quest*, 32:1, 1980. © 1980 The National Association for Physical Education in Higher Education. Reprinted by permission.

4. the legality and obligations of Title IX legislation; and
5. the participation rights of women in intercollegiate athletics (as influenced by social and cultural factors).

These conflicts are discussed through analysis of

1. the function of intercollegiate athletics in higher education;
2. historical perspective of NCAA/AIAW;
3. the comparative NCAA/AIAW programs, policies, governance, and administrative structures;
4. the impact of Title IX; and
5. the influence of social and cultural factors on athletic programs.

Finally, a summary and "views of the future" are presented.

The Function of Intercollegiate Athletics in Higher Education

Both men and women in athletics share a common belief as to the legitimate function of athletics within higher education. As an intellectual, social, and moral agency, higher education accomplishes its function through informal as well as formal education. Perhaps Whitehead best states the aim of education: "There is only one subject-matter for education, and that is life in all its manifestations."

Although some athletic personnel would wish to remain aloof from the broader function of education, most would embrace it, recognizing that in reality there is no neutrality of values: whatever is practiced in action speaks on behalf of the value system being practiced. The entire climate of learning in the athletic program including the philosophical conflicts between the male and female athletic personnel are daily visible. Programmatic abuses and differing treatment of student-athletes are obvious to the student-athlete involved. This truth makes examination of the conflicts between the men's and women's programs and striving to resolve them a most serious undertaking.

Because the governing bodies for men's and women's athletics have statements of purpose which avow similar educational interests, the philosophical conflicts between the men's and women's programs become apparent only on closer examination. The *NCAA Manual* (1979) states, in part:

Section 1. Purposes. The purposes of this Association are: (a) to initiate, stimulate and improve intercollegiate athletic programs for student-athletes and promote and develop educational leadership, physical fitness, sports participation as a recreational pursuit and athletic excellence.

Section 2. Fundamental Policy: (a) the competitive athletic programs of the colleges are designed to be a vital part of the educational system. A basic purpose of this Association is to maintain intercollegiate athletics as an integral part of the educational program and the athlete as an integral part of the student body. (p. 7)

Given the similarities between the stated purposes of the AIAW and the NCAA, we would think that women's and men's athletics could peacefully (and equally) coexist. Unfortunately, this is not yet the case.
Courtesy of University of Illinois Archives.

The *AIAW Handbook* (1979) states, in part:

Article III. Purposes. The purposes of the AIAW shall be:

1. To foster broad programs of women's intercollegiate athletics which are consistent with the educational aims and objectives of the member schools.
2. To assist member schools in extending and enriching their programs. . . .
4. To foster programs which will encourage excellence in performance of participants.

Further, the original proposal for AIAW stated:

AIAW is to be composed of member institutions which wish to uphold and promote the highest standards in women's collegiate athletic programs. As in the past, the focus is to support the individual participant in her primary role as a college student. (American Alliance for Health, Physical Education, and Recreation, Note 1, p. 80)

Because the stated purposes of each association are similar, it would appear that there is no need for a discussion of the issue, that in this best of all possible worlds, men and women share a common goal of integrating intercollegiate athletics into the setting of higher education and have a common commitment to the student-athlete. Indeed, this is not the case. More careful analysis of purpose demonstrates the roots of the philosophical difference. Different fundamental patterns of historical development have charted different policies in men's and women's athletic programs.

The clearly articulated educational purposes of the governing bodies cited above are *not* supported by current athletic policies and practices, particularly in men's athletics, which seem to be primarily an economic venture (at least in the Division I institutions of the NCAA). The success of the dollar and the win-loss record seem the important measure of the success of a program when institutions are faced with the prospect of balancing the now commonplace 1 to 5 million dollar budgets. Even when large budgets are not a consideration, some institutions have allowed the ''winning cycle'' to place programmatic priorities ahead of the educational value to the student-athlete. Whereas men readily admit their commercial priorities, women tend to place emphasis on educational experience for athletes, at times not recognizing some policy changes as departures from their stated educational purposes.

Historical Perspective of NCAA/AIAW

An analysis of the growth patterns of NCAA and the AIAW leads to an understanding of each association's present emphasis and shows the origin of the philosophical conflicts which have emerged in the actual practices of the athletic world. This analysis clarifies the pivotal points of controversy.

NCAA

The control and governance of men's intercollegiate athletics has been a subject of academic concern and debate for well over a century. Founded in 1906, the NCAA, which arose from a football reform movement, grew to over 800 member institutions with as much power, prestige, and public attention as any single association within higher education.

The early meetings of the NCAA often dealt with topics such as the dignity and high purpose of sport in education and tangled with the problems of defining amateurism and professionalism, avoiding commercialism and gaining faculty control of athletics. After faculties did assume control of policy-making from the previously student-run associations, attempts were made to curb proselytizing, professionalism, and subsidization. Another concern of the NCAA was to ensure that coaches of the college teams were not professional athletes, but rather a part of the educational environment. The development of physical education departments was encouraged by NCAA as one approach to placing coaches in a teaching situation. This procedure was helpful to both physical education and intercollegiate athletics.

The ''Golden Age of Sport'' in the 1920s brought phenomenal growth to athletics. Cries of overemphasis and flagrant violations of regulations were heard everywhere in academia as the importance of sport escalated. Institutions were pressured to expand their sports program for the entertainment of the alumni and to bring winning teams to the spectators. By 1929, when the Carnegie Foundation Report was presented by Harold Savage, "big-time" athletics were firmly established on college and university campuses. Savage noted that as matters stood, the fundamental purpose of athletics was not educational but financial and commercial. He called for a return of athletics into the intellectual life of the institution, for broader reforms of athletics without deemphasis, and for presidential intervention in athletics.

Little more than discussion and establishment of general guidelines for the conduct of athletics resulted from the Carnegie Report, and certainly no serious attempts were made to adhere to its warnings. It took another 10 years before 1939 NCAA legislation established standards for association membership. This marked the first attempt at using standards instead of ineffectual guidelines to curtail abuses found in intercollegiate athletics. The historic "Conference on Conferences" (resulting in the Sanity Code) was convened in 1946 and ultimately resulted in the passing of the "Principals for the Conduct of Intercollegiate Athletics." The policy covered

- amateurism,
- institutional control and responsibility,
- sound academic standards,
- control of financial aid to athletes, and
- control of recruiting.

Although the Sanity Code provided for a "Constitutional Compliance Committee" and a "Fact Finding Committee" to investigate all reported violations, final disciplinary action was never taken by the membership against seven large universities who were found guilty of violating the code (*NCAA*, 1950, pp. 21-23). Because of the disastrous failure of the "Sanity Code" and of the association to apply penalties for violations, further steps became necessary to strengthen investigatory and enforcement procedures. In 1954, a "Committee on Infractions" was formed, followed in 1957 by the hiring of the NCAA's first full-time investigator. In 1980, the NCAA employed at least 13 full-time investigators. Even so, NCAA enforcement procedures have been challenged by The House Subcommittee on Oversight and Investigations with respect to due process and investigation procedures. The fundamental issue before the Subcommittee was one of fairness in some of NCAA's judicial actions. Strong recommendations for changes were made in the areas of initiation of actions against an institution, investigation, hearing process, sanctions, and appeal.

The television revenue of the 1970s has reinforced the NCAA's economic priorities and made educational emphasis in athletics even more difficult. Collegiate television revenue in basketball and football has been over 25 million dollars per year over the last several years. There is little evidence that "big-time" athletic departments or the NCAA would initiate reforms which depend on interference with television. The large revenue from television has escalated efforts by institutions to gain access to television rights through winning seasons, thereby accentuating the entertainment aspects of collegiate athletics.

Hanford (1974) completed a report for the American Council on Education (ACE) demonstrating the need for a national study of intercollegiate athletics. His report pointed to the problem of commercialization, lack of proper funding by each institution, emphasis on winning, and the lack of commitment to educational objectives. Hanford's report resulted in a 3-year study by the ACE on the role of athletics. The findings of this study were published in the ACE "Educational Record" last fall. The report exposed the same difficulties expressed by Hanford (1974) and Savage (1929) with an additional warning of the need for equality for men and women athletes (American Council on Education, 1979).

Swanson lists the chief criticisms of men's athletics as involving commercialism with its subset of winning at any cost, recruiting excesses, exploitation of athletes, and a questionable relationship of "big-time" athletics to academic purpose. These criticisms lend support to the reality of a commercialized model of athletics.

AIAW

Although the above historical overview of the NCAA underscores its commercial pattern, the development of the AIAW was intentionally different because women had observed the NCAA model of athletics and were determined to avoid portions of that model. The AIAW's heritage in sport can be traced through the American Alliance for Health, Physical Education, and Recreation (AAHPER) from the first women's basketball committee in 1899 to the present National Association for Girls and Women in Sport (NAGWS). The legacy is unmistakable as one reviews the heritage of AIAW. The first direct roots of AIAW can be found in a National Joint Committee for Extramural Sports for College Women (NJCESCW) which began its work by the end of 1957. The committee was comprised of representatives from each of the three existing organizations for female physical educators, National Association of Physical Education for College Women (NA-PECW), Athletic and Recreation Federation of College Women (ARFCW), and Division for Girls and Women's Sports (DGWS) (Hunt, 1976). The Joint Committee's function was to set guidelines and standards for intercollegiate athletic competition for women. As competitive athletics continued to grow, the Joint Committee was dissolved and DGWS took over its function. This eventually resulted in the formation of a Commission for Intercollegiate Athletics for Women (CIAW) formed in 1967 to govern collegiate athletics for women. The CIAW's purpose was to encourage intercollegiate programs which were based on the general purpose of DGWS which "is to foster the development of sports programs for the enrichment of the life of the participants" (DGWS, 1969).

The AIAW was an outgrowth of the CIAW. The AIAW proposal was created to provide an organized structure for a governing body of intercollegiate athletics for women. The proposal, which passed the AAHPER/DGWS boards late in

1970, made AIAW a sub-structure of DGWS(NAGWS). The AIAW proposal contained the basis for the present philosophical tenets of AIAW; the general structure of the association; the services which would be rendered to the membership; the functions of regions, committees, and the executive board; and the requirements for membership.

The CIAW's *Procedures* booklet, as developed in 1967, provided the basis for the new eligibility regulations adopted by the new association. The same basic eligibility regulations are used today with the notable exception of the CIAW's and AIAW's early ban on financial aid based on athletic ability. While growing from its 206 charter members to over 970 institutional members, the association has sustained its four original purposes. These purposes include the concept of fostering broad programs consistent with educational aims and objectives, assisting in extension and enrichment of programs, stimulating quality leadership, and encouraging excellence in performance.

There has been one significant change in the AIAW governance structure since its conception 10 years ago. On July 1, 1979, the AIAW officially separated from AAHPER/NAGWS to become a separate association. The decision to become an independent organization came as a result of the desire for financial independence; responsibility for its own actions and contractual agreements; and finally to determine all of its own structures, policies and programs. One of the major principles of separation was the clear mandate that AIAW must continue its educational focus in programs, policies, and structure.

The first significant departure from the original purpose and regulations of AIAW was to change the fundamental belief precluding financial aid to athletes. The ban on athletic scholarship was officially lifted by AIAW in April, 1973. Because AIAW was a sub-structure of DGWS/AAHPER, the choice to permit scholarships was a joint decision made by AAHPER/NAGWS/AIAW, and it occurred in the face of a lawsuit in which several female athletes demanded access to AIAW's national tennis championship. Additional pressure came from the Educational Amendment Act of 1972 (Title IX) which required equality of opportunity for all students. A set of regulations which included financial aid based on athletic ability and recruitment was passed by a mail vote of the membership in May, 1974. This action immediately placed in jeopardy the philosophical commitment of AIAW to an educational model. AIAW reluctantly issued a statement concerning the new regulations with a warning that "A college considering the use of a program of financial aid for athletes should be cognizant of potential abuses."

Attempts were made through legislation by AIAW in both 1976 (with the provision that the NCAA follow the same legislative action) and 1977 to limit financial aid based on athletic ability to tuition and fees. When the "need-based" athletic aid legislation of the NCAA failed, AIAW also rescinded its position and permitted institutions to offer athletic aid to the extent of tuition, fees, and room and board. The leadership of AIAW saw this action as a pragmatic vote to prevent discrimination suits, not so much a change in the philosophical belief in the educational soundness of offering full athletic scholarships.

Just prior to the vote on the limitation of scholarships in 1976, the association launched a campaign for "Sanity in Sport." It resulted in the passing of a policy statement which demanded that all future legislative actions be built on the following principles:

- Fair competition for all,
- Concern for the health and welfare of the participants,
- Equality for women, and
- Institutional autonomy.

These principles, along with two initial policy statements which demanded protection of the human dignity of the college student who is an athlete and the treatment of student-athletes like other students, provide the fundamental philosophical basis for policy-making. The reality, however, is that there have been departures from these policies in recent legislative actions.

The recruitment debates by AIAW members have been the clearest indication of AIAW members' commitment to an educational model. With this model in mind, the association has denied university funding for recruitment of prospective student-athletes except for the purpose of "talent assessment." This low recruitment profile continues to be "hotly" debated, however, because of its seeming discriminatory effect on highly desirable prospective student-athletes.

The difficulty of following the established "male norm" as the measure of equality has caused the AIAW to attempt to strike a balance between equity and high caliber competition on one hand, and the educational model on the other, while avoiding problems observed in the male programs. Most observers would suggest this has been achieved in many of the new regulations; but a shift toward concern for the institution's programs has also received some attention.

The present challenge to AIAW seems to be one of redefining and reevaluating how to retain its educational focus in light of Title IX compliance legislation, increased funding, loss of decision-making power, the internal and external pressures for more economic concerns, and the phenomenal growth of women's intercollegiate athletics (206 members to 970 members in 9 years). The short history of the association seems to suggest it has ushered in a period of transition in which the vision of an educational model and student-centered program is clear; but the legislative actions demonstrate some evidence of the erosion of the philosophical commitments.

Comparative History Patterns of NCAA/AIAW

The NCAA and the AIAW have demonstrated some similar ideological growth patterns. There were, for example, prominent physical educators in each association who dedicated themselves to a crusade for an educational model of athletics and spoke to the need for the ethical conduct of intercollegiate athletics. As the formative years of NCAA passed, fewer prominent physical educators devoted their time and energies to NCAA leadership roles or to the struggle for an educational model of athletics. The same phenomenon is becoming apparent within the AIAW leadership. The early AAHPER/NAGWS leaders within AIAW have not continued to work within the Association for fulfillment of its educational goals. The partnership of physical education and athletics is disappearing in AIAW as it did in NCAA. Further, there is a slow exit of experienced female physical educators who are leaving coaching and the administration of athletics on the local level of competition.

Both AIAW and NCAA initial programs advocated the concept of "self-policing." As the men lost faith in the vigilance and integrity of their member institution, the concept of "self-policing" was replaced by a system of paid investigators. While AIAW retains its "self-policing" concept through an elected Ethics and Eligibility Committee on the national level, and elected/selected Ethics and Eligibility Committees on the regional level, that concept is under criticism by the media and to some extent by the membership. It may eventually be replaced by a judicial system of paid investigators, although it has never been seriously considered by the membership.

The NCAA and AIAW have a fundamental difference in the conduct of intercollegiate athletics which needs some explanation, although it may not properly be labeled a philosophical conflict. It does, however, affect the concept of conference versus regional identification, and minimum versus absolute regulations. The NCAA is built on the premise that it is an association primarily charged with the conduct of national championships for its member institutions. It has always encouraged the conference concept for the overall athletic programs of individual institutions, thereby setting only minimum standards for participants and institutions. It does not consider itself a true governing body of intercollegiate athletics. By contrast, the AIAW has a state-regional-national unitary membership system. As a result of this system, the AIAW accepts responsibility for the total athletic program of its institutions and all participants, therefore, setting absolute standards in all its regulations. The national championship participants are selected from regional championships in most sports. The conduct of the championships is only one of the functions of the Association. The AIAW does govern the entire intercollegiate athletic program of all member institutions.

The Comparative NCAA/AIAW Programs, Policies, Governances, and Administrative Structures

In viewing the heritage of the two organizations, it is important to note that although the issues confronting each association are similar in nature, key differences emerge in their approach to these issues. The AIAW, for example, wishes to resolve the commercial versus educational conflict, whereas the NCAA sees little need for more than cosmetic changes. This philosophical difference influences what an institution decides should be the central concern of intercollegiate athletics—i.e., whether its commitment should be student-centered or program-centered. This determination directly affects regulations, administration, and enforcement, and results in disharmony between female and male administrators.

The very real difference in viewpoint as to whether the primary role of the student-athlete should be that of the student or the athlete results in different program objectives. The economic versus human objectives are often at cross-purposes.

Because men and women share the same sphere of interest and similar programs most of the regulations and administrative policies of competitive athletics are similar. There are more similar than dissimilar policies; however, the dissimilar policies are those which result from the major philosophical conflicts under discussion. It is true that the institution's commitment is not entirely program-centered or student-centered in every respect. Nevertheless, it would be a mistake to minimize the philosophical differences resulting from the very different basic beliefs of the NCAA and AIAW.

Differing Regulations of NCAA/AIAW

The following illustrations cite critical differences in eligibility, financial aid, and recruitment regulations which result from the different philosophical commitments of each of the associations. Because the women's regulations are considered a departure from the "male norm," the differences are discussed from this vantage point.

Eligibility.   As of this writing, the most controversial eligibility rule is the transfer rule. The AIAW's transfer rule permits a student-athlete to transfer and participate immediately, but not to receive athletic aid. The men's rule is just the reverse—a student-athlete may transfer and receive athletic aid but may not participate immediately upon transfer. The women's regulation is based on the student-first concept; the men's, on athlete-first.

Female athletes enjoy more liberal amateur status regulations and may ask for more individual "waivers" of the eligibility regulations. The AIAW places no limitations on an athlete's right to participate on AAU, international, or any other outside teams. These regulations are all designed to offer more opportunity for athletes to have competitive experiences. AIAW has also sought to cooperate with the AAU and sport governing bodies to allow female athletes full participation benefits.

Financial Aid.   Because Title IX clearly identified the responsibility of collegiate institutions to provide financial aid for women if it is provided for men, there are few differences in financial aid regulations. AIAW does not regulate any financial aid received by the student-athlete except that which is based in whole or in part on athletic ability. A student-athlete may receive additional funds available to any nonstudent-athlete at the same institution who is in similar financial circumstances. In addition, loans, work/study, or employment are not considered a form of financial aid based on athletic ability. In theory, a female athlete may receive a larger total amount of financial aid per year than her male counterpart. In practice, because male athletes more often receive tuition, fee, and room and board (full ride) grants than do women, males actually receive a larger total amount of aid per athlete. In addition, male athletes are allowed to receive up to 5 academic years of financial aid based on athletic ability, whereas female athletes are limited to 4 years. The men's regulation which allows the 5th year of aid often is used to encourage athletes to transfer and/or to sit out a year while informally participating in practices. It also does assist student-athletes who need to take lighter loads per term or are injured and have an additional year of eligibility.

Recruitment.   The most significant philosophical differences are found in the recruitment regulations as cited in the history discussion. The AIAW prohibits individual solicitation of the prospective student-athlete off-campus in an effort to prevent harassment and pressures evident in open recruitment. In addition, AIAW's policy is part of an effort to keep the athletic dollar within the programs on campus to help expand intercollegiate offerings. The AIAW regulations also do, however, permit institutions to fund athletic personnel for purposes of "talent assessment" (i.e., observation of the prospective student-athlete as she performs in a scheduled athletic event). The regulations also permit on-campus auditions when a prospective student-athlete pays her own way to the campus.

A final general difference in overall regulations between the AIAW and the NCAA is that all regulations of eligibility, financial aid, and recruitment of AIAW are applied to all female athletes at all institutions and in all three divisions of AIAW. The total amount of aid differs among divisions, but the general regulations apply to each division.

Administrative and Governance Conflicts

As a result of AIAW's commitment to a student-centered program, there are several differences in regulations between NCAA and AIAW policies and procedures. The student-athletes are involved in all levels of decision-making of the association. They serve on the Ethics and Eligibility Committee's Appeal Board, each of the sport committees, and as a voting member of the Executive Board.

The adoption of liberal "request for waiver" regulations afford students assurance of individual attention in solving unique eligibility problems. There is likewise a liberal appeal board procedure which permits individual student-athletes to appeal any decision which denied them access to national championships when they were otherwise qualified for participation. Finally the single set of regulations for all female student-athletes assures each student the same opportunity for participation on an intercollegiate team and to gain access to national championships.

Perhaps the most significant administrative conflict is almost "invisible" to outside public observation. It arises because the athletic programs are being administered by male athletic directors who redirect women's programs to fit the "male norm." To illustrate, the AIAW has a commitment to broad programs of athletics without a major/minor emphasis; men's athletics often purposefully divides programs into major/minor sports according to whether or not a sport is "revenue-producing." This pattern—that is, to conduct programs toward a revenue-producing/nonrevenue-producing concept—is being forced on the women in some institutions in spite of opposition.

Women are now losing decision-making power on individual campuses. When women's athletics are combined with men's athletics, men are most often delegated as the administrators of the entire program, and the women relegated to assistants or associates. This situation has limited women's access to the "purse strings" and policy making. The lack of freedom to design and develop unique programs for women has discouraged many women administrators to the point of leaving athletics rather than finding themselves embattled in constant conflicts over athletic policy. These conflicts have made many women realize that a separate governance through AIAW seems the only possible road to freedom and the pursuit of programs which do sustain the educational viewpoint and which do not, for example, demand a major/minor split.

The basic questions on administrative conflicts and decision-making power leads to the subject of merger of the NCAA and AIAW. The recent NCAA vote by Division II and III institutions to offer national championships for women is a clear indication of NCAA's intent to include women's intercollegiate programs under their governance structure. It leaves little doubt of NCAA's commitment to "taking over" women's athletics. AIAW wishes to maintain its separate organization in order to have a governance and autonomy which enables it to develop its unique vision of intercollegiate athletics for student-athletes.

To date all NCAA policy statements regarding merger have steadfastly refused to consider equality of representation, equal decision-making power, or any promises of an athletic reform. Their statements indicate that women should merge with a minimum amount of change in the NCAA structure and a maximum loss of the decision-making power AIAW provides. Even before the NCAA displayed an interest in forming a merger, it has continuously attempted to initiate women's championships and to impose men's eligibility rules on women athletes.

One of the conflicts in a merger is AIAW's approach to affirmative action plans. As George Hanford has observed, "Women are slowly receiving parity in sports *not* because male athletic directors or even institutions believe it is morally and educationally *right* but because it is required by law and regulation." Perhaps the greatest difficulty in a merger, however, is woven into the very fabric of AIAW's educational approach. The AIAW believes that it has an opportunity and an obligation to develop a new form of athletics for women. It has a vision of freedom from the "athletic jungle" and an opportunity to lead the world of athletics into a better way of operation which is free from the business approach and the winning syndrome.

The Impact of Title IX

To the mandate of Title IX (1972) the NCAA/AIAW brought not cool heads and collected thoughts, but the passions of tribal warfare—open warfare based on acceptance by the two groups of diametrically opposed positions. NCAA spent all of its energies to assure exemption of intercollegiate athletics from Title IX while AIAW spent its energies in support of Title IX. Both governing bodies saw the overwhelming significance of Title IX, but from different perspectives. The men envisioned the remains of men's athletics as embodied by a football team wearing hand-me-downs from happier days in the local picnic area, playing to the tune of "From Riches to Rags." The women envisioned all womanhood spontaneously experiencing the miracle of self-discovery, free to move ever swifter—higher—stronger (according to the Olympic motto) after centuries of denial.

Title IX has aided women immeasurably in expansion of programs and has provided the freedom to have separate teams for women in all sports. Even in this issue men in the NCAA took offense. The NCAA's early solution for equality was to open all NCAA teams to female athletes. They preferred this policy because it saved money since few women could enter the ranks of NCAA athletes. The simple truth, argued the women in AIAW, is that as physical performers, sportswomen are far superior to nonsportswomen but are inferior to sportsmen. The bottom line is still the fact that men are stronger and faster than women in the top levels of performance. Open or mixed teams, therefore, could not answer the equity problems.

While the women busied themselves to assure final passage of the Title IX guidelines, the NCAA was equally busy attempting to block the regulations. As early as 1974, the NCAA resolved to establish that athletics were inappropriately included in the guidelines and if this failed, to have certain revisions made which would differentiate major revenue producing sports requiring special treatment on division of funds. The NCAA has made at least five different legislative attempts to exempt athletics from Title IX and/or to reject entirely Title IX.

The most significant action was a suit filed against the Department of Health, Education, and Welfare in which AAHPER/AIAW joined as friends of the court. Since the final regulations were released late in 1979, the NCAA has organized an effort to return the regulations to Congress for comment.

Whereas the men see the issue primarily in terms of dollars, spectatorism, and frank territorialism, the women see equality. The real tragedy may rest within women's governance. Big time men's athletics has long been attached to commercial motives, and Title IX legislation operates under the assumption that the male model of athletics is the *norm* for determining discriminatory action, even when women have opted for a differing model. The educational values, therefore, may be lost in the battle for equality. The women have perhaps failed to fully recognize that Title IX has proven—philosophically—a double edged sword for women.

Title IX has encouraged women's groups to demand equal rights in intercollegiate athletics even if they appear to be equal wrongs to most women in athletics. For example, in a series of articles devoted to "Revolution in Women's Sports" (1974), the comment is made that "sharing the fruits of a corrupt system is better than no fruit at all. What we want is for colleges and universities to become Equal Opportunity Exploiters" (p. 43). This concept is an anathema to most women in athletics, but it dramatizes the philosophical struggle of athletes and educators who also happen to be women. AIAW reflected the conflicts—and made a total commitment to Title IX—suspending, in part, its underlying philosophical commitments until the victory in the "war for equality" was won.

The Influence of Social and Cultural Factors on Athletic Programs

Just as sport within the setting of higher education is a peculiarly American phenomenon, American cultural expectations have proven an undeniable influence on intercollegiate athletics. Social and cultural factors have intensified the philosophical conflicts in athletics. The false equation of sport with the strenuous manly life, the myth of male superiority, commercialism, and media control of the sport experience remind all that choices regarding the nature and conduct of collegiate programs are not made extra-culturally. The NCAA is influenced by the prevailing social climate and has been since its inception.

Historically, at the dawn of a new century, President Teddy Roosevelt—along with sport advocates he encouraged—felt it necessary to lead America in a crusade for a more virile, more strenuous life in order to reestablish our sense of national purpose. The football reform movement which resulted in formation of the NCAA contributed immeasurably to President Roosevelt's effort to have the rejuvenation of manliness through sport. Since its beginning then, NCAA has seen American sport as male territory. Sport could be used to reaffirm patriotic/military loyalties in a less dangerous arena and provide a testing ground for the sex role socialization process. It is no wonder then, that the invasion of men's turf by women has seemed to men a clear attack on their territorial rights. The AIAW and Title IX may have become to the NCAA the symbol of that invasion.

American society has been built on the assumption that women's primary social role is in the family, whereas male roles are in work and in sport. Girls are the cheerleaders and men the quarterbacks. Any changes in traditional role concept would seem to be more difficult for men in athletics, because athletics is a major arena for "proving manliness." Further, the NCAA remains firmly convinced that men are the rightful recipients of the "spoils" of any athletic event because they have brought in the gate receipts and supplied the "winners."

A subset of the question of the NCAA territorialism is the use of an absolute standard of excellence in sport as the measure of whether programs ought to be funded. The fact that men can achieve a higher level of excellence in most sports is used as a reason for those in control of athletics to say women's sports are not "worthy" of large sums of money because men in sport demonstrate a "better brand of ball." There is little question that if men use the factors of speed and strength in performance, women are seen as inferior and doomed to failure. Women argue that they should develop their own standards of excellence for the performer and perhaps to educate the viewer within sport to enjoy the women's standard of excellence.

The sexism illustrated above has become institutionalized; that is, it has been built into the structure of our social and sport system. Because sexism is so deeply rooted in the value structure of the social system, the presence of large numbers of women participants alone has led to some redefining of the purpose of sport and different standards of excellence. As women increasingly participate, it will be difficult to maintain a definition of sport as a "rite of passage" for young men or as a test of manhood for adult males. Creative or new solutions to athletic dilemmas become possible as the invisible bonds constraining women gradually disappear.

However, as male athletic directors place pressure on women in athletics to become concerned about spectators, the win-loss record, and acceptance of a male standard of excellence, the women in athletics argue that the focus must not be only the spectator's viewing pleasure, and caution their male counterparts to keep spectatorism in perspective. The success or failure of spectator appeal, the AIAW argues, should neither be the measure of the success nor the standard by which excellence is to be measured in conducting intercollegiate athletic programs. Instead the measure of success must be the value of the learning experience and the joy of participation for the athlete.

Summary

The NCAA and the AIAW share a common belief in intercollegiate athletics as an integral part of higher education. Both agree that intercollegiate athletics programs should contribute to the educational experiences of student-athletes. Yet different fundamental philosophical tenets and historical developments have in reality resulted in a differing commitment to educational policies and practices by each of the associations.

The historical overview of the NCAA revealed a struggle for faculty control of athletics, for the establishment of educational purposes, for the development of standards and enforcement regulations—all in an effort to curb corruption and abuses in athletics. The final direction of the NCAA in athletics was one of control rather than curtailment of the commercial approaches to the conduct of athletics. The history underscored NCAA's commitment to the business aspects of intercollegiate athletics and to program-centered objectives.

The AIAW has its genesis with the educational domain. Its educational focus was not accidental; it knew what conflicts it wished to avoid and what educational purposes it wanted to achieve. Even with this heritage, AIAW has continually met problems in sustaining its focus and has had to adjust to frequent rule changes. These rule changes have hampered its noncommercial commitment to intercollegiate athletics. Although the vision remains clear to the association, AIAW has faced tremendous pressures in maintaining this vision in the face of the "male norm." Despite these pressures, AIAW continually strives to focus on a student-centered educational commitment.

The philosophical conflicts which have emerged within the NCAA and the AIAW athletic programs have led to differences in focus of the basic policies, program commitments, enforcement practices, and procedures of administration in each of the organizations. Major differences which are a result of the philosophical conflicts include the following:

1. For the participants: (a) fewer restrictions on eligibility, amateur status, and in participation on noncollegiate teams for the female student-athletes; (b) financial aid regulations which, in theory, favor female athletes, but in practice give male athletes the advantage; (c) recruitment regulations which are more restrictive for prospective female student-athletes; (d) liberal waiver of regulations and appeal opportunities for female student-athletes; (e) differing transfer regulations.

2. Self-policing policies of AIAW are different from the enforcement practices of the NCAA.

3. Major/minor (revenue/nonrevenue) sports in NCAA athletic programs differ from the equal emphasis for all sports in AIAW's athletic programs.

4. Student involvement in decision-making for AIAW student-athletes.

A byproduct of the primary differences between the NCAA and the AIAW policies, programs, and administration are the issues of decision-making authority and the merger of NCAA and AIAW. These two issues have caused continuing conflicts for member institutions for both the NCAA and AIAW. The AIAW is committed to a separate governance; the NCAA's disposition is to support a single governance structure under its own plan of implementation.

The Title IX legislation is of singular importance to the expansion of women's intercollegiate athletic programs. The AIAW stands committed without reservation to Title IX in spite of the accompanying possibility of a forced carbon copy of the commercial model of athletics. The NCAA is dedicated to the exemption of athletics from Title IX, or, upon failure of total exemption, it proposes special treatment of revenue-producing sports.

The practice of sexism, with its accompanying sex role expectations for sport, the practice of territorialism by the NCAA, and the question of an absolute standard of excellence has been a deterrent to the development of women's intercollegiate athletic programs. The large numbers of women now entering the sports arena with their corresponding approval by society has enhanced the acceptance of women in intercollegiate athletics.

View of the Future

1. The NCAA has displayed little interest in an athletic reform movement or in substantial changes in its commercial priorities and program-centered intercollegiate athletics. The AIAW seems eager to maintain its educational focus with student-centered programs. The best hope for the future of an educational model of intercollegiate athletics, at least for women, is for the AIAW and the NCAA to remain two separate associations. Although AIAW moves toward some duplication of the commercial model, the association is fully cognizant of its vision of an educational model for athletics which focuses on the individual participant in

her primary role as a student. At the same time, AIAW is aware of the potential corruption to be found in succumbing to the final measure of success embodied in gate receipts, crowd appeal, and the scoreboard.

2. The decision-making power and control of athletics seem destined to remain under the male domination. It would appear, therefore, that the NCAA and the AIAW would have difficulty in forming a true *partnership* which would demand equal representation and/or decision-making positions. Because a true partnership may be unattainable, continuing as a separate association might permit the AIAW to retain the power and control necessary to achieve its educational purposes. Should the NCAA initiate national championships for women in all divisions, the AIAW's commitment to the student-athlete and to the educational focus makes it appear imperative that the organization continue its own program.

3. The AIAW may legally win the battle for equity through Title IX, but it could lose the revolution for reform. The primary battleground now moves to the courtroom rather than to the Halls of Congress and HEW. The topics for debate will include discrimination against female/male athletes because of the differing AIAW/NCAA regulations and/or the failure to provide access to opportunity by the NCAA member institutions.

4. The influx of women into the sports arena has forced changes and redefinitions of the role of sport in society. These new role definitions should help the men in athletics and in the NCAA to gradually accept the importance of intercollegiate programs for women and support different standards of excellence. The acceptance of women's role in sport may free men and women for individual expression and human development and give them freedom to test human and individual potential through the media of sport and athletics.

Final Observation

Perhaps, just perhaps, the snowball teams from both the large and the small hills should be pushed *over* the cliff—and innocent and sincere new educational snowball teams (men's, women's and coed) *ought* to be created to truly fulfill the mission of the university.

CHAPTER 19

Hot Spicks Versus Cool Spades: Three Notes Toward a Cultural Definition of Prizefighting

Gerald Early

Note 1

As we enter the eighties and as the sport of boxing spotlights the lighter weight divisions where the Latin fighters tend to congregate, a new variation on the old theme of race begins to emerge. The most important, that is, the most symbolic, battles will no longer be, as in the old days of Jack Johnson, Joe Louis, and Ray Robinson, white versus black, nor, as in the sixties and seventies with Muhammad Ali, Joe Frazier, and Ken Norton, black versus black, but rather black versus Latin. No fight could more appropriately have opened the era of the eighties in boxing than the first Sugar Ray Leonard versus Roberto Duran bout for something called the World Boxing Council's welterweight championship.

No title fight of the seventies, with the exception of the Ali-Frazier clashes and, possibly the Ali-Foreman tilt, received so much publicity as this one, or reached out so far beyond the confines of the sport's enthusiasts to excite the general public. Yet no fight of this caliber in recent memory was more disappointing. To put it bluntly, it was a failure—perhaps, a poignant signal of what our slouch to the end of the century will be. The fight was surely exciting; despite complaints from some quarters about Duran's mauling and wrestling tactics, hundreds of punches were thrown by each fighter and most of them landed. The fight was performed (the most apt verb that comes to mind) at a brisk pace, and any true boxing aficionado, any dedicated devotee of what was called in 1824 ''the sweet science of bruising,'' found more than enough in the bout to keep his interest and even to elicit his admiration.

But the fight was a failure to the general public, and even the cultural instincts, the cultural radar, if you will, of the boxing aficionado sensed it to be a failure, because it was not conclusive; it ultimately gave the viewer the incredibly weird

This essay is reprinted from *Tuxedo Junction: Essays and American Culture*, by Gerald Early, New York: Ecco Press. © 1989 Gerald Early. Used by permission.

sense of experiencing a kind of rhythmless syncopation. At the end of fifteen rounds, the question of who was the best—the only relevant question in boxing and, indeed, in all sports—remained largely unanswered. Leonard and Duran seemed as if they had fought the entire fight underwater; once it was over, once they emerged from the deep, there was a lingering sense that they had never touched one another, a feeling that the fight just witnessed had never even taken place. The fight was so close that it became nearly a kind of pointless derring-do on the part of the fighters. To the public mind and to our cultural selves, it was important, to be sure, that one man come forth clearly as the best. Duran was chosen the winner almost as an afterthought.

Some said that this fight would be, metaphorically, the matador and the bull—in other words, the classy boxer against the slugger; old-timers talked about its similarity to the Jake LaMotta-Ray Robinson battles; others reminisced about Carmen Basilio and Ray Robinson or Sandy Sadler and Willie Pep; those of more recent memory said the fight was a scaled-down version of Ali versus Frazier. All of these fights were big affairs, and all of them, except Ali-Frazier, were fights between men of different races. Even the Ali-Frazier fight had a deep and bitter intraracial contrast which I will discuss shortly. So in truth the Duran-Leonard fight was, quite properly, placed in this tradition. The fight was the mythical confrontation that was to apotheosize one particular minority as the underground male image of the American collective psyche. The fight was the super-cool nigger versus the hot-blooded greaseball. Here was the monumental encounter between the hot and the cool, between the classical order of technique and the romantic impulse of improvisation; the inner-city warriors at each other for ownership of the night (one as Clark Kent in a Brooks Brothers suit, the other as Chanticleer in a sombrero).

There was Duran, whose style, like that of a jazz musician, relies so much upon the inspiration of the moment that when he is uninterested in a fight he is worse than mediocre; and there was Leonard, so completely absorbed with the intricacies of his talents that with Joycean dispassion he seemed to watch the beautiful nuances his left jab made as it traveled its trajectory through the air. George Benton, once a world-class fighter, and now the trainer of such fighters as the up-and-coming featherweight Rocky Lockridge, also seemed to be just such a combatant, enamored of the artistry of his style. One imagines that Leonard could overwhelm his opponents while not even realizing that they actually existed. Furthermore, Duran represented the old, perhaps dying order of champions, the young kid who learned his art on the street and went straight into the pro ranks at the age of sixteen. Leonard was the product of AAU meets and the extensive amateur programs in this country that threatened to make the old street-corner art of fighting obsolete (just as the old after-hours jam sessions among jazz musicians are a thing of the past; now young musicians learn jazz in the practice rooms of Juilliard).

The question arises why the first Leonard-Duran fight was the symbolic racial showdown of the black and the Latin or, to put it in the vernacular of the average white, between the nigger and the spick, as opposed to the fight between Wilfred

The racial symbolism in boxing was quite evident in the fights between Sugar Ray Leonard and Roberto Duran, shown here at a press conference along with promoter Don King. Courtesy of Holly Stein/Allsport.

Benitez, a Puerto Rican, and Leonard, in which Leonard won the title by a knockout in the fifteenth round. Benitez, who became junior welterweight champ at the age of seventeen by beating Antonio Cervantes and who became welterweight champ before he was twenty-one by beating Carlos Palomino, certainly had credentials that were as impressive as Duran's. Furthermore, while the bookmakers made Benitez an underdog in his fight with Leonard, it must be remembered that Duran was also an underdog. The answer to our question is that Benitez is black. Moreover, he anglicized his first name from Wilfredo to Wilfred, an act for which most New York Latins, among whom Benitez was once considered a young, reckless god, will not forgive him. More important, Benitez does not fight in what we have come to think of as the Latin-macho style of, say, a Duran, or a Pipino Cuevas; Benitez is a slick, polished boxer, a counterpuncher who slips his opponents' blows very well. In short, there seemed to be no real racial contrast between Benitez and Leonard for the press to exploit and the public mind to latch on.

And racial contrast is what the male politics of boxing is all about, and it has a long history. Jack Johnson, the first black heavyweight champion, avoided fighting such talented blacks as Sam Langford, Joe Jeanette, and Sam McVey during his championship reign because the ticket-buying public—that is, at that time, the white public—was interested only in seeing him fight a ''white hope.'' Even with Joe Louis, certainly the most beloved of all black boxing champions during the 1930s and 1940s, his most important and most publicized fights were those against Max Schmeling, ''Two-Ton'' Tony Galento, Billy Conn, and the final bout of his career with Rocky Marciano, all of whom were white. Granted that Louis's fights with black fighters such as Ezzard Charles and Jersey Joe Walcott were certainly major contests, one has only to check the various record books and boxing annuals to discover that only Louis's matches with whites get the pictures. Ray Robinson, the great black welterweight and middleweight champion, also had his most important fights against white opponents: Jake LaMotta, Gene Fullmer, Paul Pender, Bobo Olsen, Carmen Basilio, and for the light heavyweight title, Joey Maxim.

The Patterson-Liston bout changed the racial emphasis and then the most publicized title bouts became intraracial instead of interracial. Most of Ali's important fights, unlike Louis's or Robinson's, were against blacks (e.g., Liston, Frazier, Norton, Foreman, and Spinks). This, of course, was because there were very few white fighters left in the game. Just as the Patterson-Liston bout became in the public mind—and, now, ''public'' means black and white collectively—a fight between a ''punk'' and a ''bad nigger,'' the first Ali-Liston match became the ''crazy nigger'' versus the ''bad nigger,'' and the first Ali-Frazier fight, an encounter so fraught with political overtones that many blacks cried in the streets the day after Ali lost, became the ''politically hip'' black versus the ''homeboy.'' Ali never really needed to fight white men to create racial contrast for a bout since, with the help of the media, he was able to make over his principal opponents into whites by virtue of their politics or lack of politics; nearly every Ali opponent became a representative of the white establishment. Indeed, by the time of the Foreman fight, Ali had become a sort of Calvinist redeemer of the race and Foreman the pork-eating king of the unelect. (We must except Leon Spinks from this process. Spinks's ghetto image made Ali seem the bourgeois, overfed, conservative black. Remember, Ali never bragged, never acted the street-corner clown role, before the first Spinks fight. For the second fight, Ali became the old, wily pro, the ''old head,'' and Spinks was the green amateur, the ''young boy.'' The bout became a classic street-corner lesson in humility for Spinks. Never try to beat an old head at anything, whether it is doing the dozens or doing the dukes.)

Remembering Ali's title fights against white opponents is almost a test to discover how much trivia the mind is unable to discard. During his first championship reign there were George Chuvalo, Henry Cooper, Brian London, and Karl Mildenberger (four forgettable and largely forgotten fights in chronological order, from March through September of 1966); and during his second reign there were Chuck Wepner, Joe Bugner, Jean-Pierre Coopman, Richard Dunn, and Alfredo Evangelista. Between the two reigns there were Bugner, Rudi Lubbers, Jerry Quarry, Jurgen Blin, and Chuvalo. These fights were uninteresting not only because Ali usually did not fight at his best against these opponents, but because they were so suffocatingly passionless.

Black fighters captured Ali's easily distracted attention not only because they were better than the corps of white fighters he faced, but quite simply because they were black and were rivals for the attention of white America. And after all, Ali, since winning the gold medal at the 1960 Olympics, wanted the attention of white America, not even its adoration, though to a large degree he got that as well; but its attention was what he and, perhaps secretly in their hearts, most blacks craved. He wanted to make himself so important that whites could not ignore him, to bring the black psyche out from the underground and onto the stage, the very proscenium, of white consciousness. And he felt that he could do this better than other blacks. Ironically, Ali, while playing the role of the militant Muslim, denigrated his black opponents in ways that one would have expected only from a racist white, or a black ill at ease with his collective identity. He called them "stupid," and "ugly," he said that they "couldn't talk" and that they should not be allowed to "represent the race." In short, Ali's black opponents became symbolically that marauding mass of lower-class tricksters and berserkers who made whites flee the cities in fear, and Ali, a roguish combination of Reverend Ike and Ellison's Rinehart, a sort of jive-time, jive-assed shaman, was the middle-class, brown-skinned black who kept them at bay. If on the part of these opponents there was jealousy and envy against Ali, the "crab in the basket" mentality of the poor, then on the part of Ali there was honest abhorrence of blacks who traditionally made things "hard for the race." In some ways, Ali was as much of a striver as a hard-working, light-skinned hero from a Charles Chessnut or Jessie Fauset novel.

Since the retirement of Ali no other black fighter has been able to make an effective contrast between himself and another black fighter. If two black fighters are in the ring, the white public generally ignores it, and the black public, while on a local level supporting such endeavors of black club fighters and novices, tends to feel a bit uneasy when the fight is for higher stakes, obviously thinking that "two brothers shouldn't be beating each other up for entertainment." In effect, the Leonard-Benitez fight was two black men slugging it out. In truth, racial contrast eases the painful realization that boxing is a sort of vicious exploitation of simply being male; racial contrast gives boxing matches symbolism, a tawdry, cheap, sensational significance that the sportswriter may understate but never leaves unsaid. So with an insufficient white presence in boxing, and lack of general public interest in most black-versus-black fights, the only racial contrast that can be manipulated is black versus Latin. But the Latin must be of a certain sort.

Enter Roberto Duran, the man who, despite or perhaps because of his Indian heritage, looks both so classically and so uniquely Latin, the man with the relentless and uncompromising style—with fifty-five knockouts in seventy fights—who was champion of the lightweights for five and a half years and who exterminated the division's opposition with a degree of fury and disdain that endeared him to the television networks when they decided to recognize the existence of boxing below the heavyweight division. (We will not speak here about the level of Duran's competition while he was champion. Nor will we comment on the distinct possibility that Duran's considerable talents may be vastly overrated. Suffice it to say that it is doubtful that such mediocre fighter as Lou Bizarro, Vilomar Fernandez, and Edwin Viruet would have lasted until the thirteenth, fourteenth, or fifteenth rounds if they had been against such lightweight greats as Benny Leonard, Henry Armstrong, Joe Brown, Carlos Ortiz, Joe Gans, or Ike Williams). Here was the true Latin fighter, or at least what an uninformed American public thought was a true Latin fighter, since we know nothing about Hispanic culture and Hispanic civilization; but we do know the word "macho," a cliché that describes nothing but signifies everything. Duran is the true Latin, macho almost to the point of irritation, the man who said to Howard Cosell that he would make Leonard "fight like a man." Here was the racial contrast that made the almost unendurable publicity for the first fight possible. Duran became the prototypical Latin fighter, many people forgetting, first, the fact that not all Latins are aggressive punchers, and that the fighters who gave Duran the hardest times in the ring—the Viruet brothers, Saoul Mamby, Zeferino Gonzalez, and Vilomar Fernandez—were all Latins who understood that discretion is the better part of the manly art of self-defense, and chose to box with Duran rather than slug it out; and second, the fact that Duran, over the years, has learned to become a better than passable boxer and actually beat Jimmy Heair in a lackluster bout by outjabbing him.

Very little more needs to be said about either Duran or Leonard; they became the blond and the brunette of the romance of American sports. Duran, we know, was the little tough guy from Panama who knocked out horses as a teenager, quit school at the age of thirteen after having reached the third grade, won the lightweight title in 1972 from Ken Buchanan on a low blow, then refused to honor the return-bout clause of the contract; the man sportswriter Dick Young called "the Animal" (a term he would never dream of using to describe a black fighter) and promoter Don King called "the Little Killer." Duran's bully-boy insouciance brings to mind both the late Bruce Lee and jazz trumpeter Miles Davis, both of whom were also little tough guys, who, at the height of their fame, swaggered and swashbuckled in front of their audiences as if they were preening themselves for some secret fertility rite.

Leonard is the young man who has brought, as Howard Cosell tells us, "class" to boxing. He is articulate and handsome, smiles a lot, never discusses politics, and, aside from having one illegitimate child who was later legitimized through marriage, has very little of the taint of ghetto upon him. He gives talks about good sportsmanship to elementary school kiddies and signs autographs for Jewish ladies vacationing in the Catskills. But in truth Leonard wants so desperately to become a personality, recognizable in the same way that white movie stars and entertainers are, that he seems to be holding himself aloft for the highest bidder. Leonard, in short, wants to end up like such white ex-jocks as Bruce Jenner or Joe Namath. What we are witnessing is not the rise and fall of Sugar Ray Leonard but the selling of "Sugar." Leonard is such a shrewd young man that we can get no real sense of the army of people behind him; he seems to be the only *auteur* of this scenario. He wants to be liked, so he makes himself *likable* in about the only way a black person can in this society, by being inoffensive. (Ali, of course, was terribly offensive to this *Herrenvolk* democracy's taste and values, and he paid a dear price for that.) Leonard is not interested in airing his excesses or becoming, to use the 1920s phrase, "a race man"; he is not mythopoeic material. He is bland and cute, and gives the overwhelming impression of being harmless; his coolness is without subtlety, his manner as polished and chilled as a depthless lake in winter. Unlike other fighters, and most especially unlike Duran, Leonard anesthetizes the general public to the corruption and horrors of boxing because he does not look as if he came from a ghetto and gives the impression that boxing is not the only thing he can do. His presence, unlike, say, that of Leon Spinks, is not a *j'accuse* to the sport of boxing and to the society that supports it.

As a cultural event, as an event that produces a pattern of symbols and meanings, professional boxing, like most sports, is a social ritual, a drama in the most Aristotelian sense that elicits the feelings of pity and fear most vividly. Ideally, deep inside we should fear the winner and pity the loser, and somehow if the match fails to produce these "cleansing" emotions, then it has failed to complete us. By "completion" I mean what Clifford Geertz once said, that the involvement in our cultural forms and rituals gives us definition, finishes an "incomplete or unfinished animal." And in sports, particularly boxing, the ritual is very much like the Christian Communion; we partake of the body and soul of the athlete, the last and exquisite god, vulnerable. We have become so accustomed to racial contrast in boxing matches that they have become nearly meaningless, just so much shoddy and cheerless brutality, without it. The masks of racial identification that our fighters wear are similar to the masks worn by the actor in ancient Greece; they are not masks that hide, not psychological masks, but rather masks that reveal all, masks of the primitive which are, as it were, giant, lurid images of the ego beneath. Probably boxing comes closest, of all sports, to producing the primitive responses of pity and fear because the sport *is* so primitive—so naked, if you will. It is appropriate that boxing should now be the possession of the cool medium of television (boxers, like other athletes, have become "TV heroes"), where the drama has been modernized to adopt a tone of muted stridency.

So in our cultural hearts racial contrast and what is concomitant with it, racial identification, are important for the completion of ourselves. The cultural weight of the first Duran-Leonard fight is that it reinforced the emotional perception, if not the intellectual idea, that men are different physically and psychologically because they belong to different races. Despite the mass of scientific evidence to the contrary, we still secretly wish to believe that the mask we wear, namely our skin color and our racial background, like the ancient Greek mask, makes us what we are. Duran becomes the stereotypical fiery, macho Latin and Leonard becomes the stereotypical cool, slick boxing black.

Racial contrast awakens the still uglier need of racial identification, something that the ludicrous boxing film *Rocky* exploited in such an obvious, almost embarrassing way. Even today in boxing a cry can be heard that goes back as far as

1910: the cry for a "Great White Hope" who, supposedly, will save boxing for its white fans. As an example of how racial contrast brings about racial identification, consider Gerry Cooney, a promising young Irish heavyweight. Cooney has suddenly been propelled to the position of number-one contender in the official rankings of the World Boxing Council and the World Boxing Association, largely on the basis of beating a very inept white fighter named Dino Dennis. Now according to CBS Sports broadcaster Dick Stockton, the public is "demanding" that Cooney fight for the title (or, since nearly every division has two titleholders, it is more accurate to say "fight for *a* title")—a demand based on his very impressive win over once highly regarded Philadelphia heavyweight Jimmy Young. However, before Young lost to Cooney he was defeated by a young black fighter named Michael Dokes and beaten twice by a black Puerto Rican, Osvaldo Ocasio. The public did not "demand" that either of these fighters should immediately fight for the title. Nor did anyone think that the significance of Cooney's victory was more than slightly diluted by the fact that Young had not won an important fight since his loss to Ken Norton a few years ago. Apparently the catharsis of pity and fear produced by boxing is effected more profoundly when the viewer is of the same race as one, and only one, of the boxers.

World champions from the British Isles such as middleweight Alan Minter and lightweight Jim Watt disguise this urge of racial identification under the cloak of nationalism. Those of us with only a passing acquaintance with the history of Britain are well aware that the British nation is, in truth, the British race and that the British wish to stay as alabaster white as the heroine of an Ann Radcliffe or Jane Austen novel. Besides, when black British junior middleweight champion Maurice Hope has fought over the past few years, no band of brass-playing beefeaters file in the ring before the fight to play national airs and the British fight fans at ringside do not sing "God Save the Queen" with tears in their eyes—which is what actually happened before Minter's most recent defense against Marvin Hagler and Watt's most recent defense against Sean O'Grady of Oklahoma. (Some old-timers might mention Sugar Ray Robinson's black British nemesis, Randy Turpin, as an example that the English love of boxing transcends race. However, Turpin's ghastly suicide several years after his boxing career ended indicates that the love affair between him and his countrymen was short. Turpin died in dire poverty, so his death did not result, certainly, from a surfeit of public esteem.)

And now we must await the article in some leading sports publication such as *Inside Sports* or *Sports Illustrated* or perhaps in *Esquire* or *The Ring* that will ask the asinine question: Are black fighters better than Latin fighters? The article will then offer as possible evidence for an affirmative answer the recent successes blacks have had with Hispanic adversaries: Hilmer Kenty's knockout win over Ernesto España for the lightweight title; Aaron Pryor's knockout win over Antonio Cervantes for the junior welterweight title; Tommy Hearns's devastation of Pipino Cuevas for the WBA's version of the welterweight title; Marvin Johnson's victory over Victor Galindez for the light-heavyweight title; Jessie Burnet's victory over Galindez to become the number-one contender for the newly created cruiserweight crown; Leo Randolph's upset over Ricardo Cardona for the junior-featherweight title. But this current trend means nothing. American fighters are coming out of amateur programs better trained than many Latin fighters who fight out of foreign countries. As many of the South American countries improve their amateur athletics, their fighters will generally gain parity with black U.S. fighters. Furthermore, such brilliant Latin fighters as Roberto Duran, Wilfredo Gomez, Alexis Arguello, Wilfred Benitez, and Salvador Sanchez have had a great success against black fighters in the past and probably will continue to be successful in the future. Finally, outside of Muhammad Ali, the two most eminent fighters of the decade 1970-1980 were Duran and now retired middleweight champion Carlos Monzon. No black fighter, aside from Ali, dominated his division the way these two Latin fighters did, and neither man had, through the decade of the seventies, ever lost a title fight. Let us hope that such an article dies before it is written, since the current *slight* superiority of black fighters has absolutely nothing to do with race and we need no sportswriter to make implications to the contrary in a national publication.

Note 2

I remember very well that I could not sleep the night that Benny Kid Paret was knocked into a coma by Emile Griffith in a welterweight championship bout in March of 1962. I had watched that fight on television, and when Paret was carried from the ring, unconscious, and, for all intents and purposes, lifeless, I felt myself quivering on the inside. That night I prayed to God to save Paret's life. Indeed, I remember being on my knees and praying very hard, having learned in church that God answers those who truly believe. I thought I truly believed but Benny Kid Paret died anyway. I learned something not only about the inscrutable whimsicality of God but also about the precariousness of the life of a fighter. It was then that I felt professional prizefighting should be banned, not because it was brutal (a kid who grew up in my neighborhood could not be that morbidly thin-skinned and survive), and not even because it was absurd (whether life itself is absurd is debatable but certainly all sports are), but because it was so uncaring. Boxing as an official bureaucracy hates boxers. Some boxing bureaucrats somewhere allowed a woefully out-of-condition middleweight named Willie Classen to fight and die in the ring, allowed a flashy Philadelphian named Gypsy Joe Harris to fight although he was legally blind in one eye; these same officials and bureaucrats now tolerate a parade of bums and stiffs who, fighting under various aliases, endanger their health and degrade the sport by being allowed to fight opponents who are infinitely superior to them. In the past year, seven fighters have died as a result of beatings that they sustained in the ring, the latest being a young Welsh bantamweight named Johnny Owen, who was knocked out by champion Lupe Pintor in the twelfth round of their fight. Owen never regained consciousness and died in a Los Angeles hospital a few weeks later.

So far, the average death rate has been one fighter every two months. And yet nothing has been done to safeguard the fighters; various state boxing commissions have not coordinated their records to prevent, say, a fighter who was knocked out forty days before in Maryland from fighting in Pennsylvania or Nevada; if a ringside doctor is present at a fight, it is almost always a general practitioner, possibly an internist, doctors who are expert at examining cuts, but almost never a neurologist, a doctor who would recognize the signs of incipient brain damage; nothing has been done to change the rules of professional boxing, either reducing the number of rounds or changing the style of the gloves or introducing a standing eight count in professional fights; the only things the WBC and the WBA are concerned about is squabbling over who is the true champion of a division or compiling a ranking system often with the money of promoters and television networks in mind; so, suddenly, a very uncreditable bum becomes a contending fighter—this, of course, means that many a fighter's record is more fiction than fact.

These are the old complaints. Indeed, every few years some hard-boiled, reform-minded sports reporter like the one portrayed by Humphrey Bogart in the 1950s cinéma vérité classic *The Harder They Fall* recites this list as a kind of litany to stir the soul of the great mass of the unconcerned. The fact that these complaints are not new should tend to bother us rather than bore us. After all, these cries of reform reveal that the only major innovations that have taken place in the last 120 years of professional fighting have been placing gloves on the fighter's fists and reducing championship fights from interminable lengths to twenty rounds and, finally, to fifteen. But it should be obvious to all that professional prizefighting cannot be reformed, not with so many bogus and even criminal entities, outlaws to their very bootstraps, struggling for corporate hegemony while the boxers are seen as so much meat hanging on hooks (the most moving scene in the film *Rocky* is of Sylvester Stallone punching a carcass in a slaughterhouse. Heavy-handed but still striking symbolism). The solution for this sport is quite simple: professional fighting must go the way of cockfighting and dogfighting and be banished from our realm. Then, the amateur program, which is more sanely supervised, can be offered in colleges, and poor boys from our mean streets can be given an education and the possibility of actually qualifying for work from which they may get a pension in their old age. We have seen how, as a cultural phenomenon, boxing brings out deplorable urges to see ourselves racially, and we have only to walk into any local gym, get to know any two-bit fighter, to learn that as a nonsymbolic part of our social system fighting is an ugly sport. The one word that comes to mind more than any other watching the fighters work in the gym is "proletariat." These men are honestly, and in a most ghastly way, *toiling,* and what is more striking is how much more grotesque this work is than, say, *the* nightmare of an assembly line. And "proletariat" is such an appropriate word for fighters whom we also call stiffs and bums, words that grew out of the working-class vocabulary—a stiff being someone who is managing to survive in the working world, a bum being a stiff who has temporarily been cast out of the working world and hence is just "bumming around."

As an ardent, I might say passionate, lover of professional boxing, a follower of my boxing heroes since I was a young boy, and as one who appreciates the working-class folklore that surrounds boxing, I find it particularly difficult to call for boxing's demise. I remember listening with intense fascination while patrons in the local barbershop spoke of the exploits of Sonny Liston; I can recall the agonizing disappointment when my uncle failed to take me to see the Joey Giardello-Dick Tiger middleweight championship bout; there comes to mind the anguish when I read that the once magnificent heavyweight Cleveland "Big Cat" Williams, who was nearly shot to death a few years before, was going to fight Muhammad Ali for the title, a hopeless mismatch, and I can remember aggrieved amazement when I heard that the promising young lightweight Tyrone Everett had been shot to death by his girlfriend. Perhaps in the end, only a true lover of the sport can understand why proles deserve a better fate.

Note 3

Eugene "Cyclone" Hart was once a prospect for the middleweight title. He had a left hook that was the best that the division had seen since the days of Ray Robinson; he would whip it around his whole body, producing a crushing blow. Unfortunately, Hart was not a good defensive fighter and tended to get discouraged and disoriented if his left hook failed to produce results within the first few rounds. He had recently lost a fight by knockout to Vito Antuofermo, who was to become, briefly, the undisputed middleweight champ, when I met him in circumstances that were probably not very flattering to Hart. He had been arrested for disorderly conduct and, at that particular time, I was working with the Release on Own Recognizance Program (ROR), which was funded by the Law Enforcement Assistance Agency. My job was to interview prisoners before their arraignments to discover if they were eligible for release on their own recognizance—or as they called it, free bail. I cannot speak about other projects that LEAA gives money to but I certainly can say that my job was a monumental waste of my time and the taxpayers' money. But that topic of discussion must wait for another time. Of course, once I discovered that Cyclone Hart was "in the tank," I made sure to finagle his paperwork so I could interview him. Quite naturally, once I got him to my desk I promptly forgot his bail interview—he did not need one anyway, since he had never been arrested before and the charge was so minor that "free bail" was a foregone conclusion—and we sat and talked boxing.

"Are you still going to fight?" I asked. "Lots of people say you're washed up."

"Well, I'm still gonna try," he said. I remember how hard and strong his body was. He had the hips of a dancer, the shoulders of a halfback. "I think I can still make it. I got a few good fights in me and I might still get a title shot. That's what I'm hangin' around for: a title shot."

"I thought you were going to knock Antuofermo out of the box early," I said.

"Yeah, so did I, but he's a pretty tough cat."

We talked for a while about some other of the local fighters: Jerome Artis, Bad Bad Bennie Briscoe, Sammy Goss. When he rose to return to his cell he said:

"Yeah, I'm still hangin' in. I mean, what else can I do? My luck might change."

I had expected him to make a sort of sign with his fists when he said that, but he merely held his hands relaxed at his sides. His lack of gesture was as surprising to me as walking down a flight of stairs and anticipating a final step when none is there. Cyclone Hart was a washed-up fighter at the age of twenty-seven.

"I still might get a title shot," he said as a policeman led him away.

"Yes," I called after him, from my desk, "that's nice work if you can get it."

Postscript: Leonard-Duran II

The hardest thing to teach a young boy bent upon becoming a professional prizefighter, according to any cigar-chomping, gibbous old fight trainer, is to get up and continue fighting after being knocked down and hurt. In most cases, a fighter is knocked down by a punch he did not see, and it is only human nature to want to avoid the unknown and not to wish to continue. It takes hours and hours of the most severe sort of training to make a fighter overcome that natural instinct. Robert Jarrett, a black man who is neither a cigar-chomper nor gibbous, explained this to me one winter afternoon. He is a former professional prizefighter who now trains black youngsters in the Richard Allen projects in Philadelphia in the "sweet science." "Once a kid learns this," he pontificated, "he becomes a man." I did not disagree. But when I see a decked fighter get up and continue to fight, or, in most instances, continue to get beaten to a pulp, I know it is not "heart" or courage that makes him stand up, but a sort of Skinnerian conditioning that has effectively dulled his brain so that he has no real idea when he is hurt or how badly.

Professional boxing, in recent months, has come to resemble professional wrestling in the absurd perversity of its demeanor—lacking, however, wrestling's vulgar hilarity. Wrestling, like Roller Derby, realizes its own sense of burlesque and continually teases and insults its lower-class audience with a sort of mock drama as if it were masterminded by some Grub Street exile; boxing has now mistaken its hysteria for the most profound theater. It has, in a word, become not just a joke spoken in poor taste, but a joke gone in the teeth.

The abrupt ending of the Duran-Leonard rematch, with Duran, for whatever reason, walking away from Leonard in the eighth round, was a pathetic ending to a rivalry that had so engaged the imagination and symbolism of our culture. Perhaps Duran walked away because he was "taking a dive," although one would be hard-put to imagine what corporate interest could induce him to embarrass himself so in front of his family, friends, fans, and countrymen, or what corporate interest would want him to; or perhaps he walked away because he experienced an epiphany that revealed at once and at last to his eyes the absurdity of his profession; or perhaps, and this is more likely, he felt very sick: the once poor, lean street urchin, who when he first began as a professional was easily able to make the 135-pound limit for lightweights, may have, in acquiring fame and riches, eaten his way not only out of the lightweights but perhaps out of the welterweights as well. Crash dieting and the use of diuretics are poor methods of training. Alas, this is what happens to those who live life in the fast lane. At any rate, this poetic battle, which was to pit the war machine's frenzy against the body electric's gallantry, became just another tainted, bizarre contest. This fight that was to justify the existence of boxing wound up justifying its swift execution.

This bout kept the spirit of several other recent championship fights: Muhammad Ali's painful return, in which, donning another disguise of Melville's Confidence Man, he paid the price of passing blood for a week in exchange for $10 million and the opportunity to show the world what early male menopause is like. After acting and Third World diplomacy failed, only boxing remained for this most self-conscious man to engage his puerile exhibitionism. More recently, there was the fight for the junior welterweight championship of the world between Aaron Pryor, the black champion, and Gaetan Hart, the white Canadian challenger. Not only did this fight exploit, as usual, racial contrast and racial identification, but the network that televised the fight reminded the viewers at every opportunity that Hart had seriously injured one fighter in the ring and killed another. Implied in this grotesque reporting, and in the whole raison d'être for Hart, an extremely mediocre fighter to be fighting for the championship, was the obscene question: Would Pryor be Hart's next victim? Hart had eighteen losses on his record; normally no fighter with such a propensity for losing would have been even remotely considered for a championship fight, and the two men he severely battered in the ring were even more inept as fighters than he was and probably should not have been allowed to fight. Pryor knocked out Hart in the sixth round of a mismatch.

In early November I went to an elementary school gymnasium in Ithaca to watch a local amateur fight card. The first bout of the evening was between two ten-year-old kids, one black, the other white, representing two different boxing clubs. The white youngster was game and tried very hard but the black boy had real talent, the look and hunger of a possible future professional prizefighter, and he thoroughly thrashed his opponent and easily won the fight. As I watched the black boy being congratulated by his friends and as my eyes circled the gym and viewed Ithaca's lower class out in mass to support its relatives and friends I asked myself, Why? Why does this youngster want to be a fighter? Why would his family be proud if he became one? His chances of having a career like Ali, Duran, or Leonard—boxing's representative men of the moment—are so remote that no bookie would give any sort of betting line on the possibility. And the cost of this misplaced ambition is so much deeper and heavier than if a middle-class kid who plays tennis, another "solitary ego" sport, wished to become John McEnroe.

Tennis is a bourgeois respected recreation, second only to jogging; no stigma is attached to its pursuit by the white middle and upper classes, and failure to succeed as a tennis professional does not affect the middle-class youngster's mobility or the possibility that he can cultivate other humane or profitable interests. In other words, a tennis career and, say, an MBA degree are not incompatible. They are phenomena of the same world and they represent the same bourgeois values.

Boxing is part of another culture, available to a boy who cannot be a singer, a preacher, or a thief (which are really the only other job-training programs readily available to the lower class). His success is measured by his movement up the fight card until, finally, he becomes the featured attraction, the main event, and the high rollers of the upper class, caught between ennui and debauchery, come to watch him fight and to bet on the outcome. For the poor, any ambition is ultimately to make money, to change their lives, to make them better. But, as James Brown sang in the mid-sixties, "Money won't change you." A poor person with money is simply, to the eyes of the middle classes, the beast displaced, the tolerated savage, the simpleton with poor taste. And the poor boy himself discovers that the rage that he nurtured to become champion, the rage that pushed him from his birth, the rage against that stultifying bourgeois monolith which has made his life miserable, either still gnaws at him like a burning ulcer or has left him completely burned out by the absence of desire. Thus he finds himself naked and vulnerable, in a nest of vipers. And further, he discovers that it was the rage, and the rage alone, that not only kept him alive but made him human. Money won't change you, indeed. But as James Brown sang in the same song, "Time will take you out."

As I watched the youngster in the ring I thought for a moment about Bennie Briscoe, the Philadelphia middleweight, now an aging thirty-eight, who had several times fought for the title and each time come up empty. Losses to Carlos Monzon and Roderigo Valdes for the title and losses to such up-and-coming middleweights as Marvin Hagler (now the champion of that division) and Vito Antuofermo climaxed a career of frustration and bitterness. Bennie will never be champion and, although he continues to fight, he must hold down another job in order to live.

On any given weekday, in any gym in America, there are ten-year-old boys banging away at heavy bags and sweating in desperation as they pursue that Belle Dame sans Merci—a professional boxing title.

On any given weekday, Bennie Briscoe hauls trash in the ghetto of North Philadelphia. The long journey from the gym to the professional prize ring ended as it began: on the streets. As the corner boys say, Briscoe still "lives on the block."

Suggested Readings

Ashe, Arthur R. *A Hard Road to Glory: A History of the African-American Athlete,* 3 vols. New York: Warner Books, 1988.

Baker, William J. *Jesse Owens: An American Life.* New York: The Free Press, 1986.

Baker, William J. *Sports in the Western World.* Urbana, IL: University of Illinois Press, 1988.

Bale, John. *The Brain Drain: Foreign Student-Athletes in American Universities.* Urbana, IL: University of Illinois Press, 1991.

Berry, Robert C., et al. *Labor Relations in Professional Sports*. Dover, MA: Auburn House Publishing, 1986.

Berryman, Jack W., & Park, Roberta J. (Eds.) *Sport and Exercise Medicine: Essays in the History of Sports Medicine*. Urbana, IL: University of Illinois Press, 1992.

Chandler, Joan. *Television and National Sport: The United States and Britain*. Urbana, IL: University of Illinois Press, 1988.

Davis, Jack E. "Baseball's Reluctant Challenge: Desegregating Major League Spring Training Sites, 1961-1964." *Journal of Sport History,* 19(1992): 144-162.

Euchner, Charles C. *Playing the Field: Why Sports Teams Move and Cities Fight to Keep Them*. Baltimore: The Johns Hopkins University Press, 1993.

Fair, John D. "Bob Hoffman, The York Barbell Company and the Golden Age of Weightlifting, 1945-1960." *Journal of Sport History,* 14(1987): 164-188.

Guttmann, Allen. *A Whole New Ball Game: An Interpretation of American Sports*. Chapel Hill, NC: University of North Carolina Press, 1988.

Guttmann, Allen. *From Ritual to Record: The Nature of Modern Sports*. New York: Columbia University Press, 1978.

Guttmann, Allen. *The Games Must Go On: Avery Brundage and the Olympic Movement*. New York: Columbia University Press, 1984.

Guttmann, Allen. *Women's Sports: A History*. New York: Columbia University Press, 1991.

Hult, Joan S., & Trekell, Marianna. (Eds.) *A Century of Women's Basketball*. Reston, VA: AAHPERD, 1991.

Levine, Peter. *Ellis Island to Ebbet's Field: Sport and the American Jewish Experience*. New York: Oxford University Press, 1992.

Lucas, John A. *Future of the Olympic Games*. Champaign, IL: Human Kinetics Publishers, 1992.

Lucas, John A., & Smith, Ronald A. *Saga of American Sport*. Phildelphia, PA: Lea & Febiger, 1978.

Mandell, Richard D. *Sport: A Cultural History*. New York: Columbia University Press, 1984.

Marcello, Ronald E. "The Integration of Intercollegiate Athletics in Texas: North Texas State College as a Test Case, 1956." *Journal of Sport History,* 14(1987): 286-316.

Neal-Lunsford, Jeff. "Sport in the Land of Television: The Use of Sport in Network Prime-Time Schedules, 1946-50". *Journal of Sport History,* 19(1992): 56-76.

Rader, Benjamin G. *American Sports: From the Age of Folk Games to the Age of Spectators*. Englewood Cliffs, NJ: Prentice-Hall, 1983.

Rader, Benjamin G. *In Its Own Image: How Television Has Transformed Sports*. New York: The Free Press, 1984.

Rader, Benjamin G. "The Quest for Self-Sufficiency and the New Strenuosity: Reflections on the Strenuous Life of the 1970s and 1980s." *Journal of Sport History,* 18(1991): 255-266.

Riess, Steven A. *City Games: The Evolution of American Urban Society and the Rise of Sports.* Urbana, IL: University of Illinois Press, 1990.

Riess, Steven A. *The American Sporting Experience: A Historical Anthology of Sport in America.* New York: Leisure Press, 1984.

Roberts, Randy, & Olson, James. *Winning Is the Only Thing: Sports in America Since 1945.* Baltimore: The Johns Hopkins University Press, 1989.

Sammons, Jeffrey T. *Beyond the Ring: The Role of Boxing in American Society.* Urbana, IL: University of Illinois Press, 1988.

Smith, Thomas G. "Civil Rights on the Gridiron: The Kennedy Administration and the Washington Redskins." *Journal of Sport History,* 14(1987): 189-208.

Spears, Betty,& Swanson, Richard A. *History of Sport and Physical Education in the United States.* Dubuque, IA: William C. Brown, 1988.

Sullivan, Neil J. *The Dodgers Move West.* New York: Oxford University Press, 1987.

Tygiel, Jules. *Baseball's Great Experiment: Jackie Robinson and His Legacy.* New York: Oxford University Press, 1983.

Wiggins, David K. "The Future of College Athletics Is at Stake: Black Athletes and Racial Turmoil on Three Predominantly White University Campuses, 1968-1972." *Journal of Sport History,* 15(1988): 304-333.

Epilogue

You can see that sport has undergone dramatic changes over the course of American history. Originally informal and unencumbered by elaborate bureaucracies, sport steadily evolved into a highly structured commercial phenomenon that permeates our culture. Harness racing, originally a quaint yet popular urban recreation, was transformed into America's first commercial sport. Baseball grew from a mere backyard pastime to a national sport that now transcends international borders, intercollegiate athletics went from being student organized to being sanctioned by national governing bodies, and impromptu pick-up games somehow mutated into scripted and choreographed televised media extravaganzas. These changes coincided with increased public interest in health and physical fitness, greater government involvement in all levels of sport, and a growing cultural obsession with victory at any cost.

The changes that took place in American sport were remarkable, but perhaps no more so than the continuity evident in sport since the founding of this country. In many ways, the more things changed in sport, the more they actually remained the same. Similar to the Puritans of Colonial New England, for instance, Americans today have difficulty justifying sport merely for the joy it brings participants. Teachers, coaches, administrators, and the larger American public still have a need to rationalize sport participation in instrumental rather than intrinsic terms. Most often, sport participation is seen as a means to a greater end, an activity worthwhile because of its contribution to character development or improved health.

But the need to rationalize sport participation has *not* resulted in more balanced competition. America's obsession with winning leads many athletes to do whatever is necessary to achieve victory. For some athletes, this means adopting an overly stringent training regimen, pushing the body to the point of injury and irreparable damage. For others, the obsession leads to performance-enhancing drugs. Many athletes of both sexes from nearly every sport have turned to drugs in an attempt to outduel their opponents and improve their chances for victory.

The damage athletes inflict on their bodies through chronic drug use is just one of the many forms of violence still evident in American sport. Although gouging matches no longer take place in the Southern backcountry, blood sports are no longer condoned, and mass momentum plays are no longer permitted in football, Americans continue to be facinated by brutal and violent sporting activities seemingly without regard for the consequences. Football, hockey, and boxing remain enormously popular, attracting millions of fans enamored with the sports' brutality. Unfortunately, sport violence is not confined to the playing field but often extends to the stands. Alcohol, intense rivalries, and a mob mentality frequently combine to cause skirmishes among fans.

Less obvious, but equally as insidious as the problem of violence are the twin evils of gender and racial inequality. Although in recent years progress has been made on these fronts, persistent and deep-seeded stereotypes of women and other minority groups continue to bring them derision and limit their involvement in sport.

Conflicting interpretations of, and refusal to enforce, Title IX Legislation has caused the lack of equity in high school and college sport. Women athletes continue to receive less financial support than their male counterparts. Moreover, there was a dramatic decline in the number and percentage of women coaches and administrators in highly organized sport after the dissolutionment of the Association for Intercollegiate Athletics for Women (AIAW) in 1981. The mergers that occurred after the dissolutionment of the AIAW resulted in a loss of leadership positions for women sport and adoption of the male athletic model.

Similarly, the apparent human need to define people by skin color and ethnicity has had dire consequences for African-Americans who are often seen as having the innate physical skills required for athletic performance, while lacking the *necessities* essential for success in other fields. This contributes to the channeling of a disproportionate number of African-Americans into athletics while limiting their access to leadership positions within and outside sport. Leaders in the African-American community have protested these forms of discrimination while pointing out the dangers of blacks focusing exclusively on careers in sport. It remains to be seen if these efforts will prove fruitful.

Despite persistent evidence of drug abuse, obsession with victory, violence, and gender and racial inequality, the news in contemporary sport is not all bad. Sport provides increasing numbers of people from different backgrounds with enjoyable and meaningful experiences at all levels of competition. More and more people today turn to sport and physical activity to improve fitness. Although they are not necessarily concerned, as past generations were, with the maintenance of traditional values and toughness, Americans today use exercise and sport to achieve a sense of personal fulfillment, happiness, and pleasure.

Perhaps most importantly, sport participation allows people to fulfill their longing for camaraderie and sense of community. Similar to slaves on Southern plantations, baseball players in early America, Italian immigrants in St. Louis, and the Japanese in California's Yamato Colony, sport in today's society is a means for binding people together and forging communal identity. It provides a connectedness not often realized in a culture starving for order and common ground among divergent groups of people.

For the most gifted athletes among us, of course, sport participation provides not only intangible rewards but often great wealth. Professional athletes benefit enormously from the marketing of sporting goods and associated paraphernalia—in addition to non–sport-related merchandise. Taking the example of Albert Spalding and other early entrepreneurs to unimagined heights, today's superstar athletes enter into lucrative endorsement contracts that transform them into international media icons.

Since the days of Roone Arledge, the small screen has had a profound effect on both amateur and professional sport. Television has contributed to the expansion of professional sport franchises, provided revenue to college and professional sport, increased the popularity of some sports (and led to the demise of others), played a significant part in the recruitment of high school athletes into college sport, increased the social mobility of athletes, and been responsible for both game modifications and redefinition of the sport experience.

Not unexpectedly, sport has also exerted its influence on television. Networks reap the economic benefits of sports programs, selling advertisers one billion dollars worth of time for games and other athletic events. Sport has also led to the creation of specialized television networks—the Entertainment and Sports Programming Network (ESPN) being the most prominent among them. The popularity of sport has, moreover, greatly influenced television programming. Networks develop their weekend programming around sports and set aside prime-time evening hours for such events as the World Series, Monday Night Football, and the Super Bowl.

In the final analysis, we learn that regardless of place and time, sport plays a meaningful role in the lives of people of all ages and backgrounds. Sport has always stirred the hearts of those intent on testing their spirit, sharing a sense of community, and experiencing the beauty of human movement. History tells us that the future holds similar promise. Never as pure as its defenders would like us to think nor as morally corrupt as detractors lead us to believe, sport will continue to be a source of pleasure and sorrow for an American public enthralled with competition and the promise of victory.

Index

About the Editor

David K. Wiggins is director of undergraduate health science programs and professor of physical education at George Mason University in Fairfax, Virginia. Since earning his PhD from the University of Maryland in 1979, Wiggins has taught undergraduate and graduate courses in sport history at Kansas State University and George Mason University.

Wiggins is an expert on American sport, particularly as it relates to the involvement of black athletes in sport and physical activity. Since 1980, he has written about sport history and published articles in numerous journals, including the *Research Quarterly for Exercise and Sport, Journal of Sport History, Canadian Journal of History of Sport,* and *The International Journal of History of Sport.* His work has garnered two American Alliance for Health, Physical Education, Recreation and Dance (AAHPERD) Research Writing Awards (1984 and 1986) and significantly influenced subsequent research studies on African American involvement in sport.

In addition to his memberships in AAHPERD and the North American Society for Sport History, Wiggins has served as President of the AAHPERD History Academy and on the Publications Board of *The Journal of Sport History.* He has held editorships and memberships on various committees of professional societies dealing with sport history.

*You'll find
other outstanding
social sciences and sport
resources at*

www.HumanKinetics.com

In the U.S. call

1-800-747-4457

Australia.............................. 08 8277 1555

Canada 1-800-465-7301

Europe......................+44 (0) 113 255 5665

New Zealand................... 0064 9 448 1207

HUMAN KINETICS
The Information Leader in Physical Activity
P.O. Box 5076 • Champaign, IL 61825-5076 USA